INSTITUTIONS, PROPERTY RIGHTS, AND ECONOMIC GROWTH

This volume showcases the impact of the work of Douglass C. North, winner of the Nobel Prize and father of the field of New Institutional Economics. Leading scholars contribute to a substantive discussion that best illustrates the broad reach and depth of Professor North's work. The volume speaks concisely about his legacy across multiple social sciences, specifically on scholarship pertaining to the understanding of property rights, the institutions that support the system of property rights, and economic growth.

Sebastian Galiani is Professor of Economics at the University of Maryland. He is a Fellow of the National Bureau for Economic Research and the Bureau for Research and Economic Analysis of Development and a member of the executive committee of the Abdul Latif Jameel Poverty Action Lab at MIT. He is also associate editor of the *Journal of Development Economics*. He has published numerous papers in leading academic journals, including the *Journal of Political Economy, Quarterly Journal of Economics, American Economic Journal, Review of Economics and Statistics, Journal of Public Economics, Journal of Development Economics, Journal of Public Economic Theory, Economic Inquiry,* and *Labour Economics*. Professor Galiani received his PhD from Oxford University.

Itai Sened is Professor of Political Science at Washington University in St. Louis and Professor of Public Policy at Tel Aviv University. He has authored or co-authored several books, including *The Political Institution of Private Property* (Cambridge University Press, 1997); *Political Bargaining: Theory, Practice and Process* (with Gideon Doron, 2001); and *Multiparty Democracy* (with Norman Schofield, Cambridge University Press, 2006). He has also published numerous articles in leading journals, including *The American Political Science Review, The American Journal of Political Science, The Journal of Politics, The British Journal of Political Science, European Journal for Political Research,* and *Journal of Theoretical Politics*. He received his PhD from the University of Rochester.

Institutions, Property Rights, and Economic Growth

The Legacy of Douglass North

Edited by

SEBASTIAN GALIANI

University of Maryland

ITAI SENED

Washington University in St. Louis

&

Tel Aviv University

CAMBRIDGE
UNIVERSITY PRESS

CAMBRIDGE
UNIVERSITY PRESS

32 Avenue of the Americas, New York, NY 10013-2473, USA

Cambridge University Press is part of the University of Cambridge.

It furthers the University's mission by disseminating knowledge in the pursuit of
education, learning, and research at the highest international levels of excellence.

www.cambridge.org
Information on this title: www.cambridge.org/9781107041554

© Cambridge University Press 2014

First published 2014

A catalog record for this publication is available from the British Library.

Library of Congress Cataloging in Publication data
Institutions, property rights, and economic growth : the legacy of Douglass North / edited by
Sebastian Galiani, University of Maryland, Itai Sened, Washington University in St. Louis.
pages cm
Includes bibliographical references and index.
ISBN 978-1-107-04155-4 (hardback)
1. Economic history. 2. Econometrics. 3. Institutional economics. 4. Law and economics.
5. North, Douglass C. (Douglass Cecil) I. Galiani, Sebastian. II. Sened, Itai.
HC21.I58 2014
330.092–dc23 2013032184

ISBN 978-1-107-04155-4 Hardback

Contents

Contributors

Joseph Wallis, University of Maryland, National Bureau of Economic
rch

R. Weingast, Hoover Institution and Department of Political Science,
ord University

Contributors

Robert Bates, Department of Government, Harva

Pedro Dal Bó, Department of Economics, Brown

Sebastian Galiani, University of Maryland

Scott Gehlbach, University of Wisconsin–Madiso

Gillian K. Hadfield, Law School and Economics
Southern California

Pamela Jakiela, University of Maryland

Edmund J. Malesky, Duke University

Claude Ménard, Centre d'Economie de la Soi
Paris

Joel Mokyr, Departments of Economics and
versity; Eitan Berglas School of Economics, Te

Elinor Ostrom (1933–2012), Formerly of Indi
and Arizona State University, Tempe

Steven C. A. Pincus, Department of History,

James A. Robinson, Department of Governi
versity

Ernesto Schargrodsky, Universidad Torcuat

Kenneth A. Shepsle, Harvard University

Mary M. Shirley, Ronald Coase Institute

Preface

In the winter of 2010, we realized that Professor Douglass C. North, our mentor, intellectual leader, and friend, was getting close to celebrating his 90th birthday in less than a year. We thought the time was ripe for a big birthday party. We took it upon ourselves to put together the intellectual program, through the Center for New Institutional Social Sciences (CNISS), raise the necessary funds, and, with the help our remarkable assistant, Alana Bame, produce the event.

Many have gathered around the project. To begin, the leadership of Washington University gave us the blessing and some seed money. Then came the remarkable endorsement of the leading scholars in the field who volunteered to come to St. Louis, present papers, and contribute to this edited volume. The friends of CNISS, board members and many others, have followed with financial support and encouragement.

In a rather chilly weekend, the first weekend of November 2011, more than 300 Friends of Doug came from all over the world to celebrate his 90th birthday. And at the heart of the celebration, this volume, came to be. Two years later, after many versions and revisions, we have come to send the volume to print.

Many have made this rather unique volume come to life. We would need many pages to thank them all. We acknowledge a "short list" chosen by an intuitive but certainly not inclusive rule of thumb. Those not mentioned are not forgotten or overlooked.

We thank Alan Bame without whom none of this would have ever happened. We thank the Chancellor of Washington University, Professor Mark Wrighton, and the Provost, Professor Ed Macias, for their initial and whole-hearted support and endorsement of the project.

We thank Lee and Alexandra Benham for many years of guidance and the quiet and unrelenting support from behind the scenes. We acknowledge the very significant financial support of the Lynne and Harry Bradley Foundation as well as the Hirsch family, the Simowitch family, and a number of other CNISS board members that will remain unnamed.

We want to use this opportunity to recognize the hard work put in by our student assistant Daniel Guenther, Washington University graduate in Political Science of 2013, for his assistance editing, writing, and researching connected with the volume.

Last but not least, we are indebted to Scott Parris of Cambridge University Press for his initial endorsement of the project and his tireless work in assisting with the compilation of the volume; and to Elizabeth Case for her support in keeping us on track with the production of the volume.

Sebastian Galiani and Itai Sened
Winter 2013

Introduction

Sebastian Galiani and Itai Sened

Douglass C. North has earned himself a place of honor in the pantheon of the most influential social scientists of his era, as was recognized in 1993 when he and economic historian Robert Fogel were awarded the Nobel Memorial Prize in Economics for their work in economic history.

North was born in 1920 in Cambridge, Massachusetts. He received his undergraduate and graduate degrees from the University of California at Berkeley. He then took an appointment at the University of Washington until he moved to Washington University in St. Louis in 1983.

In 1959–1960, North cofounded *cliometrics*, an association of economic historians that systematically applied statistical methods and economic theory to the study of history. However, by the late 1960s, his ideas about institutions and their central role in the study of economics began to evolve, dominating his work. Later, during the 1970s, he also cofounded the New Institutional Economics, a group of social scientists that expanded the reach of standard economic analysis by taking into account transactions costs and the importance of institutions and organizations as critical determinants of social phenomena in terms of processes, actions, and outcomes. The group's work has had a strong effect on all of the social sciences, but its most remarkable influence is felt in political science and economics.

The purpose of this volume is to showcase the essence and the impact of North's work through several exemplars that best illustrate the breadth and depth of his influence. The volume thus speaks less of his work – which is remarkably widespread and well known – and more about his legacy. By his legacy, as the title of this collection indicates, we refer mostly to his influential work in the field of *New Institutional Social Sciences*, and more specifically on scholarship pertaining to the understanding of property rights, the institutions that support the system of property rights, and economic growth.

1

Indeed, North was a pioneer in pointing out that institutions, understood as the set of formal and informal rules and constraints that structure life in societies, are a key determinant of the process of economic growth and development. In fact, "throughout history, institutions have been devised by human beings to create order and reduce uncertainty in exchange . . . and history in consequence is largely a story of institutional evolution in which the historical performance of economies can only be understood as a part of a sequential story" (North 1991, 97).

Moreover, the institutional setup of a society in a particular moment in time can shape the way in which this society is going to evolve: "Institutions provide the incentive structure of an economy; as that structure evolves, it shapes the direction of economic change towards growth, stagnation, or decline" (North 1991, 97).

The first half of the twentieth century saw a vast expansion of the social sciences, with formal and behavioral social sciences leading the charge. Formal social sciences made quick strides in developing the foundations of social sciences from formal, logical, and mathematical principles, translating the intuitive contributions of Adam Smith and his followers into precise mathematical structures that could be tested on logical and empirical grounds. Behavioral social sciences rode a prolific wave of technological innovations in computers and other tools of measurements to record and systematically organize a wide range of observable human behaviors, whether in the marketplace or in the social and political arena in which humans interact.

By the 1960s, Professor North had matured as a scholar, and both the formal and behavioral schools of thought in the social sciences had made tremendous progress, proving the feasibility of and the promise in pursuing rigorous social sciences.

One important question, however, kept haunting the success of the social sciences at the time: How to explain the clearly observable variance in success of economics performance across regions and countries? North provided the discipline with a resounding answer: Institutions make the difference. How they make the difference is the central theme of his work, the legacy with which he leaves us, and the main subject matter of this edited volume.

Before the introduction of institutions as the critical variable in explaining the success or failure of societies and economies, the state-of-the-art explanation for this variance revolved around the concept of transaction costs. The neoclassical, general-equilibrium model of free markets established that with zero transaction costs, free and competitive markets should result in efficient allocations of scarce resources at any time in any place. What, then, explains the fact that some market allocations are seemingly very inefficient while others seem closer to being optimal? The most common answers in the 1960s, 1970s, and even beyond, referenced the concept of transaction costs. Because transaction costs are never zero, a key to the variance in the performance of different economic systems is in the extent to which they experience higher or lower transaction costs. But where would this difference in the magnitude and significance of transaction costs come from?

As the formal understanding of individual behavior developed further, the so-called collective action problem emerged as a troubling sister to the problem of transaction costs. The collective action problem was first highlighted in Garrett Hardin's 1968 article "The Tragedy of the Commons." In her contribution to this volume, Elinor Ostrom articulates her lifelong dedication to the study of this problem, which is closely related to the management challenge of common pool resources (CPR) (Ostrom 1990). The problem emerges from the violation of one of the key assumptions in the generic model of competitive markets: that individual property rights are well-defined and enforced. When property rights are not well-defined, when they are ill-enforced, or when a collective of agents rather than individual agents holds ownership rights, basic individual incentives that in competitive markets would lead, according to commonly accepted scholarship, to efficiency results instead fail, and the efficiency results vanish with them.

Research at the time resorted to two "easy solutions" to the problems of transaction costs and collective action. One trend in the literature, called constitutional economics, highlighted the role of the state in resolving these problems (Buchanan and Tullock 1962). The other trend, developed in the 1960s and 1970s, highlighted the idea of a spontaneous emergence of property rights structures (Sugden 1986).

By the late 1970s both arguments had suffered major setbacks from advances in the social sciences. The calculus of consent (Buchanan and Tullock 1962) was proven to be a whole lot more complicated and much less predictable due to a third major problem that established for itself a solid reputation in the 1960s and came to be called the problem of collective choice (Arrow 1951). Collective decision making was proven to lack the elegant transitivity condition that most of us are assumed to satisfy in our individual choices (McKelvey 1979). Contrary to the premise underlying "constitutional economics," collective decision making could not be expected to result in straightforward, elegant, or efficient policy making, regardless of the constraints imposed on the process. Politics, and collective decision making more generally, are, simply put, generically messy. While the initial discovery of the problem dates to the late-eighteenth-century writings of Marie Jean Antoine Nicolas de Caritat, Marquis de Condorcet (e.g., Young 1990), Arrow (1951) brought the issue back to the forefront of the scholarship on the topic. However, Arrow's impossibility theorem was widely overlooked. In the late 1970s and early 1980s, a group of political scientists close to Professor North at the time began to highlight the relevance of Arrow's theorem and study it carefully. A series of seminal results, often labeled collectively "the chaos theorems" (McKelvey 1979; McKelvey and Schofield 1986, 1987), presented a serious challenge to the study of economics and politics as they seemed to suggest that the outcomes of majority-rule, collective decision making may be indeterminate. William H. Riker, a leading political scientist of the era and a close friend of Professor North, went as far as to conclude that

Politics is *the* dismal science because we have learned from it that there are no equilibria to predict. In the absence of equilibria we cannot know much about the future at all, whether it is likely to be palatable or unpalatable, and in that sense our future is subject to the tricks and accidents of the way questions are posed and the way alternatives are offered and eliminated. (Riker 1981, 447)

Kenneth A. Shepsle's contribution to this volume is a generic follow-up to the debate that raged at the time and is still central to contemporary social sciences, between those who gave up on any stability in "collective" choice environments and those who suggested that institutional structures may introduce some generic stability and predictability in the spheres of public political and economic decision making. Shepsle, who Professor North would soon join as an intellectual leader at the Center in Political Economy at Washington University in St. Louis, is credited with what would become a key foundation of the new institutional social sciences: "Standing between the individual qua bundle of tastes and available social choices are institutions... frameworks of rules, procedures and arrangements – that prescribe and constrain... the way in which business is conducted" (Shepsle 1986, 51–55).

At the heart of neoclassical literature on competitive markets, a different role was highlighted for economic institutions. Economists acknowledge the role of property rights as fundamental to the functioning of free markets. For decades, leading scholars in this school tried to explain this external determinant of social order from within the framework of the friction-free competitive market (e.g., Demsetz 1967). When these efforts failed (e.g., Demsetz 1982), a considerable effort was made to explain the "spontaneous" emergence of property rights using variations of repeated games logic (Sugden 1986) by which, in equilibrium, unconstrained agents with no external government enforcement would settle on some self-enforcing governance of property rights. Research of the late 1990s disputed this argument. First, it was shown that self-enforcement is unlikely in most realistic environments. Even small groups of agents with moderate levels of future discount factors cannot hope to sustain self-enforcement property rights structures (Calvert 1995). Second, governments were shown to be rather reliable enforcers of property rights under a wide range of conditions. This established a clear role for governments as protectors of the property rights of their constituents to allow free markets to function and economies to prosper (Sened 1997).

In his seminal work, *Essays on the Political Economy of Rural Africa*, Robert Bates summarizes the state of existing empirical evidence on the origin of property rights: "[T]oo much emphasis has been placed upon decentralized systems. On the one hand, their occurrences appears to be relatively infrequent; on the other, even in so far as decentralized societies do exist, they can arguably be regarded as transitory – as societies that once were centralized or which are in the early stages towards more centralized forms" (1983, 20). In his comprehensive study of the issue, Eggertsson (1990) concludes that "the institutional equilibrium of stateless society has, in most cases eventually given away, and the state, in its various forms, has emerged" (305). In his contribution to our volume, Robert Bates goes further to argue that one limitation of the new institutional social sciences is that they fail to pay enough attention to the actors who play the central role in those political institutions. If political institutions are critical to the understanding of social phenomena, we need a better understanding not only of those institutions and how they work, but also of the central players – that is, the human leaders who make them work.

Amid this growing interest in the role of institutions in social lives, North structured a legacy that was soon to move into the sphere of academic social sciences and far beyond. In this volume, both John Joseph Wallis as well as Claude Menard and Mary Shirley submit two well-documented histories of the ascendance of North's legacy and its history. In this introduction we limit ourselves to a series of short comments on its essence.

Following the concern with the uncertainty and instability that political structures introduced into society, Professor North's first intuition was that "the major role of institutions in society is to reduce uncertainty by establishing a stable (but not necessarily efficient) structure to human interactions" (1990a, 52).

What are institutions exactly? North (1990a) offers the following definition: "Institutions are the rules of the game in a society or, more formally, are the humanly devised constraints that shape human interaction." Thus, he emphasizes that institutions, in consequence, "structure incentives in human exchange, whether political, social, or economic" (54).

Once the importance of institutions was recognized, North set out to understand the reasons why inefficient institutions persist and, more broadly, the process and dynamics of institutional change. Institutional persistence and change has been the main theme of his work since the 1981 publication of *Structure and Change in Economic History*. This theme led North to investigate both path dependence and transaction costs, achieving a theory of the state in which, under the presence of transaction costs, political systems do not inevitably evolve into efficient institutions.

North's work also makes an important distinction between institutions and organizations. Institutions are hard to define because the rules that apply include written laws, formal social conventions, informal norms of behavior, and shared beliefs about the world. In contrast, organizations are concrete. They are made up of specific groups of individuals pursuing a mix of common and individual goals through partially coordinated behavior. This way he opened a large venue to the possibility of a dynamic relationship between the interests and incentives facing the organizations and the structure of the rules of the game that govern their actions and interactions. Ultimately, North paved the way for an integrated theory of the state that incorporates coercion as a tool of government.

North's view represented a significant novelty in the field of economic development as well. Economic growth theories traditionally ignored the institutional dimension of development by focusing on capital accumulation and technological change in a world where property rights were perfectly enforced. However, Ronald Coase's (1960) seminal work showed that creating, specifying, and enforcing property rights is costly and, thus, property rights will never be perfect.

The new institutional approach to development economies pioneered by North recognizes this and assumes that, in a world with positive transaction costs, enforcement of property rights has a cost that affects the allocation of resources and thus has an effect on growth. Hence, institutions that assure those rights become a relevant piece in the economic architecture that the process of growth and development is built on. As Douglass North and Paul Thomas (1973, 76) stated: "The factors we have listed (innovation, economies of scale, education, capital accumulation, etc.) are not causes of growth; they are growth." Factor accumulation and innovation are only proximate causes of growth. In North and Thomas's view, the fundamental explanation of comparative growth is differences in institutions.

Following his seminal work on the origin of institutions and their critical role in shaping economic systems, North led his scholarly journey to the frontier study of how both beliefs and ideological persuasions persist, and thus make all institutional change incremental at best. This idea plays a central role in *Institutions, Institutional Change and Economic Performance* (1990a) and is the central focus of *Understanding the Process of Economic Change* (2005).

In his most recent work, *Violence and Social Orders* (2009, with Wallis and Weingast), North poses a conceptual framework to understand recorded human history. The salient feature of this work is the attempt to assemble an equilibrium theory of the state and its role in shaping different social orders, through which we can understand the history of societies, from primitive ones to modern developed societies where open orders prevail.

Science in general progresses when curious people pose smart questions and then answer them. This is precisely what Douglass North has been doing throughout his entire academic career – at least fifty years of making progress in understanding human social history. The result has been an enormous impact on social sciences, which we hope is reflected in the broad collection of topics covered in this volume by a distinguished group of scholars working in the domain of the questions North's work has stimulated.

***

In Chapter 1 of this volume, Claude Mènard and Mary M. Shirley thoroughly review the rise of New Institutional Economics, giving special attention to the evolution of North's ideas and how they shaped the emerging field.

In Chapter 2, John Joseph Wallis recounts the evolution of North's ideas, but he does so through the lenses of the persistence and change of institutions in society. His essay explores North's intuitive reaction to the literature on the persistence of institutions and his insistence that the problem we should be investigating is institutional change.

Robert Bates in Chapter 3 goes a step further in advancing the field of New Institutional Social Sciences, arguing that this school of thought has failed to pay enough attention to those who play the central role in all political institutions. He explains that the environment from which politicians come has a significant effect on how they deal with the institutions at hand or lack thereof. Comparing the "path-dependent" respective developments of Kenya and Uganda, he shows how the unique pattern of relationships between politicians and their respective constituency has led to very significant divergence of the final outcomes in each case.

Kenneth A. Shepsle's contribution to this volume (Chapter 4) represents a central debate in contemporary social sciences, between those who do not see any stability in collective choice environments and those who suggest that institutional structures may introduce some generic stability and predictability in the spheres of public political and economic decision making. Examples drawn from the U.S. Congress are used to exhibit the ways in which rules arise, change endogenously, and are sometimes even violated.

In Chapter 5, Nobel Laureate Elinor Ostrom revisits and further articulates her lifelong dedication to the study of the problem of the management of common pool resources (CPRs). The problem of CPR management emerges from the violation of a key assumption in the generic model of competitive markets: that individual property rights are well-defined and enforced. Property rights in CPRs are ill-defined, ill-enforced, or defined and enforced collectively in a way that individual incentives do not lead, at least given commonly accepted scholarship, to the efficiency results expected in perfectly competitive markets.

In Chapter 6, Sebastian Galiani and Ernesto Schargrodsky present a study of the causal effects of property rights. Douglass North's research has shown the importance of the institutional dimension in the process of economic development. Among the institutions that foster growth, the enforcement of property rights appears most prominently. Land rights are particularly important in the process of economic development. Relying on a unique natural experiment of land titling at the outskirts of Buenos Aires, Argentina, Galiani and Schargrodsky review the effects of titling the poor on their physical and human capital investments, household decisions, access to credit, earnings, and beliefs.

Gillian K. Hadfield and Barry R. Weingast in Chapter 7 highlight North's influence on the emerging field of research of law and society. Scholars agree that a legal system providing for impersonal exchange is important for long-term economic growth. In their paper they explore the complex questions of what law is and what its components are. They ask why law has the attributes characteristically associated with the rule of law, why law involves public reasoning, and how this system is sustained as an equilibrium.

In Chapter 8, Joel Mokyr addresses the issue of culture, institutions, and economic growth. Following on the work of North in *Understanding the Process of Economic Change*, Mokyr examines the role of innovative grand ideas and the "intellectual entrepreneurs" that help spread them in the evolution of culture, suggesting ways in which we can understand cultural change and how it affects the economy. He then applies this framework to provide an understanding of a special case of considerable interest to students of economic change, namely the British economy on the eve of the Industrial Revolution.

Steven C. A. Pincus and James A. Robinson in Chapter 9 revisit a key debate in economic history. The Glorious Revolution of 1688–1689 is one of the most famous instances of institutional change. It fascinates scholars because of the role it may have played in creating an environment conducive to making England the first industrial nation. This claim was advanced forcefully by North and Weingast (1989). And yet, existing literature in history and economic history dismisses their arguments. Pincus and Robinson argue that North and Weingast were correct in arguing that the Glorious Revolution represented a critical change in institutions. In addition, and contrary to the claims of many historians, most of the things they claimed happened, such as parliamentary sovereignty, did happen. But Pincus and Robinson argue that they happened for reasons different from those North and Weingast put forward. This chapter shows that rather than being an instance of a de jure "re-writing the rules," as North and Weingast argued, the Glorious Revolution was actually an interlinked series of de facto institutional changes that came from a change in the balance of power and authority and was part of a broader reorientation in the political equilibrium of England. Moreover, it was significant for the economy not because it solved a problem of credible commitment, but because the institutional changes meant that after 1688, party politicians rather than the king set the economic agenda, and also because the ministries were dominated by Whigs with a specific program of economic modernization.

In Chapter 10, Scott Gehlbach and Edmund J. Malesky address the issue of institutional change in Eastern Europe and the former Soviet Union. Their essay traces the evolution of the literature on this topic, showing how the study of transition has responded and contributed to our understanding of the emergence and evolution of key political and economic institutions.

Pamela Jakiela (Chapter 11) and Pedro Dal Bó (Chapter 12) close the volume with two examples of the imprints of North's legacy on the field of experimental social sciences. Jakiela investigates informal institutions, with moral preferences at the heart of her research in experimental economics. Dal Bo applies the tools of experimental economics to the study of formal institutions. His essay reviews part of the extensive experimental literature on the workings of democratic institutions, starting with the description of the existing literature studying the determinants of efficient institutional change. That is, when will people choose institutions that provide incentives for them to take socially optimal actions? Results from original experiments he conducted with his research collaborators show that whether subjects vote for efficient institutions may depend on their understanding of the environment. The essay summarizes the recent literature, showing that democracy can affect behavior itself, in addition to its effect on the choice of policies and regulations.

The Contribution of Douglass North to New Institutional Economics

Claude Ménard and Mary M. Shirley

1. Introduction

New Institutional Economics (NIE) began to take shape around some relatively vague intuitions only in the 1970s, yet in less than twenty years, the field has produced four Nobel laureates; significantly impacted major policy debates on a range of topics from antitrust law to development aid; increasingly penetrated mainstream journals; and developed a large and growing body of adherents, research, and data. Many actors were important to this successful evolution; in another essay (Ménard and Shirley 2012b) we have focused on three in particular. Ronald Coase, Douglass North, and Oliver Williamson transformed early intuitions about institutions into powerful conceptual and analytical tools, spawning a vigorous base of empirical research. Although she started somewhat later than the first three, Elinor Ostrom's work quickly had a major impact as well, especially on political science and environmental and development economics.

Today's robust institutionalization of NIE is especially remarkable when we consider that from the beginning it was divided into distinct schools of thought. One school of thought is identified with Coase and Williamson and analyzes property rights and contracts at the firm level; another, identified with Douglass North, analyzes broader institutional environments and the role of the state.[1] Ostrom was one of the small but growing number

---

[1] There are a number of other schools of thought that developed simultaneously and are closely associated with or even part of NIE that we do not have space to cover adequately here. These include, for example, the theories of Mancur Olson, public choice theory and the work of Buchanan and Tullock, and the work of positive political scientists such as Ken Shepsle and Barry Weingast. Closely associated with NIE is the work of Harold Demsetz, in the continuation of the property rights approach. However, when it comes to the history of how ISNIE was born and developed, we think that the two branches on which we focus here led the way and represent the dominant group of participants. Our *Handbook of New*

of institutionalists whose empirical work encompasses both Williamson's transaction cost economics and North's institutional analysis.[2] This review focuses on the contribution of Douglass North and the school of thought associated with his work to the development and institutionalization of NIE. The chapter's main contribution is a succinct overview of North's evolving ideas about institutions and an explanation of how his work shaped the emerging field of New Institutional Economics with important repercussions for economics and the social sciences more broadly. For example, North's research changed many economists' view of development from a process of growth spurred by new technology and capital accumulation to a dynamic process of institutional change. North's ideas also helped set the agenda for scholars studying the post-communist transition, as Gehlbach and Malesky argue in their chapter in this volume. This review of North's work offers a valuable lesson of how persistent and well-placed confidence and hard work can productively transform the status quo.

Section 2 of this chapter summarizes how the key concepts that underlie all institutional analysis were formulated in response to puzzles not well explained by the standard neoclassical paradigm, in particular: the decision to make, to buy, or to look for alternative organizational arrangements and the explanation of why some countries are rich and some countries are poor. NIE accepts much of the standard neoclassical paradigm, although with important exceptions that give NIE its revolutionary character.[3] Section 3 then traces the special contribution of Douglass North to the transformation of NIE from early ideas to analytical tools, analyzing the evolution of his ideas on institutions, and Section 4 describes the dissemination of NIE in general and North's ideas in particular. Section 5 concludes with a brief discussion of the challenges for future research and the possibility that growing mainstream acceptance will erode NIE's revolutionary character, creative focus, and interdisciplinary nature. How best can institutionalists avoid the risk of uninspiring and narrow-minded orthodoxy? The remarkable scholarly life of Douglass North offers a stellar example of how creativity, insight, and innovation can be preserved and strengthened over the course of many decades.

Institutional Economics (2005) includes a relatively wide spectrum of the contributors to NIE, including the four Nobel laureates, although some other major names (e.g., Barzel and Demsetz) are missing.

[2] Other examples of this synthesis are found in Greif (2006) and the case studies of urban water reform in Shirley (2002).

[3] In Ménard and Shirley (2012) we examine these exceptions in detail.

2. The Intellectual Origins of NIE[4]

Virginia Woolf once asserted that "on or about December 1910 human character changed" (Woolf 1928, 4). We cannot be so bold in determining when economics changed,[5] but we can date the origins of the changes introduced by NIE. They emerged from the confluence of several major contributions: two pioneering papers from Ronald Coase, "The Nature of the Firm" (1937/1988b) and "The Problem of Social Cost" (1960/1988a), two defining books – Davis and North on *Institutional Change and American Economic Growth* (1971) and North and Thomas on *The Rise of the Western World: A New Economic History* (1973), and Williamson's landmark book *Markets and Hierarchies* (1975). Although there were predecessors, as there are with all schools of economics, these contributions laid the foundation for the transformation of NIE's initial intuitions into a useful analytical apparatus.

As we mentioned, new institutional economics arose in response to two puzzles: Why make or buy? Why rich or poor? Solving the first puzzle required an explanation of why economic activity was organized into firms, markets, bureaus, franchises, and other modes of organization, to understand what went on inside the firm, and to explain firm decisions about mergers versus contracts. Solving the second puzzle demanded an explanation for the vast disparities in economic performance and why these disparities persist despite countless efforts at reform and decades of foreign aid and advice.

The standard neoclassical paradigm viewed the economic system as adjusting supply to demand and production to consumption automatically, under the coordination of the price mechanism. Neoclassical economists long treated the firm as a black box, a production function that turned inputs into outputs, responding to changes in relative prices and available resources in ways that maximize profits. This system worked under certain simplifying assumptions that troubled the founders of NIE, such as the assumptions that information is perfect, individuals are rational wealth-maximizers with stable preferences, and exchange is instantaneous and costless. New institutionalists also questioned mainstream assumptions that different rates of development were purely the result of different endowments of resources and human capital or of different rates of investment and adoption of new technologies. Another puzzle that particularly concerned North was the nature of the state; namely, why political markets do not function like

---

[4] This section draws from Menard and Shirley (2012).
[5] We might note that Ronald Coase was born in December 1910.

economic markets and under what circumstances states protect property rights even when they possess unchallenged power to expropriate property and subjugate individuals?[6]

NIE's answers to these fundamental economic puzzles rest on three key concepts – transaction costs, property rights, and contracts – the "golden triangle" of NIE. These concepts, combined with NIE's increasingly radical behavioral assumptions (e.g., North 2005), progressively structured NIE's two leading schools. Let us consider briefly the origin of those three key concepts.

The concept of transaction cost arose when Ronald Coase first challenged the standard description of the economy as an automatic process that equilibrates supply with demand by means of the price mechanism in his 1937 paper "The Nature of the Firm." Coase asked, why are there firms?[7] The answer, as he later described, was that "although production could be carried out in a completely decentralized way by means of contract between individuals, the fact that it costs something to enter into these transactions means that firms will emerge to organize what would otherwise be market transactions whenever their costs were less than the costs of carrying out the transactions through the market" (Coase 1988a, 7). In the market, a would-be trader must find someone with whom to trade, determine price and quality, reach an agreement between buyer and seller, and monitor and enforce that agreement. By eliminating the need for bargains among the many owners of the factors of production, a firm can sometimes reduce these transaction costs (Coase 1960).

Steven Cheung later enriched Coase's idea, arguing that a firm would lower transaction costs whenever discovering a price through the market required numerous transactions or information about many different components of a product or required measurement of attributes that change frequently, vary greatly, or may not be conveniently stipulated in advance; and/or whenever the different contributions of inputs cannot be easily separated (Cheung 1983).[8]

---

[6] This has also been a prime concern of Robert Bates, whose lucid and compelling book, *Beyond the Miracle of the Market* (1989), cogently analyzes how economic institutions change political choices, using Kenya as a case study.

[7] At the same time that Coase wrote his paper, Commons (1934, 4) introduced the idea that "the ultimate unit of activity . . . must contain in itself the three principles of conflict, mutuality, and order. This unit is a transaction." Coase was unaware of this development, but later Williamson (1975, 6; 1996, 7) integrated it into his approach to transaction costs.

[8] Cheung also showed how transaction costs affect contractual arrangement in different sectors, most notably agriculture (1969, 1973).

Williamson operationalized the concept of transaction costs by asking what are the specific factors that determine the choice between market and firm and how a firm decides whether to make, to buy, or to rely on alternative arrangements such as franchising, joint ventures, strategic alliances, and so forth. His answers focused in particular on the role of asset specificity, uncertainty, and the frequency of transacting, as we explore in greater detail in "From Intuition to Institutionalization: A History of New Institutional Economics" (Ménard and Shirley 2012).

In later work Coase argued that transaction costs profoundly influence not only individual firms but the size and activities of the entire economy. "If the costs of making an exchange are greater than the gains which that exchange would bring, that exchange would not take place and the greater production that would flow from specialization would not be realized. In this way transaction costs affect not only contractual arrangements but also what goods and services are produced" (Coase 1992, 716). Continuing this idea, North used the concept of transaction costs to address why some countries are rich and some countries are poor.

North extended the concept of transaction costs to explain the state and some of its fundamental characteristics (1990b). Political markets are more prone to inefficiency than economic markets. The cost of measuring and enforcing agreements is higher in political markets, North argued, because what is being exchanged – promises for votes – is inherently difficult to measure. Voters may find it hard to judge if the actions of their representatives produce outcomes that favor voter interests; voters may not even know what their interests are under certain policy choices. And voter ability to judge their representatives' effectiveness is clouded by beliefs: Representatives do not only make policy promises to their constituents, they also sell themselves on the basis of ideological frameworks that appeal to voters' preferences and prejudices. Competition, which plays a powerful role in economic markets, is weaker in political markets, where representatives can be held accountable only in infrequent elections. Nondemocratic political markets lacking even electoral competition operate with far less transparency, so political transaction costs are even higher.

NIE's second central concept is property rights. Standard neoclassical economics assumed that people trade physical commodities and services, but Coase argued in "The Federal Communications Commission" that they actually trade rights – the rights to perform certain actions – and that those rights with their duties and privileges are established by the legal system (Coase 1959). This view of property rights was further developed by Armen Alchian in a contribution initially published in *Il Politico* in 1965, where he defined property rights as a set of rights to take permissible actions to use, transfer, or otherwise exploit or enjoy property. These rights are sometimes enforced by law but more often are enforced by etiquette, social custom, and social ostracism.[9]

Unlike standard neoclassical economics, which assumes contracts are complete and costlessly enforceable through the judicial system, Williamson's work on contracts also implied that property rights would be vulnerable to opportunistic predation and that legal systems are usually a more costly remedy for disputes than private ordering. North focused on how property rights and their enforcement affect the ways societies develop and differ. North contrasted the robust property rights of powerful elites with the vulnerable or absent rights of non-elites in societies where non-elites have little access to legal or political remedies.

Ostrom expanded and enhanced our understanding of property rights with her work on alternative ways to organize common property resources such as irrigation systems or fishing grounds to those postulated by mainstream economics: private ownership or state regulation. Ostrom argued that under certain circumstances governance by local user groups is superior to poorly defined and enforced private property rights (leading to the tragedy of the commons), as well as to government regulation or state ownership. Through meticulous and extensive field work and laboratory experiments Ostrom showed that where the boundaries of the users and the resources are clear, monitoring and enforcement by small, tightly knit groups with strong social norms and procedures for making rules and enforcing sanctions produces superior outcomes. Ostrom's evolving theoretical framework provided a foundation for scientific analysis of highly complex and heterogeneous institutions through carefully designed comparative microanalytics.

NIE's third core concept is contract. In the standard neoclassical paradigm, contracts are agreements between parties that are perfectly complete and perfectly enforced. Once again the concept of contract was progressively developed along different paths by the two main branches of NIE. Williamson stressed the issue of incomplete contracts as early as 1971 in a paper on vertical integration. In his formulation, opportunism – the

---

[9] Demsetz (1967) substantiated Alchian's view in his controversial analysis of the emergence of private property rights among the Montagnais, a tribe of Northeastern Canada, in which he argued that property rights arise when it becomes economically beneficial for them to do so.

idea that parties to an exchange may defect from the spirit of cooperation when the stakes are high – overturned neoclassical behavioral assumptions that ignored these human traits. To Williamson, a contract is "an agreement between a buyer and a supplier in which the terms of exchange are defined by a triple: *price, asset specificity,* and *safeguards*" (ital. from Williamson 1996, 377). Williamson's approach to contracts became central to NIE's analysis of governance, and, as emphasized by the Nobel Committee in 2009, the source of many successful empirical investigations, operationalizing the Coasian approach in microeconomics and industrial organization.

The Northean branch emphasized early on the key role of contract enforcement and the institutions it requires, particularly the polity (North 1981, ch. 4).[10] Contract enforcement and especially the role of coercion in protecting property rights and individual rights later developed into a theory of its own. North highlighted the trade-off between the high cost of private protection of property using private police, private armies, and the like versus the risk of state protection of property, which might reduce private costs but invite state encroachment on rights (see North et al. 2009; and also North and Weingast 1989; Weingast 1993; Greif 2005). The risk of state predation led North, Weingast, and others to emphasize ways the state might credibly commit to respect private property rights, a theme that united the two branches of NIE.

Transaction costs, property rights, and contracts are not the only concepts developed by NIE, but they encapsulate its core and make its paradigm distinctive. One reason NIE differs radically from the orthodox approach is because these core concepts reject standard neoclassical assumptions of perfect information, perfect rationality, and zero transaction costs.

3. From Early Ideas to Analytical Tools: The Contribution of Douglass North

In the late 1960s and early 1970s, these early ideas about transaction costs, property rights, and contracts were already evolving into the core concepts of what Williamson christened New Institutional Economics (Williamson 1975, ch. 1). A research program progressively blossomed, challenging some of the main assumptions of standard neoclassical economics. As we

---

[10] See also the influence of Buchanan and Tullock (1962) on North; and Buchanan (1975) on Williamson. Barzel's contribution to the analysis of property rights and the violence of the state also deserves mention here (e.g., 1989).

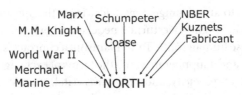

Figure 1.1. Early roots of North's ideas

have mentioned, this program developed almost simultaneously along two branches. In another paper we consider both branches and their interactions, but here we focus on the contribution of Douglass North to the branch that we call institutional analysis.

Douglass North's earliest intellectual roots were as a Marxist when he was an undergraduate at the University of California at Berkeley (see Fig. 1.1). Another early influence was World War II: North had to think profoundly about violence and societies when he decided to join the merchant marine because, as he put it, "I did not want to kill people." Later he was exposed to the ideas of Joseph Schumpeter through the entrepreneurial school of Arthur Cole at Harvard. Schumpeter had a strong influence on North's thinking, as did his interactions with the economists he met when he spent a year at the NBER in the mid-1950s, including Solomon Fabricant and Simon Kuznets.

In the later 1950s and early 1960s North became a leader in the first efforts to apply economic theory and quantitative methods to history and in the process became a founder of the new field of cliometrics (another subject in its own right and beyond the scope of this paper). His emphasis on institutions began later and developed gradually. The rest of this section summarizes the main milestones in North's institutional theories, which we illustrate in Figure 1.2.

In his 1961 and 1966 books, North followed the standard economic model. For instance, he attributed economic growth to three factors: technology, human capital, and efficient economic organization, giving primacy to technological change (North 1961, 1966). But North was beginning to question the applicability of mainstream economics in the 1960s when he turned to study European history. Increasingly he concluded that the tools of neoclassical economics "were not up to the task of explaining the kind of fundamental societal change that had characterized European economies from medieval times onward" (North 1993, 3).

North departed noticeably from a strictly neoclassical approach in his famous 1968 paper in the *Journal of Political Economy* (one of the most

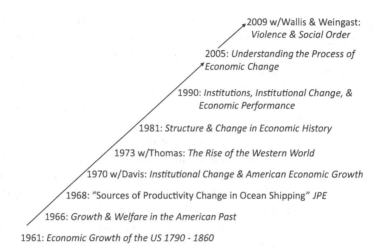

2009 w/Wallis & Weingast:
Violence & Social Order

2005: *Understanding the Process of Economic Change*

1990: *Institutions, Institutional Change, & Economic Performance*

1981: *Structure & Change in Economic History*

1973 w/Thomas: *The Rise of the Western World*

1970 w/Davis: *Institutional Change & American Economic Growth*

1968: "Sources of Productivity Change in Ocean Shipping" *JPE*

1966: *Growth & Welfare in the American Past*

1961: *Economic Growth of the US 1790 - 1860*

Figure 1.2. North's evolving view of institutions as reflected in his major publications

quoted research works in economic history, according to the Nobel committee). This paper explains the reasons for productivity gains in ocean shipping since 1600. Prior to this paper, as North puts it, "Among economic historians, technological change has always held the pre-eminent position as a source of economic growth" (North 1993, 953). North's 1968 paper knocked technology off its throne.

The genesis of the paper was exceptionally hands-on. While pondering the puzzle of productivity gains in shipping, North toured a maritime museum in the Netherlands. North noticed that the ship models did not display any major technology improvements, but had carried fewer and fewer armaments over time. He went home and built models of ships from historical kits to confirm his observations. North knew firsthand from his experience in the merchant marine the importance of weight and labor costs to productivity in ocean shipping, and the paper shows how a decline in piracy and privateering permitted ships to reduce both heavy armaments and manpower and also lowered insurance costs. Additional key factors in productivity improvements were the development of bigger markets and the aggregation of goods in fewer ports, which allowed ships to transport goods in both directions and reduced turnaround time in port. Through a combination of practical experience, keen observation, and meticulous research, North opened a new perspective on productivity improvement.

North's 1971 book with Davis, *Institutional Change and American Economic Growth*, further diminishes the priority assigned to technology as the explanation for growth. North and Davis specified a theory of institutional change, which they applied to facets of U.S. economic history. Despite its unorthodoxy, the book showed strong neoclassical roots, especially in its hypothesis that institutional innovation occurs when the expected net gains exceed the expected costs.

North's 1973 book with Robert Paul Thomas, *The Rise of the Western World: A New Economic History*, similarly moved toward giving organizational and institutional change a greater role in determining growth. North and Thomas asserted that "efficient economic organization is the key to growth" and that efficient economic organization entails "the establishment of institutional arrangements and property rights that create an incentive to channel individual economic effort into activities that bring the private rate of return close to the social rate of return" (North and Thomas 1973, 1). The book argued that new institutional arrangements such as written contracts enforced by courts were largely responsible for successful European economic development because they enabled units "to realize economies of scale (joint stock companies, corporations), to encourage innovation (prizes, patent laws), to improve the efficiency of factor markets (enclosures, bills of exchange, the abolition of serfdom), or to reduce market imperfections (insurance companies)" (North and Thomas 1973, 5–6). North and Thomas stressed that fragile property rights are an important obstacle to economic development and Galiani and Schargrodsky's chapter in this volume provides strong evidence of the effects of land titling on the poor in Buenos Aires.

Yet the North and Thomas framework still showed neoclassical roots. For instance, it assumed that institutions change when the net benefit from change outweighs the cost, although North and Thomas documented that the fiscal benefits to government sometimes lead the state to protect inefficient property rights for a very long time – as in Spain – a forecast of North's future direction.

Increasingly, North began to ask how these efficiency assumptions could be true when for centuries most countries had suffered under persistently inefficient institutions that caused persistently poor economic performance. He sought a more realistic explanation for why societies choose the institutions they have and why they choose to change them. In his breakthrough book, *Structure and Change in Economic History* (North 1981) he abandoned the assumption that institutions were efficient, and he also introduced the role of ideology in fostering or hindering change, foreshadowing his later interest in beliefs.

North's book *Institutions, Institutional Change, and Economic Performance* (1990a) went further in abandoning the neoclassical assumptions of efficiency and rationality. North answers his pertinent question of wealth and poverty as follows: "Third World countries are poor because the institutional constraints define a set of payoffs to political/ economic activity that do not encourage productive activity" (North 1990a, 110). Institutional change occurs when economic or political entrepreneurs who have the bargaining strength to change institutions perceive "that they could do better by altering the existing institutional framework on some margin. But their perceptions crucially depend on both the information the entrepreneurs receive and how they process that information" (North 1990a, 8). Their information is often incomplete, their models imperfect, and their reforms "path dependent" – constrained by the existing set of institutions and incentives.

North began to go beyond information problems and path dependency, arguing that radical reforms are also constrained by societies' inherited belief systems. "Societies that get 'stuck' embody belief systems and institutions that fail to confront and solve new problems of societal complexity" (North 1994, 6). The sticky nature of beliefs and institutions helps explain why underdevelopment has been so persistent in most of the world and why efforts to reform by importing rules, laws, and constitutions from elsewhere have been so unsuccessful. But a new puzzle arose. If rules and norms resist change because of beliefs, then what determines beliefs? North turned to cognitive science to understand better how human beliefs are affected by their "mental models." Human beings use mental models to explain and interpret the world. These models are shaped by individuals' personal experiences and their inherited belief system – the belief system that they share with other members of their society. Because learning is filtered through this shared belief system, the past affects how people solve problems today (North 2005, 77).[11]

Having developed an institutional framework to explain European and American history and then having adapted it to explain the history of underdevelopment, North joined John Wallis and Barry Weingast to interpret all of recorded human history (North et al. 2009). Their analysis starts ten thousand years ago when humans were still dominated by warring tribes. In some of these tribes, small groups of powerful elites formed coalitions around specialists in violence who could protect nonmilitary elites, such as traders or the clergy, and limit outsiders' access to valuable resources – land,

---

[11] In this same vein Chapter 13 in this volume, by Dal Bò, presents experimental evidence that people's willingness to demand efficient institutional change depends on their understanding of the environment.

labor, capital – and valuable activities – trade, worship, education (North et al. 2009, 30). Limiting non-elite access gave elites exclusive control over resources and activities that generated rents. These rents in turn motivated elites to agree not to fight each other but to share power, creating a stable equilibrium for expanded trade and production – and additional rents. This equilibrium was so stable that limited-access orders came to dominate most societies through most of human history; they became the "natural state."

The natural state encompasses a large and varied group; some societies are "fragile," tottering on the brink of chaos and war; others are "basic" with more durable and stable state organizations; and some are "mature" with many of the formal trapping of open access such as secure property rights, regular elections, and apparently open trade. But all natural states, even the mature ones, enforce property rights and rule of law only for elites, and all have institutions designed to limit access. Access is limited in basic and fragile natural states by laws and norms that allow only elites to engage in trade or to create or dominate corporations, unions, political parties, clubs, and other organizations. Non-elites may not be explicitly excluded from starting businesses or going into politics in mature natural states, but if they try they will face such high transaction costs that they will not be able to compete with elites. For example, it will be much cheaper and easier for elite-run businesses to obtain credit or government contracts because banks and state agencies are run by their cronies. Elites in natural states use the law, the state, social networks, and tradition to limit access and retain control, but that does not mean that the specific elite group that controls power and wealth never changes. To the contrary, the personalities with power and wealth change frequently through coups, revolutions, and even elections. What seldom changes are the institutions that exclude the bulk of society from access to the means of power and wealth. When non-elite groups manage to wrest control from elites, the new insiders usually use the same exclusionary institutions to limit access for everyone outside their circle.

Open-access societies are still the exception. They emerged only recently, after the industrial revolution in Europe, and spread to the countries that now compose the developed world. They operate very differently from limited-access orders; they are distinguished by shared belief systems emphasizing equality, sharing, and universal inclusion. Open-access institutions ensure that the political system controls the use of violence, laws are enforced impartially, and citizens across society have access to competitive economic and political organizations at relatively low transaction costs. Not only is access open, the risks of market participation are reduced and the gains across society are shared through such means as universal education, social insurance programs, and widespread infrastructure and public goods (North et al. 2009, 111).

In North, Wallis, and Weingast's framework, economic development takes on a new meaning: "In addition to capital accumulation, being developed economically entails having sophisticated economic organizations and credible enforcement of property rights and other contractual commitments.... Being developed politically entails having rule of law, a constitutional setting in which all major players accept changes of power, effective legal recognition of organizational rights independently of who is in power, and state control of organized violence" (2009, 3).

This 2009 work is the latest in North's evolving insights about how institutions explain long-run economic performance, insights that have stimulated a large body of applied research. Simultaneous with this rising interest in Northean institutional analysis, there has been a rising interest in NIE more broadly, and we document both trends in Section 4.

4. The Diffusion of NIE in General and Institutional Analysis in Particular

North's work contributed to a general diffusion of New Institutional Economics, and the feedback from this expanding network also fed into his evolving theory. The diffusion of NIE was also spurred by the creation of an international society, in which North also played an important role.

4.A. The Diffusion of New Institutional Economics

During the late 1980s and early 1990s, a growing number of researchers were attracted to NIE, and its influence over economics and other disciplines began to expand. Scholars increasingly cited Coase, North, and Williamson in the literature; presentations and sessions on institutional research at international conferences multiplied; and the subject attracted adherents in political science, management, law, sociology, and anthropology, among others. We can get a partial picture of this trend by looking at the increase in articles referring to NIE in refereed journals. The number of publications listed in Google Scholar with "New Institutional Economics" in the title grew from one in the 1970s to fifty in the 1980s to close to 200 in the 1990s and more than 400 in the 2000s.

With the spread of articles on New Institutional Economics, a network of new institutionalists began to emerge. At first the network was informal and unorganized: scholars with an interest in institutions simply attended each other's presentations at meetings in economics, managerial sciences, history, political science, and other social sciences. This informal network got a boost in 1983 when Rudolf Richter began to organize, initially with Eirik Furubotn, an annual research seminar on institutions in Germany.[12] All leading institutionalists attended this conference at one time or another, and their contributions were published in the *Journal of Institutional and Theoretical Economics*.

Still, this informal network was largely sustained by sporadic and haphazard encounters of like-minded institutionalists in conferences devoted to other topics. The sporadic nature of these contacts frustrated some scholars who in the early 1990s began to discuss the creation of a more formal network. In a process that we have documented in another paper (Ménard and Shirley 2012), these scholars' activities led to the creation of the International Society for New Institutional Economics (ISNIE), with annual meetings that gave a large boost to the diffusion of the field.

Douglass North played a key role in the creation of ISNIE. He was highly supportive of the idea of a more formal network from the first time Claude Ménard proposed it in a 1994 conference in Paris. He continued to be enthusiastic throughout the start-up of the new organization, providing strong support to initiatives led by Lee and Alexandra Benham, Claude Ménard, and Mary Shirley, later reinforced by John Drobak and others. North cosigned a letter with Ronald Coase inviting a large group of scholars to join the new society in October 1996. He participated actively in the early planning meetings and agreed to join the board of directors and to serve two terms (1998–2000) as the second president of the new society (Ronald Coase was the first). He continued thereafter to lend his strong support to ISNIE as a board member and regular speaker at the meetings. As we report elsewhere (Ménard and Shirley 2012), ISNIE has provided institutional scholars with a regular point of contact, attracted new adherents to NIE, and accelerated the dialogue between the two main branches and across disciplines.

4.B. The Diffusion of Northean Institutional Analysis

Initially the branch of institutional analysis identified with Douglass North captured a wider audience, while Coasian-Williamsonian ideas were highly influential in specific fields, such as industrial organization, managerial

---

[12] Held in Mettlach for the first two years then in Wallerfangen, under which name the seminar became known.

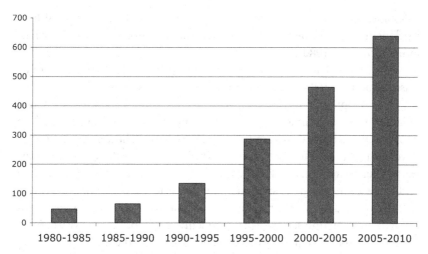

Figure 1.3. Citations of North's articles. *Source: Web of Science.*

science, and law and economics.[13,14] We can see the spread of North's ideas in Figure 1.3, which shows the rise in citations of North's articles. Since many of North's most influential publications are books, this figure gives a very partial indication of his impact but it does show the strong upward trend.

North's work had an impact on a number of fields. For example, his work was one of a number of important influences shaping the direction of the new political economy. Initially new political economy largely focused on the United States and democracy, voting, legislative rules, and bureaucracy, but more recently there has been an upsurge in studies analyzing a broader set of institutions and covering polities in European and developing and transitional countries. Northean institutional analysis also influenced how scholars study utilities, such as telecommunications, water, or electricity, and common-pool problems and management of small communities, such as Ostrom's work. Increasingly these scholars are analyzing how broader political, constitutional, and societal institutions affect sector or locality

---

[13]   By the early 2000s, the Coasean-Williamsonian branch had begun to win wider adherents as well, and both branches of NIE became well-established. For specifics on NIE's diffusion see *The Handbook of New Institutional Economics*. The references provided in the different chapters substantiate the richness of analysis already available at the time the book was published. Further evidence can be found in the collection of papers in Furubotn and Richter (1991), in the seven volumes by Ménard (2004b), in Brousseau and Glachant (2008), and in the synthesis already proposed by Furubotn and Richter (1997). See also partial surveys provided in Shelanski and Klein (1995), Klein (2005), Ménard (2004a).

[14]   North's enormous impact on historical analysis is beyond the scope of this paper; indeed we cannot truly do justice to his huge impact on economics and other disciplines.

rules and performance.[15] Similarly, in law and economics, studies of how legal institutions frame market exchanges and investor incentives have ballooned since the 1980s.[16]

North's ideas had an especially strong impact on development economists, practitioners in the aid community, and policy-makers and scholars in developing countries. The collapse of planned economies opened a Pandora's box of choices, and scholars and practitioners alike seized on Northean institutional analysis to help inform them. Those studying underdevelopment turned to North as one of the few prominent economists offering persuasive new answers to the question of why some countries are rich and some countries are poor. Starting in the mid-1990s the importance of institutions to development was increasingly accepted among development scholars and practitioners. North was first invited to speak at the World Bank in 1994 and spoke frequently to aid agencies, consulted with presidents and top officials of developing countries, and gave speeches to packed audiences in developing countries around the world. The World Bank devoted a flagship publication, the 2002 World Development Report, to institutions and development, and institutional issues were also taken up in many subsequent WDRs as well as in World Bank Policy Research Reports, starting with *Bureaucrats in Business* (World Bank 1995). Other international agencies adopted the same focus (see, e.g., InterAmerican Development Bank 2003, International Monetary Fund 2003, 2005). Critiques of development assistance were also strongly influenced by North. These critiques cite the failure and even inability of foreign aid to deal adequately with institutional barriers to growth (see, e.g., Easterly 2002; Martens et al. 2002; Shirley 2008). One reason for this apparently paradoxical influence was the tendency of some in the aid community to ignore those aspects of institutional analysis that conflicted with their belief that outside assistance can change institutions (e.g., Shirley 2008).

The implications of Northean institutional analysis for growth also began to have a large impact on macroeconomists. So-called new growth economists increasingly included aggregate measures of institutions in Solow-style growth models. Unlike the earlier frustrating experience of scholars who tried to correlate growth to democracy with ambiguous

[15] See for example, Ostrom's work on common-pool resources and case studies of local management; Levy and Spiller (1996) on telecommunicatons; Shirley, ed. (2002) on water supply and the chapter on regulation of public utilities by Spiller and Tommasi in the *Handbook of New Institutional Economics* (2005/2008).

[16] See for example, the several chapters on legal institutions in the *Handbook of New Institutional Economics* (2005/2008).

results, these economists discovered that institutional variables had statistically strong, positive correlations with growth. These strong correlations led even some previously disdainful mainstream economists to use them in their own work. As one economist described the situation: "Growth economists who, as mentioned earlier, used to rely almost uniquely on pareto-optimal-complete-market-perfectly competitive neoclassical models, now systematically abandon their traditional paradigms **without being ashamed** and they discuss the role of institutions **without thinking they are doing second-rate research**" (Sala-i-Martin 2002, 17, emphasis added). Furthermore, these "institutional" measures were easily accessible. For example, Knack and Keefer (1995), in one of the earliest papers to use an aggregate measure of institutions in regressions and perhaps the one that launched this trend, used widely available commercial risk ratings as proxies for institutional quality. The subsequent upsurge in studies employing this and similar variables has been a mixed blessing, because the variables are abstract and general, running counter to NIE's emphasis on increasing precision and specificity in economics. But they did spur wider interest in institutions among mainstream economists.

Initially, most applied institutional analysis focused largely on formal, written institutions, neglecting North's emphasis on societal norms and beliefs.[17] Among the few authors to defy this trend was Elinor Ostrom, who emphasized social norms in the success of community groups in managing common property. Avner Greif is another institutionalist who treats social norms seriously. For Greif, beliefs, norms, and organizations are as much a part of institutions as Northean rules. Indeed, for Greif, institutions are such powerful motivators precisely because they incorporate individuals' beliefs and internalized norms about the world, including their expectations of how others will behave and will expect them to behave. Joel Mokyr also emphasizes beliefs, which he defines as including knowledge and attitudes toward science and technology as well as religious beliefs and ideology. In his chapter in this volume he argues that beliefs, values, and preferences shared by some subset of society encompass culture. For Mokyr, culture and cultural entrepreneurs are an important part of the explanation of why some economies evolve institutions that enable them to develop more quickly.[18]

---

[17] The same is true of econometric studies regressing growth on institutional variables. Of fifty-nine such studies that were categorized by Shirley, only six dealt with informal institutions, specifically trust and social capital (Shirley 2005).

[18] In Chapter 12 of this volume, Jakiela uses cross-country experiments to measure effects of informal institutions.

5. Conclusion

As we have shown, research on NIE spread rapidly, and the diffusion of the Northean branch was especially fast. But institutional analysis faces some major challenges for the future. One is to develop a satisfactory general theory of NIE that integrates Northean institutional analysis with Williamsonian transaction cost economics. A general theory would explain how the institutional framework (described by North as the scaffolding for human transactions) interacts with the structure of governance (defined by Williamson as the matrix in which the integrity of a transaction is organized). This raises a lot of issues explored by Ménard 2006, issues that will likely shape much future research. A foremost issue will be: How do the (Northean) rules that determine the security and functioning of property rights or the laws that affect contractual credibility and enforcement shape the choice of (Williamsonian) modes of governance and of the ways to organize transactions? A related question is: What are the comparative costs of different institutional schemes, such as different judicial systems for implementing contractual laws?

Beyond this daunting challenge of bridging the gap between a society's general institutional framework and its specific transactions and modes of governance, there are also areas where institutional analysis needs to be developed further. North himself has challenged NIE to produce better theories, especially a theory of the state, and better explanations of growth and innovation.[19] NIE needs a better theory of institutional change as well. Some aspects of current institutional theory make change seem almost impossible. North has long argued that change in deeply rooted institutions is fundamentally gradual and incremental (e.g., North 1990b). Change is gradual because long-standing beliefs and conventions are usually slow to change, even though formal institutions can change rapidly in response to deliberate policies. But the abrupt changes in Eastern Europe, Taiwan, or South Korea present a challenge to this theory, as do sudden changes in informal institutions.[20,21]

These challenges notwithstanding, the future for NIE broadly and for institutional analysis specifically looks very bright. Acceptance and

---

[19] North's emphasis on the need for a better understanding of politics is echoed by Bates in Chapter 4 in this volume.

[20] For example, the convention of foot-binding in China, which had been practiced for millennia, was ended in a decade (Mackie 1996).

[21] Shepsle, in Chapter 5 in this volume, also challenges North's view of rules as exogenous constraints.

adherents continue to grow, and new research is pushing out the frontiers of the field. Indeed, one of the most daunting challenges for NIE is to maintain its revolutionary character and be open to good ideas from across disciplines without abandoning the powerful tools of economics. Further conceptual breakthroughs depend on rising to this challenge. It is true that cross-disciplinary work has drawbacks. The expansion of institutional analysis across the social sciences has resulted in a host of sometimes confusing and contradictory theories.[22] Yet powerful partnerships have also emerged, for example, in political economy or in law and economics. One of the strengths of NIE is that, unlike some schools of economics, it has not isolated itself from the rest of the social and physical sciences. Here the founding thinkers have led the way. They all have freely adopted from other fields, most notably, Coase from law, Williamson from managerial sciences and organizational theory, and North from political science, cognitive science, and history.

The increasing mainstream acceptance of New Institutional Economics may tempt some institutionalists to demand greater methodological orthodoxy, which could stifle NIE's creativity. North stands as a living example against this danger; he continues to exemplify the revolutionary roots of NIE. As our brief summary of his work indicates, North's creativity has never ebbed, and his research always seeks new frontiers. He has often been the first to challenge his own conclusions and has never let his past work become a hindrance in his search for radical new approaches. This has kept institutional analysis in the forefront, attracting new adherents in pursuit of new research directions.

---

[22] In Chapter 6 in this volume Ostrom mentions the confusing treatment of institutions in policies proposed to increase the sustainability of ecological systems. In Chapter 4, Bates attributes some of the confusion in the analysis of institutions to the implicit use of different time frames.

2

Persistence and Change in Institutions

The Evolution of Douglass C. North

John Joseph Wallis

1. Introduction

Throughout his career, Douglass North has been concerned about the importance of human institutions and how they affect economic performance and development. His early work provided evidence that institutions mattered quantitatively, and his later work focuses on how we conceptualize institutions and institutional change through time. Over the last two decades economists and economic historians have made enormous progress in quantifying the effects of institutions: They do matter. Institutions are important because they structure human interaction. In part, institutions make behavior more predictable, and once adopted they persist for long periods of time. Their persistence provides econometric leverage that helps us unravel whether societies with better institutions have better economic performance because better institutions lead to higher incomes or because higher incomes lead to better institutions. Rather than being overjoyed at these new empirical findings, North has accepted them as necessary evidence to show economists what they already should have known – that institutions matter – but he remains skeptical about whether the results help us answer a more interesting and challenging question: How do institutions change over time?

North's deepest contribution as a scholar has been his powerful intuition about which questions we should be asking next. This essay explores North's intuitive reaction to the persistence literature and his insistence that we investigate institutional change rather than institutional persistence. In the end, it gives a slightly different interpretation of the importance North has placed on the ever-changing nature of the world around us, shifting attention toward the ever-changing nature of the world that humans make.

North is partly to blame for the emphasis on persistence because his early work stressed the importance of past institutional changes on current economic performance, that is, persistence. I begin with a brief review of North's major contributions to economic history and institutional economics. Then I show that the finding that institutions have persistent effects involves a subtle sample-selection bias. If we want to see whether institutions matter, we have to look at institutions that exist for long enough to exert an effect. But why would an institution persist if it did not affect human behavior? If we want to formulate and test hypotheses about institutional change, then the sample including only persistent institutions is clearly a biased one. Many institutions are created and then disappear with little or no effect. Understanding institutional change requires us to understand both how institutions are created and the process of social dynamics that lead some institutions to persist and others to disappear.

The idea that two separate social processes, one that generates institutional change and another that winnows out institutions, may be at work is implicit in the idea that institutions evolve. In a sense, the persistence literature requires a winnowing process, because some institutions eventually come to persist only if others are eliminated. Not all institutions have long lives. By deliberately thinking about two separate processes that generate and winnow institutions North's recent fascination with cognition, beliefs, and our ever-changing world comes into a better focus.

2. Institutions over Time

North has long emphasized the importance of history and of neoclassical economics. He criticizes scholars in both disciplines for their complacency about the adequacy of the current conceptual and methodological consensus on how history or economics should be conducted. In North's framework, individuals act intentionally (neoclassical economics matters) and perceive the world through cognitive lenses that are part inherited from their culture and part derived from their own experience (history matters). Individual actions are governed by interests shaped by relative prices, endowments, and constraints (institutions) as well as by perceptions of how the world works (cognition and beliefs). Social outcomes are the sum of individual actions, but the summation process is not a simple adding up of these actions because interactions between individual decisions and beliefs critically influence the behavior of everyone.

The evolution of North's thinking has continuously shaped his willingness to pursue the interesting questions he was unable to address in his last book

or paper, not by what is currently hot in the profession. Testimony to
the power of his insight is that the profession has followed him, for he
certainly has not followed the profession. This process – North's moving on
to new questions – manifests itself in his first book, *The Economic Growth
of the United States, 1790–1860.* The introduction states his conceptual
approach:

This study is based on the proposition that U.S. growth was the evolution of a
market economy where the behavior or prices of goods, services, and productive
factors was the major element in any explanation of economic change. Institutions
and political policies have certainly been influential. They have acted to accelerate
or retard growth on many occasions in our past, primarily by affecting the behavior
of the prices of goods, services, or productive factors either directly or indirectly. But
they have modified rather than replaced the underlying forces of a market economy.
(North 1961, vii)

Can you imagine a conceptual statement that more inaccurately predicts
the path that North's research eventually followed?

Economic Growth was one of the first examples of quantitative economic
history, or cliometrics, North's first major contribution to the study of
economics and history. The book presented a very neoclassical theory of
economic development that emphasized the importance of geographic specialization and division of labor, which led North to investigate the sources
of falling transportation costs over the nineteenth century. His 1958 paper
in the *Journal of Economic History* laid out a technology-based neoclassical framework for thinking about declining ocean freight rates, but ten
years later, in his 1968 *Journal of Political Economy* paper, North noted:
"The conclusion one draws is that the decline of piracy and privateering
and the development of markets and international trade shared honors as
primary factors in the growth of shipping efficiency over this two-and-a-
half-century period" (967). Essentially, the costs of shipping were falling
because costs other than the costs of operating ships were falling. Those
cost reductions were the result of institutional change. The paper marks
North's turn toward both transaction costs and institutions as important
elements of economic change over time.

This turn did not mean a turn away from neoclassical economics, however. The assumption of zero transaction costs and unchanging institutions
could be relaxed within the context of neoclassical theory, as North argued
in 1971 (118–119): "What we need is a body of theory which encompasses
the traditional models of the economist and both widens its scope and
allows us to include an explanation of the formation, mutation and decay
of organizational forms within which man cooperates or competes." North

was moving toward a neoclassical theory of institutions in which the form of institutions or organizations were themselves determined by traditional neoclassical rationality and constraints:

> Let us begin on a positive note. Briefly stated, the model specifies the process by which an action group (an individual or group) perceive that some new form of organization (institutional arrangement) will yield a stream of benefits which makes it profitable to undergo the costs of innovating this new organizational form. These new arrangements have typically been profitable to realize potential economies of scale, reduce information costs, spread risk, and internalize externalities. These institutional arrangements account for a vast array of the "economic institutions" with which economic historians have traditionally been concerned. However, the formation (and mutation and decay) of these organizational forms can now be an integral part of the economic analysis rather than a descriptive addition to the analysis. Moreover, since a great many were realizable without substantial redistribution of income, their formation is at least in principle predictable from the model. Perhaps even more significant than the ability to integrate economic analyses and institutional formation is the implication of this theoretical model for the study of productivity increase. Economic historians have focused on technological change as the source of growth but the development of institutional arrangements from the above mentioned sources are a major historical source of the improvement in the efficiency of product and factor markets. The development of more efficient economic organization is surely as important a part of the growth of the Western World as is the development of technology, and it is time it received equal attention. The few cases of which I am aware that have attempted to measure productivity change attributable to improving economic organization certainly support this contention. (North 1971, 119–120)

The idea that neoclassical theory could be used to explain why institutions functioned as they did was a fundamental breakthrough and North's second major conceptual contribution. The idea was implemented in a series of papers with Lance Davis and with Robert Paul Thomas, which led to two more books, *Institutional Change and American Economic Growth*, published in 1971 with Davis, and *The Rise of the Western World*, published in 1973 with Thomas. The heart of the argument in both books is that we can explain changes in the organization of human interaction (institutions) on the basis of the rational interests of individuals attempting to structure the world around them in ways that maximize net benefits. The classic application of the technique is North and Thomas's explanation of how the rising price of labor in fourteenth-century Europe as a result of the Black Death led to the institution of wage labor in Western Europe and a return to the institutions of serfdom and slavery in Eastern Europe. The same relative price shock led to two different, but both rational, institutional changes.

Two lines of thinking emerged from the idea of neoclassical institutions, and they were not entirely consistent with one another. In one line, institutional change occurs because of short-run variations in relative prices that create, at some point in time, the incentives to restructure human organizations. For some reason these changes persist. This idea led North to investigate both path dependence and transaction costs. Transaction costs play a key role because they are both a reason to change institutions (to reduce or increase transaction costs) and because transaction costs subsequently can make it difficult to change institutions and so contribute to institutional persistence.

The other line was a growing dissatisfaction with neoclassical economics altogether as a way to understand the process of economic growth specifically, and more broadly to understand the process of economic change over time. North's third significant breakthrough was the realization that neoclassical theory was not just inadequate, but unable to explain long-term economic and institutional change in any society, growing or not. While acknowledging the important contribution that economic theory and quantitative techniques made in advancing our understanding of historical processes, North directed his first clear criticism at economic historians:

From my quite subjective perspective, the new economic history has made a significant contribution to revitalizing the field and advancing the frontiers of knowledge. Yet I think it stops short – far short of what we should be accomplishing in the field. Our objective surely remains that of shedding light on man's economic past, conceived in the broadest sense of those words; and I submit to you that the new economic history as it has developed has imposed strictures on enquiry that narrowly limit its horizons-and that some of my former revolutionary compatriots show distressing signs of complacency with the new orthodoxy. (1974, 1)

His criticism of neoclassical theory in economic history, development, and growth would culminate in *Structure and Change in Economic History* (1981), which many (including myself) believe is North's best book. The introduction and a second chapter extend the argument that we must have more than a history of markets to understand economic change. The third chapter, "A Neoclassical Theory of the State," lays out a logical neoclassical argument for why, in the presence of transactions costs, political systems do not inevitably evolve institutions that promote economic growth. Indeed, as long-term economic history suggests, the tendency is for political systems to evolve that do not support growth. Chapters four and five argue that we need a theory of organizations as well as a theory of beliefs and ideology, to complement a theory of the state if we are to understand long-term change, long-term change that does not inevitably produce growth and development.

The contradiction is clear in *Structure and Change*. On the one hand, there is a strong argument that neoclassical economics is incapable of delivering the full range of explanations necessary to understand economic change, particularly ideologies and beliefs. On the other hand, there is a strong argument that rational individual behavior is consistent with institutional choices that retard, rather than promote, economic growth. Is the question, then, to be neoclassical or not to be neoclassical? I don't think so.

The real question the book is trying to grapple with is: persistence or change? Going back to *Rise of the Western World*, institutions change when there are gains from doing so, but then persist because of the high transaction cost of changing them. In *Structure and Change*, beliefs and ideologies persist. Because beliefs (and norms and culture) are based on the cumulative experience of society passed down through culture and formed through repeated interactions of many people through norms of behavior, beliefs do not change quickly, and it is extremely difficult to for social actors to manipulate beliefs in real time. As a result, beliefs are always a function of what happened in the past and can impede change in the present for good or ill. The persistence of beliefs and institutions from the past (culture) explains why changes in the present often produce results that impede rather than promote growth and development. The importance of beliefs in North's framework plays a major role in *Institutions, Institutional Change, and Economic Performance* (1990) and is the central focus of *Understanding the Process of Economic Change* (2005).

The *Structure and Change* framework includes two different time patterns of institutional change. One is episodic and discontinuous, like the move toward wage payments after the Black Death in Western Europe. The other is continuous and marginal. Changes in beliefs and ideologies, in norms, and in informal and formal rules occur constantly, and, while changes sometimes persist, they need not. Neither continuous nor episodic institutional change is necessarily persistent. Fleshing out these ideas in the 1980s produced a classic example of change during a crisis that persists – North and Barry Weingast's "Constitutions and Commitment" (1989) on the effects of the Glorious Revolution in Britain. The paper's emphasis on institutional mechanisms explains why particular institutions are self-enforcing and persist over time. North was writing *Institutions, Institutional Change, and Economic Performance* at the same time. Persistence plays a large role in *Institutions*, which regularly emphasizes that the function of an institution is to provide stability and predictability to human behavior.

The big contribution of the book, however, is the definition of institutions that North calls the sports analogy. Institutions are the rules of the game and the means of enforcement, and organizations are the teams that play the game. The definition motivates three behavioral choices that organizations can make: 1) maximize under the rules; 2) devote resources to changing the rules; and/or 3) cheat. The alternatives are not mutually exclusive, and they comprise a framework for understanding the dynamics of institutional change.

North's fourth major contribution was to separate institutions and organizations. Since his earliest books, North always included a discussion of the importance of organizations, but organizations were treated as manifestations of institutions. Organizations usually disappeared from the conceptual framework, which was always neoclassical in its focus on individuals. By defining institutions as the rules of the game and means of enforcement and then separating the rules from the organizations that actually play the game, the possibility of a dynamic relationship between the interests and incentives facing the organizations and the structure of the rules became possible. The descriptive concept that comes out of the dynamics is adaptive efficiency. In some societies, the interaction of institutions and organizations produces a series of institutional changes that incrementally improve, rather than a sequence that is sometimes good and sometimes bad for economic performance.

Rather than resolving (or integrating) the tension between the long- and short-term forces leading to institutional change, *Institutions* exacerbated it. The rules of the game included formal rules, informal rules, and norms of behavior. By stressing the function of institutions as providing stability and predictability, and emphasizing the importance of beliefs and norms, the book effectively claimed that the persistence of institutions was not a matter of real-time economic and political forces, but an outcome of the natural limits of human capacities for cognition and culture. North pressed farther down this road with his 2005 book, *Understanding the Process of Economic Change*. The interaction between organizations and institutions was not revisited until *Violence and Social Orders* in 2009, but by that time, the economics profession's empirical understanding of institutions had taken a different turn entirely.

3. Institutional Persistence: Inputs or Outputs?

The availability of a much wider cross section of national income and product data for societies around the world, including for the first time, developing societies, changed our empirical understanding of institutions in the 1990s. Combining measures of economic performance with survey data on the quality of institutions produced clear and robust evidence that institutions have a significant effect on income (Knack and Keefer 1995, 1997). Questions about whether high-income countries have better institutions because they have higher incomes, and not the reverse, remains a controversial question. But the work of Acemoglu, Johnson, and Robinson (2001, 2002, and 2005b), Rodrik (1999, 2007) and Rodrik, Subramanian, and Trebbi (2004), La Porta, Lopez-de-Silanes, and Shleifer (1997 and 2008), Nunn (2008, 2009), and now many others addressing the endogeneity question have resolved the basic empirical question of whether institutions matter in narrow quantitative measures of economic performance: They do. Engerman and Sokoloff (1997, 2002, 2005a, 2005b, 2008) provided empirical, but noneconometric, evidence on the importance of patterns of institutional development over very long periods of time.

As with all new results, the data raised as many questions as they answered. One of the surprising results was the detectible influence of institutional arrangements in the distant past on present institutions and outcomes. It may seem like ingratitude for someone who thinks that institutions matter, as I do, to react to empirical studies that show the lasting effect of institutional arrangements by arguing that they show *too much* persistence. But that is just what I want to do in the remainder of the paper. The research is valuable, but the point of the research is to show that institutions are important and have lasting effects and often to use institutional persistence as a statistical tool to identify causal relationships. The papers in this literature are often not designed to tell us how institutions change. This section of the paper discusses the problem of measuring and perceiving institutions, and the following section examines the problem of sample selection and institutional dynamics.

If we keep within the boundaries of North's definition of institutions, when we look for institutions in history or the contemporary world we should be looking for formal rules, informal rules, or norms of behavior (listed in order of the ascending difficulty of documenting each aspect). What passes for institutions in much of the economics literature, however, are really outcomes, not institutions. Secure property rights, governments that make credible commitments, rule-of-law, impersonal exchange, and trust are all real phenomena, but they are the results of institutions; they are not themselves institutions. They are outcomes rather than inputs. Acemoglu and Robinson (2006) acknowledge the problem in their paper about institutional persistence:

These observations suggest that we need to develop a framework in which changes in certain dimensions of institutions are consistent with overall institutional persistence. In this paper, we make an attempt to highlight some important mechanisms for understanding simultaneous change and persistence in institutions. Institutional persistence, in this context, refers to the persistence of *a cluster of economic institutions*, such as the extent of enforcement of property rights for a broad cross section of society (Acemoglu et al. 2001). . . . Such lack of property rights enforcement may be driven by quite different specific institutions, e.g., risk of expropriation, entry barriers, or economic systems such as serfdom or slavery.

Since many specific institutional arrangements can support the same outcome, Acemoglu and Robinson shift our attention from the details of institutions to the persistence of outcomes. Engerman and Sokoloff (2008, 121–122) reach a similar conclusion in their review of the institutional literature. They caution against placing too much weight on specific institutional arrangements because institutional structures that appear very different have often been found to be reasonable substitutes for each other. In the antebellum United States, for example, the North and South both grew relatively rapidly with their sharply contrasting institutions of labor. The historical record, therefore, does not seem to support the notion that any particular institution, narrowly defined, is indispensable for growth. Engerman and Sokoloff stress the importance of endogenous institutions and, again, that perhaps we should not be too worried about specific institutional arrangements but instead about the overall pattern of institutional outcomes.

North, Davis, and Thomas laid the intellectual foundation for a neoclassical theory of institutions and institutional change in *Institutional Change and American Economic Growth* and *The Rise of the West*. Economic conditions create situations in which a change in institutions may produce large gains. Institutions change as a result and then persist through time because of path dependence, the transaction costs of changing them, inertia built into culture, the slow change of beliefs, and ideologies, but they persist nonetheless. Is this a good way to conceptualize and explain how institutions change over time? The answer is no. If we do not follow the time pattern of specific institutions unfolding over time we will never understand the process of institutional change. By focusing on outcomes we take our eye off the ball.

4. Two Selection Problems: Institutional Change and the Nature of Social Dynamics

Scholars who work on institutions are aware of the problems of measuring outputs rather than inputs. If we are concerned with producing better institutions in specific societies, then it is not enough to know that if relative prices lined up correctly in the distant past a society gets good institutions that persist. A pattern of institutional change through time must underlay persistence. North laid out the notions of continuous versus episodic change in *Institutions* (89–91) as part of his discussion of adaptive efficiency. Since the formation of beliefs and norms is based in part on past experience and inherited culture, in a changing world those beliefs are always at least a little bit out of alignment with the external world. Adaptive efficiency is a descriptive term for institutions and beliefs that adjust to a changing world in ways that produce (on average) better rather than worse social outcomes. Occasionally situations arise in the world where current institutions are so far out of line with the possibilities inherent in the existing resource endowments, technology, demography, and relative prices that a discontinuous episodic change in institutions is warranted. Over time, institutional change is the result of both continuous and episodic change.

One of the major problems facing societies in real time, and researchers who later try to figure out why societies behaved as they did, is that no one really knows what the impact of an institutional change will be until a significant amount of time has passed. Seemingly small, incremental changes can have very large and discontinuous effects on a society. Apparently revolutionary changes often have little or no effect at all. An appreciation of unintended consequences is a part of every good economist's intellectual toolkit. Unintended consequences pose two important problems for our understanding of institutional change.

The first and most serious problem from a methodological point of view is sample selection bias. Institutional change is continuous, and most institutional changes are not successful. Changes either do not persist and/or they have little or no effect on society. Yet our studies of institutional change – every study mentioned so far in this paper – are about successful institutional change that persisted through time. We have concluded that institutions are important because their effects persist for very long periods of time, and we have tested that proposition by looking only at institutional changes that have persisted!

You can immediately see the problems that this raises, theoretically and empirically. A test of the hypothesis that institutions matter or of the hypothesis that institutional effects persist ideally begins with a random sample of institutional changes that are then tracked through time. An episodic institutional change that received extended treatment from North and Weingast (1989) as well as many others, including Pincus (2009) and Pincus and Robinson in this volume, are the institutional changes in Britain in 1688 and the years immediately following, the Glorious Revolution. Institutional change was so important in seventeenth-century England that a series of revolutions and wars were fought over what the changes should be. There is no doubt that institutions changed in the late seventeenth century and that the changes mattered.

But why did they change? Any explanation of institutional change would not take just the sample of changes from 1688 into account, but also the institutional changes from years like 1603, 1642, 1649, 1660, and 1685. Similarly, any test of whether institutional change mattered should take the entire sample of institutional changes into account. Pincus argues that James II engaged in an aggressive and thorough attempt to change the institutional structure of English society between 1685 and 1688. Most of the institutional changes put in place by James, however, did not persist. Should they be ignored? No, because the institutional changes that failed to persist were an integral part of the pattern of institutional change in the late seventeenth century that produced the changes that did persist after 1688. It is as important to understand the social process that winnowed out institutional changes as it is to understand the institutional changes that persisted. Once we see that we select biased samples from past institutions and institutional changes when we attempt to answer the question what effects do institutions have, then the reasons that these studies do not tell us very much at all about how institutions change over time is clear.

The second problem posed by the continuous and episodic generation of institutional change is the need to understand the dynamics of social change that winnow out institutions. A steady stream of continuous institutional change and a lumpy stream of episodic changes feed into society every day, month, and year. Some of these changes are local, others regional, and others affect the entire society. Most of these changes amount to little or nothing, some make incremental improvements or degradations in social outcomes, and still others have large positive or negative implications. The dynamics of social interactions political, economic, religious, military, and educational determine which changes are rejected, which are sustained, and which changes persist, ultimately having a large impact.

As North argued in *Structure and Change* there is nothing inherent in the process of social change to suggest that good outcomes are more likely than bad outcomes. As North, Weingast, and I argued in *Violence and Social Orders*, if we use a simple summary metric of economic performance like per capita income, then for all of human history until 200 years ago the periods of increasing income are offset by periods of decreasing income. The persistence of economic growth in the last 200 years is extremely unusual. Any model of how societies work must be a model in which growth is not inevitable. We need models in which the pattern of social change (economic, political, demographic, and technological) goes up and down, advances and retreats (like a Malthusian population model). A fundamental question then becomes whether the differences in institutions across societies or over a single society through time are due to differences in the process that generates institutional change or in the dynamic process that winnows out institutions.

The title of this section is "Two Selection Problems." The first selection problem arises when social scientists draw samples of institutions from a history that is biased toward institutions that persist over time and find, not surprisingly, that institutions both persist and matter. The second selection problem is quite different. A steady but lumpy stream of institutional changes occurs in every human society. What dynamic process of change leads societies to sustain (or select) some changes but not others? How do social dynamics winnow the wheat from the chaff? In fact, we must ask as well whether societies winnow out the wheat or the chaff. Why do societies sometimes move away from institutions that work well toward institutions that work less well? When North introduced the idea of adaptive efficiency in *Institutions*, he was implicitly talking about the process of social dynamics that govern which institutional changes were sustained. Did he get it right?

5. Persistent Problems, Social Dynamics, and Institutional Winnowing

Persistence is the repeated appearance of a pattern over time. There are many persistent elements in human life. People breathe, eat, procreate, and eventually die. All of those are persistent problems that cannot be permanently solved. Some problems can be solved forever, but most problems in structuring human interaction are persistent. The rule that Mom cooks dinner and Dad takes out the garbage may be a clear and workable solution to the division of household tasks in principle, but there are inevitably days when the rule (an institution) does not work because either Mom or Dad is not home. Even clear and simple rules may not be the solution to a problem but instead are patterns of behavior to which people regularly recur in order to address coordination problems that persist. That is why informal rules and norms are just as important as formal rules in structuring behavior.

North emphasizes that the world changes every day and that no two situations are exactly alike. Because our beliefs are based on past experience, they are always a bit inconsistent with the world we actually face. Yet, even in a perfectly stable external physical world, institutions change constantly.

Because institutions are rules, there are always groups and individuals who have an incentive to change the rules. Think, for example, about a perfectly competitive market equilibrium where there are no Pareto-improving real-locations. Individuals do not have incentive to change their behavior by producing or consuming more or less or to changing the price at which they sell or buy. The market outcome, however, presumes a set of rules that supports those outcomes. Every individual in the market (and even people who are not actively in the market) could potentially benefit from some change in the rules.

It takes a heroic set of assumptions to specify the conditions under which the cost to everyone of changing the rules is greater than the benefits they would receive from a rule change, and thus make the current rules a sustainable equilibrium. Even if conditions in the physical world were constant, the interaction of human behavior produces continuous small changes in the rules and the expectation of future changes because there are always potential benefits to someone from changing the rules of human interaction. As a result, all societies must deal with constant debate over changes in the rules – formal, informal, or norms that structure coordination between individuals. The process of continuous institutional change stems from our nature as human beings, our social nature if you will. Continuous change is inevitable.

Economists can be handicapped when thinking about the winnowing process by their notions of equilibrium. We think of a market as a persistent institution that works because at the market equilibrium no one has an incentive to change his or her behavior. The market, however, is not a very good analogy for institutional change. First, as noted, even in a competitive market there are still plenty of incentives for people to change the rules. The socially optimal and individually credible behavior that neoclassical economics describes within a market depends on existing institutional arrangements that underlay the market. A market equilibrium does not neutralize interests that groups and individuals may have in changing the market rules. Second, the market equilibrium concept is that individuals do not have an incentive to change their behavior in the equilibrium. There are no institutional equilibria, however, where individuals do not have incentive to change their behavior, because all institutional equilibria are about the rules. Unless we want to call on the existence of some meta-rules or natural laws that are somehow fixed by an exogenous force and not subject to manipulation by intentional or accidental human behavior, there are no social outcomes where no one has an interest in changing the rules to promote his or her interests. Institutions, then, are always changing because there is no possibility of an institutional equilibrium where no one could be better off by changing the rules.

To be clear about the general argument: The forces that generate institutional change are not necessarily the forces involved in the winnowing process that determine which institutional changes persist. New institutions are continuously generated and the winnowing process runs constantly without ever reaching a point at which everyone is satisfied with the rules as well as their realized outcomes under the rules. Because people can change institutions merely by changing their individual behavior or by attempting to coordinate with other people through the norms of social interaction, the scale on which institutional change can be implemented ranges from norms to informal rules to formal rules. Whether these institutional changes persist depends on the dynamics of social interaction. This is what I think North really wants to convey in his conceptual view that the world is constantly changing. He is not saying that true Knightian uncertainty stems primarily from unpredictability of the external physical world, but instead from the unpredictable nature of social dynamics.

What then can we say about the dynamics of winnowing processes? One important element is that the dynamics of the winnowing process are not the same as the dynamics of the process generating institutional changes. North's emphasis on the limitations of human cognitive processes bears on the process of generating changes. People rarely know ex ante which institutional changes will persist, and all of human history is an object lesson that institutions rarely turn out to do what they are designed to do. If the process of generating institutional changes correctly anticipated the winnowing process, then unintended consequences would be much less of a problem.

North emphasizes the limits of human cognition in order to explain why societies do not select efficient institutions over inefficient ones. I suspect that cognitive limits are less important in the winnowing process than they are in the process of generating institutional change. All proposed institutional changes are the result of backward-looking analysis of how society has worked in the past. Institutional changes produce real-world effects that are experienced and perceived by social actors in the future. On the basis of those effects social dynamics determine what changes persist. Cognition informs the winnowing process, but the process depends more on what actually happens in the wake of an institutional change than on people's expectation of what will happen. Unsuccessful institutional changes don't work very well and often simply fade away, rather than being replaced by another round of deliberate institutional change.

6. Institutional Change in History

Institutions really do change all of the time, but we are predisposed to think of institutions as things that change slowly. The apparent persistence of institutional rules is often an illusion. The world is too complicated to learn everything about it, so we focus on specific parts of interest and assume that other parts are not changing. Careful scholars are constantly aware of these kinds of assumptions. The illusion also stems from how we learn about institutions. Actually studying how an institution works in reality is a much different process than learning about an institution through the description and analysis of another scholar. Secondary treatments necessarily edit, select, elide, and otherwise organize information, and the institution inevitably looks more unchanging than it really was.

Much of the winnowing process, both what is retained and what is discarded in the process of institutional change, is in the details that do not make it into the secondary histories. I am not talking here about the small change that turns out to have large unanticipated consequences. The process of institutional change over time is the result of hundreds and thousands of small decisions and changes that make up the process of a sustained institutional change. We cannot see the winnowing process at work historically if we look only at the big picture, because the process works in the little picture.

We are not yet in a position to gather empirical information about the winnowing process. No one, to my knowledge, has attempted anything like a complete census of institutional changes in a particular society over a particular period of time. Just the thought of it is daunting. We therefore lack appropriate samples to test theories of institutional change.

Property rights in land in the United States are good example of how institutions change constantly but are, nonetheless, perceived as relatively unchanging. The United States is often held up as an example of how secure and easily alienable private property rights in land contribute to economic and political development. There is little doubt that property rights in land in the United States have been secure, since the late eighteenth century, but that is an outcome rather than an institution. Did the institutional structure of property rights in land change? And does it continue to change?

The structure of property rights in land in colonial America was rooted in British land law. In early seventeenth-century Britain, a single piece of land was typically owned by several individuals, each of whom had the right to a particular aspect of the land, its product, or a payment associated with the land. The Virginia Company charter required that the colony establish land tenure in "free and common socage." Free and common socage implied that there were at least three owners of each piece of land – the King, the Company, and the landowner. The owner enjoyed the use of the land in perpetuity with the right to devise land by will, in return for which the landowner owed the Company (the landlord or donor) a fixed and certain payment. Eventually, colonial and then state governments came to occupy the place of landlords. Individual landowners owned their land as long as they met certain requirements, and if they failed to meet those requirements that land would escheat (revert) to its ultimate owner, the state. In the United States, the only "allodial" owners of land – that is, owners who owned land free and clear with no obligations, were state governments and, on public land, the national government.

Property rights in land, therefore, had many dimensions. One aspect was the rights to use, exclude, alienate, and derive income from particular pieces of land, and the tax burdens applied to individuals who possessed those rights. Another dimension was the right to sell, appropriate, and tax land possessed by various governments (national, state, and local). A third dimension of rights was the procedures by which land was transferred between governments and private individuals, and the procedures governing land transfers between private individuals.

There is little doubt that typical landowners in the early nineteenth-century United States enjoyed greater security in their rights to use land and exclude others from its use than was common either by the standards of the nineteenth century or the twenty-first century developing world and that this security stretched back in time to the earliest colonial founding. Yet issues over who ultimately owned the land and how it would be distributed to and among private individuals were actively debated and periodically changed from the 1750s until at least the 1840s. After the French and Indian (or Seven Years') War, the British altered colonial land policy west of the Appalachians in the Quebec Act, which transferred control of western land policy from the colonies to the British government. Schofield (2000) argues that this was a major impetus to the events that led to the revolution in 1776.

The revolutionary government, the Continental Congress, wrote its first constitution, the Articles of Confederation, in 1777. The chief bone of contention among the states over ratification of the Articles was who should control the disposition and settlement of western lands and the establishment of new states. The Articles were not ratified until 1781, after an agreement over western lands was finally reached. The new national public land policy was codified in the Land Ordinances of 1785 and 1787. Under the Ordinances, nationally owned public lands were to be surveyed and transferred to private individuals through a process of auctions and direct sale. Once land had been transferred to private individuals, allodial owner-ship and the ability to tax the land passed from the national government to the states. The Ordinances also established the framework through which new states would be created and admitted to the Union.

Even if individuals remained secure in their rights to use land, the arrange-ments between governments, the British and their colonies, or the national and state governments, were critical parts of institutional arrangements that enabled individual rights to persist through time. Individual rights were affected by institutional arrangements at the level of governments. The value of an individual piece of land was affected by the ease with which title could be proved, protected, and transferred; various rights and restric-tions on the use of the land; and expected tax burdens associated with land ownership, to mention three important effects. The institutions that affected land values were subject to a process of continual change in the sixty years following the Ordinances. When Ohio was admitted to the Union in 1803, its enabling act embodied a deal between Congress and the state in which the state was given 5 percent of the land revenues to develop transportation infrastructure to and within Ohio, in return for which the state agreed not to tax land for five years after it had been sold to a private individual. This provision was repeated in enabling acts up to 1837 and had direct effects on the rights and value of land. State enabling acts embodied deals between Congress and the new states. These deals varied widely across states.

The Ordinances required that all land be sold to private individuals. But the original Ordinances underwent several subsequent modifications. Because the land was to be surveyed before it was auctioned, some indi-viduals took up residence on public land before they established clear title. These squatters were important parts of the community in western states, where new migrants made up a large part of the population. Western states pressured Congress to grant the squatters to clear title through preemption acts that granted the first settlers rights to purchase land rather than the person who paid the highest price at auction. A series of *ad hoc* preemption acts allowed squatters to claim title at the minimum price in different states and regions. In 1841, a general Preemption Act allowed anyone to claim up to a quarter section (160 acres) through preemption. The long series of preemption acts and changes in terms of sale, including the minimum purchase price at auction, credit terms, and the minimum (and later maxi-mum) acreage available to individuals, all affected the rights and values that individuals possessed in their lands.

Yet another aspect of property rights in land is the relationship between governments and individuals with respect to ultimate ownership. The most obvious manifestation is eminent domain, the ability of the government to reenter into the use of land under certain conditions. Lamoreaux (2011) neatly shows that ideas about the sanctity of property rights have always been an integral part of the beliefs that Americans hold about their social contract. Nonetheless, she traces the numerous times when state or local governments have changed the way eminent domain is used and documents how the Supreme Court has facilitated and legitimated the changes. Lamoreaux shows that while security of individual property rights vis-à-vis the government has always been protected, that protection has never been absolute, and the terms of the protection are subject to change.

And yet, Americans continue to believe that sanctity of property rights are an unchanging and persistent element of American institutions. Why?

Despite the many involuntary reallocations of property that have occurred repeatedly since the formation of the republic, Americans still strongly believe that their property rights are secure, and they act in their economic lives accordingly. I have suggested that the key to resolving this mystery is the widespread ownership of property, which makes redistribution in favor of the bottom unlikely and prompts voters to mobilize whenever they think redistribution in favor of the top is getting out of hand. (Lamoreaux 2011, 301)

Lamoreaux effectively documents the continuous process of institutional change, even in a society that prides itself on the security of property in land and the unchanging nature of the institutions that protect it.

Property rights in land in the United States are not an outlier with respect to the continuous nature of institutional change, but they are a well-studied and important set of institutions. Despite the continuously changing nature of property rights institutions in the United States, social scientists continue to regard them as essentially static and persistent. Such views are pernicious. We cannot understand why property-rights outcomes have remained stable over time unless we understand how the institutions that sustain property rights have changed through time. Moreover, and perhaps more important, we will never figure out how to establish secure property rights in a society without them unless we understand the dynamic process of institutional change and institutional winnowing that produce sustained outcomes in successful societies.

7. Conclusions

Douglass North has made four fundamental conceptual contributions to economics, history, economic history, and the social sciences in general. The importance of economic theory and quantitative analysis in history; the neoclassical interpretation of institutions; the neoclassical theory of the state capable of producing good and bad outcomes; and defining institutions as the rules of the game and the means of enforcement and organizations as the teams that can abide by the rules, change the rules, or cheat. In addition to these fundamental contributions, he has pointed to the importance of explicit theorizing, quantification, organizations, transaction costs, path dependence, culture, cognition, and beliefs. North's genius is figuring out what question to ask next, which often comes as an answer to the question of what cannot be explained with the current conceptual framework.

To do this requires a very unusual combination of humility and confidence. North has repeatedly said: I know I was wrong about the last way I tackled the problem of explaining economic performance through time, but I am sure I am right about the current way I am explaining it. How rare is it in academia for someone to genuinely admit that they got it wrong? This feature makes North, in Weber's terminology, a charismatic leader, where charisma is understood be a manifestation of grace. North is not tall and handsome, he is not a great speaker, nor does he write particularly well. He has the endearing characteristic of always picking fights with people who are bigger than him, intellectually, and showing kindness toward those who are smaller. But his charisma comes from the finely honed power of his intuition about what is the next important question to ask.

The empirical accomplishment of the persistence literature in demonstrating the importance of institutions as determinants of economic performance are impressive, but I share North's uneasiness that we learn little from these studies about how institutions change over time. At the worst, we gain the impression that institutions really do not change very much and that when they do change, they do so in response to unusual combinations of relative prices. I do not think that the authors of the persistence studies try to make that argument, but it is one way their results can be read.

I have tried to sharpen North's intuition that understanding institutional change is more important than understanding institutional persistence if we are to understand how institutions affect economic performance. North is more than partly to blame for the influence of the persistence school – he is a founder of it!

It seems clear that the process by which institutions are generated is different than the social process by which institutions are winnowed out. Our understanding suffers from a sample selection bias if we use the persistence studies to understand how institutions change. To understand change we need the full sample of institutions that persist as well as fail.

I suspect that North's emphasis on the limits of human cognition and the importance of beliefs plays a larger and intentional role in the process of generating institutional change than in the process of institutional winnowing. Likewise, North's emphasis on understanding social dynamics should be directed at the process of institutional winnowing. Generating institutional change and the social dynamics that produce persistent institutions are not independent processes. Perhaps North's next intuitive insight will show us how to think of them separately.

Acknowledgments

This paper was prepared for the conference on Douglass North's Legacy. I received helpful comments at the conference as well as the anonymous referees from Cambridge University Press. Itai Sened, Sebastian Galiani, Stan Engerman, Martin Schmidt, Peter Murrell, Roger Betancourt, Lee Alston, Barry Weingast, and Douglass North gave me valuable suggestions as well.

3

The New Institutionalism

Robert Bates

1. Introduction

Whether in the guise of formal theory (e.g., Persson and Tabellini 2000) or empirical research (e.g., Acemoglu, Robsinson, and Johnson 2001), in the study of political economy, "institutions rule" (Rodrik, Subramanian, et al. 2002).

If anyone can lay claim to being a founder of the new institutionalism, it would be Douglass North. In this paper, I attempt to account for the reception accorded North's work. While doing so, I probe the origins and foundations of the field, which lie in both formal theory and applied economics. I then appraise it. On the one side, I see confusion: a multiplicity of notions as to what constitutes an institution and what does not. On the other, I see unrealized promise. Those who work in this field, I contend, have yet to extract the full implications of its deepest insight: that power, if properly deployed, can create value. I then engage in remediation by, on the one hand, proposing a way of introducing greater clarity in the field and, on the other, by outlining a productive form of political analysis. The first response reminds us of the field's deep preoccupation with time, whereas the second shifts its focus from the economics of institutions to the politics that shapes their behavior.

Three major themes emerge from this discussion. As already intimated, one is the importance of time and a second is that coercion can be a source of value. The third is that people expend political effort to create institutions not only to privilege particular claims but also to increase the likelihood and magnitude of future outcomes. To create an institution is to invest; to destroy one is to extinguish future possibilities. Institutions, we learn, are a form of capital.

2. The Reception

I begin by analyzing the reception accorded North's work, thereby complementing the contributions of John Joseph Wallis (Chapter 2) and Claude Ménard and Mary M. Shirley (Chapter 1) to this volume, which survey both the development of North's ideas and of the field he helped to found. As they note, the new institutionalism was rapidly incorporated into the academy and quickly gained influence in the policy world. One reason for this, I argue, is that advances in theory and methods attuned academic audiences to North's arguments. And in the policy-making community, his work served the pragmatic needs of the development agencies: It provided a means for bridging professional differences within them and for reorienting their programs from the promotion of "market fundamentalism" to the promotion of "good governance."

The Academy

Traditionally, in economics, markets, not institutions, rule. People do not starve, Smith famously argued, because of the benevolence of the butcher, the brewer, or the baker; rather, the latter sustain the former because in so doing, they could reap profits in markets for food (Smith 1976). It was because of the market, Smith argued, that the pursuit of individual self-interest could be aligned with the interests of society.

Market Failure: The fundamental theorems of welfare economics established the conditions under which Smith's conjecture was valid. In doing so, the theorems also prepared the ground for the study of non-market institutions, and in two ways. Firstly, the proofs highlighted an embarrassing inconsistency: Notable by their absence were the rational, maximizing individuals that stood at the core of neoclassical theory. On the supply side stood firms, and on the demand side families. An opening therefore beckoned, and ambitious scholars surged into it, with some, like Coase (1988a) and Williamson (1985), asking why profit-maximizing individuals would move transactions out of markets and imbed them in firms and others, like Becker (1981), applying economic reasoning to the behavior of households. The theory of the firm and the theory of the family represent two of the earliest contributions to the new institutionalism.

Secondly, by establishing the conditions under which markets align self-interest with the social welfare, the theorems highlighted as well the conditions under which they would fail to do so. In imperfect markets, individuals, behaving rationally, might choose strategies that yield equilibria, but an equilibrium can be inefficient. And when markets fail, there will therefore be alternatives that some prefer and no one opposes; incentives will then exist, it was argued, to inspire a search for alternative ways of generating collective outcomes. For example, when information is costly, people might find it useful to signal, as by offering collateral when seeking a loan or by passing an exam to exhibit their skill. The very conditions that lead to the failure of markets thus lead to the creation of remedies, some in the form of institutions.

To be noted is the functionalist nature of this reasoning: By such arguments, the origins of an institution lie in its consequences (Stinchcombe 1958, Elster 1979). To provide a causal account, in Section 4, I will distinguish between the demand and supply of institutions and call for closer attention to politics – as do, for example, Pincus and Robinson in Chapter 9. Those who emphasize the implications of market failures address demand for institutions. To account for their supply, we need to explain why politicians might choose to insert power into economic life and why they would do so in ways that secure the creation rather than the mere redistribution of wealth. I return to this theme toward the end of this chapter.

From Normative Debate to Positive Theory

The proof of Smith's conjecture thus led to the recognition that institutions rather than individuals dominate markets and that incentives are often such as to drive people to devise them. James Buchanan and Gordon Tullock (Buchanan and Tullock, 1962) were among the first to build on these insights; under their influence, the study of institutions took the form of public choice theory. Public choice theorists divided the world into two spheres: the sphere of choice, where markets ruled, and the sphere of coercion, where the powerful governed. In the one, exchanges were voluntary and generated welfare gains. In the other, those who dominated institutions involuntary transfers; one person might gain, but possibly at the expense of another. Liberty thrived in the one realm; tyranny threatened in the other.

Initially compelling, public choice soon became sterile. Stasis in the field can be attributed, at least in part, to its technical foundations. While Buchanan and Tullock (1962) made use of cooperative game theory, they lacked the tools of noncooperative game theory and thus had largely to ignore matters of sequence and timing. Almost of necessity, their arguments therefore portrayed economic activity as if it consisted of simultaneous exchanges. Within that framework, transactions would of necessity be consensual, which implied in turn that they generated improvements in welfare. It was the study of noncooperative games in extensive form that made possible a less obvious insight: that coercion could be socially productive. In these games, as in the real world, agents would encounter opportunities to profit from duplicitous behavior. At one moment, they might receive goods and promise subsequent payment; later, they would be tempted to renege. But because of the passage of time, agents could condition their choices on the actions taken by others; agents could therefore threaten to respond by punishing those who behave opportunistically. And when the conditions are such that their threats were credible, then mutually beneficial transactions could take place, even in environments suffused with temptation (Kreps 1990). When cast in extensive form, noncooperative games thus suggested that, *contra* public choice theory, the insertion of power into economic life makes possible the creation of value.

Employing noncooperative game theory, researchers began to explore the properties of nonmarket institutions. In particular, they probed the manner in which, by imposing sanctions, such institutions could alter the behavior of those responding to the perverse incentives that prevail in imperfect markets.

To illustrate, consider a market for labor. Specifically, consider what would occur were information costly and employers, ignorant of the individual abilities of those applying for a job, offered wages based on their assessment of the average ability of the applicants. As each job candidate knows his or her own ability, those with above-average skills would find the wage offered too low while those with low abilities would find it attractive. The result would then be a downward shift in the average quality of the applicant pool. And should the employers revise downward her assessment of the average quality of the job applicants and adjust her wage offer accordingly, the market would begin to unravel. Workers of high quality would withdraw their services, even though employers desire them and would be willing to reward them with higher wages. The market would fail (Akerlof 1970).

The remedy to this failure lies in costly signaling, that is, in acts that demonstrate one's willingness to be penalized, as by being dismissed from one's job. Workers confident of their abilities might voluntarily incur such a risk; they might agree to let themselves be fired should they fail to perform. They could do so by acceding to a contract under which they would serve an initial period of probation, while their work is monitored, followed either by selection for permanent employment (if judged to be of high quality) or dismissal (if judged to be inept). As only those sure of their success would agree to such an offer, the provisions of the contract enable the skilled to "reveal their type" and a market to function.

Note the role of sequence and coercion. By choosing at time t to agree to being punished at time $t+2$, should he or she not perform at time $t+1$, a job candidate can signal his or her ability. The existence of punishments and the possibility of coercion make it possible for a candidate to reveal previously hidden information in a credible manner. By allowing the market to form, they also allow welfare-enhancing bargains to be made and higher levels of welfare to be attained.

North argued that by modifying the environments within which agents make choices, institutions ameliorate market failures, thus aligning the pursuit of private interest with the social welfare and enhancing the performance of economies. In advancing these arguments, he was laboring on grounds that had been well-prepared by advances in economic theory, and, in particular, the theory of noncooperative games. North's work was well-received in part because he mobilized data at the macro level that appeared to confirm the implications of the reasoning that others were developing at the micro level. Had these advances in micro theory not taken place, contemporary political economy might well have remained the provenance of public choice theory; instead, "institutions rule."[1]

The Policy Community

As did those in academia, economists in development agencies quickly recognized the cogency of North's arguments and the manner in which they resonated with intellectual trends in their field. Other practitioners came from the ranks of sociology, anthropology, and political science, however. They too were certain of the value of their insights into the development process and, in particular, into the economic significance of institutions other than markets. When, under the influence of North's work, development economists too converted to the new institutionalism, these noneconomists found their arguments validated. By championing the new institutionalism, they forged common ground with economists in the development community.

The political realities confronting this community further contributed to the favorable reception accorded North's arguments. During the Reagan-Thatcher years, governments were commonly viewed as part of the problem rather than part of the solution to underdevelopment. In the 1970s and 1980s, the World Bank and the International Monetary Fund, fortified in their bargaining position by the magnitude of the debts owed them, insisted that governments lay off employees, sell off public-sector firms, free up markets, and reduce public spending. By allowing private markets, rather than public programs, to determine the allocation of resources, they contended, resources would be allocated efficiently, and the developing world would

---

[1] See also Chapter 1 by Ménard and Shirley.

once again grow. But despite strenuous efforts at structural adjustment and policy reform, economies in the poorest regions of the world continued to stagnate. Attitudes toward government therefore began to alter. And a consensus formed that for economic incentives to promote productive behavior, markets had to be imbedded within institutions: legal systems that defined and enforced property rights, bureaucracies that provided public goods, and regulatory structures that enabled capital markets to form. Rather than inferior substitutes for private markets, it was realized, public institutions might better be viewed as productive complements. North's work then provided a neoclassically based justification for the rehabilitation of the public sector, aimed at strengthening rather than undermining institutions.

3. The Current Disarray

Thus the favorable reception accorded North's work and the rapid rise of the new institutionalism in the academic and policy communities. In Section 3, I address two shortcomings in the field. The first is the conceptual disarray arising from the various and divergent notions of what constitutes an institution. The second is what I regard as the unwarranted reluctance of those who subscribe to the new institutionalism to pursue the implications of the basic insight of the field: that coercion can be socially productive. Both of these critiques lead to positive insights, the first regarding the importance of time and the second the importance of politics.

Institutions?

Just what counts as an institution? As noted in Chapter 1 by Ménard and Shirley and Chapter 2 by Wallis, in *The Economic Origins of the Western World*, North makes little effort to define the term; his discussion suggests, however, that the word "institution" refers to whatever brings the "private rate of return close to the social rate of return" (North and Thomas 1973, 1) and ensures the efficient use of resources. In *Institutions, Institutional Change, and Economic Performance*, North instead emphasizes the element of constraint. Institutions, he states, "include any form of constraint that human beings devise to shape human interaction. Are institutions formal or informal? They can be either, and I am interested in both formal constraints – such as rules... and informal constraints – such as conventions codes of behavior" (North 1990a, 4).

As stressed by Shepsle in Chapter 4 in this volume, North thus tends to cast institutions as if they were external forces, capable of limiting choices made by human beings.

While others in the field concur in emphasizing the element of constraint, they appear less ready to reify; rather than casting institutions as external sanctions, they view them as internalized restraints. Some, such as sociologists, speak of "norms," whereas others, appealing to game theory, refer to "self-enforcing" patterns of behavior. Viewed either way, institutions are seen as patterns of conduct from which people are reluctant to deviate (Shepsle 1979; Schotter 1981; Weingast 1995; Medina 2007).

And where do institutions come from? In responding to this question, practitioners of new institutionalism again diverge, some viewing them as chosen and others as bequeathed.[2] In one of his most famous papers, North joins Weingast in analyzing the origins of Parliamentary sovereignty and the Bank of England (North and Weingast 1989), which they treat as the product of design. In doing so, their paper echoes others, such as Riker's study of the constitutional convention (Riker 1984); Shepsle and Weingast's (1987) and Gilligan and Krehbiel's (1997) studies of legislative rules; and McCubbins, Noll, and Weingast's papers on the design of bureaucracies (e.g., McCubbins and Schwartz 1987). Others – most notably Greif (2006) and Acemoglu and Robinson (2012), perhaps – treat institutions as inherited rather than chosen; that is, they treat them as the product of long-term historical processes and deeply embedded cultural practices.

Those who champion the new institutionalism thus hold divergent conceptions of the nature and origin of institutions. If, as some proclaim, "institutions rule" (Rodrik, Subramanian, et al. 2002), one would think it better that it not be because institutions can be anything.

Upon reflection, it is possible to discern order amid this disarray. It is not an order that derives from a narrowly bound consensus, however; rather, it is an array. The order highlights that the new institutionalism is not a single approach but rather several and that what distinguishes them is the temporal scale they presume. To make this point, I invoke Marshall's (1890) distinction between the short and the long term and then shift to *la longue durée*, a time scale more frequently employed by historians than by economists (Braudel 1992).

Marshallian Time and La Longue Durée

Differentiating between the short term and the long, Marshall made reference to factors of production. While producers can change their use of labor in the short run, he noted, to alter their use of capital, they have to allocate resources inter-temporally; the change requires the passage of time. In the short term, some factors are thus fixed and others variable; but in the long

---

[2] See once again Chapter 4 by Shepsle.

term, factors that were once treated as fixed can be altered. In seeking to bring greater clarity to the analysis of institutions, I appropriate Marshall's distinction.

The Short Term: When speaking of the constraining role of institutions, scholars, I argue, are viewing them within a short-term time perspective. In the short term, institutions are fixed; they therefore constrain, allowing only actions that influence outcomes at the margin. In the short run, they themselves are not subject to alteration.

The Long Term: When analyzing the creation of an institution, scholars then shift to Marshall's second period, one in which actors are not seeking to influence current outcomes but rather to generate future benefits. In this time frame, maximizing decisions are not single period; rather, they are inter-temporal. Institutional design is thus an investment decision in which people seek to increase the magnitude of future payoffs as well as the certainty with which they will occur.

Marshall's second period is that in which capital is formed and investment occurs. Viewed in this light, it is intriguing that both investors and politicians speak of "policies" and that in both settings the word signifies flows of future payoffs. They also speak of "portfolios," bundles of financial instruments in the economic realm; the distribution of power in the political; and, in both, an assemblage of value-yielding assets. The very language thus suggests that we view institutions as a form of capital – as indeed we should, now that we inhabit Marshall's second period.

La Longue Durée: For historians, institutions are best viewed within yet another temporal scale, *la longue durée*. Within this setting, we treat institutions as structures (Braudel 1967). Structures map variables into the set of choices and the set of constraints; they determine what can be decided and what must be taken as fixed. They also embody the technology that determines the interactions that can take place and the consequences that follow from them; the ramifications of, say, a given financial decision will vary, depending on the era in which one lives and the kind of economy – agrarian, commercial, or industrial – that prevails. Structural variables are very slow moving; they include the demographic composition of a population (Ladurie 1976), its productive technology, and its *mentalité* (Braudel 1967; Mokyr in Chapter 8 of this volume), or the beliefs and assumptions that govern the way in which people perceive each other and the world about them. In this setting, the term institution – as Shepsle notes – refers to the game form.

The new institutionalists thus come in several varieties. Some, such as (Greif 2006), focus on issues that arise in *la longue dureé*; the fine-grained features of institutions little preoccupy him. Others (e.g., Shepsle and

Weingast 1981) take institutions as fixed and demonstrates how their structures and rules constrain the strategies that people can chose and the outcomes that can prevail in equilibrium. Still others, such as Riker (1996), explore institutions' "founding." This diversity of approaches, I argue, results not from disagreements among these scholars as to what is, or is not, an institution, but rather from differences in time scale that they inhabit.

Persistence

Focusing on the temporal nature of institutions thus enables us to discern order in a field that might at first glance appear in disarray. It also leads us to recognize that institutions persist over time. Indeed, as is widely recognized, they are longer lived than those they govern. In this section, I turn to the different explanations advanced for the longevity of institutions.

Internal and External Defenses: Institutions possess defenses. One set is internal: Those who create institutions often recruit the institutions' top officials as well. They recruit persons who share their goals and confer upon them legal mandates and the resources with which to implement them. Thus chosen and thus empowered, the staff is equipped to defend the institution and its mission. Those who serve in the lower ranks of an institution also defend it, but for a different reason. While working their way up its ranks, they acquire site-specific skills. Because these skills are not portable, the private prospects of the staff depend upon the health and durability of the institution in which they serve. In the words of Huntington (1968), the institution then itself acquires value.[3]

Institutions acquire external lines of defense as well; they generate constituencies whose fortunes depend upon the policies that the institution propounds and its ability to implement them. By way of illustration, consider those that generate projects, the returns to which depend upon the maintenance in place of their policies. Encouraged by the Department of Commerce, for example, manufacturers may import costly equipment and install production lines behind a panoply of protective tariffs; should the Ministry of Finance, say, then seek to promote free trade, the Department of Commerce will be well-positioned to rally defenders for its protective policies. The institution thus creates rents which it shares with those who

---

[3] The creation of an effective vaccine marked both a triumph and a disaster for the March of Dimes; while it had achieved its mission, it had also lost its reason for being. Its members responded by redefining its mission, Sills reports, thus keeping he organization alive. See Sills, D. L. 1957. *The Volunteers: Means and Ends in a National Organization.* New York: Free Press.

return a portion in the form of costly effort in defense of the institution and its programs. Protected by external defenders, the institution endures.

Overlapping Generations: In part as a result, institutions outlive those who create them. Being longer lived than those who staff them, they are manned by overlapping generations. Writing in 1992, Soskice, Bates, and Epstein applied the logic of overlapping generation games (Kandori 1992) to Max Weber's (1985) characterization of an institution and thereby derive this ability to endure. Among the properties of an institution, Weber (1985) lists:

A division of labor.
Hierarchy, i.e. the division of labor by rank.
Ambition.
Rule governance.
That the organization is longer lived than its members.

Soskice, Bates, and Epstein (1992) argue that given the fourth, the other three imply that policies will be stable, rules will persist, and the institution will replicate itself over time.

Returning to Soskice, Bates, and Epstein (1992), we can trace their argument, which begins with a society that has been endowed with a valuable asset. The senior members of this society would like to consume the asset; the juniors would prefer that it be preserved so that they could consume it later. But if governed by an institution bearing Weberian attributes, the authors contend, the society will be able to resist pressures to consume the resource. If the initial state in this society is defined by the existence of the asset, future states will be as well. The features that characterize institutions, the authors argue, promote permanence and stability.[4] By condition (4), institutions contain overlapping generations. When seniors command, and juniors implement (conditions 1 and 2), then juniors can check the efforts of the seniors; they can undermine the efforts of elders to use power to despoil. But what would prevent seniors from bribing juniors, as by sharing with them a portion of the resource? The answer lies in the desire for high office (condition 3) and in the rules (condition 4) that deem expropriation a delict of sufficient gravity to disqualify someone from holding it. Given the desire for high office, then, countering efforts to suborn becomes a sub-game perfect strategy. If there is ambition to advance in the ranks

---

[4] Note that these properties distinguish institutions from organizations, which are often less hierarchical, less rule governed, and less internally differentiated. As a corollary, organizations are also less long lived; founded to advance a particular cause, they are likely to atrophy after attaining their objective (but see Sills 1957).

of the institution, then, given the characteristics above, its rules will be observed.

The attributes listed by Weber (1985) characterize most institutions. By the logic advanced by Soskice, Bates, and Epstein (1992), "institutionalized" orders will persist over time.

Institutions as Predetermined Variables: A third approach adopts the language of time series and casts an institution as a predetermined variable. Viewed in this manner, the properties of an institution are initially determined "in the model": The institution is created in response to social or economic forces. While at first endogenous, a predetermined variable subsequently becomes exogenous; it acquires causal power. So, too, an institution, once created, is able to influence the very forces that lead to its creation.

Proceeding a step further, the analogy offers a theory of change – one whose properties share elements in common with those stressed by Wallis in his chapter. Over *la longue durée*, slow-moving forces alter. The institution continues to shape outcomes and to determine behavior; it continues to be a causal variable. But because societies and economies change – be that change ever so slow moving – a gap opens up between the welfare-maximizing choice of policies and the policies actually chosen. Rather than promoting desirable outcomes, the institution begins to impede their selection; as a result, it is increasingly viewed as imposing costs rather than promoting welfare. Slow-moving forces that operate over *la longue durée* can thus lead to demands for reform (Greif and Laitin 2004).[5] Returning to the analogy with structural equation models, it is as if the model reverts to the initial period; economic and social variables that have been being shaped by the institution now shape it instead.

Institutions, such as monarchies or "central planning," that once may have been viewed as providing valuable solutions to society's needs were later viewed as imposing barriers on the attainment of what is desirable. This "contradiction" between the nature of the polity and forces shaping their social and economic environment provides points of entry for reformers and revolutionaries. In much the same way as Pincus and Robinson discuss the origins of the glorious revolution (see also Jha 2010), the tensions between the polity and the society it governs prepare the ground for institutional change.

---

[5] Among the approaches discussed by Shepsle in his chapter, this argument thus adheres to the assumptions that underlie the approach of Calvert and Schotter, rather than those that characterize the thought of Riker – or Shepsle himself.

There are of course other interpretations. Most prominent among them, perhaps, is the theory of path dependence (Arthur 1994; Pierson 2007). While presented as a dynamic theory, however, path dependence is better at accounting for persistence than for change. Institutions limit the range of choice, its proponents note, and political changes will therefore be incremental and cumulative rather than discontinuous and revolutionary. Because institutions vest power in those who benefit from their policies, those proposing changes find themselves powerfully opposed. And if institutions propound and defend broadly held values, then it is easier to coordinate in support of them than to rally in opposition. Once created, institutions are therefore likely to endure or, if they do change, to do so incrementally. Where they start therefore determines where they end up.

4. From Clarification to Critique

This paper began by exploring the diverse forms of the neoinstitutionalism and by seeking to account for its reception. It then attempted to impart order to what had become a disorderly field. As noted at the outset, to my mind, at least, the approach remains incomplete, in two ways. Having emerged from the analysis of market failures, it provides a theory of the demand for but not the supply of institutions. For related reasons, it therefore too often fails to realize the implications of its basic insight: that coercion can be productive. Taken together, I argue, these criticisms suggest that for its completion the new institutionalism must recenter on the study of politics.

To motivate this argument, consider the institution of property rights. Where the legal system defends property rights, then the fear of punishment provides an incentive to refrain from trespassing, thereby strengthening incentives to expend productive labor and to invest. Now, however, consider Weingast's (1995) pithy rejoinder: that someone powerful enough to create a system of property rights is powerful enough to violate them. If one acknowledges the validity of the point – as I believe we all must – then we must also look beyond institutions themselves when seeking to account for their existence and their impact on economic life.

Will an institution employ its powers so as to promote the creation of wealth, or will it use them to seize and distribute it? Given that one of the goals of the new institutionalism is to account for economic growth and development, no question could be more fundamental. And yet, when we look for an answer, the new institutionalism appears to have little to offer. To remedy that deficiency, I would argue, we need to turn to the study of politics. Politicians create institutions; they determine how that power is employed and how, therefore, institutions will behave.

To advance this argument, I turn to some of my own work and explore the impact of political institutions on the agricultural economies of Africa. In doing so, I add more material to that provided in this volume by Jakiela in Chapter 11, Gehlbach and Malesky in Chapter 10, Galiani and Schargrodsky in Chapter 6, and even more directly, Pincus and Robinson in Chapter 9, who stress the importance of partisan politics to the creation of British institutions.

Lessons from Kenya

Agriculture constitutes the single largest sector of the economies of most nations in Africa. In the 1970s, growth rates in Africa declined and, in some instances, turned negative. My research (Bates 1981) led me to believe – and others to concur – that government policies toward agriculture constituted a major reason. Governments intervened in agricultural markets, enabling bureaucrats and politicians to extract wealth from the rural economy. Public institutions failed to furnish protection to farmers; rather, they engaged in predation, thereby discouraging farmers from committing their resources to the expansion of production. The resultant decline of the rural sector was both a symptom and contributor to the decline of Africa's economies.

For many, the remedy appeared obvious: Governments should withdraw from the industry and let market forces prevail. Defenders of this position cited Kenya, whose government cheerfully endorsed the private pursuit of wealth and proclaimed itself "capitalist," and whose economy continued to grow while others' declined.

When I turned to the study of Kenya (Bates 1989), I was therefore surprised to find its rural sector was marked not by the prevalence of free markets but rather by high levels of government intervention. Most farmers faced but one licensed buyer; less than 40 percent of total agricultural production was freely marketed. Farmers were compelled to join government-sponsored cooperatives that processed, stored, and marketed their crops; furnished seasonal loans; and sold farm inputs – seeds, fertilizers, and pesticides. Crop authorities – for cotton, sugar, coffee, or tea, for example – prescribed and enforced farming practices and imposed conservation measures. The government may have proclaimed itself capitalist and a friend of the market, but it maintained a powerful presence in Kenya's rural economy.

In contrast to what I had found elsewhere in Africa, in Kenya, many farmers tolerated high levels of regulation by nonmarket institutions and indeed opposed proposals to introduce market competition. For in Kenya, not only did the agencies offer prices that approximated those in global markets, they also provided additional benefits, the most prized being seasonal credit. And the farmers acknowledged that it was precisely because the agencies were given sole right to purchase the crop that were they willing to advance loans: Where land rights remained unclear, they recognized, the crop served as the best collateral.

In Kenya, institutions corrected for market failures in credit markets, but also helped to promote the formation of public goods and the amelioration of externalities (Bates 1989). By deducting fees from their payments to farmers, cooperatives funded laboratories, which developed crop varieties that produced more fruit and succumbed to fewer diseases. They also imposed fines on those who failed to employ proper cultivation methods. If farmers planted their coffee or tea bushes too closely, rendering them difficult to inspect for pests or plant diseases; or if they continued to harvest from infected trees, then diseases would infect their farms and spread to neighboring *shambas*. By penalizing individuals who engaged in such practices, government agencies altered private incentives in ways that enhanced the welfare of the industry.

Institutions, I have argued, introduce power into economic life. As stressed by the public choice school, and as confirmed by my earlier research, that power can be employed to predate. Alternatively, as argued here, it can also be employed to instill incentives and to constrain choices and thereby counter the perverse incentives that prevail when markets fail. The contrasting manner in which institutions operate in Africa highlights a major weakness in the new institutionalism: As presently constituted, the approach offers little insight into the issue of under what conditions the power of government institutions promote or forestall the creation of wealth.

The Turn toward Politics

To remedy this defect, I argue, the new institutionalism needs to focus on politics. In support of this argument, I return to East Africa, focusing first on the divergent fate of coffee growers in Uganda and Kenya and then on changes within Kenya itself.

Uganda and Kenya in the 1970s: As in Kenya, the coffee industry in Uganda was governed by a marketing board; indeed, the enabling statutes of the two boards are virtually identical, empowering them both to serve as sole purchaser of the crop, to provide research and agricultural services, and to promote, in these and other ways, the prosperity of the coffee sector. Despite possessing similar institutions, in the 1970s, the boards behaved in a strikingly different manner. In Uganda, the coffee board imposed prices that enabled it to extract more than 60 percent of the revenues generated from coffee exports; by contrast, Kenya's board extracted less than 10 percent, and it converted a major portion of the revenues it seized into public goods and productive services for the industry.

The origin of this contrast lay not in the institutions themselves, which closely resembled each other, but in the political environment within which they operated. In Uganda, political power lay in the hands of politicians from the north, which was arid and poor; capturing power at the national level, these politicians used the coffee board to extract resources from the south, which they then spent on northern "development projects." In Kenya, by contrast, power lay in the hands of politicians from the coffee-growing regions: Jomo Kenyatta, Kenya's president, and his colleagues from Central Province. In exchange for the votes that kept them in office, they used their power to enhance the wealth of their constituents and to defend the wealth of the industry from efforts by other regions to lay claim to its resources. In both Uganda and Kenya, institutions inserted power into economic life. The manner in which power was employed was not determined by the institutions themselves, however, but rather by politicians.

Explanations based on institutions are thus not complete; they need to be grounded on an understanding of the incentives that shape the choices of the politicians who oversee them. Changes that took place in Kenya after the death of Jomo Kenyatta help to drive this point home.[6]

Kenya over Time: Upon the death of Kenyatta, power passed out of the hands of the Central Province and into the hands of Daniel Arap Moi, a politician from Western Kenya. Western Kenya grows much grain and little coffee; by comparison with Central Province, its people are therefore disadvantaged. In the months following his rise to power, Moi unleashed teams of auditors and public prosecutors upon the coffee board and the cooperatives in Central Province. Filing charges of corruption and mismanagement, he shifted their funds to institutions that financed the planting, purchasing, and storage of grain in the West.

With the shift from Kenyatta to Moi, new interests animated the use of power by the institutions that governed farming. When the political order changed, so too did the performance of institutions. Rather than using the institutions of the coffee industry to safeguard its interests, politicians employed them to seize and redistribute its revenues.

---

[6] Note that his within-country variation helps to identify my causal claim. For an elaboration, see Chapter 10 by Gehlbach and Malesky.

5. The Productive Margin

Data from the field thus underscores that institutionalist arguments are wanting and require political analysis for their completion. As adumbrated in our discussion of the public-choice school, institutions are Janus-faced: instilling power into economic life, they can redistribute or destroy value or they can facilitate its creation. The key question, then, is: When will politicians find it politically rewarding to mobilize power for the one purpose or the other? Under what conditions will they fashion and employ institutions to promote the creation of wealth, thereby promoting development? Such questions, I argue, mark the productive margin of this field.

4

The Rules of the Game

What Rules? Which Game?

Kenneth A. Shepsle

1. Introduction

Imagine we are on Capitol Hill in early January of an odd-numbered year. A new Congress is about to convene, the even-year election having been concluded the previous November. But is it a new Congress? As we will see, this is a constitutionally controversial matter, one that lies at the heart of more abstract matters concerning the nature of institutions of self-governing groups.

For the House of Representatives, this is a settled matter. The previous House had adjourned *sine die* before the election and, from a constitutional perspective, is now an entirely new body. The newly convened House will operate under "general parliamentary law" until it has sworn in its members, elected a presiding officer, and adopted rules.

For the Senate, on the other hand, this is *not* a settled matter. For two-thirds of the senators, the election of the previous November in no way interrupted their respective careers. They are sitting senators who were not "in cycle" for the election – their staggered terms did not require them to face contract renewal in November. Under one constitutional view this senate is the same collective body as the one that existed before the election; it never adjourned permanently and only a portion of its membership may have changed. More generally, the senate of time t is the same as the one of time $t - 1$. By induction, a current senate is the same body as the one that convened in 1790! There is never a new senate. This is the continuing-body theory of the Senate (Bruhl 2010).

The continuing-body theory has interpretive consequences for rules, consequences that follow from three provisions. The first is Article I, Section 5 of the Constitution. This reads in part: "Each House may determine the Rules of its Proceedings...." That is, each chamber is a self-governing group. The Constitution is otherwise modest in restricting internal features of each chamber.[1]

The second provision is a standing rule, created by Article I, Section 5 authority. Rule V of *The Standing Rules of the Senate* states:

1. No motion to suspend, modify, or amend any rule, or any part thereof, shall be in order, except on one day's notice in writing, specifying precisely the rule or parts proposed to be suspended, modified, or amended, and the purpose thereof. Any rule may be suspended without notice by the unanimous consent of the Senate, except as otherwise provided by the rules.

2. The rules of the Senate shall continue from one Congress to the next Congress unless they are changed as provided in these rules.

A third provision, also a standing rule of the Senate, prescribes how standing rules may be amended as permitted by Rule V. According to Rule XXII.2, if sixteen senators sign a motion to bring debate on any measure to a close, then the presiding officer

shall at once state the motion to the Senate, and one hour after the Senate meets on the following calendar day but one, he shall lay the motion before the Senate and direct that the clerk call the roll, and upon the ascertainment that a quorum is present, the Presiding Officer shall, without debate, submit to the Senate by a yea-and-nay vote the question: "Is it the sense of the Senate that the debate shall be brought to a close?" And if that question shall be decided in the affirmative by three-fifths of the Senators duly chosen and sworn – *except on a measure or motion to amend the Senate rules, in which case the necessary affirmative vote shall be two-thirds of the Senators present and voting* [emphasis added] – then said measure, motion, or other matter pending before the Senate, or the unfinished business, shall be the unfinished business to the exclusion of all other business until disposed of.[2]

---

[1] Article I, Section 5 lays out a short list of requirements. Each chamber is the judge of elections to it; a majority constitutes a quorum; it may compel attendance of its members and set penalties for violations; it may punish members for disorderly behavior; it may expel a member on a two-thirds vote; it must keep a journal of proceedings and publish it; and it may not adjourn for more than three days without the consent of the other chamber. In addition, Article I, Section 2 specifies that the House shall choose a Speaker and other officers, while Article I, Section 3 designates the vice president of the United States as the president of the Senate and implores the Senate to choose other officers including a president pro tempore who presides in the absence of the vice president.

[2] As an aside, note that a vote on cloture that is not a rules change requires the support of three-fifths of the senators "duly chosen and sworn," not sixty senators. Of course, when the Senate possesses a full complement, the number is sixty. After the presidential inauguration in January 2009, however, there were only ninety-seven senators "duly chosen and sworn" in the 111th Congress. Neither Barack Obama's seat from Illinois nor Joseph Biden's seat from Delaware had been filled. And the election result for the seat from Minnesota had

As a self-governing group, in sum, the Senate may formulate its own rules of procedure as well as rules governing the revision of those rules (Article I, Section 5 of the Constitution), but absent such rule-governed amendments to the rules (requiring majority support to pass, but two-thirds support to close debate as specified in Rule XXII.2 of the Senate's standing rules), the rules of one Congress continue to the next (as specified in Rule V.2 of the standing rules).

Now imagine the following choreographed exercise.[3] At the opening of a new Congress, the majority leader, who, according to Senate rules, possesses priority in recognition, rises in the well of the Senate and announces,

As the Senate is not a continuing body, its first order of business, under Article I, Section 5 of the Constitution, is to select standing rules for the new Congress in accord with general parliamentary procedure. I move the re-adoption of the standing rules of the previous Congress, with two exceptions. Rule V.2 is deleted. And the special treatment given to cloture as applied to amendments to standing rules in Rule XXII.2 [italicized in the previous paragraph] is removed.[4]

After this motion is read, chaos breaks out in the chamber. The presiding officer, the vice president, gavels the chamber to order and recognizes the minority leader who, with great agitation, seeks recognition: "I rise to make a point of order. The Senate *is* a continuing body and thus is governed by the rules today that were in effect in the last session, not by general parliamentary procedure. This is clearly stated in Rule V.2. Thus it is possible to revise the rules only in compliance with Rule XXII.2, even if the objective is to revise said rule." The key question to be ruled upon by the presiding officer is whether the previous Senate can bind its successor (as Rule V.2 would seem to do).

Since the majority leader has invoked a constitutional basis for moving to adopt rules, the presiding officer would normally yield to the norm of not ruling on a constitutional point himself; instead he would entertain a motion to table the point, thus allowing the fate of the minority leader's intervention to be determined by the full Senate. If the motion to table the minority leader's point succeeds, the majority leader's motion then becomes the unfinished business before the Senate. (If it fails, then the

---

not been resolved. So, for a few weeks, only fifty-nine affirmative votes were required for cloture. Throughout the rest of the 111th Congress, the Senate was not always at full force, but the ranks were never so depleted as to reduce the cloture number below sixty. Note also that the cloture number for a rules change is two-thirds of those present and voting.

[3] I thank David Rohde for first bringing this possibility to my attention.

[4] The most important feature of general parliamentary procedure is that decisions are taken by a simple majority, subject to a quorum being present.

majority leader's motion is effectively off the agenda.) A second key question arises – if the motion to table succeeds, is the subsequent unfinished business (the majority leader's motion to adopt rules) to be debated under the old Senate rules or according to general parliamentary procedure? The presiding officer rules that if the point of order is tabled, the Senate will proceed immediately to the majority leader's motion under general parliamentary procedure. The minority leader then appeals the chair's ruling, arguing that it makes no sense to consider the majority leader's motion under general parliamentary procedure since this is precisely what the majority leader's rules-change motion aims to establish but has not yet done; the motion must, in the humble opinion of the minority leader, be taken up under existing Senate rules. When the motion to reverse the presiding officer's ruling is put to a vote, a majority votes to sustain the ruling. (Senate majorities rarely overturn rulings of the presiding officer.) The objection is thus tabled, and the majority leader's motion is taken up under general parliamentary procedure. A simple majority then approves his motion. *Voila!* A revision of the rules – in effect a reduction in the threshold to end filibusters on amending the rules – has been accomplished by a simple majority. And a precedent has been set that the Senate is not a continuing body.

This is just a story. But it illustrates several points that will be the focus of this paper:

- Self-governing groups create the rules according to which their proceedings are governed.
- Self-governing groups may change their rules – suspend, amend, override, even disobey.
- Let me repeat this last point. Self-governing groups may even flout the rules upon which they have previously agreed (as they did in regard to Rule V.2 in the illustration just given).

2. Two Views of Institutions[5]

Douglass North (1990a, 3; also see Mantzavinos, North, and Shariq 2004) is famously associated with characterizing an institution as a game form. It is "the rules of the game in a society or, more formally... the humanly devised constraints that shape human interaction." North urges us to think

---

[5] This is more fully developed in Shepsle (2006a, 2006b) and independently developed in Munger (2010).

flexibly about this definition: Institutions range from informal constraints like taboos, customs, conventions, codes of behavior, and traditions to formal rights, responsibilities, and constraints like those found in contracts, official procedures, and modern constitutions. An institution specifies the players whose behavior is bound by its rules; the actions the players must, may, must not, or may not take (Crawford and Ostrom 1995); the informational conditions under which they make choices; their timing; the impact of exogenous events; and the outcomes that are a consequence of these choices and events. The game form is transformed into a game when players are endowed with preferences over outcomes.

The game-form view of institutions, one to which I adhered in earlier work on the role of institutional structure on political outcomes (Shepsle 1979), is silent on three significant matters. First, it says little about the sources of institutions. Institutional arrangements are taken as given with the objective of tracing the implications of these rules for behavior and outcomes. Attention is riveted on the subsequent play of the game governed by these rules and the outcomes that arise from this play, not on the origins of the rules. Second, there is little consideration given to the durability of rules. Because they are taken as exogenous, they are not, themselves, part of the play of the game. They are assumed to endure.[6] Third, the constraints entailed in the rules are regarded as self-enforcing. There is no provision made for deviating from the rules. An agent, at any node in the game tree to which he or she is assigned, has a fixed repertoire of alternatives as specified by the branches emerging from the node and must choose from among these. It would never occur to a majority leader of the U.S. Senate, as he stares into his shaving mirror in the morning, to contemplate announcing, contra Rule V.2, that the Senate is not a continuing body.

The equilibrium view of institutions – an alternative perspective associated with the work of Schotter (1981) and Calvert (1995) – does not focus primarily on institutional origins either, but it does have something to say about their durability and prospects for departures from their strictures. According to this approach, the game form itself is an equilibrium.[7]

---

[6] This is a slightly unfair characterization of North's approach; his formulation allows organizations like firms to invest in organizational elaborations in order to enhance their profits.

[7] For a treatise weaving together game theory and economic history to develop an elaborate theory of endogenous institutions, see Greif (2006). Greif is one of the exceptions in focusing on institutional origins as well as on equilibrium properties (137ff. and Chapter 7). Greif's approach differs slightly from Calvert-Schotter's, mainly at the level of nuance, so I will group the three together for present purposes.

What North took as exogenous, Calvert (1995), Schotter (1981), and Greif (2006) view as the endogenous product of a more primal environment. There are really two parts to equilibria of interest: the one induced by a particular body of rules – institutional or structure-induced equilibrium (Shepsle 1979) on which North focuses, and the one arising in the primal environment where rules are chosen and maintained – equilibrium institution (Shepsle 1986). The combination of these two elements is what Calvert, Schotter, and Greif have in mind as an institution: It is "an equilibrium of behavior in an underlying game.... It must be rational for nearly every individual to almost always adhere to the behavioral prescriptions of the institution, given that nearly all other individuals are doing so" (Calvert 1995, 58, 60). Or as Greif (2006, 136) observes, "institutionalized rules and the beliefs they help form enable, guide and motivate most individuals to adopt the behavior associated with their ... position [in the game] most of the time."

This means that the rules themselves are part of the equilibrium. Perturbations in the primal environment may undermine the existing rules equilibrium, possibly providing opportunities to change them. If, for example, an exogenous change in constituency preferences – caused, say, by the bursting of a housing bubble, a technological development, a natural resource discovery, or an environmental disaster – were to generate a change in the composition of legislators, this, in turn, may provide the circumstance for changing institutional rules – say, the elimination of the filibuster in the Senate.[8]

Many institutions provide avenues for precisely this to take place – they provide the means to suspend or revise existing rules. This has already been mentioned for the Senate – Rule XXII describes how the Senate may amend its standing rules. The House, on the other hand, devises routine procedural routes around its standing rules, either by a suspension-of-the-rules motion (requiring two-thirds support of those present and voting) or by the majority adoption of a special rule brought to the floor by the Committee on Rules (Doran 2010). These, respectively, suspend the standing rules and move directly to a vote or replace them with a specially crafted procedure, in either case only provisionally to take up a specific measure.[9]

---

[8] Greif (2006, chapter 7) emphasizes the effects of perturbations in the primal environment on beliefs (about the efficacy of following equilibrium behavior and the prospects of others doing so) as a potentially disequilibrating result.

[9] Whether the successful use of an institutionally permissible method of rules revision produces the same institution or a new one is a terminological matter. It certainly changes the game form.

There is a second methodological possibility this broader view of institutions permits. The North view of institutions does not countenance departures from the rules. They are assumed to be obeyed, although this remains implicit. In the Calvert-Schotter-Greif formulation, on the other hand, deviation is entirely possible. The Senate majority leader *can* announce that the Senate is not a continuing body, even though Rule V.2 declares that it is (so long as a majority is prepared to support this departure). The Senate is a self-governing group and can depart from its rules as it wishes. The more comprehensive equilibrium view of institutions associated with the Calvert-Schotter-Greif approach does not *assume* that compliance with the rules necessarily occurs, and therefore allows for deviation.

3. Endogenous Procedures to Change Rules

There are multiple mechanisms by which rules change. That some such mechanisms exist at all is partially due to the self-awareness of institutional designers at a constitutional moment that they are not omniscient. Mechanisms are provided ex ante to fill unanticipated gaps and to adapt to changing circumstances. They are also provided to deal with circumstances that could be imagined but are too unlikely or too convoluted to accommodate at the constitutional stage.

One conspicuous instance of these is a constitutional clause that describes the method by which the constitution itself may be amended. This is the role played by Article V of the U.S. Constitution. At the constitutional convention of 1787, many participants made clear that they sought a less-than-unanimous procedure, given the unanimity straitjacket into which the Articles of Confederation had placed the existing regime, but one that could not be exploited easily.

Bodies of rules, likewise, often possess amendment procedures. Rule XXII of the Senate's standing rules is, as we have seen, one such instance. Suspension of the rules, special rules from the Committee on Rules, and motions to waive points of order (that would otherwise be in order) are examples drawn from the U.S. House that temporarily eliminate a constraint on procedure. Other sources of institutional change include interpretive courts, escape clauses (in treaties and labor-market agreements), nullification arrangements, emergency powers (see Loveman 1993 on "regimes of exception"), devolution, redistricting, and expansion (contraction) of (s)electorates.

Without going into further detail, it should be clear that rules are provisional in the sense that they do not possess permanent status. They continuously face a Nash conjecture – is it in any agent's interest to deviate from

behavior required or expected of them by the existing institutional arrangements? Such arrangements may possess self-altering procedures (Article V
of the Constitution); they may be altered in the primal environment (as
happened to the Articles of Confederation); and they may be disobeyed
(as we shall see).

4. Institutions as Constraints, Except When They're Not: Examples from the U.S. Congress

From the discussion thus far, it is evident that self-governing groups have
a commitment problem. Rules may serve a variety of purposes and confer conspicuous advantages, but by its very nature a self-governing group
cannot commit to sticking to them. There is no bond to post, no hostage
to give. Like the all-powerful Hobbesian state, itself, a self-governing group
can break any promise it makes. Its members may *choose* to obey its rules
and follow its procedures, but then again they may choose otherwise in any
particular situation. Lest one think this merely an abstract problem with no
practical significance, I offer next a set of illustrations of rule-breaking.

- *The Senate as a continuing body* (Riddick 1981, 991–995). The Senate
  has only rarely made changes in its rules. One of its most controversial,
  though not apparent at the time, occurred in 1806 when, in an effort
  to clean up a cluttered set of rules, the Senate (possibly inadvertently)
  eliminated the method of calling the previous question, which would
  have permitted a simple majority, a quorum present, to shut off debate.
  Thereafter, until 1917, the only way to close debate – on *any* matter,
  including rules changes – was by unanimous consent. In 1917, in the
  wake of inaction on a Wilson administration proposal to arm merchant
  ships to deal with attacks by the German navy (a proposal blocked by
  "a small group of willful men" as President Wilson declared), and the
  subsequent public outcry, the Senate agreed to Rule XXII, providing a
  method to bring closure to debate. This prevailed for some thirty years.
  But from 1949 onward, at the opening of almost every Congress, a resolution to revise the rules, especially the filibuster rule, was introduced
  and debated, only to be blocked because a super majority was unwilling
  to close debate. In 1959, the Senate went a step further (backward?),
  not only retaining the existing super-majority requirement for closing
  debate, but also adding a proviso on the continuation of rules from
  one Congress to the next unless revised by procedures laid out in the
  current rules (essentially language identical to that of Rule V.2 cited

earlier). Further efforts to revise the rules over the next sixteen years
consistently ran up against Rule V.2 and Rule XXII.2; resolutions to
proceed to consider a revision were defeated by a failure to bring debate
to a close.

In 1975, there was a modicum of success. The 1975 revision resulted
in a reduction in the cloture requirement to "three-fifths of those duly
chosen and sworn" for ordinary motions, and "two-thirds of those
present and voting" for rules revision (both requiring a quorum to be
present). What is of relevance to the present discussion about institutions is the method by which this was accomplished.[10] S. Res. 4,
introduced by Walter Mondale, Democrat from Minnesota, and James
Pearson, Republican from Kansas, sought to reduce the cloture requirement for all measures to three-fifths of those present and voting, a
quorum present. To expedite matters, Pearson offered a motion with
three parts:

1. That the Senate proceeds to the consideration of S. Res. 4.
2. That under the rulemaking powers found in Article 1, Section 5 of
   the Constitution, debate on this motion to proceed be brought to
   an immediate conclusion.
3. That on the adoption of this motion, the presiding officer put the
   question on the motion to proceed without further debate.

Majority Leader Mike Mansfield, Democrat from Montana, raised
a point of order against Pearson's motion, citing Rule V.2 and the
continuing nature of Senate rules. He claimed that quite apart from
his own views on the filibuster, Senate rules prohibit the procedure
provided by the Pearson motion. Vice President Rockefeller submitted
the point of order to the full Senate. Before a vote was taken on whether
to table the point or not, he was asked whether, if the point were tabled
and the Senate proceeded directly to a consideration of S. Res. 4, he
would follow the procedure outlined in Pearson's motion. Rockefeller
responded that his interpretation of events would lead him to affirm
these procedures because the Senate's act in tabling the point of order,
in effect, gives him the green light to do so.

Senator James Allen, Democrat from Alabama, the master parliamentary expert of the era, pointed out to Rockefeller the inconsistency of
his interpretation. How can the Senate follow the procedure provided
in the Pearson motion when it hasn't even agreed to that motion yet?
The current rules would require that Pearson's motion, like any other,

---

[10] The full details are found in Gold (2008).

be taken up under *existing* rules, in particular under the direction of Rule XXII.2, since the Senate is a continuing body according to Rule V.2 (citing the reaffirmation of this position in the last rules revision in 1959). Gold (2008, 61) puts it thus: "In other words, how can the Senate be bound by the terms of a motion it refused to table but has not yet adopted?" Rockefeller stood his ground, stating that by tabling the Mansfield point of order, the Senate is expressing its willingness to proceed in this manner. Gold continues, "Although Pearson's motion runs contrary to the Senate rules, Rockefeller will abide by it because, when it tabled Mansfield's point of order, the Senate expressed its will that he do so."

For the rest of this story, the reader should consult Gold. For our purposes, the interesting thing to note is that, even though the rules specify that the Senate is a continuing body – that the rules of the Senate in Congress t carry over to Congress $t + 1$ – and, therefore, that its rules for amending the rules must follow the procedures laid out in those existing rules rather than general parliamentary procedure at the opening of a new Congress, a majority, by sustaining the "illegal" interpretation of the presiding officer (at least in Senator Allen's opinion), may choose to violate its own rules.[11]

- *Byrd's breaking of the post-cloture filibuster in the Senate.* The 1975 reform in the filibuster rule – Rule XXII.2 quoted earlier (a compromise worked out with Mondale and Pearson) – made it easier to bring debate on a measure to a close. This provided incentives for the invention of clever parliamentary tactics. The master, as noted, was James Allen of Alabama, who invented the post-cloture filibuster. According to the filibuster rule newly in place, once cloture is secured, each senator is limited to one hour of speaking time. But the rule did not obviate the need to dispose of amendments to the measure that had already been introduced or limit the number of those amendments (so long as an amendment was germane and had been introduced before the cloture vote). Additionally, it did not limit the reading of amendments, quorum calls, or roll call votes. In short, there was still no limit on how much time could be devoted to a measure, *even after cloture had been voted.* This procedure was actively utilized by Allen, bringing the Senate to a standstill on many occasions. It reached its zenith (nadir?) in 1977 when Howard Metzenbaum, Democrat from Ohio, and James Abourezk, Democrat from South Dakota, in advance

---

[11] Whether the Senate should be regarded as a continuing body is analyzed by Bruhl (2010).

of cloture, submitted hundreds of amendments to a natural gas dereg-
ulation bill, which the Senate was compelled to take up after cloture
had been voted. This filibuster by amendment lasted thirteen days,
and still neither senator (nor other senators) had used his one hour of
permitted speaking time.

Robert Byrd, Democrat from West Virginia, in his first year as majority
leader, aimed to break this device by closing the loopholes in Rule
XXII that permitted it. If he had tried to do this by introducing a
rules revision, it would have been necessary, first, to secure cloture on
any measure he proposed (a rules change, recall, required two-thirds
support) and, second, to overcome a post-cloture filibuster on his
measure to end post-cloture filibusters. This posed a tactical dilemma.
Byrd chose a course of action in the debate on the natural gas deregu-
lation bill, a course that by reasonable interpretation violated existing
Senate rules. By existing rules, a post-cloture motion can be ruled out
of order by the presiding officer only in response to a point of order; he
does not have independent authority to do so. And any ruling on a point
of order by the presiding officer can be appealed and debated, consuming more time. This is what made Allen's post-cloture filibuster tactic
so effective. Byrd's heresthetical maneuver was to secure a ruling from
the presiding officer, Vice President Walter Mondale, that, post-cloture,
any amendment introduced before cloture had been voted, but deemed
defective, could be ruled out of order without the necessity of a point
of order. (I do not know why this ruling was not challenged.) Having
secured this ruling, Byrd began calling up the amendments that were
being used by Metzenbaum and Abourezk to obstruct consideration of
the unfinished business before the Senate. Mondale would rule one out
of order as defective and, before an appeal of his ruling could be made,
Byrd, using his priority right of recognition as majority leader, would
call up another amendment. This way, the majority leader, in cahoots
with the vice president, disposed of the many amendments being used
for obstructionist purposes. The parliamentary dance choreographed
by the vice president and the majority leader was clearly not sanctioned
by the rules.

In 1979, Byrd succeeded in formally amending Rule XXII, putting a
one-hundred-hour cap on post-cloture activity, thereby allowing for
only limited post-cloture obstruction. Note that Byrd did not do this
initially, instead circumventing (breaking?) existing Senate rules.

- *(Non) right of recognition and disappearing quorums in the House.* Perhaps the world record for rule innovation by rule violation is held by

late-nineteenth-century speaker of the House Thomas Brackett Reed, Republican from Maine, who earned the sobriquet "Czar."

In the fifty-first Congress, the Republicans held a slim majority. After an ordinary legislative day on January 21, 1890, a minority motion to adjourn was offered. On a voice vote, the Speaker declared it defeated. Congressman Bland, Democrat from Missouri, appealed for a teller vote. As reported by Mary Parker Follett (1902, 191), the appeal for a teller vote, in which proponents and opponents of a measure present themselves to tellers in the well of the House chamber for a precise count, is regarded as appropriate when it is possible the presiding officer has mistaken the relative size of the opposing sides based on a voice vote. Indeed, she opined that it is "an inherent privilege of all legislative bodies" to check the accuracy of a presiding officer's count. But Reed believed, as Follett reported, that "it was apparent to all" that Bland's motion was "purely dilatory." Reed refused to entertain the request, thus flouting a privilege typically accorded rank-and-file members, with neither precedent nor rule in his support (but see below). Subsequently, whenever someone rose to seek recognition, the Speaker queried, "For what purpose does the gentleman rise?" and refused recognition if he judged the purpose obstructionist.[12]

The first session of this Congress had opened in December 1889, with limited attendance. The majority party, given its slim advantage, was unable to provide a quorum on its own, which was necessary to conduct business. This proved a tempting opportunity for the minority Democrats to obstruct the majority. With increasing frequency they demanded quorum calls, requiring a time-consuming roll-call vote, but refused to answer to the clerk's call of their names. When the majority members' responses to the clerk's call did not constitute a quorum, the minority demanded another quorum call. On January 30, 1890, the yeas and nays were called on to consider a contested election case. The vote stood at 161 yeas, 2 nays, and 165 (Democrats) present but not voting. The objection of "no quorum" was made by minority members (who had demanded the roll call in the first place, but then did not answer to their names when the roll was called).[13] Instead of ordering a

---

[12] Recognition is deemed within the discretionary power of the presiding officer. But the discretion has more to do with who is recognized than with the purpose for which recognition is sought. Reed expanded this authority by his heresthetical maneuver. On recognition in the House generally, see Deschler (1975).

[13] Why the Democrats didn't all simply vote no and defeat the motion (they appeared to have the votes at this time) is unclear to me. Perhaps they desired not to oppose directly

call of the roll, Speaker Reed instructed the sergeant at arms to lock the doors to the chamber, instructed the clerk to record the names of those who were in attendance but not responding to their names as present, ordered the clerk to continue as chaos prevailed, and then announced the final tally in favor of the yeas with a quorum participating. One of the minority members appealed the Speaker's decision, but this was tabled by a majority of a quorum (not a majority of the House), and the final tally stood.[14] Reed announced that, as a quorum had been determined by the House, he would no longer tolerate quorum calls that were purely dilatory, even if they were in order according to the rules.

Follett (1902, 194) describes Reed's accomplishments as follows:

> His two most important parliamentary decisions were: first, that a vote is valid if a quorum be actually present, though the quorum may not vote; and secondly, that motions obviously and purely dilatory, designed only to block the doing of business, need not be entertained.

Follett (1902 [1974], 194–216) provides a passionate defense of Reed's actions, citing occasional idiosyncratic uses of these tools by previous speakers, their use in state legislatures and in the House of Commons, and possible interpretations of the Constitution consistent with these actions. Nevertheless, at the time they were deployed, these practices were not part of the Standing Rules of the House of Representatives. On February 14, 1890, several weeks *after* Reed's preemptive strikes, they were formally incorporated into the rules. Once again, then, we see that rules are constraints, except when they're not.

- *Violating scope of the differences.* The U.S. Congress is a bicameral legislature. The presentment clause of the Constitution requires that each chamber pass a bill in identical form before it may be presented to the president for his signature. When different versions of a bill pass each chamber, these differences must be resolved. One approach is to "message" between the chambers. One chamber accepts the other's version, but with an amendment in the nature of a substitute, that is, the members strike everything after the enacting clause in the other chamber's bill and substitute the language from their own bill. This is messaged back to the other chamber, which may accept it (and end the

---

a constitutional obligation of each chamber to judge elections. See Follett (1902 [1974], 192ff.).

[14] Reed reportedly asked of one minority member who personally objected that Reed had named him "present and counting toward a quorum" whether he really wanted to insist he wasn't present, and observed that if he did, that very insistence would constitute evidence that he was.

process), or accept it with amendments and send it back the other way. This ping-pong-like process works satisfactorily on relatively simple bills. But a several-hundred-page bill with many complexities cannot practically be handled in this manner. A conference committee is convened, consisting of a delegation from each chamber, that fashions a compromise between the two versions. This compromise is sent back to each chamber under a closed rule (no amendments) and is voted up or down there. If both chambers approve, then the bill is sent along for the president's signature.

There are, however, restrictions on what the respective conferees can agree to. Known as the scope of the differences, conferees are effectively required to produce a convex combination of the two chamber-approved bills. This means

○ Any negotiated outcome must lie within the interval defined by the two bills.[15]

○ Any initial agreements in the two bills must be reflected in the conference report.

○ Matters contained in neither initial bill may not be introduced into the report.

The normal practice is to observe these constraints, except when they are not observed. Imagine an agriculture appropriations bill in conference, where the conferees are drawn primarily from the committees in each chamber with original jurisdiction.[16] A particular subsidy may have been kept low in the chamber-specific versions in order to secure passage; a majority of legislators in each might oppose a higher support level. In conference, the conferees, with ties to agricultural constituencies and interests, would prefer a level higher than in either chamber's bill. Nominally, they are limited by the scope of the differences. But, in fact, they are limited by what they can get away with when each chamber votes on the conference report in its entirety under a closed rule. While it is possible for a legislator in one of the chambers to offer a point of order against a conference report for violating the scope of the differences, if it succeeds then the entire bill is placed in jeopardy. This has the practical effect of permitting violations in the rules, as long as they are not so egregious that a majority in the chamber is willing

---

[15] This is unambiguous when the difference is quantitative, but requires judgment when it is not.

[16] For appropriations measures it is almost always the full agriculture subcommittee on Appropriations of each chamber.

to take on the risk of sinking the whole bill by sustaining a point of order against it.

5. Rule-Breaking: Some Further Considerations

With these illustrations in mind, let me raise a few additional theoretical issues. Violating a rule in a given instance is one thing; formally changing a rule is another. A revised rule subjects all future considerations to the new constraint. But legislators, lacking omniscience, may be quite uncertain what future considerations might fall within the purview of the new rule. Under a lower threshold for cloture in the Senate, for example, *any* measure will have an easier route to a final-passage vote than under a more stringent threshold. Sometimes, senators are prepared to take this leap – the filibuster criterion was, in fact, changed in 1917 and 1975. But many attempts in the intervening years failed. Why? Perhaps because many a senator anticipated he or she might actually benefit from a more stringent cloture threshold, not always but often enough and on issues of great enough significance to the senator compared to those on which he or she would be disadvantaged. Indeed, for this very reason the imaginary scenario with which I introduced this paper – in which the Senate majority leader's heresthetical maneuver resulted in abolishing the super-majority requirement altogether – might not succeed. Many in the majority may be loathe to participate in the majority leader's procedural ploy.

Pervasive uncertainty about the contents of the future domain of a revised rule is often sufficient to deter rules changes – better the devil you know, and all that. But it is not necessary. Even if legislators know that many, even most, will be beneficiaries of the change, so long as they remain uncertain about the identity of beneficiaries, they may still balk at making changes. Uncertainty about future incidence produces a status quo bias (Fernandez and Rodrik 1991). This status quo bias means that permitting the occasional "breach" or temporary "reinterpretation" of the rules may be superior to tampering with standing rules (or a constitution for that matter) directly.

This is a variant of time inconsistency in which the circumvention of a particular rule on a particular occasion is a temptation too attractive to resist at the time. It is not unusual for majorities simultaneously to agree to standing rules ex ante but also to leave loopholes that may be exploited in particular circumstances. The provision of such loopholes and the antic-ipation of their occasional use does not indicate that collective choice on standing rules suffers from time inconsistency; rather it identifies how the collectivity anticipates the occasional circumvention. But toleration for actually *breaking* rules, as some of the examples given earlier illustrate, is a horse of an altogether different color. That is, arranging a procedure for suspending rules in a particular circumstance and providing some regulation of its use (e.g., a super-majority requirement) is one thing. But permitting a simple majority to sustain an outright violation – indeed, as in the Reed example, a simple majority of a quorum – damages the rules-as-constraints vision of institutions. It is the time inconsistency of "remote majoritarianism" (Krehbiel 1991) with a vengeance.

6. Conclusion

Through a series of examples drawn from historical experiences in the House and Senate, I have tried to contribute what I believe are novel points about our treatment of institutions. The concept of institutions as constraints has been a workhorse in the positive political theory and political economy fields – Baron-Ferejohn bargaining games, Shepsle-Weingast amendment games, Romer-Rosenthal agenda games are some examples. Collective practices are taken as fixed exogenously, providing a strategic context in which agents interact. In taking practices as fixed, equilibrium is established where deviations from the game form are ignored (or repressed) and compliance is taken for granted. The game form is given ex ante, and there is no choice on whether to play it as opposed to some alternative game form. This is not a bad starting point, since even if practices are endogenous choices, these choices must be informed by what (equilibrium) consequences are anticipated. As an application of backward induction, the equilibria associated with various alternative institutions must be determined before agents can rationally select which one to impose.

The institutions-as-equilibria approach, however, allows a deeper appreciation of institutional life by taking on board the possibility that departures from the rules are possible. Self-governing groups, in a manner like the Hobbesian state, cannot commit to enforcing their rules always and everywhere; thus, individual agents may find circumstances in which it does not always pay to comply with existing rules. Prospective departures, however, are not all of the same type. I have identified four different senses in which departures from a given body of rules are possible.

First, an institution is, as Calvert, Greif, and Schotter remind us, embedded in a primal environment. If the institution initially is in equilibrium, then an environmental perturbation may be sufficient to provide incentives for agents to "move against" the institution. A regime in place may be replaced by an alternative arrangement peacefully (e.g., the Articles of Confederation regime) or violently (e.g., the *ancien régime* in France).

Second, a body of rules may contain its own mechanisms for revision. Article V of the U.S. Constitution and Rule XXII of the Senate's standing rules are examples. Election rules, as well as those governing redistricting and reapportionment, might also be regarded as self-referential mechanisms of change. Unlike departures of the first type (in the previous paragraph), where the impetus for change comes from the primal environment, mechanisms of change here are prearranged by forward-thinking designers at a constitutional moment.

Third, rules may be temporarily suspended in accord with institutionally specified regulations. Suspension and special rules in the House, unanimous consent agreements in the Senate, escape clauses in treaties and contracts, and emergency powers in constitutions are examples. They share in common the belief that once the issue at hand is resolved, a return to "normal order" is expected.

Finally, rules may be broken. Declaring the Senate not a continuing body, in direct contradiction of a standing rule, or direct violations of the scope-of-the-differences requirement for conference reports were mentioned earlier. For a generation, the U.S. South found "massive resistance" to Supreme Court edicts to integrate public schools attractive. A collectivity may have the means to reverse outcomes based on rules violations or to punish deviations but may lack the will to do so.

All of these departures from rules raise concerns with the institutions-as-constraints approach. Rules may, as North states, consist of "humanly devised constraints." But what humans devise, they can revise. Thus, institutions are constraints except when decisive coalitions decide they are not. The examples given earlier suggest that clever institutional politicians are on the prowl for heresthetical opportunities to bend, evade, and even break the rules, especially when the stakes are large.

A second concern revolves around the difference between revising rules and breaking them. Revising is forever (or at least until the next round of revision). Breaking is issue- and time-specific. The policeman looks the other way when a motorist travels 40 miles per hour in a 35-miles-per-hour zone; he neither enforces the rule nor attempts to have it revised. Likewise, legislative majorities often ignore scope-of-the-differences violations in conference reports. Small departures, some of the time, appear to keep an institution intact. It remains equilibrium-like, that is, it persists despite occasional violations and is resistant to revision.

Lest I be accused of committing the fallacy of the two opera singers – in which a judge gave a role to the second opera singer immediately after having heard only the audition of the first – let me note a difficulty with the rules-as-equilibrium approach. There may be no such equilibrium in the primal environment. Riker (1981) makes this point in the context of majority rule in what has been coined the "inheritability hypothesis." When majority preferences over outcomes are cyclic (almost always in multidimensional spatial contexts), and institutional arrangements map into unique social outcomes, then collective preferences over institutions inherit the cyclicity of collective preferences over outcomes. In such cases, we have two diametrically opposed circumstances – the potential disequilibrium in the primal environment on the one hand, and the structure-induced equilibrium of a well-functioning institution on the other. What we observe in many empirical settings, however, seems to be something in between, neither the chaos of the former nor the stability of the latter. Institutions are revised occasionally, rules are violated with some frequency, and policy outcomes change over time but often exhibit only small variations around some central tendency. The puzzle is how to account for this in-between state of affairs. Maybe what we are looking for is a theory of friction, but whatever it might be, more thinking needs to be directed toward it.

Acknowledgments

Prepared for presentation at "The Legacy and Work of Douglass C. North: Understanding Institutions and Development Economics," a conference at the Center for New Institutional Social Science, Washington University in St. Louis, November 4–5, 2010. The author thanks Robert Bates for constructive comments.

5

Institutions and Sustainability of Ecological Systems

Elinor Ostrom

1. Introduction

Douglass North has had an incredible influence on my life and research and that of many other scholars. As an economic historian, he stressed the importance of individuals, not just governments, crafting important rules that enable them to solve tough problems. This challenged the presumption that we always need "the state" to solve all problems and was a major foundation for my work (North 1981, 1986, 1990a). North stressed that the term "institution" was used far too loosely. Some scholars thought of institutions as buildings, others used the term to mean organizations, and others to denote rules humans use to provide structure to their lives and interactions. Trying to explain human behavior by the presence or absence of a county jail is not a satisfactory theoretical effort, but examining how rules change incentives and outcomes is.

Digging into the rules that individuals have crafted on their own, why they work, how they enforce them and what are the consequences of diverse rule systems is an important theoretical and empirical endeavor that Douglass North (1978, 2005) stimulated. His work has been pathbreaking for me and numerous other scholars.

It is a pleasure to share with you that my own book, *Governing the Commons* (1990), would not have been written but for Doug North. He invited me to Washington University to give a talk in the fall of 1986. In that presentation, I described the diversity of rules that pumpers from several groundwater basins in California had devised, using a variety of arenas, ranging from their own private association, drafting legislation and having it passed by the state legislature, to having an election to create a special district, and negotiating new rules in the shadow of the court. I talked about the database we had developed on common-pool resources, some of the initial analysis that we were undertaking in the study of the impact of rules, and my own frustration that there were no particular rules that always made a difference.

This was the first in a series of events that led me to write *Governing the Commons* (Ostrom 1990). At the time of my lecture, Doug urged me to engage in writing a book-length manuscript. I had not dreamed of doing that prior to his urging. Then, Doug and Jim Alt invited me to write a book in their series, "The Political Economy of Institutions," at Cambridge University Press. That was a strong motivation in and of itself. Later, I had the good luck of having a sabbatical to spend the spring semester of 1988 in Bielefeld with a group that Reinhard Selten organized. It gave me an opportunity to try out ideas and discuss them with colleagues, particularly Reinhard Selten and Franz Joseph Weissing. In the late spring of 1988 Jim Alt and Kenneth Shepsle invited me to give a series of lectures at Harvard University. The combination of having a place to write and think, being invited to write a book, and then being invited to give a series of lectures really motivated me to move ahead. I probably would not have written *Governing the Commons* but for all of those positive pressures.

When I started the book, I was very upset that I could not find a specific set of rules that were consistently associated with self-organization and long-term sustainability. Finally, I got the insight that I had to move up to a more general level instead of focusing on specific rules. What boundary rules users agreed on – related to who was authorized to use a resource of some sort – was not crucial when looking across a large N of cases. Crucial, however, was that they *had* boundary rules. At the time, I called this broader level "design principles." I did imply that individuals self-consciously designed these long-surviving institutions but rather that these principles could be used by theorists to understand why some were successful and others failed.

Building on North's work and that of many other political economists, we are slowly developing a cumulative, cross-disciplinary framework and theory that provides a coherent explanation of the presence or absence of collective action across a rich array of situations. A great deal of North's work focused on institutional change over time and the contributions of individuals and organizations, other than governments, to institutional change. A great deal of my work has focused on how to understand what is contained within an institution. We can talk about property rights or rules related to use of a resource, but the terms "common property" or "private property" are not very descriptive. Thus, we have developed a way of modeling the impact of rule changes on behavior using game theory and placing some of those theoretical models into an experimental lab where we have been able to test changes in the rules and examine their impact. Further, we have done an immense amount of case analysis. Some of these studies we have done ourselves and with others we resorted to meta-analysis (see Poteete, Janssen, and Ostrom 2010).

There is a lot more to cover as we dig into the Northean question of how rules affect incentives, behavior, and outcomes. Over time, we have become more and more aware that the number and type of rules that people use to solve difficult problems is an amazing array. Here is where a focus on formal games has turned out to be very useful. When we are able to make a tight formalization, we can develop a strong theoretical analysis related to the incentives facing participants and predicted outcomes using game theory.

For the last three decades, we have been using and developing a framework consistent with game theory that enables us to deal with institutions of a wide diversity of kinds across the world. Thus, I will talk first of the institutional analysis and development (IAD) framework. Then I will talk about how we have analyzed specific combinations of rules to assess their impact on resource sustainability. Then, I will discuss how polycentric governance systems are more likely to be effective in changing rules to fit ecological systems than centralized systems.

For scholars and policymakers interested in issues related to how different governance systems enable individuals to solve problems democratically, the IAD framework helps to organize diagnostic, analytical, and prescriptive capabilities. It also aids in the accumulation of knowledge from empirical studies and in the assessment of past efforts at reforms. Markets and hierarchies are frequently presented as fundamentally different "pure types" of organization. Not only are these types of institutional arrangements perceived to be different, but each is presumed to require its own explanatory theory. Such a view precludes a more general explanatory framework and closely related theories that help analysts make cross-institutional comparisons and evaluations.

Without the capacity to undertake systematic, comparative institutional assessments, recommendations of reform may be based on naive ideas about which kinds of institutions are "good" or "bad" and not on an analysis of performance. One needs a common framework and family of theories in order to address questions of reform and transition. Particular models help the analyst to deduce specific predictions about likely outcomes of highly simplified structures. Models are useful in policy analysis when they are well-tailored to the particular problem at hand. Models can be used

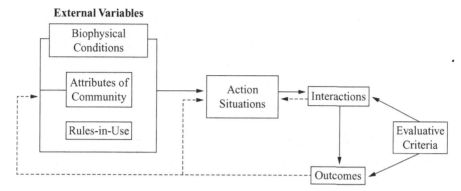

Figure 5.1. A framework for institutional analysis. Adapted from E. Ostrom (2005, 15).

inappropriately when applied to the study of situations that do not closely fit the assumptions of the model.

2. Institutional Analysis and Development Framework

An institutional framework should identify the types of structural variables that are present in all institutional arrangements, but whose values differ from one type of institutional arrangement to another. The IAD framework is thus a multitier conceptual map (see Figure 5.1). By now, we have integrated the IAD into a broader framework for examining social-ecological systems, but I will not address that broader framework in this chapter (see, e.g., Ostrom 2007, 2009).

A key part of a useful framework for the analysis of institutions is the identification of an action situation, the resulting patterns of interactions and outcomes, and the evaluation of these outcomes. An institutional analyst can then dig deeper to inquire into the factors that affect the structure of an action arena. From this vantage point, the action situation is viewed as a set of variables dependent upon other factors. The factors affecting the structure of an action arena include three clusters of variables: (1) the rules used by participants to regulate their relationships, (2) the attributes of states of the world that are acted upon in these regulations, and (3) the structure of the general community within which a particular arena is placed (see Kiser and Ostrom 1982).

The term "action situation" is used to refer to an analytic concept that enables an analyst to isolate the immediate structure affecting a process of interest to the analyst for the purpose of explaining regularities in human actions and results and potentially to reform them. As illustrated in

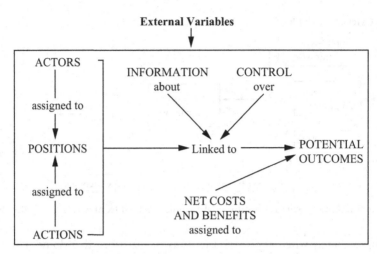

Figure 5.2. The internal structure of an action situation. Adapted from E. Ostrom (2005, 33).

Figure 5.2, a common set of variables used to describe the structure of an action situation (or a game) includes (1) the set of actors, (2) the specific positions to be filled by participants, (3) the set of allowable actions and their linkage to outcomes, (4) the potential outcomes that are linked to individual sequences of actions, (5) the information available to participants about the structure of the action situation, and (6) the costs and benefits – which serve as incentives and deterrents – assigned to actions and outcomes. Finally, (7) whether a situation will occur once, a known finite number of times, or indefinitely affect the strategies of individuals. When one is explaining actions and cumulated results within the framework of an action arena, these variables are the "givens" that one works with to describe the structure of the situation. These are the common elements used in game theory to construct formal game models.

Rules, states of the world, and the nature of the community affect the types of actions that individuals take, the benefits and costs of these actions and resulting outcomes, and the likely outcomes achieved. This chapter focus is on rules, given the core role they play in North's work.

3. The Concept of Rules

Rules are shared understandings among those involved that refer to enforced prescriptions about what actions (or states of the world) are required, prohibited, or permitted. All rules are the result of implicit or explicit efforts to achieve order and predictability by creating classes of persons (positions) that are then required, permitted, or forbidden to take classes of actions in relation to required, permitted, or forbidden states of the world (Crawford and Ostrom 2005; V. Ostrom 1991).

One may also want to ask where the rules that individuals use in action situations originate. In an open and democratic governance system, many sources of rules exist. It is not considered illegal or improper for individuals to organize themselves and craft their own rules, if the activities they engage in are legal. In addition to legislation and regulations of a formal central government, there are apt to be laws passed by regional, local, and special governments. Within private firms and voluntary associations, individuals are authorized to adopt many different rules about who is a member of the firm or association, how profits (benefits) are to be shared, and how decisions will be made. Each family constitutes its own rule-making body.

When individuals genuinely participate in the crafting of multiple layers of rules, some of that crafting will occur using pen and paper. Much of it, however, will occur as problem-solving individuals interact trying to figure out how to do a better job in the future than they have done in the past. Work teams frequently craft their own rules when they plan who will do which future activities over a coffee break or lunch. This is not a self-conscious rule-making process. In an open and democratic society, problem-solving individuals do this all the time. They also participate in more concrete decision-making arrangements, including elections to select legislators.

Thus, when we do a deeper institutional analysis, we attempt first to understand the working rules that individuals use in making decisions. Working rules are the set of rules to which participants would make reference if asked to explain and justify their actions to fellow participants. Although following a rule may become a "social habit," it is possible to make participants consciously aware of the rules they use to order their relationships. Individuals can consciously decide to adopt a different rule and change their behavior to conform to such a decision. Over time, behavior in conformance with a new rule may itself become habitual (see Shimanoff 1980; Toulmin 1974; Harré 1974). The capacity of humans to use complex cognitive systems to order their own behavior at a relatively subconscious level makes it difficult for empirical researchers to ascertain what the working rules for an ongoing action situation may be.

The stability of rule-ordered actions depends upon the shared meaning assigned to words used to formulate a set of rules. If no shared meaning exists when a rule is formulated, confusion will exist about what actions are required, permitted, or forbidden. Regularities in actions cannot result

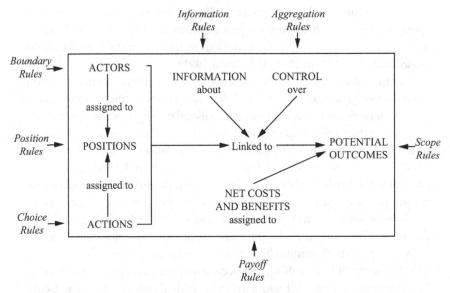

Figure 5.3. Rules as exogenous variables directly affecting the elements of an action situation. Adapted from E. Ostrom (2005, 189).

if those who must repeatedly interpret the meaning of a rule within action situations arrive at multiple interpretations. Because "rules are not self-formulating, self-determining, or self-enforcing" (V. Ostrom 1980, 312), human agents formulate them, apply them in particular situations, and attempt to enforce performance consistent with them. Even if shared meaning exists at the time of the acceptance of a rule, transformations in technology, in shared norms, and in circumstances more generally change the events to which rules apply: "Applying language to changing configurations of development increases the ambiguities and threatens the shared criteria of choice with an erosion of their appropriate meaning" (ibid.).

What rules are important for institutional analysis? A myriad of specific rules are used in structuring complex action situations. Scholars have been trapped into endless cataloging of rules not related to a method of classification most useful for theoretical explanations. But classification is a necessary step in developing a science. Anyone attempting to define a useful typology of rules must be concerned that the classification is more than a method for imposing superficial order onto an extremely large set of seemingly disparate rules. The way we have tackled this problem using the IAD framework is to classify rules according to their impact on the elements of an action situation or a formal game (see Figure 5.3).

4. Rule Configurations

A first step toward identifying the working rules can thus be made by overtly examining how rules affect each of the variables of an action situation. A set of working rules that affect these variables should constitute the minimal set of rules needed to offer an explanation of actions and results based on the working rules used by participants to order their relationships within an action situation. Because states of the world and their transformations and the nature of a community also affect the structure of an action situation, working rules alone never provide both a necessary and sufficient explanation of the structure of an action situation and results.

Seven types of working rules can be said to affect the structure of an action situation. As illustrated in Figure 5.3, these are boundary rules, position rules, scope rules, choice rules, aggregation rules, information rules, and payoff rules.

Boundary rules affect the number of participants, their attributes and resources, whether they can enter freely, and the conditions they face for leaving. Position rules establish positions in the situation. Choice rules assign sets of actions that participants in positions at particular nodes must, may, or may not take. Scope rules delimit the potential outcomes that can be affected and, working backward, the actions linked to specific outcomes. Choice rules, combined with the scientific laws about the relevant states of the world being acted upon, determine the shape of the decision tree, that is, the action-outcome linkages. Aggregation rules affect the level of control that a participant in a position exercises in the selection of an action at a node. Information rules affect the knowledge-contingent information sets of participants. Payoff rules affect the benefits and costs that will be assigned to particular combinations of actions and outcomes, and they establish the incentives and deterrents for action. The set of working rules is a configuration in the sense that the effect of a change in one rule may depend upon the other rules in use.

Let us return to the challenge of conducting an analysis of common-pool resources and focus on a series of questions that is intended to help the analyst get at the rules-in-use that help structure an action situation. Thus, to understand these rules, one would begin to ask questions such as:

- ***Boundary rules:*** Are the appropriators from this resource limited to local residents; to one group defined by ethnicity, race, caste, gender, or family structure; to those who have obtained a permit; to those who own required assets (such as a fishing berth or land); or in some other way limited to a class of individuals that is bounded? Is a new participant allowed to join a group by some kind of entry fee or initiation? Must an appropriator give up rights to harvest upon migrating to another location?

- *Position rules*: How does someone move from being just a "member" of a group of appropriators to someone who has a specialized task, such as the chair of a management committee or a water distributor-guard?
- *Scope rules*: What understandings do these appropriators and others have about the authorized or forbidden geographic or functional domains? Do any maps exist showing who can appropriate from which region? Are there understandings about resource units that are "off-limits," for example, the historical rules in some sections of Africa that particular acacia trees could not be cut down even on land owned privately or communally?
- *Choice rules*: What understandings do appropriators have about mandatory, authorized, or forbidden harvesting technologies? For fishers, is a particular net size required? Must forest users use some cutting tools and not others?
- *Aggregation rules*: These affect the choice of harvesting activities. Do certain actions require prior permission from, or agreement of any subset of individuals involved?
- *Information rules*: These imply what information must be held secret or made public.
- *Payoff rules*: How large are the sanctions imposed for breaking any of the rules identified above? How is conformance to rules monitored? Who is responsible for sanctioning nonconformers? How reliably are sanctions imposed? Are any positive rewards offered to appropriators for any actions they can take?

The problem for the field researcher is that many rules in use do not exist in written form nor can they be sorted out by asking a random sample of respondents about their rules. Many of the rules in use are not even conceptualized by participants as rules. In settings where the rules in use have evolved over long periods of time and are understood implicitly by participants, obtaining information about rules in use requires spending time at a site and learning how to ask nonthreatening, context-specific questions about why they adopt some strategies and not others.

5. Individuals Using Common Pool Resources

The sustainability of resources is affected by rules as well as by a wide diversity of biophysical factors at multiple scales, such as solar radiation, temperature and precipitation, the chemical composition of the atmosphere, and topography, as well as by a wide diversity of biological phenomena such as seed dispersal, competition, and herbivory. In analyzing human decisions as they impact ecological systems, we need to assume that:

1. Within tiers of decision making, individuals make decisions that are intended to increase net benefits to self and potentially to others.
2. Individuals learn from their own experiences and from those of others that are communicated to them.
3. Human decisions at all tiers are affected by the cultural values of the individuals, the resources they possess, the information they obtain, the incentives and disincentives they face, the internal learning and choice processes used, and the time horizon invoked.
4. Physical and biological processes also affect the information, the incentives, and the time horizon that are used in human choice and are themselves affected by human choice.
5. Individuals often try to change the structure of situations in which they find themselves.

We have found that the parallel efforts by local resource users to search out and create local rule configurations may find better rule combinations over the long term while top-down design processes are more limited in their capacities to search for and find appropriate rules. All forms of decision making have limits. That is why it is important to build polycentric governance systems with considerable overlap so as to combine the strengths of parallel search and design processes with the strengths of larger systems in conflict resolution, acquisition of scientific knowledge, monitoring the performance of local systems, and the regulation of common-pool resources that are more global in their scope. Since the resulting polycentric governance systems are not directed by a single center, they tend to be more complex yet more adaptive systems.

6. Using Rules as Tools

Users of a common-pool resource must understand the biophysical structure of the resource and how to affect one another's incentives so as to support sustainable use for the long term. Instead of being given a set of instructions with the transformation function fully specified, they have to discover the biophysical structure of a particular resource that will differ on key parameters from similar resources in the same region. Further, they have to cope with considerable uncertainty related to the weather, complicated growth patterns of biological systems that may at times be chaotic in nature, and external price fluctuations affecting the costs of inputs and value of outcomes (Wilson et al. 1994; Wilson 2002). In addition to the physical changes that they can make in the resource, the tools they can use to change the structure of the action situations they face consist of seven clusters of rules that affect the action situations.

Given the nonlinearity and complexity of action situations, it is rarely easy to predict the effect produced by changing a particular rule. For example, a change in a boundary rule to restrict the entry of users simultaneously reduces the number of individuals who are tempted to break choice rules, but it also reduces the number of individuals who monitor what is happening or contribute funds toward hiring a guard. Thus, the opportunities for rule-breaking may increase. Further, the cost of a rule infraction will be spread over a smaller group of users and thus the harm to any individual may be greater. Assessing the overall effects of a change in boundary rules is a nontrivial analytical task (Weissing and Ostrom 1991a, 1991b). Instead of conducting a complete analysis, users are more apt to use their intuitions to experiment with different rule changes until they find a combination that seems to work.

To understand the types of tools that are available to users somewhat better, let us examine in some detail the kind of boundary, authority, payoff, and position rules that are frequently used in field settings. These four clusters of rules are the major tools used to affect the management of common-pool resources; information, scope, and aggregation rules are used to complement changes induced by these four clusters of rules.

7. Affecting the Characteristics of Users through Boundary Rules

The most frequent recommendation concerning boundary rules in the policy literature is to limit the number of persons allowed to appropriate from a common-pool resource so that the level of appropriation is reduced. If contingent cooperation is perceived to be a possibility, then an important way to enhance the likelihood of using reciprocity norms is to increase the proportion of participants who are known in a community, have a long-term stake in that community, and would find it costly to have their reputation for trustworthiness harmed. Reducing the number of users but opening the resource to strangers willing to pay a license fee, but who lack a long-term interest in the sustainability of a particular resource may reduce the level of trust and willingness to use reciprocity and thus increase enforcement costs substantially.

At least twenty-seven distinct boundary rules are being used in at least one common-pool resource somewhere in the world (E. Ostrom 1991). Some systems use a single boundary rule whereas many use several rules in combination. Boundary rules can be broadly classified in three general groups defining how individuals gain authority to enter and appropriate units from a common-pool resource. The first type of boundary rule relates to an individual's citizenship, residency, or membership in a particular organization. Many forestry and fishing user groups require members to have been born in a particular location. A second broad group of rules relates to ascribed or acquired personal characteristics of users. A third group of boundary rules relates to the relationship of an individual with the resource itself. Using a particular technology or acquiring appropriation rights through auctions or lotteries, are examples of this type of rule. About half of the rules relate to the characteristics of the users themselves. The other half involves diverse relationships with the resource.

Schlager (1990, 1994) coded thirty-three out of the forty-four groups identified as having some rules regarding the use of fishing resources. All thirty-three groups depended on a combination of fourteen different boundary rules (Schlager 1994, 258). None of these groups relied on a single boundary rule. Thirty of thirty-three groups (91 percent) limited fishing to individuals living in a nearby community. Thirteen groups also required membership in a local organization. Thus, most inshore users' organized groups restrict fishing to individuals who know each other, have a long-term time horizon, and are connected to one another in multiple ways (Taylor 1982; Singleton and Taylor 1992).

After residency, the next most frequent type of rules, used in two-thirds of the organized subgroups, involves the type of technology that fishers must be willing to use. Such rules are often criticized by policy analysts because gear restrictions tend to reduce the "efficiency" of fishing. Gear restrictions have many consequences, however. Used in combination with choice rules that assign fishers different types of gear for distinct areas, such restrictions solve conflicts among noncompatible technologies. Gear restrictions also reduce the scale of the fishery and help to sustain the resource.

Other rules were also used. Some groups used ascribed characteristics: age – two groups; ethnicity – three groups; race – five groups. Three types of temporary use rights included government licenses (three groups), lottery (five groups), and registration (four groups). Seven groups required participants to have purchased an asset such as a fishing berth; three groups required ownership of nearby land. Schlager did not find that any particular boundary rule was correlated with higher performance levels, but she did find that the thirty-three groups that had at least one boundary rule tended to be able to solve common-pool problems more effectively than the eleven groups who had not crafted boundary rules.

Much of the diversity of boundary rules attempt to ensure that users relate to others who live nearby and have a long-term interest in sustaining the productivity of the resource. This is a way of coping with the commons by increasing the proportion of participants who have a long-term interest, are more likely to use reciprocity, and who can be trusted. Central governments tend to use a much smaller set of rules, and some of these may open up a resource to strangers without a long-term commitment to the resource.

8. Affecting the Set of Allowable Actions through Choice Rules

Choice rules are also regularly used to regulate common-pool resources. Some rules involve a simple formula. For example, forest resources are often closed to harvesting during one period of the year and open for extraction by whoever meets the boundary rules during other periods. Most choice rules have two components: an assignment and a basis. Fishers, for example, might be assigned to a fixed fishing spot or to a fixed rotational schedule. A member of the founding clan may be authorized to cut timber anywhere in a forest. Assignment used in most choice rules require a basis for the assignment. Fishers might be assigned to a location based on a number drawn in a lottery, on the purchase of that spot in an auction, or on the basis of historical use.

If bases were combined with assignment possibilities, there would be 112 different choice rules (8 assignment formulas times 14 bases). A further complication is that the rules for one product may differ from those of another product in the same resource. In regard to forest resources, for example, children may be authorized to pick fruit from any tree located in a forest for their own consumption, women may be authorized to collect so many head loads of deadwood for domestic firewood and certain plants for making crafts, and *shaman* are the only ones authorized to collect medicinal plants from a particular location in a forest (Fortmann and Bruce 1988). Appropriation rights to fish are frequently related to a specific species. The exact number of rules used in the field is difficult to compute since not all bases are used with all formulas, but many rules focus on specific products. A still further complication is that the rules may regularly change over the course of a year depending on resource conditions.

Schlager (1994, 259–260) found that all thirty-three organized subgroups used one of five basic formulas in their choice rules. Each group in Schlager's study assigned fishers to fixed locations using a diversity of bases including technology, lottery, or historical use. Spatial demarcations are a critical variable for inshore fisheries. Nine user groups required fishers to limit their harvest to fish that met a specific size requirement. Seven groups allocated fishing spots using a rotation system, and seven other groups allowed fishing locations to be used only during a specific season. Four groups allocated fishing spots for a particular fishing day or a fishing season.

An important finding – given the puzzles addressed in this chapter – is that the choice rule most frequently recommended by policy analysts (Anderson 1986 1995; Copes 1986) was *never* used. No attempt was made "by the fishers involved to directly regulate the quantity of fish harvested based on an estimate of the yield. This is particularly surprising given that the most frequently recommended policy prescription made by fishery economists is the use of individual transferable quotas based on estimates on the economically optimal quantity of fish to be harvested over the long run" (Schlager 1994: 397). In an independent study of thirty traditional fishery societies, James Wilson and colleagues also noted the surprising absence of quota rules:

All of the rules and practices we found in these 30 societies regulate 'how' fishing is done. That is, they limit the times fish may be caught, the locations where fishing is allowed, the technology permitted, and the stage of the life cycle during which fish may be taken. None of these societies limits the 'amount' of various species that can be caught. Quotas – the single most important concept and tools of scientific management – is conspicuous by its absence. (Acheson, Wilson, and Steneck 1998, 397; see also Wilson et al. 1994)

Just in order to succeed as fishers, fishers have to know a great deal about the ecology of their inshore region including spawning areas, nursery areas, the migration routes of different species, and seasonable patterns. Over time, they learn how "to maintain these critical life-cycle processes with rules controlling technology, fishing locations, and fishing times. Such rules in their view are based on biological reality" (Acheson, Wilson, and Steneck 1998, 405).

The diversity of rules devised by users greatly exceeds the limited choice rules recommended in textbooks. Given this diversity of rules, it is particularly noteworthy that rules assigning users a specific quantity of a resource are used infrequently in inshore fisheries and irrigation systems. They are used more frequently in allocating forest products where the quantity available and the quantity harvested are easier to measure (Agrawal 1994). To assign a user a specific quantity of a resource unit requires that those making the assignment know the total available units. In water resources where there is storage of water from one season to another and reliable information about the quantity of water is available, such rules are more frequently utilized (Blomquist 1992; Schlager, Blomquist, and Tang 1994).

9. Affecting Outcomes through Payoff and Position Rules

One way to reduce or redirect appropriations made from a common-pool resource is to change payoff rules so as to add a penalty to actions that are prohibited. Many user groups adopt norms that those who are rule breakers should be socially ostracized or shunned, and individual users tend to monitor each other's behavior rather intensively. Three broad types of payoff rules are used extensively: (1) the imposition of a fine, (2) the loss of appropriation rights, and (3) incarceration. The severity of each of these types of sanctions can range from very low to very high and tends to start out on the low end of the scale. Inshore fisheries tend to rely heavily on shunning and other social norms and less on formal sanctions.

Passing rules that impose costs is relatively simple. The difficult task is monitoring behavior to ascertain whether rules are being broken. Self-organized fisheries tend to rely on self-monitoring more than the creation of a formal position of guard. Most inshore fishers now use short-wave radios as a routine part of their day-to-day operations, allowing a form of instant monitoring to occur. An official of a West Coast Indian tribe reports, for example, that "it is not uncommon to hear messages such as 'Did you see so-and-so flying all that net?' over the short-wave frequency – a clear reference to a violation of specified gear limits" (cited in Singleton 1998, 134). Given that most fishers will be listening to their short-wave radio, "such publicity is tantamount to creating a flashing neon sign over the boat of the offender. Such treatment might be preceded or followed by a direct approach to the rule violator, advising him to resolve the problem. In some tribes, a group of fishermen might delegate themselves to speak to the person" (ibid.).

Many self-organizing forest governance systems create and support a position of a guard since resource units are highly valuable, and a few hours of stealth can generate substantial illicit income. Monitoring rule conformance by officially designated and paid guards may make the difference between a resource in good condition and degradation. In a study of 279 forest *panchayats* in the Kumaon region of India, Agrawal and Yadama (1997) found that the number of months a guard was hired was the most important variable affecting forest conditions. The other variables that affected forest conditions included the number of meetings held by the forest council (when infractions are discussed) and the number of residents in the village.

It is evident from the analysis that the capacity of a forest council to monitor and impose sanctions on rule-breakers is paramount to maintaining the forest in good condition. Nor should the presence of a guard be taken simply as a formal mechanism to ensure protection. It is also an indication of the informal commitment of the *panchayat* and the village community to protect their forests. Hiring a guard costs money. The funds are generated within the village and earmarked for protection of the resource. If there is scant interest in protecting the forest, villagers have little interest setting aside the money necessary to hire a guard (Agrawal and Yadama 1997, 455).

Boundary and choice rules also affect the difficulty of monitoring activities and imposing sanctions on rule infractions. Closing a forest or an inshore fishery for a substantial amount of time, for example, has multiple impacts. It protects particular plants or fish during critical growing periods and allows the entire system time to regenerate without disturbance. Further, during the closed season, rule infractions are highly obvious to anyone as any user in the resource is breaking the rules. Similarly, requiring users to use a particular technology may reduce the pressure on the resource, help to solve conflicts among users of incompatible technologies, and also make it very easy to ascertain if rules are being followed. Changing payoff rules is the most direct way of coping with commons dilemmas. In many instances, dilemma games can be transformed into assurance games – a much easier situation to solve.

10. Affecting Outcomes through Changes in Information, Scope, and Aggregation Rules

Information, scope, and aggregation rules complement boundary, authority, payoff and position rules. Many smaller and informal systems rely entirely on a voluntary exchange of information and on mutual monitoring. When resource units are more valuable and groups are larger, information requirements are added that must be kept by users or officials. Scope rules limit harvesting activities in some regions that are being treated as refugia. By not allowing any appropriation from these locations, the regenerative capacity of a system can be enhanced. Aggregation rules are used in collective-choice processes and less in operational settings, but one aggregation rule that is found in diverse systems is a requirement that harvesting activities be done in teams. This encourages mutual monitoring and reduces the need for special guards.

11. The Daunting Search for Better Rules

The search for rules to improve the outcomes obtained in commons dilemmas is a complex task involving a potentially infinite combination of specific rules that could be adopted. To ascertain whether one has found an optimal set of rules to improve the outcomes, one would need to analyze how diverse rules affect each of the components of such a situation and the likely effect of a reformed structure on incentives, strategies, and outcomes. Since there are multiple rules that affect each of these components, conducting such an analysis would be a time and resource-consuming process. Further, how these changes may affect the outcomes in a particular location depends on the biophysical characteristics of that location and existing community relationships. No set of analysts would ever have sufficient time or resources to analyze all the combinations of rule changes and resulting situations, let alone all of the variance in these situations.

12. Experimenting with Rule Changes

Instead of assuming that designing rules that approach optimality, or even improve performance, is a simple analytical task that can be undertaken by distant, objective analysts, we need to understand the policy design process as involving an effort to tinker with a large number of component parts (Jacob 1977). Those who tinker with any tools – including rules – are trying to find combinations that work together more effectively than other combinations. Policy changes are experiments based on more or less informed expectations about potential outcomes (Campbell 1969, 1975a, 1975b). Whenever individuals agree to add a rule, change a rule, or adopt someone else's proposed rule set, they are conducting a policy experiment. Further, the complexity of the ever-changing biophysical world combined with the complexity of rule systems means that any proposed rule change faces a nontrivial probability of error.

13. Self-Organized Resource Governance Systems as Complex Adaptive Systems

For many scholars, the concept of organization is tied to central directors who design systems to operate in a particular way. Consequently, self-organized systems are not well-understood. Many self-organized resource governance systems are invisible to the officials of their own country or those from donor agencies. A classic example of this occurred in the Chitwan Valley of Nepal several decades ago when an Asian Development Bank team of irrigation engineers recommended a very large loan to build a dam across the Rapti River to enable the farmers there to irrigate their crops. The engineering design team did not see the eighty-five farmer-managed irrigation systems that already existed in the valley and had achieved relatively high performance. Most farmers in the Chitwan Valley already obtained three irrigated crops a year as a result of their participation in the activities of these irrigation systems (Benjamin et al. 1994).

In contrast to forms of organization that are the result of central direction, most self-organized groups – including the types of locally organized fisheries, forests, grazing areas, and irrigation systems discussed above – are better viewed as complex adaptive systems. Complex adaptive systems are composed of a large number of active elements whose rich patterns of interactions produce emergent properties that are not easy to predict by analyzing the separate parts of a system alone. Holland (1995, 10) views complex adaptive systems as "systems composed of interacting agents described in terms of rules. These agents adapt by changing their rules as experience accumulates." Complex adaptive systems "exhibit coherence under change, via conditional action and anticipation, and they do so without central direction" (ibid., 38–39). Holland points out that complex adaptive systems differ from physical systems that are not adaptive and that have been the foci of most scientific effort. The physical sciences have been the model for many aspects of contemporary social science. Thus, the concepts needed to understand the adaptivity of systems are not yet well-developed by social scientists.

14. Advantages and Limits of Parallel Sets of Local Users in Policy Experiments

A series of relatively autonomous, self-organized, resource governance systems may do a better job in policy experimentation than a single central authority. In this section, I discuss the advantages and limits of a fully decentralized system where all responsibility for making decisions related to smaller-scale common-pool resources is localized. In the last section, I discuss why a polycentric governance system involving higher levels of government as well as local systems is able to cope more effectively with tragedies of the commons.

Among the advantages of authorizing the users of smaller-scale common-pool resources to adopt policies regulating the use of these resources are:

- **Local knowledge.** Users who live and appropriated from a resource system over a long time develop relatively accurate mental models of how the biophysical system itself operates, since the very success of their appropriation efforts depends on such knowledge. They also know others living in the area well and what norms of behavior are considered appropriate.
- **Inclusion of trustworthy participants.** Users can devise rules that increase the probability that others are trustworthy and will use reciprocity. This lowers the cost of relying entirely on formal sanctions and paying for extensive guarding.
- **Reliance on disaggregated knowledge.** Feedback about how the resource system responds to changes in actions of users is provided in a disaggregated way. Fishers are quite aware, for example, if the size and species distribution of their catch is changing over time.
- **Better adapted rules.** Users are more likely to craft rules that are better adapted to each of the local common-pool resources than any general system of rules.
- **Lower enforcement costs.** Since local users have to bear the cost of monitoring, they are apt to craft rules that make infractions highly obvious so that monitoring costs are lower. Further, by creating rules that are seen as legitimate, rule conformance will tend to be higher.
- **Redundancy.** The probability of failure throughout a large region is greatly reduced by the establishment of parallel systems of rule making, interpretation, and enforcement.

There are, of course, limits to all ways of organizing the governance of common-pool resources.

- **Users may not organize.** While many local users invest considerable time and energy into their own regulatory efforts, other groups of users do not. There are many reasons why some groups do not organize, including the presence of low-cost alternative sources of income and thus a reduced dependency on the common resource, conflict among users along multiple dimensions, lack of leadership, and fear of having their efforts overturned by outside authorities.
- **Some self-organized efforts will fail.** Given the complexity of the task involved in designing rules, groups may select combinations of rules that generate failure instead of success. Further, they may be unable to adapt rapidly enough to avoid the collapse of a resource system.
- **Local tyrannies.** Not all self-organized resource governance systems organize democratically or rely on input of most users. Some groups

are dominated by local leaders or power elites who only change rules to their advantage. This problem is accentuated when exit costs are high and reduced if users can leave when local decision makers are not responsive to their interests.

- **Stagnation.** Local ecological systems are characterized by considerable variance. Experimentation can produce severe and unexpected results, leading users to cling to systems that have worked well in the past and stop innovating before they develop rules that improve outcomes.

- **Inappropriate discrimination.** Joint recognition of identity frequently increases the level of trust and rule conformance. Reliance on ascribed characteristics can, however, exclude some individuals from access to sources of productive endeavor unrelated to their trustworthiness.

- **Limited access to scientific information.** Time and place information is extensively articulated by local groups, but they may lack access to scientific knowledge.

- **Conflict among users.** Without access to an external conflict-resolution mechanism, conflict within and across common-pool resource systems can escalate and provoke violence.

- **Inability to cope with larger-scale common-pool resources.** Without access to larger-scale jurisdiction, local users may have difficulties regulating a part of a larger-scale common-pool resource. They may not be able to exclude others who refuse to abide by the rules that a local group would prefer to use. Given this, local users have no incentive to restrict their own use and watch others take away all of the valued resource units that they have not appropriated.

15. The Capabilities of Polycentric Systems to Cope with Tragedies of the Commons

In a polycentric system, citizens may organize multiple governing authorities at differing scales (V. Ostrom, Tiebout, and Warren 1961; V. Ostrom 1991, 1997, 2008). Each unit may exercise considerable independence to make and enforce rules within a circumscribed scope of authority for a specified geographical area. In a polycentric system, some units are general-purpose governments while others may be highly specialized. Self-organized resource governance systems may be special districts, private associations, or parts of a local government, nested in levels of general-purpose governments that provide civil, equity, and criminal courts.

In a polycentric system, users of each common-pool resource would have some authority to make at least some of the rules related to how that particular resource will be utilized. Thus, they would achieve most of the advantages of utilizing local knowledge and the redundancy and rapidity of a trial-and-error learning process. On the other hand, problems associated with local tyrannies and inappropriate discrimination can be addressed in larger, general-purpose governmental units who are responsible for protecting the rights of all citizens and for the oversight of appropriate exercises of authority within smaller units of government. It is also possible to make a more effective blend of scientific information with local knowledge where major universities and research stations are located in larger units but have a responsibility to relate recent scientific findings to multiple smaller units within their region. Because polycentric systems have overlapping units, information about what has worked well in one setting can be transmitted to others who may try it out in their settings.

Polycentric systems are themselves complex, adaptive systems without one central authority dominating all of the others. Thus, there is no guarantee that such systems will find the optimal combination of rules. One should expect all governance systems to operating at less than optimal levels given the immense difficulty of fine-tuning complex, multitiered systems. Empirical research, however, has documented that polycentric systems frequently outperform either fully centralized or decentralized systems when citizens are expected to contribute significant efforts to use resource systems sustainably (Marshall 2009; Lubell et al. 2002; Fernández-González and Aylward 1999; Scholz and Wang 2006).

Coping with potential tragedies of the commons is not easy and never finished, but those dependent on these resources are not forever trapped in situations that will only get worse. Governance is frequently an adaptive process involving multiple actors at diverse levels. Such systems look terribly messy and hard to understand. The scholars' love of tidiness needs to be resisted. We need to develop better theories of complex adaptive systems, particularly those that have proved themselves able to utilize renewable natural resources sustainably over time.

16. Looking Forward to a More Robust Social Ecological Systems

Local users may manage smaller- to medium-scale resources more effectively than national agencies. One reason is the diversity of local environmental conditions. The variation in rainfall, soil types, elevation, scale of resource systems, and plant and animal ecologies is immense, even in small countries. Some resources are located near urban populations while others are remote. Given environmental variety, rule systems that effectively regulate access, use, and the allocation of benefits and costs in one setting are unlikely to work well in different environmental conditions. Efforts to pass national legislation establishing a uniform set of rules for an entire country are likely to fail in many of the locations most at risk. Users managing their resources locally may be more effective in dealing with diversity across sites.

A second potential advantage of local organization are benefits obtained from husbanding of resources, when future flows of benefits are taken into account. The costs of monitoring and sanctioning rule infractions at a local level are relatively low. These advantages occur, however, only if local users have assurances that they may receive the long-term benefits of their investments.

Nevertheless, local participants do not uniformly expend the effort needed to organize and manage these resources. Some potential organizations never form at all. Some do not survive more than a few months. Others are dominated by local elite who divert communal resources to achieve their own goals at the expense of others. In some cases, a local resource may be almost completely destroyed before local remedial actions are taken (Blomquist 1992). These actions may be too late. Still others do not possess adequate scientific knowledge to complement their own indigenous knowledge. Making investment decisions related to assets that mature over a long time horizon is a sophisticated task. In highly volatile worlds, some organize themselves more effectively and make better decisions than others.

The romantic view that anything local is better than anything organized at a national or global scale is not a useful foundation for a long-term effort to improve understanding of what factors enhance or detract from the capabilities of any institutional arrangement to govern and manage resources wisely. Any organization or group faces a puzzling set of problems when it tries to govern and manage complex multispecies (including Homo sapiens) and multiproduct resource systems whose benefit streams mature at varying rates. Any organization or group will face a variety of environmental challenges stemming from too much or too little rainfall to drastic changes in factor prices, population density, or pollution levels.

Long ago, Hayek (1958, 30) recognized that many factors are acquired by local citizens over time as they interact with their environment. He posited that through the mutually adjusted efforts of many people, more knowledge is utilized than any individual possesses or than it is possible to synthesize intellectually. It is through such utilization of dispersed knowledge that achievements are made possible more than any single mind can foresee. It is because freedom means the renunciation of direct control of individual efforts that a free society can make use of so much more knowledge than the mind of the wisest rule could comprehend.

Hayek stressed the importance of mechanisms of mutual adjustment of individuals as a core foundation for making effective rules. Further, he concluded that order based on knowledge dispersed among many people cannot be established by central direction. Rather, mutual adjustment of participants to the events that act immediately on them was necessary to achieve a form of learning, institutions which Hayek called "a spontaneous order" (1958, 159). Thus, a key to the successful design of polycentric institutions is their multiple scales and their generation of information that allows participants operating at many scales to learn from experience. The complexity of the environments involved is simply more than any single corporate entity can absorb and manage.

Acknowledgments

This chapter was originally presented at the conference on "The Legacy and Work of Douglass C. North: Understanding Institutions and Development Economics," Washington University in St. Louis, Missouri, November 4–6, 2010. Support from the National Science Foundation and the wonderful editing skills of Patty Lezotte are greatly appreciated.

6

Land Property Rights

Sebastian Galiani and Ernesto Schargrodsky

1. Introduction

One of the necessary conditions in order for trading activity to take place is that the relevant agents must be able to appropriate the gains yielded by their transactions. If the gains are appropriated by only one of the parties, then there is no incentive for other parties to engage in the exchange. Indeed, economic growth will occur only if property rights make it worthwhile to undertake socially productive activities (North and Thomas 1973). It is therefore clear that poorly specified property rights pose a major obstacle to economic development and that knowledge about the institutions that enforce those rights is crucial to an understanding of countries' economic performance (see, among others, North and Thomas 1973; Acemoglu et al. 2001; Johnson et al. 2002).

Douglass North was a pioneer in pointing out that institutions – understood as the set of formal and informal rules and constraints that structure life in society – are a key dimension of the process of economic growth and development. In fact, he wrote, "Throughout history, institutions have been devised by human beings to create order and reduce uncertainty in exchange . . . and history in consequence is largely a story of institutional evolution in which the historical performance of economies can only be understood as a part of a sequential story" (North 1991, 97).

Moreover, the institutional setup of a country at a given point in time can shape the way in which it is going to evolve: "Institutions provide the incentive structure of an economy; as that structure evolves, it shapes the direction of economic change towards growth, stagnation, or decline" (North 1991, 97).

North's view was an innovation in the field. In fact, economic growth theories traditionally ignored the role of institutions and instead focused exclusively on capital accumulation and technological change in a world where property rights were assumed to be perfectly enforced. Coase (1960), however, pointed out that creating, specifying, and enforcing property rights are costly undertakings and will therefore never be perfect (see, in particular, Barzel 1997). The new institutional approach to development economics that North pioneered recognizes this and asserts that, in a world with positive transaction costs, the enforcement of property rights has a cost that influences the allocation of resources and thus has an effect on growth. Hence, institutions that ensure that those rights will be upheld become one of the cornerstones of the economic architecture underpinning growth and development.

Barzel (1997) emphasizes that, because of the costliness of accurately measuring all of an asset's attributes, rights are never fully delineated, and property is consequently in danger of appropriation by others. Property rights facilitate specialization so long as they are enforced. However, by the same token, the preservation of property rights following their conveyance requires costly institutions and resources (Arruñada 2011).

Indeed, North (1990a) argues that a society's inability to develop effective, low-cost methods of enforcing contracts is the single most important cause of underdevelopment. In developed countries, effective judicial systems include clearly delineated bodies of law and well-identified agents, and people have some degree of confidence that the merits of a case, rather than private payoffs, will be the decisive factor in determining its outcome. In contrast, enforcement in poor countries is uncertain, not only because of ambiguities in legal doctrine, but also because of uncertainty with respect to the behavior of the judicial system.

Property rights are not an all-or-nothing affair. There is a spectrum ranging from no rights at all to a complete set of rights. Indeed, even in the absence of legal or formal rights, individuals still hold economic rights over assets (i.e., informal rights) that are equated with their ability, in terms of expectations, to directly consume the services associated with an asset or to consume it indirectly through exchange (Barzel 1997).

Following Schlager and Ostrom (1992), we can characterize property rights based on (1) the scope of the group exercising those rights and (2) the degree of control given to the group exercising those rights. In line with this characterization, we can divide property rights into private and collective property rights, with the latter being further subdivided into government property and open property.

Thus, it is important to emphasize that the answer to the question as to whether or not a more completely defined set of property rights (i.e., formal private property rights) will be socially beneficial will depend on the magnitude of common pool losses, the nature of the contracting costs involved in resolving such losses, and the economic costs of defining and enforcing property rights.[1]

Land rights play a particularly important part in the economic development process. Land is obviously the main production asset for agricultural activity. Moreover, due to its immobility and relative indestructibility (Binswanger and Rosenzweig 1986), it lends itself to its use as wealth and collateral. However, for historical, economic and political reasons, land rights, to a large extent, tend to be weakly defined even in today's world. Indeed, among all rival and excludable assets, land is probably the asset for which rights are the most poorly defined, in particular in developing countries.[2] This entails a potential efficiency loss for society, and it is therefore worthwhile to take a closer look at the exact nature of those costs.

Investigating this question is no easy matter, however. Identifying the causal effects of land property rights necessitates the assessment of the missed counterfactual – that is, what would have happened in the absence of those rights. Thus, any attempt to answer this question has to compare the outcomes associated with titled and untitled land. However, the allocation of property rights across units is usually not random but is instead based on wealth, family characteristics, previous investment levels, and/or other mechanisms built on differences between the groups that acquire those rights and the groups that do not. Exogenous variability in the allocation of property rights is necessary to solve this selection problem. In a series of recent papers, Galiani and Schargrodsky (2004), Di Tella, Galiani, and Schargrodsky (2007), and Galiani and Schargrodsky (2010) address this selection problem by exploiting a natural experiment in the allocation of urban land titles to a very deprived population group in Argentina. In this essay, we rely on the findings obtained from exploiting this natural experiment to shed light on the question of what the effects of land titling are among poor households, which tend to be untitled in developing countries.[3]

In Section 2 we present a brief theoretical discussion. In Section 3, we discuss identification issues and relate them to the empirical literature on land titling. Section 4 summarizes the natural experiment in Argentina that is the focus of this review. Then, in Section 5, we discuss the lessons learned

---

[1] See, for example, Ostrom (1990).

[2] In a conservative review of De Soto's (2000) estimates, Woodruff (2001) speculates that the value of untitled real estate in developing countries could be as much as US$5,000 per household.

[3] For a survey of the literature on land property rights, see Galiani and Schargrodsky (2012).

from the studies that have drawn upon this natural experiment in Argentina. Finally, we present some conclusions.

2. Land Property Rights: A Brief Theoretical Discussion

The theoretical framework devised by North leads us to conclude that the establishment and enforcement of ownership rights to factors of production are crucial to a country's economic development. Land property rights are particularly important in this sense. As stated above, land lends itself to be used as wealth and collateral. Historically, it was one of the two most prevalent factors of production in the Western world before the Industrial Revolution (the other being labor). It is still a relatively abundant asset in many developing economies, as indicated by World Bank estimates (2006). However, among all rival and excludable assets, land is probably the one for which ownership rights are the most weakly defined, in particular in developing countries. One of the clearest manifestations of this is the fact that millions of people are living in slums or underprivileged urban areas without any kind of formal title to the plots of land that they occupy (Deininger 2003; Banerjee and Duflo 2006). Unclear and weak property rights lead to an efficiency loss in society. This effect can be transmitted through several channels.

First of all, insecure land rights expose owners to the risk of expropriation. Underinvestment may occur as a result. People will not invest – or will do so only to a limited extent – if they have little chance of appropriating the fruits of their investments (Demsetz 1967; Alchian and Demsetz 1973). Another cause of underinvestment is the illiquidity of an asset whose legal ownership is unclear.

Second, obstacles to the transfer of parcels of land from one agent to another that are associated with poorly defined ownership rights may interfere with resource allocation (Besley 1995). In fact, legally established land titles help to promote the transfer of land from agents that generate less value added to those that generate more, as well as facilitating renting.

Third, because land can be used as collateral, the absence of titling can limit credit access (Feder et al. 1988; De Soto 2000). In the case of the urban poor, for instance, the lack of clear, legally defined land rights constrains the supply of credit, because banks may foresee difficulties in repossessing low-quality dwellings in poor neighborhoods, and the gains from their sale may be very limited (see Deininger and Feder 2009).

Fourth, there is also the possibility that insecure land rights may have an influence on other decisions made by households. For instance, households with incompletely defined legal rights to the land that they occupy may need to spend additional resources to defend their possessions. If households are resource-constrained in terms of labor supply, land rights can stimulate efficiency by diminishing the resources needed to maintain property rights (Lanjouw and Levy 2002; Field 2007). Similar situations may arise in connection with decisions concerning procreation and household size. There are several potential reasons this may happen. Insurance-related motives seem to be the most important. The poor lack access to proper insurance markets and pension systems that could protect them during bad times and support them during retirement. With limited access to means of risk diversification, savings instruments, and the social security system, their need for insurance has to be satisfied by other means. A traditional provider of insurance for the poor is the extended family. Another possibility is to use children as future insurance providers. All of this, naturally enough, has long-term implications for aggregate productivity and poverty reduction.

Finally, the status of property rights also has a broader, systemic effect. The literature has drawn attention to the implications that countries' institutional features have for the beliefs held by their populations (see Denzau and North 1994; Greif 1994), which in turn have been seen to play a central role in shaping economic outcomes. A prominent example of this is provided by the literature on the reasons Europe and America are so different when it comes to giving government a role in the production and distribution of income (see, for example, Piketty 1995; Benabou and Ok 2001; Benabou and Tirole 2006; Rotemberg 2002; Alesina and Angeletos 2003). Two broad channels for the link between property rights and beliefs are proposed. First, property rights may affect beliefs by influencing the experiences that individuals have, as explained by Piketty (1995), who argues that, in a costly learning process, an "accidental" initial belief may become accepted if further experimentation is not justified by early experience. Alternatively, property rights may also change the incentives that individuals have to engage in belief manipulation.

All these arguments support the notion that a lack of secure land ownership rights may limit the scope for investment, credit access, and development. This is what has prompted numerous bilateral and multilateral institutions to sponsor programs that focus either on registering land titles or on improving the way in which land administration institutions function.

3. Identifying the Effects of Land Property Rights

The empirical evaluation of the effects of land titling poses a major methodological challenge. As mentioned earlier, the allocation of property rights across households is typically not random but is instead correlated with both observable and unobservable variables – for instance, the possession of land titles could be correlated with family inheritance or the willingness of households to invest resources in acquiring legal rights to the land that they occupy. Moreover, the individual characteristics that determine the likelihood of possessing land titles are also probably correlated with the outcomes under study. The unobserved heterogeneity of the households in question creates a selection problem that obstructs the proper evaluation of the effects of property rights acquisition.

A first quasi-experimental strategy for resolving that endogeneity problem would be to rely on an instrumental variables analysis. This method consists of "instrumenting" the endogenous variable by an exogenous one: that is, by a variable that is not correlated with the unobserved characteristics that have an impact both on the outcomes that are of interest here and on the possession of land rights. Alternatively, a fixed-effect analysis can also potentially solve the endogeneity issues by controlling for the unobserved heterogeneity that is time-invariant. This approach has been used, for instance, by Do and Iyer (2008). On a relatively aggregate level, they examined the impact of Vietnam's 1993 Land Act, which gave households the power to exchange, transfer, lease, inherit, and mortgage their land-use rights after years of collectivization. Exploiting the variation across regions in the speed of implementation of the reform (a variation assumed to be strictly exogenous) using a two-way fixed-effects model, Do and Iyer found that the issuance of land titles led to a statistically significant– albeit small in magnitude – increase in the share of total area devoted to long-term crops, a result suggesting that possession of legal land rights increases investment. On the other hand, they did not find evidence of increased access to credit.

Using a similar approach, and on a more micro level, in a series of papers Erica Field has analyzed the impact of a large titling program for urban squatter settlements in Peru. Her identification strategy rests on what might be described as a difference-in-difference approach that exploits the staggered timing of the program, assumed to be exogenous, and the differential household ownership status prior to the program. Her main findings suggest the presence of large transaction costs associated with the lack of titles, combined with binding labor constraints. Controlling for household size, Field (2007) found that the lack of title reduces the total household labor supply by about 14 percent. Moreover, titling allows households to substitute work in the outside market for work at home and to substitute adult labor for child labor. Her interpretation is that adults in untitled households appear to have to stay at home in order to protect their informal tenure. She finds significant effects on housing investment associated with titling, but she also finds that this investment is financed without the use of credit (Field 2005). In particular, titling has no effect on formal credit from private banks (Field and Torero 2003). A final finding (Field 2003) is that a negative association exists between land titling and birth rates.

However, inasmuch as unobserved heterogeneity varies across time, fixed-effect models are not able to solve the potential endogeneity problem associated with the possession of land titles. In this sense, an ideal way to address the selection issues discussed above would be to randomly assign land rights among the relevant units of analysis (which could be households, communities, or neighborhoods). Under full compliance, randomization guarantees the possession of land titles would be exogenous. Though this is feasible in principle, it has not yet been done. The closest research design to randomization would be a natural experiment: a design where treatment – in this case, the possession of land rights – is considered exogenous in a cross-sectional analysis even though no deliberate randomization has occurred. Indeed, such a research design has been employed by Galiani and Schargrodsky (2004), Di Tella, Galiani, and Schargrodsky (2007) and Galiani and Schargrodsky (2010), who studied the effects of titling by exploiting a natural experiment based on land occupation in the outskirts of Buenos Aires, Argentina, in 1981.

4. A Natural Experiment

The natural experiment that Galiani and Schargrodsky (2004), Di Tella, Galiani, and Schargrodsky (2007) and Galiani and Schargrodsky (2010) took advantage of began in 1981, when, with the help of a Catholic chaplain, about 1,800 landless families took over a wasteland in the San Francisco Solano area on the outskirts of Buenos Aires. At the time of the occupation, the squatters thought the land belonged to the state, but they later found out that it was private property. The occupied area, which turned out to be made up of thirteen tracts of land belonging to different private owners, was partitioned by the squatters into small, urban-shaped parcels for each household. The squatters resisted several eviction attempts mounted by the military government. After Argentina's return to democracy in 1984, the Congress of the Province of Buenos Aires passed a law expropriating the land from the former owners, who were to be provided with monetary compensation by the government, and allocated it to the squatters.

The resulting titling process was, however, incomplete and asynchronous. The government offers were very similar (in per-square-meter terms) for the thirteen land tracts. Each of the original owners had to decide whether to accept the expropriation compensation proposed by the government or to initiate legal proceedings in an effort to obtain a larger sum. In 1986, eight former owners accepted the compensation offered by the government. The formal land titles that secured the property rights to those parcels were then transferred by the state to the squatters in 1989. (These squatters were thus in what can be described as the early treatment group.) However, five former owners did not accept the compensation offered by the government and disputed the expropriation payment in Argentina's slow-moving courts. One of these trials was brought to a conclusion in 1998, and that particular tract of land was later transferred to the squatters (who thus formed the late treatment group). The squatters occupying the other plots of land, however, remain without title (and thus constitute the control group). As a result, a group of families now has formal property rights, while the families of another group, who arrived at the same time and under the same conditions, are still living on parcels to which they have no title. The allocation of land titles and its timing was exogenous to the quality of the land, as well as to the squatters' behavior and characteristics. This is a straightforward situation, since in 1981 no squatter knew which tracts of land would ultimately be surrendered by the owners, and the occupation of the plots was therefore absolutely random in this sense. Two surveys – performed in 2003 and 2007 – provide the data utilized for this study (for a detailed discussion, see Galiani and Schargrodsky 2010).

A statistical comparison of the characteristics of the households of these two groups prior to the point in time where they were differentiated (that is, prior to the time that one group received titles and the other did not) shows that the hypothesis of exogenous assignment of land titles during this natural experiment stands up to the facts. There were no significant differences between the treatment and control groups in terms of age, gender, years of education or any other characteristic of the family member who was the head of household at the time of the occupation. There were also no differences in plot characteristics. Moreover, the squatters played no part in the lawsuit brought against the government by the former owners, and the values of the dwellings they constructed were explicitly excluded from the calculation of the expropriation compensation.

The squatters' success or failure in obtaining property rights depended on whether or not the original owners decided to challenge the expropriation and on the outcome of the legal proceedings. Because these factors were exogenous to the squatters, it is possible to study the effect of the intervention "to give property rights" by comparing individuals who received and did

Table 6.1. *Effect of land titling on investment and household structure*

	Land titling	T-statistic>	Control group mean	% difference
Housing investment				
Good walls (=1)	0.20***	−3,47	0,5	40,00%
Good roof (=1)	0.15**	−2,49	0,32	46,87%
Floor space (m^2)	8.27**	−2,34	67,63	12,23%
Concrete sidewalk (=1)	0.11**	−2,18	0,67	16,42%
Overall house appearance index	8.42***	−3,65	22,71	37,08%
Household structure				
Number of household members	−0.95***	−2,81	6,06	−15,68%
Other relatives (no spouse or offspring)	−0.68***	−3,53	1,25	−54,40%
Schooling				
Secondary school completion (=1)^	0.27*	1,93	0,26	103%

* Significantly different from zero at 10%, ** at 5%, *** at 1%.
^ Refers to the effect on the early treatment group only.
Source: Galiani and Schargrodsky (2010).

not receive land titles but who live in very close proximity, had similar pre-treatment characteristics and have been exposed to similar life experiences (with the exception of the treatment).[4]

5. Main Lessons

Table 6.1 summarizes the main results reported by Galiani and Schargrodsky in their studies of 2004 and 2010. The evidence indicates that land titling has a statistically significant effect on different kinds of housing investments (e.g., improvements in the quality of walls and roofs, amount of floor space and the likelihood of there being a concrete sidewalk). An aggregate index of household appearance shows that there has been nearly 40 percent more investment in houses on property to which the occupants hold title. The estimated effects are large and robust,[5] and they seem to be the result of changes in the economic returns to housing investment induced by land

[4] For an in-depth discussion of the strengths and statistical challenges of this natural experiment see Galiani and Schargrodsky (2010).
[5] See Galiani and Schargrodsky (2010) for a series of robustness checks on the results reported in this table.

titling. Thus, this micro evidence supports North's hypothesis that securing property rights significantly increases investment levels.

Titling was also found to be related to changes in household structure. The average household size fell from six to five members in titled parcels, with this decrease being accounted for by at least two different factors: First, there are more (0.68 members) nonnuclear relatives in untitled households; second, the head of household in titled households has fewer offspring. The effect on fertility is made plausible by the fact that the impact is concentrated among parents in the appropriate age group – that is, parents whose children were born after the title allocation.

In line with this reduction in fertility, titled households also exhibit higher investments in education: The likelihood that children in households that hold title to their properties will complete secondary school is 27 percentage points higher than it is for those in households that lack title to their land. This result is seen only in the early treatment group, however. The logic for this is that the early treatment group had the time to significantly adjust fertility as a result of the treatment. Thus, this result is consistent with the analysis in Becker and Lewis (1973), who posited the presence of parental trade-offs between quantity and quality in terms of their procreation choices. This trade-off appears because parents' limited time and resources can be spread over more or fewer children. Thus, if land titling leads to a reduction in fertility, it may also induce households to increase their investment in their children's education.

The reduction in the presence of extended family members that is associated with titling may reflect the need for extra protection of the tenure rights of untitled households, as argued by Field (2007). Galiani and Schargrodsky (2010), however, do not find a differential presence of adult males in untitled households. They discuss two additional mechanisms. One is that the property owned by titled households and the incremental housing investment provide an insurance tool for use during old age and bad times, whereas insurance for untitled households is provided through higher fertility and the presence of nonnuclear family members. The other is that a lack of title increases intra-household transaction costs. In the absence of a land title, the division of property among household members becomes more complicated, forcing relatives to remain in the same house in order to protect their informal rights.

Galiani and Schargrodsky (2004) also find better nutrition and lower teenage pregnancy rates for children in titled households. In the sample under study, the authors report that teenage pregnancy is a serious problem: 11.4 percent of girls between 14 and 17 years of age who answered the question on teenage pregnancy were pregnant or had been pregnant at least once. Galiani and Schargrodsky find that the pregnancy rate was substantially higher among the households in the untitled parcels (20.8 percent) than in the titled parcels (7.9 percent).

As mentioned earlier, the possession of formal property rights could make it possible to use land as collateral, which would provide poor people with greater access to credit markets. Moreover, land titling may have direct labor-market effects if it frees families from the need to leave adults at home in order to protect their houses from occupation by other squatters. However, Galiani and Schargrodsky (2010) find very small effects on formal credit and no effects on earnings or labor supply. The small credit effects are not surprising, given the population under consideration. Potential lenders may feel that they would have little chance of success in legally evicting families in these socioeconomic groups in the event of default (Arruñada 2003) or that the market value of their parcels is too low to offset the legal costs involved. Additionally, the ownership of real estate does not appear to be a sufficient condition to qualify for formal credit, which, in Argentina, is generally accessible only to formal workers who have held their current job for a certain number of years and who earn relatively high wages. In consequence, only 4 percent of titled households have ever received a mortgage-based loan.

As far as labor supply is concerned, it should be noted that these results differ from those of Field (2007), who reports an increase in labor supply and a reduction in child labor for titled households in Peru. In an effort to reconcile these results, the theory suggests that it may be helpful to investigate whether households are constrained in their labor supply (Besley and Ghatak 2010). This is not the case for the urban households in the natural experiment studied by Galiani and Schargrodsky (2010), which display high levels of adult unemployment and nil levels of child labor.

Galiani and Schargrodsky (2010) point out, however, that the absence of earnings and credit effects does not necessarily imply that land titling entails no progress for poor people. By providing access to a savings tool, allowing households to reduce fertility, and paving the way for improved educational achievement, land titling may help to reduce poverty in the next generation.

Finally, we recall the argument presented earlier about the link between the enforcement of property rights and the formation of beliefs. Given that beliefs are influential in determining economic performance, it is useful to analyze the effects that land titling has upon household members' beliefs about economic issues. Di Tella, Galiani and Schargrodsky (2007) took advantage of the same natural experiment in Buenos Aires to study this issue

Table 6.2. *Effect of property rights on beliefs*

Statement	Land titling	T-statistic	Control group mean	% difference
It is possible to be successful on your own (=1)	0.169***	2.56	0.330	51.21%
Money is indispensable/very important for happiness (=1)	0.188***	2.76	0.503	37.38%
People who make an effort end up much better off than those who don't (=1)	0.022	0.39	0.735	3,00%
You can trust others in this country (=1)	0.139**	2.13	0.335	41.49%
Individual index of pro-market beliefs (0 to 4)	0.520***	3.90	1.906	27.28%

* Significantly different from zero at 10% ** at 5% *** at 1%.
Source: Di Tella, Galiani and Schargrodsky (2007).

and found that titled squatters report beliefs that are closer to the types of beliefs that are conducive to the workings of a free-market economy. Thus, insofar as these beliefs encourage effort and enterprise, this could be an additional channel through which property rights may enhance the welfare of the poor and promote economic development.

As Di Tella et al. (2007) point out, at least since the time of Adam Smith, a large body of work in history and economics has put forward the argument that individualism, materialism, and meritocratic approaches are conducive to the operation of the market. More recent work has emphasized that trust also belongs in this category.[6] Accordingly, in their 2003 survey, this team of researchers posed questions related to each of these topics to the households included in their random sample.

Table 6.2 presents the responses obtained for each question. The last row shows an index of "pro-market beliefs," which is the sum of the dummies for the four preceding questions. The results indicate that titled families were more individualistic, materialistic, and prone to trust others, while land titling had no significant impact in terms of meritocratic beliefs.[7]

---

[6] See Arrow (1971), Coleman (1990), Putnam (1993), Schotter (1998), Durlauf (2002), and Glaeser et al. (2002).
[7] This is not surprising, however, given the fact that, in this particular case, squatters with and without land titles reported meritocratic beliefs at a rate comparable to those of the population of the greater Buenos Aires metropolitan area (see Di Tella, Galiani, and Schargrodsky 2007).

The change in beliefs resulting from the treatment applied in this natural experiment is consistently in the direction of what can loosely be called "pro-market beliefs." A person who holds materialist and individualist beliefs is unlikely to demand market regulation. Similarly, trust (when it is not naive) fosters cooperation, which is valuable in a market where contracts are difficult and costly to write. This is interesting because of the strong similarities in the lives of squatters with and without titles. Moreover, the estimated causal effect is sufficiently large so as to make the beliefs of squatters with legal titles comparable to those held by the population of the greater Buenos Aires metropolitan area, in spite of the striking differences in the lives that these two groups lead.

6. Conclusion

The ideas of Douglass North, which made a fundamental contribution to the school of thought associated with the New Institutional Economics approach, underline the fact that, in order for countries to develop, property rights to productive assets should be efficiently provided and enforced. A world in which property rights are not well-defined – or are weak because the institutions that are supposed to enforce them are not strong enough – is inherently inefficient. Since land is one of the most abundant assets in many parts of the world, it is important to understand the causal effects of land property rights.

Land property rights can influence the efficiency of resource allocation through a number of different channels. First, the possession of land titles may enhance investment incentives by limiting expropriation risk and may reduce the need to divert private resources to the protection of property. Second, land titling facilitates transferability and therefore stimulates trade. Third, by improving collateralization, land titling may enhance credit transactions. Fourth, secure land rights may affect the intra-household allocation of resources. Finally, land property rights may influence economic outcomes through changes in the belief system of the population.

In this chapter we have summarized the findings of a unique natural experiment concerning land titling in Buenos Aires in order to shed light on the effects of land titling on physical investment, household structure, human capital accumulation, access to credit, and earnings and beliefs. The study of this natural experiment shows that land property rights have a significant and positive effect on home investment. However, this positive result does not appear to be the result of improved access to credit. Furthermore, no effects of land titling on labor income were detected. Land titling also influences household structure, as it appears to reduce household size by favoring the residence of nuclear family members over nonnuclear ones and by reducing fertility. Once fertility is reduced, the evidence also suggests that there is a large positive effect on human capital accumulation. Lastly, we have reported that the possession of property rights encourages pro-market beliefs, which can undoubtedly have a strong impact on individuals' economic behavior and, in turn, on the institutional system (North 2005).

7

Constitutions as Coordinating Devices

Gillian K. Hadfield and Barry R. Weingast

1. Introduction

Why do successful constitutions have the attributes characteristically associated with the rule of law, such as generality, stability, universal applicability, publicity, and consistency? Why do constitutions involve public reasoning? And how is such a system sustained as an equilibrium? In this paper, we adapt the framework in our previous work on the question of what is law to the problem of constitutions and their enforcement (see Hadfield and Weingast 2012, 2013a, b).

Most accounts of constitutions take constitutions as given and study its effects. This holds for the vast majority of works in both law and economics and positive political theory and the law.[1] Most traditional legal scholarship focuses on the development of constitutional doctrine by clause of the constitutions or studies a wide range of normative issues raised by constitutions.

The issue of constitutional enforcement is important because most constitutions in the world fail. Only about two dozen or so current constitutions have been in place for sixty or more years. The median democratic constitution last is only sixteen years (Elkins, Ginsburg, and Melton 2009, table 6.1). Indeed, new leaders often radically alter constitutional rules following violent regime change. Moreover, violent regime change is surprisingly common. Using data from 1840 through the present, Cox, North, and Weingast (2013) show that the median number of years between violent regime changes for regimes worldwide is eight. These dim facts suggest the difficulty in creating a constitutional equilibrium.

---

[1] Epstein (1985), Posner (2007, part 7) are emblematic of the law and economics literature; as are Epstein and Knight (1998), Eskridge and Ferejohn (1992), and Gely and Spiller (1992) for the positive political theory and the law literature.

In recent years, a small body of work has studied how constitutions are enforced. Many scholars have observed that a central role of constitutions is to help people coordinate, and nonauthoritarian constitutions are more likely to survive when they create a coordination equilibrium (Hardin 1989; Mittal and Weingast 2013; Ordeshook 1992; Weingast 1997). Yet none of these approaches explain why successful constitutions have the truly characteristic features we associate with law. In the highly abstract accounts we find in the existing literature, a constitution is just a focal point.

Consider two characteristic features of law associated with successful constitutions. The first concerns the nature of law itself. Fuller (1964), for example, argued that law is a system of governance by rules characterized by eight attributes: generality, promulgation, clarity, noncontradiction, nonretroactivity, stability, feasibility, and consistency between rules as announced and rules as applied. In this chapter, we will call attributes of law such as these "legal attributes." Fuller argued that these criteria must be met not to satisfy an external moral principle but for what he called "the enterprise of subjecting human conduct to the governance of rules" to be recognizable as law as such, distinct from the exercise of arbitrary power. From this perspective, laws must be general, for example, because judgments of wrongdoing that cannot be organized into rule-like generalizations reflect a system of decision making by "patternless exercises of political power" (Fuller 1964, 48) rather than law. People cannot govern their behavior in accordance with law if the law lacks any knowable and predictable pattern. "A total failure in any [of the eight attributes] does not simply result in a bad system of law; it results in something that is not properly called a legal system at all" (Fuller 1964, 39).

A second characteristic feature of law concerns the process of law, namely its structure as a system of distinctive and abstract or impersonal reasoning and normative processes for reasoning and decision (Friedman 2003, Waldron 2008, 2011). Law is not simply another way of reaching an economic or political result, although law may accomplish both these ends. We recognize the presence or absence of law in a society by its structure, not simply by its results.

In this essay, we draw on our recent work to present an account of law as an institution characterized by the two features noted above: a system of distinctive reasoning and process that is grounded in economic and political functionality; and a set of legal attributes, such as generality, stability, publicity, clarity, noncontradictoriness, and consistency.

To do so, we begin with the observation that no external agent exists to enforce the constitution. Instead, constitutions must be self-enforcing in the sense that all relevant actors – political officials, citizens, and groups – have incentives to abide by the constitution's prescriptive rules. A major part of this enforcement, therefore, involves the actions of decentralized citizens in the absence of coercion, a setting we argue applies to law in general (Hadfield and Weingast 2013a).

Decentralized enforcement often requires that members of the community simultaneously but independently make a decision about whether to participate in a collective punishment of an action of another agent, such as a merchant, the sovereign, or a neighbor. Widespread decentralization of enforcement therefore requires that members of the relevant community have both the incentive and the ability to coordinate. Yet people face major problems with this type of decentralized enforcement. Typically, a successful boycott requires a minimum number of individuals to refuse to deal with the rule violator. Individuals contemplating whether to participate in an enforcement action thus must act on the basis of their beliefs about how others will act. They must also prefer the outcome under coordination to the alternative without coordination. Decentralized enforcement thus poses substantial coordination and incentive challenges. First, a sufficient number of individuals must individually conclude that coordination is preferred to the alternative. Second, these potential enforcers must all believe that a sufficient number of others will choose to participate in enforcement. Third, to coordinate the enforcement actions of willing participants, individuals must all share similar beliefs about what the law requires – what is right and what is wrong. Fourth, all these beliefs must be common knowledge.

We argue that constitutions have developed their distinctive structure, at least in part, to coordinate beliefs among diverse individuals and thus to improve the efficacy of decentralized rule-enforcement mechanisms. In our account, constitutions involve a specialized system of reasoning that seeks to converge on the categorization of actions as either "constitutional" – that is, acceptable – or not, the latter warranting punishment/action. We contend that a designated system of specialized reasoning helps coordinate beliefs by undertaking two tasks: reducing ambiguity and thus serving as a focal point around which people can coordinate their enforcement behavior as well as providing a process of public reasoning (Hadfield and Macedo 2012) that, among other things, extends and adapts existing rules to novel circumstances.

One of the principal mechanisms in enforcing constitutional rules is citizen resistance, an idea emphasized by Locke in his *Second Treatise on Government* (1689). A central concern therefore is the question of when will an individual participate in action against unconstitutional behavior despite a potential collective action problem.

Others have approached this problem using cultural beliefs or preferences (Greif 1994); standard subgame perfect arguments where people who fail to punish are themselves punished (e.g., Milgrom, North, and Weingast 1990); evolutionary game theory that demonstrates the fitness benefits of heritable strategies that punish wrongs (Boyd, Gintis, and Bowles 2010); or, in an important line of experimental work on altruistic punishment, to the presence of negative emotions such as anger toward wrongdoers (Fehr and Gachter 2002).

We take a different approach in which individuals are concerned about the beliefs of others; specifically, beliefs about whether political officials might act unconstitutionally in the future, and whether other citizens might participate in resisting such officials. Suppose there exists a partition, R, that divides actions into constitutional and unconstitutional. By participating in an act to resist political officials using R as the standard to judge official behavior, an individual j can affect others' beliefs so as to influence the likelihood that they participate in resistance in the future, in particular, that they will participate in resisting an unconstitutional action against i. A political official considering violating a constitutional rule makes his choice in part based on an estimate of the likely size of response. We show that there exist circumstances where it is rational for j to undertake costly actions to change the beliefs of others (e.g., both potential enforcers and potential wrongdoers) about j's willingness to resist unconstitutional harms (against anyone) defined by R. Thus, j's participation today in resisting increases the likelihood that a future unconstitutional harm against another is effectively resisted by the group by giving members of the group confidence that they will not participate in costly resistance without adequate numbers of others doing so as well. In this way, j's actions help create a coordination equilibrium; j will undertake the costly actions to change people's beliefs when the benefits to j of coordinating under R exceed j's costs.

This perspective on constitutions – emphasizing constitutional law and legal procedure as coordinating diverse people's actions and reactions – generates a new understanding about the ability to sustain a system of order with legal attributes. Consider generality. A legal system fails to be general if its judgments depend entirely on case-by-case specific features. In our account, legal rules need to be framed in general terms in order to give individuals a basis for predicting how the law will treat situations the details of which the law will learn about only in the future. Predictability is necessary to secure their incentive to participate in collective punishments under a common classification of "wrong" or unconstitutional.

Similarly, widely shared, generally available and impersonal reasoning (for example, reliance on popular principles, maxims, or simple concepts) also promotes coordination. The coordinating function of law is less effectively performed if few can conduct the reasoning (or buy expertise in the reasoning system) themselves or if judgments depend on who is doing the reasoning. Generally available principles and reason increase the chances that decentralized coordination occurs, especially under widely varied circumstances.

The coordination function of constitutional law sheds new light on several of the attributes Fuller claimed were definitive of legal order. We argue that fulfilling this coordination function requires that law be stable, clear, general, prospective, and publicly accessible. Moreover, the coordination function of law predicts attributes of law that do not appear in Fuller's list. We argue, for example, that to effectively coordinate decentralized enforcement activity, constitutions must be organized to achieve unique classifications of behavior as right or wrong and that to accomplish this a legal system is likely to place classification under the authoritative stewardship of a unique and recognized entity, such as a legal profession and hierarchical court system with clear jurisdictional boundaries. We also argue that, to accommodate the idiosyncratic perspectives and preferences of the individuals whose participation in punishment is required for efficacy, legal rules are likely to be immanent, subject to elaboration in open and public processes that allow individuals to demonstrate how their idiosyncratic information and reasoning comports with the common reasoning implemented by law. A legal system also must be universal in order to be effective in our account: The legal rules has to offer the people who play a role in decentralized enforcement the benefits of deterring acts against themselves that they consider wrongful. A legal system that considers actions wrong only if the victim belongs to a particular class of people cannot draw on the enforcement support of other classes.

Others have proposed that law and legal conventions, such as property rights, can serve as a focal point for the purposes of coordination (Sugden 2005; Weingast 1997; Cooter 1998; Basu 2000; McAdams 2000; Mailath et al. 2001; Myerson 2004; Dixit 2004). This literature focuses on interactions that are themselves coordination problems. Sugden (1986), for example, offers an account of the spontaneous emergence of property rights to coordinate strategies in a hawk-dove game in which rival claimants to an object are able to coordinate which claimant plays hawk (claiming the object) and which plays dove (relinquishing the object) by referring to a focal concept of ownership. Myerson (2004) expands the idea of law as coordination to include an account of deliberate equilibrium selection by a recognized leader in games with multiple equilibria.

Our account differs in three key respects that significantly expand the explanatory framework of a coordination model of law. First, we focus on coordination of the decentralized enforcement activity that supports inter-actions rather than coordination of underlying interactions themselves. Our account is therefore not limited to explaining the role of constitutional law in coordinating a particular subset of underlying interactions (coordina-tion games with multiple equilibria) but rather to explaining the role of law in coordinating decentralized enforcement of rules to support any type of interaction. An interaction beset by the risk of opportunism, for example, is not a coordination game. Our account, however, can help to explain the role of law in mitigating the problem of opportunism.

Second, and related, because the underlying enforcement game is not a pure coordination game, our approach brings to the fore an incentive compatibility constraint. It is not enough just to coordinate individuals to support a constitution. It must also be common knowledge that those who are capable of punishing sovereigns who transgress the constitution, and who will bear the costs of doing so, believe they benefit from the constitutional order.

The third key difference between our account and that of the existing literature is that we expressly focus on understanding the structure and process of law as an institution in light of its role in coordination. The existing literature, by contrast, focuses on the equilibrium selection function per se and does not distinguish constitutional law as a coordinating device from other types of coordinating devices. Myerson (2004), for example, proposes that a leader can announce equilibrium strategies and thereby coordinate agents in their strategy choices. But, as Mailath, Morris, and Postlewaite (2001) propose, any entity with "authority," including a dictator, can do this. Our perspective suggests that many dictators create order in the sense of an absence of violent conflict, but they do not create law. The existing law-as-focal-point literature does not help us understand why law has the particular attributes that it does or to distinguish between order coordinated by law and order coordinated by other means, such as social norms, authority, or tyranny.

We develop our argument as follows. Section 2 develops the theoret-ical approach to law as the solution to a coordination problem. Section 3 discusses the implications of this perspective for our principal questions about constitutional enforcement. Section 4 suggests that the principal ele-ments of our approach have been understood by political theorists for several centuries. In Section 5 we apply our approach to three moments of constitutional change, the English Glorious Revolution of 1689, the early U.S. Constitution, and the recent constitution of Chile. Our conclusions follow.

2. The Theory of Decentralized Constitutional Enforcement

We begin our theoretical discussion by considering an environment without coercion.[2] Consider a generic situation with a single large player, a political official whom we will label the sovereign, or S. S interacts in a similar way with many citizens, c_i (a framework developed in Weingast 1997). With each individual c_i, S has the opportunity to behave according to the constitutional rules or to violate those rules, imposing a loss on c_i. We suppose that S's behavior with respect to an individual b_i is observable by all. After observing S's behavior, each c_i chooses whether or not to retaliate against S. Critically for our results, we assume that for punishment to be effective in deterring undesired behavior by S, many individuals must participate in the punishment. (For concreteness we assume all c's must participate for the punishment to be effective in changing S's behavior.) As long as the one-time value of violating the constitution for S is less than the discounted present value of behaving according to the constitution in each period, the threat of retaliation by the c's polices S's behavior.

Many problems exist with the standard approach to modeling interactions between S and the c's. The one we highlight is that, in standard accounts, S's behavior is unambiguously classified as either constitutional or not. This holds, for example, in the many models that employ the repeated prisoners' dilemma. Yet in most real world settings, S's behavior generally has many dimensions. In the context of a sovereign and a citizen S's actions often involve ambiguities about what is "necessary and proper" to undertake public actions. For example, can an individual's rights of privacy be violated in the interests of national security? Does a national emergency constitute sufficient reason to compromise citizen rights?

In general, no obvious or unique answer exists to these questions. The public official and the citizens are likely to have different understandings of the various constitutional provisions – or at least to profess such differences, keeping any information to the contrary private. More importantly for our purposes, other members of the community who have to decide whether to participate in punishment of a prospective constitutional

---

[2] This section summarizes the model developed formally in Hadfield and Weingast (2012).

violation are likely to disagree about how to partition various actions into constitutional and unconstitutional categories. Heterogeneous views about honorable and wrongful behavior make it difficult for diverse individuals to coordinate their retaliation against wrongful behavior (Weingast 1997). Milgrom, North and Weingast (1990) show that coordination for decentralized punishment breaks down when members of the community act on their idiosyncratic information.

To gain purchase on this problem, we assume that each individual possesses an idiosyncratic logic to classify S's behavior as constitutional or not. Most importantly, this setting implies that each individual c_i has preferences over the classification of S's behavior in c_i's interactions with S. We assume idiosyncratic logic is not accessible to others, at least not at reasonable cost. An individual c_i faces a problem: c_i wants S to expect that behavior toward c_i that c_i classifies as wrongful will result in punishment by the entire community of c's. But the other c's do not know what c_i considers wrongful. A possible solution to that problem of course would be for c_i to announce when S's behavior toward c_i is wrongful. But this then poses an incentive problem: What incentive do the other c_j's have to participate in a costly collective punishment to deter behavior that c_i judges (in an inscrutable way) to be unconstitutional?

We propose a solution to this incentive problem in the designation of a common logic – accessible to all – that classifies S's behavior in its interactions with all individual c's, designating actions as either constitutional or unconstitutional. Call this common logic R (for reasoning). If all c's participate in a collective punishment whenever S engages in behavior – to any individual c – that is classified as unconstitutional by R, then the community of c's can deter S from R-unconstitutional behavior. An individual c_j then benefits from collective punishment coordinated by R if R is sufficiently convergent with c_j's idiosyncratic logic; that is, if R results in a threat of punishment in response to what c_j considers to be unconstitutional sufficiently often.

Our model shows that, for collective punishment of R-unconstitutional behavior to be a subgame perfect equilibrium, it must be that each individual c is not better off deviating from the collective punishment strategy – supporting S's actions, for example. We argue that this incentive can be found in c_j's self-interest in ensuring that S and the other c's all maintain the belief that R is sufficiently convergent with idiosyncratic logics to generate a benefit for each individual c. By participating in collective punishment in reaction to R-unconstitutional actions, each individual c helps to ensure that there is common knowledge observation of an effective punishment if S engages in unconstitutional behavior. Failing to do so leads S and other c's to believe that R is not capable of coordinating the citizens.[3]

Note that we do not start with the idea that the parties simultaneously search out a uniquely salient focal point – such as Schelling's (1960) separated parachutists searching for a landmark on a common map – from the landscape. Rather we start with the idea that citizens have an incentive to help identify a coordinating device for collective punishment because they will benefit from communicating to a third party that they have coordinated. In our formal model, we study two citizens who would benefit from coordinating punishment of unconstitutional behavior by the sovereign. Recognizing this, one citizen has an incentive to retaliate against the sovereign and announce that the retaliation follows a logic accessible to the other – "the right of free speech," "the ancient constitution of England," or "the sanctity of private property," for example. The second citizen has an incentive to join the withdrawal of support of S under that announced logic if that logic would serve to coordinate punishments that provide sufficient benefit to that citizen. The second citizen will participate in the retaliation if he or she judges the announced common logic to be sufficiently convergent with his or her idiosyncratic logic. By participating, the second citizen engages in observable behavior – completing an effective retaliation – that communicates the information that the second citizen benefits from punishments coordinated on the announced common logic and hence alters the beliefs of the first citizen and the sovereign. By engaging in costly self-conscious efforts to identify a coordinating logic (echoing the self-consciousness of the coordination problem that Schelling argued would lead to the identification of a focal point), the citizens generate a coordinating device. What makes it salient is its proposal by one citizen willing to bear the costs of waiting to learn whether it is acceptable to the other.[4]

---

[3] In this sense, each participant in the boycott is a pivotal participant. For an evolutionary game theoretic approach to collective punishment that predicts the emergence of equilibria in which each participant in a collective punishment is pivotal, see Boyd, Gintis, and Bowles (2010).

[4] In Hadfield and Weingast (2012), we do not expressly model this proposal process; we evaluate the stability of equilibrium under a candidate system R given beliefs about the likelihood that individuals judge R to be good enough to support participation. It is relatively straightforward to generalize to a proposal process, which would imply that the gains from coordination are sufficiently great and the grounds for expecting others to participate sufficiently strong that a first-mover is willing to attempt to secure coordination. For a model that considers how players who lack a common language to describe a game might learn to coordinate by taking observable actions, see Crawford and Haller (1990).

For a common logic R to coordinate collective punishment, it must be the case that it is more than a focal point. R must also be sufficiently convergent with the idiosyncratic logic of individuals needed for the punishment to be effective. More precisely, all individuals have to be able to reach the conclusion that R is sufficiently convergent with their own idiosyncratic logic that the threat of collective punishment of R-unconstitutional actions generates sufficient benefit for the individual to overcome the cost of participating in punishments to demonstrate coordination.

Our claim is that a common logic – both the reasoning of the classification system itself and the institution that implements it – that can achieve equilibrium coordination in the face of substantial idiosyncratic reasoning will possess certain distinctive attributes. Those attributes, we claim, are the attributes that characterize law. We turn to a discussion of those attributes in the next section.

3. Law and Legal Process as the Solution to the Coordination Problem

The approach has thus far left abstract the nature of the principles – the common logic, R – around which people coordinate. In this section, we discuss what characteristics a logic must have in order to serve as a coordinating device for decentralized punishment and explore the claim that these are the characteristics we associate with law.

Legal Attributes

We emphasized that, for a common logic to serve as a coordinating device, individuals must be able to assess the logic and reach the conclusion that it is sufficiently convergent with their idiosyncratic reasoning so that they will benefit from coordination on a proposed logic. We predict, therefore, that the logic must be universal in its coverage: It must contain rules that address, at least to some extent, the circumstances of all those who participate in supporting it. Universality is in fact one of the most distinctive features of constitutional law, typically prescribing rights that apply to all citizens. We recognize the existence of the rule of law in a society in large part on the basis of whether neutral and independent courts that follow the law are available to all who may be the victims of wrongdoing. Our approach suggests a new reason why universal coverage is an attribute of legal and constitutional order.

A legal system that lacks universal coverage – for example, a system that protects only particular people or classes – makes it less likely that those excluded from the law's protections will value the system sufficiently to participate in its (costly) enforcement. Recall our framework with a single S interacting with many diverse c's. A common logic that benefits exclusively a subset of c_i's is unlikely to gain support among other c_j's so that they will help c_i resist S.

To attract the support of others in helping defend against potential problems from S, c_i must rely on a logic that benefits others rather than a rule that primarily benefits him or herself. Others in the community are far more likely to follow a logic with universal coverage that applies to c_i today but will equally apply to themselves when they interact with S in the future. In this way, universality helps facilitate the community-wide reciprocity system whereby all the b's coordinate their retaliations against S.

Our account of the coordination function of law also sheds light on several of the legal and constitutional attributes emphasized by legal philosophers. In the conventional account, legal attributes are explained by the need to create a workable system in which individuals are able to guide their behavior in order to comply with law. Constitutions must be publicly expressed in general terms – abstract principles – so that people can reason from these public expressions of the law's content (announcements of decisions or codified rules) to determine how the law will apply to their particular circumstances in the future so that they can coordinate their resistance when necessary. Legal rules must be prospective, open, clear, noncontradictory, capable of being followed and stable because, as Raz (1977, 198–199) puts it, "One cannot be guided by a retroactive law [and] if it is to guide people they must be able to find out what it is." Furthermore, Raz writes, "an ambiguous, vague, obscure or imprecise law is likely to mislead or confuse at least some of those who desire to be guided by it" and "stability is essential if people are to be guided by law in their long-term decisions" (Raz 1977, 199). Similarly, those who are subject to the law must anticipate that the rules as announced will be consistent with the rules as applied. "Litigants can be guided by law only if the judges apply the law correctly" (Raz 1977, 201).

Our model predicts these same attributes as part of the equilibrium that supports the compliance (deterrence) of S. But our focus on the coordination problem facing the c's offers a different perspective on several of them. Consider:

- *Generality* is definitive of Fuller's concept that law is the "enterprise of subjecting human conduct to the governance of rules." Generality is necessary for the same reason as *prospectivity*: Individuals must be able to predict from the public pronouncements of the law how it will treat particular situations that it may not yet have encountered. But the capacity to evaluate how the law will treat particular situations in our account follows from the need to predict whether one will be a beneficiary of the law, not (only) from the need for guidance to avoid running afoul of the law.

- *Stability* is also central to constitutional law. In our coordination account, stability plays an additional role, beyond that predicted by a focus on compliance. Coordination considerations predict that in equilibrium law will show stability over a longer time horizon than that strictly needed to support compliance. The incentive compatibility-constraint for individuals to support the constitutional order requires that individuals have positive expectations about how constitutional principles will apply to situations they care about in the future. Because unstable rules raise uncertainty about the future value of today's rules, instability lowers the value of the rule and hence of participating in decentralized punishment for wrongful behavior. Instability therefore lowers the likelihood that people will coordinate today. Because instability implies much higher costs of coordination, people are likely to fail to coordinate when the rules change frequently.

- *Clarity* serves a straightforward role in reducing ambiguity. The clearer a set of principles, the more adequately they distinguish between the circumstances considered right and wrong. Clarity therefore makes it easier for citizens to partition constitutional from unconstitutional behavior. As the conventional account recognizes, clarity reduces ambiguity so that potential wrongdoers can more easily comply with the law. But it also increases the number of circumstances under which people are likely to succeed in coordinating decentralized enforcement against wrongful behavior. "Brightlines" – constitutional provisions that are unambiguous so that citizens can readily and independently understand violations – are an important feature of clarity that helps coordinate resistance. Examples of brightlines include the U.S. Constitution's provision that grants the power to regulate interstate commerce solely to the national government; or the supremacy clause that says in the event of a conflict between a state and a national law, the national law is supreme.[5]

- *Noncontradictoriness* is equally straightforward: Constitutional rules that contradict one another imply circumstances where different rules

---

[5] Mittal and Weingast (2013) discuss the theoretical importance of brightlines; Jacobi and Weingast (2013) demonstrate that a surprising number of provisions in the U.S. Constitution involve brightlines.

present conflicting prescriptions about compliance. They also interfere with coordination by generating ambiguity in the predictions made by enforcers about when they should participate in enforcement and how the logic they are supporting will treat them.

- *Publicity* also facilities both compliance and coordination. The coordination account, however, emphasizes a wider public than the compliance account. To serve a coordination function, both the principles partitioning constitutional from unconstitutional behavior and the logic underlying the partition must be known by the entire enforcement community, not merely those who need to know what is required of them for compliance and the avoidance of penalty. Moreover, coordination requires publicity not only of constitutional rules but also of the logic on which the rules are based, in order to allow those who must decide whether to participate in collective punishment to determine how the rules, once elaborated, would apply to their idiosyncratic circumstances. Public announcement thus facilitates a coordinated equilibrium by members of a decentralized community.
- Finally, consider *consistency* between an announced rule and its implementation. Inconsistencies are likely to lead to coordination failure. As with clarity and promulgation, an inconsistency raises the problem that some people will know the announced rule and use that to guide their choices (including their punishment choices) while others use the rule as implemented. When these conflict, compliance and coordination failure is likely.

In short, the legal attributes identified by legal philosophy are all consistent with promoting the coordination function of constitutions. By eliminating a degree of ambiguity in prediction about how others will interpret conduct today, these attributes facilitate both compliance and coordination of punishment of unconstitutional behavior. The stability of law promotes compliance today and in the future. This approach also generates some of the most fundamental aspects of the rule of law: generality, universality, impersonality, and stability (Hayek 1960).

Law and Legal Reasoning

In addition to providing a deeper account of the legal attributes emphasized by legal philosophers, our coordination model brings to the fore features of law that have been overlooked, deemphasized, or treated as controversial by legal philosophy. Waldron (2008, 2011), for example, has argued that the conventional concept of law is too thin an account of what we understand as a legal system, being too narrowly focused on formal rule-attributes, such as those listed by Fuller and the even narrower account offered by Raz (1977) to keep the concept of law distinct from the rule of law. Waldron argues that the concept of law should include procedural and argumentation requirements such as open courts that hear evidence and reasoning from both sides in formal processes. Dworkin (1986) claims that law inherently includes the ideal of integrity of reasoning and the concept that there is a "right answer" to hard legal questions, however contested they may be (particularly in the domain of constitutional law) in practice.

Our positive model predicts that constitutional law that succeeds in coordinating decentralized enforcement will have features like those emphasized by these more controversial accounts. Widely shared, generally available reasoning (for example, reliance on popular principles, maxims, simple concepts) also promotes compliance and coordination. A constitution's coordinating function is less effective if few can conduct the reasoning (or access expertise in the reasoning system) themselves. Generally available logic and principles increase the chances that decentralized coordination occurs. Moreover, because the world is constantly changing and presenting new circumstances, compliance and coordination require some form of judicial process to deal with them. New and unforeseen circumstances bring the risk of coordination failure. An important role of constitutional process, therefore, is to make rulings that reduce ambiguity, fostering private coordination.

Coordination requires not only that the judiciary rule in a particular case but that they announce a reason articulating why they ruled in this manner. These reasons help a decentralized community extend the logic of the specific circumstances of the case to other circumstances. The more important and the more complex the issue, the greater number of cases will emerge, thereby moving the law toward the goal of greater thoroughness, reducing ambiguity, and fostering private coordination.

A publically accessible logic must be such that all players can use it to make common-knowledge predictions about future classifications, in particular about the classification of possibly as-yet unobserved and unknown sets of circumstances. This conclusion follows from the premise that the behaviors citizens engage in and the impact of sovereign intervention are in some fundamental sense made valuable by the private information and idiosyncratic reasoning processes of individuals. The set of classifications cannot be based exclusively on already-observed characteristics that describe circumstances experienced in the past. For this reason, the community must have a logic and not merely an accumulated set of observations about classification: Even if the logic is derived from observed classifications, it must contain generalizable principles to predict the classification of new and perhaps unimagined circumstances. Moreover, the application of these generalized principles to new circumstances that are (at least initially) inaccessible to some of the players must lead to a relatively unique classification: The community must possess a means of deciding what the logic uniquely implies about classification.

This conclusion suggests that the constitution's common logic must be under the stewardship of an authoritative person, body, or mechanism. The community is therefore likely to create a specified system of reasoning – with specialized keepers of the reasoning (lawyers, judges, and, earlier, wise men, rabbis, clerics). This conclusion also suggests that the process of determining the implications of the logic for a new and/or initially private set of circumstances must be to some degree open: Individuals must see an opportunity to introduce evidence and argument based on their private circumstances in an effort to allow the stewards of legal reasoning to apply and elaborate the common logic on the basis of that information. The process must also be public[6]: The application of the logic can lead to common knowledge classifications only if the information and reasoning with which the logic is elaborated in novel and otherwise private circumstances are shared.[7] Because multiple ways typically exist to extend an existing logic to new circumstances, a system of constitutional law must have some form of final arbiter that resolves these differences. Failure to have such an arbiter leads to coordination failure and even potential conflict as different groups seek to promote their approach to coordination at the expense of others.

The Constitution as an Equilibrium

The coordination approach also offers an explanation for how constitutional order is sustained. The coordination features of law support an equilibrium. The third party enforcement aspects of the law require that individuals use the same definition of honoring and wrongful behavior. Once coordination has been established, citizens have no incentive to deviate from it, so long as the coordinated outcome is at least as good as the uncoordinated outcome (as Hume 1739–1740; Schelling 1960; and Hardin 1989 have emphasized). Moreover, this conclusion holds even if individuals disagree about the best way to coordinate so that many prefer a different way to coordinate to the

---

[6] Compare, here, Macedo (2010) and his concept of "public reason."

[7] The qualifiers "relatively" and "to some degree" are intended to reflect the fact that a robust coordination could tolerate some noise but that if these features of generalizability, clarity, openness and so on were not present in the main then the proposed logic would likely fail to coordinate sufficiently to support an equilibrium.

adopted focal solution. The decentralized coordination equilibrium means that third parties will help punish when S has acted unconstitutionally according to the focal system of reasoning R and not otherwise. Therefore, acting alone and using a different logic to guide a given c_i's actions makes i worse off; this deviation from the focal point is costly to i and, because i acts alone, it does not affect S's behavior.

Summary
Taken together, these implications of the coordination function of constitutions help answer the larger questions we asked at the opening of this chapter. Constitutional law is at once a body of rules and principles that facilitate private ordering and decentralized coordination on enforcement; a system of public reasoning to explain and extend that system; and an equilibrium that sustains stability. Many countries have a system of announced rules. But if those systems do not also possess legal attributes, they are likely to support authoritarian regimes rather than constitutional law because they will have to depend exclusively on centralized coercion, with no role for decentralized enforcement.

Our approach helps us theorize about constitutional process. Taken together, the ever-changing nature of the world and our inability to conceive of all possible contingencies mean that new contingencies are constantly arising. As mentioned, these effects lead to an organization that provides stewardship over the law. To maintain their position, the stewards have incentives to create and maintain value for the community. Failing to create value – for example, by announcing a potential focal solution that inadequately fosters compliance or decentralized coordination – holds the risk that people simply ignore the constitution. For this reason, stewards have incentives to extend the existing focal solution to cover new circumstances and to reduce ambiguities as they arise.

Moreover, the coordination perspective suggests that there exists many different ways to define the specifics of law so that the law is not unique. Nonetheless, the participation constraint for individuals requires that the law provide value for citizens, so the substance of the constitution cannot be arbitrary; it must be structured so as to make most citizens better off.[8]

---

[8] Alberts, Warshaw, and Weingast (2012) show that successful constitutions must also protect the interests of those with the power to disrupt the constitution if they are made worse off. Examples include slaveholders in the early United States and those associated with the pre-constitutional regime in Chile, Spain, and South Africa. Because the interests with such power differ across states, every constitution must be different.

Our approach differs from normative legal literature in that we do not, for example, begin with normative principles and derive their consequences for doctrine or constitutional process. Instead, we build a positive model of how constitutional law emerges and is sustained. We then show that, as part of the equilibrium, the system sustains desirable characteristics. Universality and impersonality, both central features of a rule of law (Fuller 1964; Hayek 1960; Raz 1977), emerge as elements to support coordination. Our model suggests that the content of the rules in a legal system also possesses certain normatively attractive features: individuals in the system must perceive themselves to be better off with the rules than without them. This does not mean that they will all be equally well off, or that the benefit is large – the outcome without coordination may be sufficiently bad that almost anything is better. We do not explore these normative features in depth here. Our principal observation is that the study of how normative principles are sustained in equilibrium is a potentially important addition to the normative literature, as Binmore (1994) and others have observed.

4. Political Theorists Have Understood Many of These Principles for Centuries

In this section, we show that principal elements of our approach to sustaining constitutions have been understood for several centuries. Importantly, the two main theorists whose ideas we report were both deeply involved with critical moments creating constitutional stability: Locke with the Glorious Revolution and Madison at the U.S. founding.

One of our basic principles is that constitutions must be self-enforcing in the sense that political officials and citizens have incentives to abide by the rules. Hobbes, in *Leviathan* (1651), famously argued that mere rules are not self-enforcing: "Covenants, without the Sword, are but Words, and of no strength to secure a man at all" [II, 17; 117]. Madison echoed these sentiments in *Federalist* 48: "The conclusion which I am warranted in drawing from these observations is, that a mere demarcation on parchment of the constitutional limits of the several departments [of the federal government], is not a sufficient guard against those encroachments which lead to a tyrannical concentration of all the powers of government in the same hands" (Hamilton, Jay, and Madison [1788: 326]).

We argue that the principal mechanism in enforcing constitutional rules is citizen resistance. When citizens react in concert to resist unconstitutional actions by political officials, they can either force those officials to back down or remove them from office. This principle has been understood by

political theorist for centuries. Demosthenes, discussing the maintenance
of democracy in fourth century BCE Athens, observed:

And what is the power of the laws? Is it that, if any of you is attacked and gives a
shout, they'll come running to your aid? No, they are just inscribed letters and have
no ability to do that. What then is their motive power? You are, if you secure them
and make them authoritative whenever anyone asks for aid. So the laws are powerful
through you and you through the laws. You must therefore stand up for them in
just the same way as any individual would stand up for himself if attacked; you must
take the view that offenses against the law are common concerns. (Demosthenes
speech 21, Against Meidias, sections 223–225)

Locke, writing during the constitutional controversies of the late-
seventeeth-century England, argued in his famous *Second Treatise on Government* (1689), "If the king... sets himself against the body of the commonwealth, whereof he is the head, and shall, with intolerable ill usage,
cruelly tyrannize over the whole, or a considerable part of the people, in this
case the people have a right to resist and defend themselves from injury"
[118, §233].

In 1689, Locke's thesis about resistance was a radical doctrine. It remained
so a century later during the American Revolution when the founders used
this logic to support their resistance to the British. The Declaration of
Independence declared: "When a long train of abuses and usurpations,
pursuing invariably the same Object evinces a design to reduce them under
absolute Despotism, it is their right, it is their duty, to throw off such
Government, and to provide new Guards for their future security."

Locke also understood the idea of publicity and stability. He argued:

The ruling power ought to govern by declared and received laws, and not by extem-
porary dictates and undetermined resolutions: for then mankind will be in a fare
worse condition than in the state of nature... [If one man can] force them to obey
at pleasure the exorbitant and unlimited decrees of their sudden thoughts, or unre-
strained, and till that moment unknown wills, without having any measures set
down which may guide and justify their actions. [72–73, §137]

Central to Alexander Hamilton and James Madison's concerns in the
Federalist Papers at the founding of the United States were problems of
arbitrary power and tyranny: "In every political institution, a power to
advance the public happiness involves a discretion which may be misapplied
and abused" (Hamilton, Jay, and Madison 1788, 260). Further, Madison,
emphasizing the role of ordinary citizens in controlling government, can
be read as recognizing that this form of control rests at least in part on
"auxiliary precautions" – that is, constitutional provisions that expressly

obligate political officials to observe limits; we can understand these internal controls as coordinating the external controls of the citizenry:

If men were angels, no government would be necessary. If angels were to govern men, neither external nor internal controls on government would be necessary. In framing a government which is to be administered by men over men, the great difficulty lies in this: you must first enable the government to control the governed; and in the next place oblige it to control itself. A dependence on the people is, no doubt, the primary control on the government; but experience has taught mankind the necessity of auxiliary precautions. (Hamilton, Jay, and Madison 1788: 337)

In logic closely paralleling our view of the citizen resistance in the face of the coordination problem underlying constitutional enforcement, Hamilton and Madison explained at several points in the *Federalist Papers* how citizen coordination would work, often through their agents at the state level. Both writers used the term "encroachment" to mean unconstitutional actions, such as abusing citizen rights or grasping powers that were not delegated by the constitution; further, both saw collective resistance as the primary means of enforcing constitutional limits on the federal government.

Hamilton argued in *Federalist* 26:

The state legislatures, who will always be not only vigilant but suspicious and jealous guardians of the rights of the citizens against encroachments from the federal government, will constantly have their attention away to the conduct of the national rulers, and will be ready enough, if anything improper appears, to sound the alarm to the people, and not only to be the voice, but, if necessary, the arm of their discontent. (Hamilton, Jay, and Madison 1788: 163–164)

Pursuing this line, Madison further argued in *Federalist* 46 about the important role of the states in monitoring the federal government and in organizing states, citizens, and their militias against possible violations and abuse:

But ambitious encroachments of the federal government, on the authority of the State government, would not excite the opportunity of a single state, or a few States only. They would be signals of general alarm. Every government would espouse the common cause. A correspondence would be opened. Plans of resistance would be concerted. One spirit would animate and conduct the whole. (Hamilton, Jay, and Madison 1788: 309)

Madison also understood the importance of the bill of rights as helping to coordinate citizens and resistance. In his view this worked somewhat differently in constitutional monarchies than in popular governments. The bill of rights following the Glorious Revolution in England, a constitutional monarchy, contained a great many brightlines. For example, taxation was the sole domain of Parliament: "That levying money for or to use of the crown, by pretence of prerogative, without grant of Parliament, for longer time, or in other manner than the same is or shall be granted, is illegal." As another example, the king had to obey the law: "That the pretended power of suspending of laws, or the execution of laws by regal authority, without consent of Parliament, is illegal."

The English bill of rights improved clarity, reduced ambiguity, and therefore facilitated citizen resistance. Madison explained this in a letter to Thomas Jefferson dated October 17, 1788:

The efficacy of a bill of rights in controlling abuses of power – lies in this: that in a monarchy the latent force of the nation is superior to that of the Sovereign, and a solemn charter of popular rights must have a great effect, as a standard for trying the validity of public acts, and a *signal for rousing & uniting the superior force of the community.* (emphasis added)

The bill of rights in the U.S. Constitution also aided citizens in the face of "usurped acts of the government" from which "evil may spring." As Madison explained to Jefferson, in the face of such acts, "A bill of rights will be good ground for an appeal to the sense of the community. Perhaps too there may be a certain degree of danger, that a succession of artful and ambitious rulers may by gradual & well timed advances, finally erect an independent Government on the subversion of liberty."

Public reasoning was also a major part of the U.S. constitutional experience and design. The ratification debates, pitting Federalists against Anti-Federalists, focused public attention on key issues involving the meaning of the proposed constitution. Indeed, the *Federalist Papers* themselves represent a monumental effort to explain the constitution and make clear the meaning of a wide variety of its provisions. In a similar manner, the English bill of rights made public the new rules of the constitutional process in a manner that settled and clarified many of the constitutional debates at issue during the contentious rule of the Stuarts prior to the revolution (i.e., 1603–1688). More than this, however, the U.S. Constitution committed the political process to the protection of a platform for public reasoning, guaranteeing freedom of the press and laying the groundwork for federal courts to assume a central role as stewards of public conversation about constitutional principle.

This short section demonstrates that several of the historic political theorists and constitutional architects understood, even if in fragmented ways, many of the central aspects of our approach. We thus see our contribution as one that is well-grounded in existing constitutional theory but provides a more concrete formulation of these key components of constitutional stability.

5. Coordination and Equilibrium in Particular Constitutional Contexts

As we observed at the outset, sustaining a constitution in practice is a difficult problem. Coordination problems arise in policing potential unconstitutional actions by the sovereign against the citizens; for example, when the sovereign violates citizen rights, as is so common in constitutional failures; or when the sovereign begins issuing and enforcing decrees that ignore constitutional procedures to produce laws. When the c's (the citizens) all act in concert, they can police S's (the sovereign) actions and prevent unconstitutional transgressions of their rights. When the b's lack the ability to act in concert, the S can exploit them and avoid punishment. Creating a long-term, stable constitutional equilibrium therefore requires solving a complex form of coordination game. A host of issues central to creating a constitution reflect this form of coordination problem: What rights should citizens have? What should the process of producing sovereign commands be?

In practice, coordination difficulties arise because no natural or unique solution exists for the specification of citizen rights or the processes that produce sovereign commands. Indeed, too many solutions to these problems exist. The U.S. Constitution has a right to bear arms, while many others do not. Some have proportional representation and parliamentary systems while others have a presidential system with winner-take-all elections. Other constitutions charge the military with a duty to protect public peace, allowing them legal authority to suspend the democratic government (see Loveman 1993).

The wide range of possible constitutional provisions implies that, here too, the different positions and experiences of citizens are likely to produce widely varying preferences over procedures and rights, making organic or spontaneous coordination especially difficult. Rational citizens can disagree about the appropriate form of government or the best rights to enshrine in a constitution. Because citizens' situations differ so markedly, they will typically prefer to coordinate on different forms of rights and governmental procedures. Therefore, no natural focal solutions exist to the coordination problem. In terms of the model, if citizens use their own idiosyncratic logic to decide when to punish the sovereign or government, they will fail to coordinate effective resistance. To solve this coordination problem, a focal point that is incentive-compatible for all the citizens needed for enforcement must be constructed.

The approach developed in this paper helps explain how such coordination may arise. Suppose the two players (that is, two c's) represent members of two opposing groups in society; the Federalists and Anti-Federalists in the 1780s United States; the Whigs and Tories in late-seventeenth-century England; the royalists and the republicans in nineteenth-century France; and the left and the right in both mid-to-late-twentieth-century Spain and late-twentieth and early-twenty-first-century Chile.

In each of these settings, two sides held opposing views about the appropriate constitution, the allocation of political power, and the constitution's specification of citizen rights. Abstractly, creating a stable constitution by means of a focal point-coordination equilibrium requires rules that benefit both groups. To succeed in creating a constitution that fosters coordination, neither side can impose a set of rules that provides benefits exclusively to its group (for example, if one of the c's forms a coalition with S against the other b). Instead the players must arrive at a set of constitutional principles that are sufficiently convergent – and hence valuable – to members of both groups so that both are willing to participate in a constitutional coordination equilibrium. Put another way, the incentive-compatibility constraint requires that both players be better off under the constitution for them to be willing to take costly actions to defend it.

Constitutions with impersonal rights for all citizens are unlikely to emerge if one of the two sides has the upper hand and dominates politics. Under these circumstances, it is generally not feasible to create a focal solution that supports law and legal attributes. A dominant side typically has little incentive to foster creation of a focal solution that grants rights to the other faction. By virtue of domination, this side gets what it wants without attracting the support of its opponents. Dominant groups instead create societies with privileges rather than rights, excluding the opposition, in what North, Wallis, and Weingast (2009) call natural states. In so many of these societies, allowing the opposition to participate does not lead to open access with a stable democratic constitution, but risks a change in the dominant party in which the former opposition takes power and suppresses the previous dominant party.

For this reason, many new constitutions emerge during crises or settings where neither party dominates, so the two parties must accommodate each other, creating a constitution that makes both sides better off. Elster (2000, ch. 2) observes that most long-term stable constitutions emerged during crises.[9] The U.S. Constitution emerged in the crisis over the failure of the

---

[9] Crises are not a sufficient condition for stable constitutions. As North, Wallis, and Weingast (2009, ch. 2–3) observe, most natural states face recurrent crises that alter the natural state (e.g., who holds power) but do not move the natural state along the transition to open access order.

Articles of Confederation; Spain's constitution during the unstable years following the death of long-term dictator Francisco Franco; Fifth Republic France emerged during the failures of the Fourth Republic and threats of a military coup; and Chile's during the transition to democracy in the wake of a coup followed by a military government.

In each case, the new constitution represented a pact or compromise between the opposing factions. These pacts had several features that made them self-enforcing in the sense that all the parties to the pact had incentives to maintain it (Mittal and Weingast 2013). First, neither side dominated. Second, both sides were made better off by the pact. Third, the pact created new rights and public procedures of government. Finally, each side was willing to help defend the constitution, including the provisions that protected their opposition. The latter holds when both sides are better off under the constitution and when failing to defend the constitution destroys it, making them worse off.

For our purposes, we consider the third feature of self-enforcing pacts, namely, rights and process. Impersonal, universal rights are attractive when creating a focal-point solution to help citizens coordinate against sovereign transgressions. First, universal rights provide protections for those out of power. Universal and general rules are also attractive to each side because they structure the absence of privilege. Treating citizens in like circumstances alike – achieving a particular kind of generality – limits the ability of those in power to take advantage of those out of power. Finally, generality and universality are economizing. As we have emphasized, coordination to police sovereign transgressions requires that decentralized citizens react in concert to sovereign behavior. Systems of privilege are more difficult to police because they require more information and they reduce the benefits to those not privileged; they are therefore less likely to foster coordination among large groups of decentralized citizens. Other attributes of legal process are important here as well. As with private law, in constitutional law, stability of the rules, clarity, public promulgation, and consistency, for example, all foster economizing and coordination; and they help limit the ability of the majority to take advantage of the minority.

As an example, consider seventeenth-century England, where two groups were the Whigs and Tories. These groups had markedly different understandings of the constitution, and as a consequence failed to coordinate against the king who favored the Tories while transgressing the rights of the Whigs. Tories followed Filmore (1690), who argued for the "divine right of kings." In the constitutional context, this doctrine implied that while kings could do wrong, citizens nonetheless had a duty to obey. In this view, citizens had no right to resist. Whigs, in contrast, were followers of Locke, a major Whig theorist, who argued that citizens had the right to resist unconstitutional actions by the king (Locke 1689). Because the citizens were so deeply divided over constitutional issues, they failed to coordinate against the king, who abused citizen rights.

This setting characterized much of post-Restoration England, from 1660 until the Glorious Revolution of 1688, which occurred when King James II turned on his own supporters, the Tories. A sufficient number of Tories at this moment set aside their beliefs in the divine right, coming to agree with the Whigs so that, in concert, they made several constitutional changes. First, taking active resistance to the king, they displaced King James and brought William and Mary to the throne. Second, they made an explicit agreement, negotiated in Parliament, which explained the reasons for this action and announcing that any future king who violated these constitutional provisions would risk the same treatment as James.

During the Glorious Revolution, Parliament assumed the role of constitutional steward. The new rules limiting the king, as embodied in the bill of rights, had the various features of legal attributes predicted by our model. For example, the constitution became general and universal in practice, which it had not been before. Similarly, although the constitution had always held kings to respect laws of Parliament, both Tudor and Stuart monarchs honored this in the breach. Laws of parliament became sacrosanct following the Glorious Revolution, regardless of whom they benefited or harmed. Kings who violated them were subject to resistance. The rules were also prospective, clear, and public.

In the United States of the mid-1780s, the failure of the first constitution, the Articles of Confederation, meant that Americans could not provide valued public goods, some desperately needed, especially national security, but also a common market and a stable monetary system. At this time, the Federalists proposed to improve the national government's powers to accomplish these goals while the Anti-Federalists opposed new powers as dangerous to liberty. Under the Articles of Confederation's unanimity rules, the Federalists failed. Finally, in 1787, the Federalists proposed a new constitution that took into account many of the Anti-Federalists' concerns, incorporating a series of rights and governmental procedures designed to mitigate the Anti-Federalists' fears of a national government too strong. They did so by creating a new focal point that embodied legal attributes in the new document, thereby helping citizens to coordinate, including the well-known system of checks and balance, a series of brightline constitutional restrictions (such as limits on direct taxation or the taking of property), a national government solely of enumerated powers targeted to national problems, and a strong system of federalism that at once decentralized powers to the states and ensured that states would remain strong and be vigilant monitors of the national government. As our quote from Madison in the previous section emphasized, states would monitor "encroachments" by the national government and not only sound the alarm, but coordinate citizen action to resist the national government.

An important part of the constitution's success, including its ability to become a stable focal equilibrium, involved legal attributes. Creating a constitution characterized by universality, generality, stability, public promulgation, clarity, and consistency all worked to secure support of pivotal Anti-Federalists. In particular, the Federalist founders did not create a system of privilege that advantaged holders of national power. They instead created a system that fostered the provision of widely valued public goods while protecting citizen rights and limiting the national government's potential intrusion in other policy areas. A wide variety of universal general rights, including the Bill of Rights, applied to the Anti-Federalists even if the Federalists were to control the national government (as most believed would occur with Washington likely to become the first president).

Hofstadter (1969) describes the emergence of another important piece of constitutional liberty, namely, that the opposition party came to be seen as a necessary and legal part of a competitive democracy rather than as a form of sedition. This shift in perspective changed the notion of honorable and wrongful behavior, making it more general and universal and less personal – that is, less tied to which party held power at any given moment.

To see how this shift in perspective came to be, we observe that two parties arose very quickly under the new U.S. Constitution, the Federalists under the leadership of Washington, Adams, and Hamilton, and the Republicans under Jefferson and Madison. Each party questioned the other's legitimacy and sought to vanquish it. This period did not embrace the idea of the loyal opposition.

With the demise of the Federalists in the second decade of the nineteenth century, many Jeffersonians thought they would be able to implement their programs without opposition. They failed. Instead, the Jeffersonians fell into different factions, each vying to implement their own vision of the Jeffersonian legacy. Martin Van Buren, a major political innovator (creating, for example, the party nomination convention), understood the problem. He realized that absence of an opposition led to the infighting among different factions of the party. The presence of political competition, he argued, forced factions in each party to make the difficult political compromises necessary for a party to win.

The idea of a loyal opposition emerged in this context, when people recognized that party competition for power was a positive thing (Hofstadter 1969). This idea also represented a coordination equilibrium in which citizens came to see that political competition by parties had positive effects and that restrictions against the opposition were illegitimate. The new coordination equilibrium had legal attributes, treating those out of power in the same way as those who held power today. In order for individual factions of the ruling party to participate in upholding the rules – to punish their fellow faction members for attempting to silence opposition; or not to punish the opposition, for example, for voicing difference – they had to know what the rules defining "loyal" opposition were. The same point holds for members of the opposition – they had to punish each other for overstepping the bounds of loyal opposition. Finally, the system had to exhibit universality – members of all parties had to be confident that the boundaries of loyal would be applied equally to themselves whenever their party was in the opposition. Throughout the country, states began to pass new laws regulating party entry and competition, including creating primary systems.

Chile's transition from a natural state to a stable constitutional democracy took a different path but nonetheless reflects the lessons of our approach.[10] As with the United States, the process of writing a new constitution began with action by one side – the authoritarian dictatorship of President Augusto Pinochet, representing the political Right. Members of this faction designed a constitution that benefitted themselves. The constitution included various forms of authoritarian "enclaves" as they are called – counter-majoritarian constitutional features that included senators appointed for life – and the removal of various issues from politics, such as property rights and retribution for the authoritarian regime's actions. The political Left acceded to participate under this constitution, but did not consider the constitution legitimate, notably because the Right's control of the military meant ongoing military threat.[11] In addition, the constitution's counter-majoritarian features protecting the Right not only constrained the government in ways

---

[10] This discussion draws on Alberts, Warshaw, and Weingast (2012), Londregan (2000), Scully (1996) and Valenzuela (1994).

[11] Despite being forced to operate under the military-imposed constitution, the opposition (and subsequently the new government) "wanted to avoid giving Pinochet any excuse to renege on the constitutional deal that had been struck" (Siavelis 2008: 193).

that the Right sought to protect, but also hobbled the government's ability to address many important policy problems.

By design, the constitution created divided government – allowing the Right to retain veto power over the government through its control of the senate, in part through its enclaves. The Right accurately forecasted that they would win about 40 percent of the vote. Adding senators for life appointed by the Right granted the Right a majority in the senate and hence veto power over all legislation. Importantly, the constitution also allowed the Left to govern as the Left won majorities for both the presidency and the lower chamber for two decades.

Over time, the political environment changed in several ways. The Left retained power in part because it continued to promote stable economic growth and did not threaten the Right's biggest concerns. Perhaps most important, the original appointees to various enclaves changed, some through expiration of their long terms and others through death of the officeholder. This allowed the left government to replace many right-wing holders of enclaves with individuals sympathetic to their interests. Throughout, the Left moderated many of its views, for example, no longer questioning property rights. These factors combined with the successful economy and the government's gradual control over the enclaves to allow the left to alter the constitution, removing many of the veto enclaves. Importantly, it did so within the existing rules for constitutional amendment, enhancing the legitimacy of the changes. This constitutional change completed the transition to stable, constitutional democracy.

The success of the revised constitution is consistent with our model. The Pinochet constitution failed to obtain widespread legitimacy because the Left acceded to it by threat. The Left had no incentive to support this constitution over the long term, although the Left constrained its behavior due to the threat of military intervention. Over time, the Left came to control more of the veto enclaves and the military. Economic success, widely valued and supported by most Chileans, became an element of the Left's political success. Over time, the Left had greater incentives to honor the rules as they allowed the Left to compete successfully in elections. With the 2005 constitutional changes, the Left removed the most inimical features of Pinochet's constitution, such as all nonelected senate seats and eliminating the provisions prohibiting the president from naming, firing, and promoting high-level military officials. The Left nonetheless retained the constitution's essential core.

With these revisions in place, both sides came to support the constitution. The Left had strong incentives to enforce the constitution. The revisions at once removed the parts the Left deemed illegitimate; and, as we have observed, the constitution allowed them to rule. Because the Left came to support and honor the constitution, the Right had far less to fear from the Left: The constitution protected the Right's more important interests by guaranteeing property rights and protection from prosecution for misdeeds during the authoritarian period. The new constitution therefore fostered decentralized coordination of both the Left and the Right to protect constitutional provisions and rights, including those that were subject to uncertainty in the democratic regime that preceded the military coup in 1973. In terms of our model, the modifications in the constitution allowed both Right and Left to see the constitutional order as sufficiently convergent with their interests over time as to make the new constitution an equilibrium.

5. Conclusions

We ask how is a stable constitutional order sustained? To address this issue, we develop a new perspective on constitutions to explain three distinct aspects of constitutions – first, that constitutions have a series of legal attributes, often associated with the rule of law, such as generality, stability, consistency, publicity; second, that constitutions involve a process of public reasoning, particularly as they are applied over time and in new circumstances; and third, that successful constitutions support an equilibrium in which citizens of divergent views and interests are willing to coordinate to uphold the constitution and retaliate against those who violate constitutional provisions. Our answer builds on earlier insights, notably, that constitutions reflect in part a coordination game (Sugden 1986; Weingast 1997; Cooter 1998; Basu 2000; McAdams 2000; Mailath et al. 2001; Myerson 2004; Dixit 2004) and that, to be sustained, constitutions must be incentive compatible (Binmore 1994, 1998; Weingast 1997).

Our approach begins by emphasizing that sustaining a constitution involves decentralized coordination of resistance. No higher authority exists with coercive power to exogenously enforce a constitution. But coordination raises significant problems: What should the constitution entail? How do a large number of dispersed and disparate individuals with a potentially wide range of idiosyncratic views about constitutional issues rely on similar rules so that their resistance strategies deter unconstitutional actions?

In order for a constitution to be an equilibrium, citizens must have incentives to abide by the constitution and, importantly, to participate in decentralized enforcement of the constitution. We argue that, to do so, a constitution must have several characteristics. First, it must create a focal solution to the coordination game so that citizens can rely on a single set of rules. Second, that focal point must secure a constitutional order that is sufficiently convergent with the interests of diverse citizens to incentivize enough of them to participate in upholding the constitution. Third, the constitutional regime must have legal attributes. These attributes help citizens coordinate because they raise the value of coordination to a large number of people; they support confidence in the durability of an order that citizens prefer to the alternatives; and they economize on the costs of coordination by ruling out more complex systems of rules, such as those that involve not only the circumstances of the case, but personal variables, such as where a person sits in the social hierarchy. Fourth, the constitution must include a system for creating public logic around legal rules. The reason is that the circumstances under which citizens interact with the state are so varied that successful constitutions cannot simply be comprised of a list or algorithm about constitutional and unconstitutional behavior; it must instead be a common knowledge set of rules in combination with a logic so that people can extrapolate the logic from rules into a wide variety of new circumstances.

Our approach differs from standard philosophy of the law and constitutions in several ways. We agree about the normative value of many of the legal attributes, such as generality, stability, and consistency. Yet we emphasize that constitutions must also be unique; that is, among the many possible legal (coordination) equilibria, the constitution must create a unique set of rules and legal reasoning around which people can coordinate. Reflecting the ever-changing world, the legal system must have an authoritative steward, such as a hierarchical court system with a supreme or constitutional court. The system of stewardship extends existing rules to new circumstances in a unique way, resolving problems of ambiguity – which threaten coordination – when multiple and conflicting interpretations can be extrapolated from existing rules. This system may also arbitrate differences among lower courts, again, to create a unique set of rules.

We applied this perspective to issues in constitutional law, suggesting that our approach yields important lessons about how constitutions are sustained. Given that most constitutions fail, assuring defense of the constitution is a major – and clearly difficult – function. Many have observed the coordination function of a constitution (Hardin 1989; Ordeshook 1992; Weingast 1997). We build on the observation that constitutions facilitate coordination, adding that constitutions that systematically incorporate legal attributes are more likely to induce citizen participation in defending the constitution against violations.

Acknowledgments

The authors thank Brian Tamanaha for helpul comments.

8

Culture, Institutions, and Modern Growth

Joel Mokyr

1. Introduction

In his *Understanding the Process of Economic Change*, North for the first time came to grips with the economic significance for economics of cultural beliefs and ideology. He repeatedly referred to them as "scaffolding" for institutions.[1] He pointed out that human beings try to "render their environment intelligible" and erect scaffolds, platforms that allow us to stand on and do things together. Scaffolds are thus constructions that "define the formal structure of incentives and dis-incentives that are a first approximation to the choice set. But they also are the informal structure of norms, conventions, and codes of conduct... and the way the institutional structure acts upon and reacts to other factors that affect... changes in the stock of knowledge."[2]

In what follows, I propose to do three things. First, I will unpack these definitions and come up with a meaningful and useable definition of some Northean terms that could bear a bit of clarification. Second, I will propose to take a look at culture through the perspective of cultural evolution and suggest ways in which we can understand how and why culture changes. Third, I make an attempt to apply ideas from this framework to provide an understanding of a special case of considerable interest to students of

[1] The term in this context originates apparently in Andy Clark (1998). It refers to the cognitive structures such as language, religion, and other shared cultural beliefs that allow us to interpret our social and physical environment.

[2] In recent years, economists and economic historians have "rediscovered" culture. Early work by Greif (1994) and Peter Temin's presidential address (1997) are examples of this development in economic history. In theoretical economics, the work of Samuel Bowles (2004) and Roland Benabou (2008) stands out, while in applied work, the pioneering paper by Zak and Knack (2001) and that of Guido Tabellini (2008) should be mentioned.

economic change, namely the British economy on the eve of the Industrial Revolution.

Culture, institutions, and behavior can actually be easily and usefully separated and understood in terms of evolutionary theory. North, like the rest of us, was interested in understanding economic *behavior* and stressed that institutions are essentially incentives and constraints that society puts up on individual behavior. Institutions are in a way much like prices in a competitive market: individuals can respond to them differently, but they must take the parametrically and cannot change them.[3] Human behavior is first and foremost conditioned by "culture," and in his 2005 book North argued forcefully that without understanding culture, we cannot really understand why societies have the institutions they do. The definition of culture he borrowed from Hayek, as the "transmission in time of our accumulated stock of knowledge," but here "knowledge" was defined as including a kitchen-sink of "habits, skills, emotional attitudes" and, confusingly enough, "institutions." This needs clarification. How should we separate "institutions" from "culture," and how do they both affect economic outcomes?

Institutions, that is, the rules by which society operates – both formal laws and social norms and customs – are heavily conditioned by what is believed by its members. Human behavior is something we observe, much like an individual phenotype, while culture is the "information" that underlies this, much like a genotype. "Institutions" in this kind of analogy constitute the environment that determines how cultural elements lead to behavior. But social theory is not precisely like biology: in human history, culture shaped institutions. If this were all there was to it, things would be simple enough: all we had to do is develop a theory of why people believe and like the things they do, and we would have arrived at a good explanation of their institutions and thus economic performance. Unfortunately, two major factors intervene here: first, institutions have

---

[3] McCloskey (2010, 300) criticizes this view, arguing that incentives are overrated and that behavior is only at times described as responding to incentives and at other times it is best described as "improvisational comedy." Instead she prefers "complex and interacting system of norms, structures, and cultural understandings that shape . . . behavior." Leaving aside the vagueness of terms such as "system" and "structures," she misses the point that the existence of prices and rewards to certain behavior does not require that all agents respond to them rationally – all it says is that such costs exist and that individuals who fail to observe the rules pay some price. In that sense, indeed, thinking of institutions as analogous to budget constraints (which are set by relative prices) is quite helpful. She is, of course, correct in that institutions must be understood in conjunction with beliefs, that is, culture. In equilibrium, in order to be legitimate, institutions have to correspond to the beliefs of the society on which they are imposed.

a large aleatory component to them, so that seemingly similar cultures can lead to violently different institutional outcomes, as in the cases of North and South Korea or Costa Rica and Nicaragua. Small differences at critical junctures can make a big and persistent difference.[4] Second, there is a feedback from institutions to what people actually believe, although this feedback is not well-understood. By setting school curricula and influencing the media, existing powers can affect what people actually believe. At times it works to legitimize existing institutions, but not always. Seven decades of Marxist rules in Russia somehow failed to convert the bulk of Russians into believing in the class struggle and the principles of Leninist revolution.

But it is not by culture and luck alone that institutions evolve. Acemoglu and Robinson (2012) point out that institutions reflect political power and are set up to benefit the allocation of resources in favor of those who have political power. A very different perspective has been provided recently by Douglas Allen (2012). He sees institutions as determined by information costs, geared to produce workable incentive structures in activities in which principals hired agents but found it very difficult to monitor them.

2. Culture and Evolution

Defining culture once again might seem foolhardy, except that many scholars concerned with it seem not to bother with precise definitions, which may lead to misunderstandings.[5] Culture is about those pieces of the mind that are not inherited and hard-wired in the brain. It is about elements that are learned from others. A definition consistent with much of the literature in cultural anthropology and that is sufficiently restrictive would be: *Culture is a set of beliefs, values, and preferences, capable of affecting behavior, that are socially (not genetically) transmitted and that are shared by some subset of society.*[6] There may be legitimate doubt whether this – or indeed any – definition of culture will ever be operational, for instance, by asking which subsets ascribe to what beliefs. But, as I shall try to show in Section 3, even if cultural groups are inevitably open-ended ("*who* are the Jews?" for instance), we can identify cultural elements they share. I also submit that

---

[4] This is one of the main arguments of Acemoglu and Robinson (2012).

[5] Eric Jones's otherwise perceptive book (2006) does not provide a precise definition and thus opens itself to possible misunderstanding (Grantham 2007).

[6] The definition is very similar to the one proposed by Boyd and Richerson (1985, 2; 2005, 5).

using evolutionary terms will be a first step in making the concept more operational (Mesoudi 2011).

This definition requires a bit more elaboration: **beliefs** contain statements of a positive or factual nature that pertain to the state of the world, both the physical and metaphysical environment and social relations.[7] **Values** pertain to normative statements about society and social relations (often thought of as ethics and ideology), whereas **preferences** are normative statements about individual matters such as consumption and personal affairs. Clearly culture is decomposable, that is, it consists of cultural elements or features and such traits are largely shared by people of the same culture (much like genes that are shared by members of the same species), but each individual is unique in that it is unlikely that two people share precisely the same combination of cultural elements. It is important that culture is *collective*: a single individual cannot have "culture" that is not shared by others anymore than one can be a member of a species without sharing the vast majority of one's genes with others. Indeed, some would go as far as to say that culture can exist only as an interpersonal or social entity, though that definition is not useful for my purposes. Furthermore, as has been pointed out many times, culture is a Lamarckian system in the sense that culture involves social learning, and that beliefs, values, and knowledge that are learned from others can be transmitted further.

What about outcomes (or, to pursue the analogy, phenotypes)? It seems useful to separate observable *behavior* (i.e., actions) from *culture* that motivates and guides it. In determining these outcomes, cultural and hard-wired motives are intertwined, but the hard-wired component is largely identical across societies. Not all beliefs matter to economic (or any) behavior. A great deal of culture, much like junk DNA, that does not code for any known proteins, just "is" in our minds, and conditions no identifiable actions. Yet, an analogy that sees culture as "genotypical" and actions as "phenotypical" is only very approximate, and caution is called for in employing it.

The third element in this setup is institutions. Institutions, of course, were central to North's interpretation of history. Greif (2006), in his magisterial attempt to define historical institutions with care, points out a problem with the basic "institutions-as-rules" idea, namely that without a meta-rule

---

[7] As such, "beliefs" should be interpreted as to contain *knowledge*, both codifiable and tacit, as well as human skills and capabilities. Greif's (1994) notion of cultural beliefs concerning expectations about the behavior of others would be included in this definition, as would religious beliefs and useful knowledge.

that rules should be respected and followed, rules and laws may well be empty. Moreover, as Szostak (2009, 234) notes, many institutions are little more than the "codification" of beliefs. Thus, an aversion of violence in a society may lead to formal legislation against it. Here we can find a clue to an operational distinction between the two. A cultural belief that the use of drugs is harmful will give rise to an institution that mandates prison terms for drug use.[8] For my purposes, then, it seems best to define culture as something entirely of the mind, which can differ from individual to individual and is, to some extent, a matter of individual choice, whereas institutions are socially-determined conditional incentives and consequences to actions. As noted, these incentives are parametrically given to every individual and therefore create the structure of incentives in this society. Institutions as "rules" can be seen as a special case: the rules specify a certain behavior to be proper and legal, but also specify the penalties for breaking them and the rewards for meeting them.[9] Greif solves the problem he sets forth by stressing that the set of cultural elements includes the *legitimacy* of existing institutions – that is, a belief that these institutions are just and beneficial and that therefore the rules should be complied with, and that those who break them should be punished. Indeed, as he has pointed out, institutions do not arise by decree alone. Those who issue them, from Hammurabi to Napoleon, must have some authority assuring that people are willing to live by the decrees that they issue. All the same, legitimacy can be and is often contested, and thus the political struggles around institutions, and the need to punish those who violate the rules.

How have economists employed the concept of culture in trying to understand economic change as well as persistence over time?[10] The mechanism through which culture is believed to have affected economic performance is primarily through ideas of trust and cooperativeness, as well as willingness to abstain from free-riding behavior and individuals' beliefs regarding

[8] Indeed, narcotics illustrate the full gamut of our definition of culture: "beliefs" contains a concept that narcotics may harm one's or others' health; "values" the notion that a society in which others use drugs is a bad society or that there is something ethically wrong with drugs; "preferences" simply means that one does not like to use them. All three contribute to a society that sets up institutions that heave penalties on their use.

[9] This view is a variation on Bowles (2004, 47–48) who defines institutions as "laws, informal rules, and conventions that give a durable structure to social interactions . . . and make conformity a best response to virtually all members of the relevant groups."

[10] The literature on the topic has been growing by leaps and bounds. Especially striking examples are Guiso, Sapienza and Zingales (2008); Dell (2010); and Voigtländer and Voth (2011).

the behavior of others.[11] The importance of these elements was already pointed out by John Stuart Mill and has recently been shown to explain income differences between nations (Zak and Knack 2001; Guiso, Sapienza, and Zingales 2006; Tabellini 2008). The main mechanism through which this works is through the notion that trust and reputation reduce transaction costs and opportunistic behavior and thus make commerce easier and cheaper, reduce rent-seeking, improve the supply of public goods, and lead to a more efficient allocation of *existing* resources.

More recently, economists have also become interested in preferences relevant to economic growth: attitudes toward education, work, time, patience, self-control, discipline, and similar areas. They also help determine, for instance, whether preferences might be "other-regarding" – that is, whether the consumption of others affects one's well-being and whether preferences might be "process-regarding" – that is, whether the utility one derives from a good depends on the way a certain state was reached rather than on the intrinsic quality of the state (Bowles 2004, 109; Bowles and Gintis 2009). Both types of preferences are not normally part of economic preferences, but there is no inherent reason they should not be. Such preferences affect economic growth in multiple ways: more "patience" – that is, a lower rate of time preference – leads to the accumulation of physical and human capital and more and harder work. Attitudes about the welfare of others affect individuals' ability to cooperate on public projects and common-resource management.

Can evolutionary models help us understand the role of culture in economic change? In recent years economists such as Galor and Moav (2002), and Clark (2007) have come back to Darwinian models of culture and tried to find in them keys to modern economic history. Their arguments are basically that certain subsets within society displayed cultural characteristics that increased their fitness and at the same time exhibited certain characteristics consonant with economic growth. Hard-working entrepreneurial types who believed in educating children had more surviving offspring. Through differential reproduction, then, these groups increased their relative size in the population to the point where they could alter the trajectory of the economy. There is nothing wrong with this approach in principle, except that differential reproduction of human individuals seems too slow a process to accomplish a transition from a slow-growing to a modern

---

[11] In Greif's (1994, 915) terms, cultural beliefs are expectations that individuals have about the actions that others will take. To that we should add the further belief that individuals hold regards the morality of a particular action.

economy even a few centuries. More importantly, it leaves out the more interesting aspects of culture, namely that beliefs and preferences are not received just from one's parents but absorbed from others, such as peers, teachers, and influential strangers in what is known as horizontal or oblique transmission.[12]

A more plausible way to use evolutionary models in economic growth is to take cultural elements such as ideas, beliefs, or "memes" to be the units of selection rather than carriers. This is what I will call "choice-based social learning."[13] The historical argument I will make is that not *all* culture is absorbed vertically from one's parents or from a "random" individual in society as in the Bisin and Verdier (2001) model. People can be *persuaded* by others; they learn and imitate and in so doing, they make choices of what to learn and from whom. They accept some options and reject others. While their capability to do so is highest at a young age, it never quite goes away, as the example of Douglass C. North's intellect proves abundantly. What matters to history is that the proportion of culture absorbed from non-parents changes over time as technology and modes of transmission transform and that the content individuals absorb from others changes. This points to an important difference between cultural and natural evolution: in the former, the speed of change depends not only on the frequency of innovations ("mutations"), but also on the rate of cultural transmission. All the same, this difference does not invalidate the analogy.

Darwin was the first to point out in his *Descent of Man* that culture exhibited certain evolutionary characteristics.[14] The analogy consists of three elements. One is that cultures, much like species, have a broad *variation* of traits, and many of these traits are shared among certain groups of individuals and distinguish them from those belonging to other groups. Yet the lines are often blurry, as they are between species, and overlaps are

---

[12] In her popular *The Nurture Assumption*, Harris (2009) amasses a great deal of evidence to show that the cultural impact of parents on their children in today's society is very limited. In her view, based on a great deal of evidence, social behavior is largely the result of the interactions of children with their peers, that is, other children, and that parents have only limited effect on their children past the toddler years.

[13] In principle, the three types of choice take place simultaneously on multiple levels: selection on cultural elements, selection on individuals displaying these traits, and selection on societies in which such individuals are common.

[14] Darwin made this point especially poignantly with respect to language, one of the main components of any culture Darwin (1859/1871, 466). The classic works in the mid 1980s were by Cavalli-Sforza and Feldman (1981) and Boyd and Richerson (1985). It has since become a cornerstone of a certain line of cultural argument associated with Richard Dawkins and his followers, who have tried to identify units of cultural analysis equivalent to genes.

common. The second is that culture, much like genes, is passed on from generation to generation, through mitosis in eukaryotic cells and through socialization and choice-based social learning in cultural processes. Children are being socialized at a high rate by other individuals, but the socialization of young individuals is not all there is to choice-based cultural evolution; adults can be subject to persuasion and other forms of cultural ontogeny and engage in choice-based learning albeit at a declining rate as they age.[15] The third is that change is adaptive in that when there is a change in the environment, there is a tendency of cultural traits to change through the retention of some and the elimination of other elements. The exact unit (or level) on which this selection operates is at the very center of the story, as we shall see below. Again, it is important not to push the evolutionary analogy too far, looking for units such as memes that would be similar to genes and even be "selfish" like them. Evolutionary models are larger than Richard Dawkins, even larger than Charles Darwin.[16]

What is actually gained from an evolutionary approach? Economists still committed to a Popperian notion that science should make some kind of falsifiable predictions will find little of use here, but historians trying to make sense of the past may find some of its implications helpful. Below I list some of the main advantages of an evolutionary approach to an economic history that tries to account for cultural elements.

First, evolution is about the interaction between a pre-existing environment, in which an innovation is introduced, and the innovation itself. The exact nature of innovation remains a stochastic variable, even if innovations are not purely random (as mutations are in a purely Weissmannian world). We may never know precisely why a certain idea occurs to an individual at a particular time, and why in some societies certain ideas never seem to have occurred to anyone. But even if the nature of innovations were predictable, we would not be able to predict with much certainty their success, unless we could establish in advance their "fitness" relative to the environment in which they take place. Yet, as has been pointed out many times before,

---

[15] Social values may be part of the life cycle, as illustrated by the famous and often misattributed quote, now a cliché, implying that people are liberal or socialist at a young age and become more conservative with age. The original statement appears to be due to the nineteenth-century French politician François Guizot.

[16] Alex Mesoudi (2011) makes a persuasive case that the neo-Darwinian principles are not needed for an evolutionary theory of culture. These principles were formulated after Darwin. They include the Weismann barrier (acquired characteristics are not passed on to following generations); the random ("blind") occurrence of mutations (so that all direction is imparted by selection); and the particulate nature of transmission in discrete units (genes).

there is clearly an impossibility theorem here: we cannot predict the fitness of an idea because when it "infects" more and more individuals, it may start changing institutions and thus the environment in which it operates. Recall that for an individual the institution is parametrically given, but a sufficiently large number of people can bring about institutional change and thus change the "environment" in which the innovation finds itself. Evolutionary models, most emphatically, forewarn us against hindsight bias, the mistaken belief that eventual outcomes were inevitable or even highly probable ex ante. Steven Jay Gould has asked if we rewound and replayed life's tape, whether the history of life would look the same, and answered in a resounding negative (Gould 1989, 48). How different, exactly, it would be is of course disputable.

Second, evolutionary systems are characterized by a fundamental *duality* between information and action, between genotype and phenotype. Distinctions between genotype and phenotype are hazardous to extend to cultural history, but all the same, it seems, something can be learned. Culture is about matters of the mind; behavior and actions are the observable outcomes of preferences and knowledge. But, as already noted, there is no easy mapping from beliefs to behavior any more than there is from genes to phenotypes; at best there are loose statistical associations. One reason is that beliefs, much like other genotypical processes, affect "adjacent" beliefs. We can indeed speak of cultural pleiotropy, much like in evolutionary processes. *Pleiotropy* means that a certain genotypic change leads to more than one phenotyical effect, because of the spillover effects on genes in the proximity of the mutation, in a sort of genetic packaging. A similar packaging exists in cultural beliefs.[17] A mirror-opposite phenomenon is *epistasis*, in which more than one piece of information is required to jointly bring out a certain trait or behavior. Such "bundling" occurs very often in economically relevant beliefs. The rise of "capitalist behavior" may have required a growth in the belief in the virtue and dignity of commercial activity (McCloskey 2010), together with a growth in the belief in the value of useful knowledge, as well as a growth in the taste for luxury goods.[18]

---

[17] Thus being an evangelical Christian or a liberal democrat normally involves a certain package of cultural beliefs and preferences about many social and political matters, ranging from abortion to Pinot Grigio.

[18] A good example can once again be found in the history of technology. In Mokyr (2002) I distinguish between propositional knowledge and prescriptive knowledge. There is no easy mapping between the two. There are times when techniques are used with virtually no understanding of why and how they work. At other times, the necessary underlying knowledge may well be there, but the techniques fail to emerge. The most rapid progress,

Third, the dynamics of evolutionary systems is produced by superfecundity and selection. The system throws up more variants than it can possibly accommodate, and so some form of winnowing must take place. The notion of natural selection in biology is purely metaphorical, but in cultural systems the idea of choice-based cultural evolution requires that people actually make conscious decisions to choose one cultural element over another and then display the behavior implied by this choice. Choices are made by agents who choose cultural variants neither as perfectly rational agents of standard economics nor as mindless mechanical replicators of biological models. They are somewhere in between. In Bowles's words, they are "adaptive agents" who learn when exposed to new cultural variants and choose whether to adopt them or not (Bowles 2004, 60) using a variety of criteria or "biases." As John Ziman (2000, 50) pointed out, selectionist models consist of dynamical magnification of *rare events*. This is as true when we think of successful mutation or recombination in nature as when we think of macro invention and cultural innovation in human history. After all, cultural choices are made, but they are made very infrequently – few people are pro-life on Monday and pro-choice on Friday.

Fourth, evolutionary models are rich in that they allow change to occur on different selection levels. To see this, consider a cultural trait offered to an individual in a particular society. If the individual chooses the variant and not another, this is one level of selection at which choice-based cultural evolution occurs. Now assume, however, that the variant in question increases the fitness of this individual and thus extends her life expectancy and/or the number of surviving children who resemble her. Higher fitness increases the chances that the trait will be passed on, either vertically through the socialization of offspring or horizontally through infecting her immediate neighbors. Finally, suppose that society has now adopted the trait, and that it increases the fitness of this society (e.g., through more cooperation or adopting a superior technique); this may mean a higher population growth rate in a society that has adopted this trait and thus is likely to increase its frequency in the global population. Because cultural evolution happens at all levels, it can be at times lightning fast and at others move at a tectonic rate, as Eric Jones (2006, 47–48) has noted.

Fifth, like all evolutionary systems, culture is resistant to change. In the technical language of evolutionary dynamics, prevalent cultural variants are evolutionary stable strategies with respect to most conceivable innovations

---

however, occur when the two types of knowledge (say, theoretical mechanics and mechanical engineering) emerge together.

("mutants"). There are built-in mechanisms that maintain a certain stability, but the effectiveness of such mechanisms is itself a function of the content of the system. For instance, a religious culture that is out of tune with other cultural elements may adapt to reflect new beliefs, or cling to increasingly antiquated beliefs if the power structure within the organizations depends on these beliefs (as may be the case with the Catholic church today). But no matter what kind of cultural system we are looking at, there will some resistance to change, and many seemingly "fit" innovations will fail in a hostile institutional environment.

Sixth, evolution implies that easy generalizations about speed and direction of cultural change are doomed. Most of the time culture changes at a tectonic pace, surviving dramatic institutional and political shocks. But there are instances when culture changes quickly as a result of weakened resistance, perhaps, or some powerful exogenous shock that challenges existing cultural beliefs. An example would be attitudes toward race and women's rights in the United States in the last decades of the twentieth century, or the attitudes toward Zionism following the Holocaust. Thus, predictions about the precise direction of cultural change are hard to make. Much like evolutionary science, the strength of the methodology is in helping us make sense of the past rather than predict the future with precision. Because the unit of analysis continuously interacts with its environment and due to few time-invariant relations, it becomes unpredictable (Saviotti 1996, 31). If cultural change were less chaotic, history would have not been as sad or as interesting.

3. Biases in Cultural Evolution

If socialization occurs through nonparental (oblique or horizontal) channels, choice-based social learning or cultural transmission can be subject to what Boyd and Richerson call "biases." What is meant by bias here is that cultural choices follow certain identifiable patterns that make people choose one cultural element over another (Richerson and Boyd 2005). The type of bias and the rate of bias depend on the technological parameters of cultural transmission and on the cultural and institutional structure themselves. The more individuals are exposed to "menus" of cultural variants different from those offered by their parents, the more important such biases will be. The printing press, open science, mandatory schooling, and mass communications are natural developments that clearly affected the significance of such biases. At times, of course, even with oblique or horizontal transmission, parental culture was reproduced. If parents choose teachers much like themselves, or if there is little cultural variance in the community – for instance, in the Israeli kibbutz before 1970, where children were not socialized by their parents as much as by representatives of the community – the bias may be quite small. But in most societies, we can discern the operation of a variety of biases. They can be classified into the following categories.

Content-based bias: People pick cultural variants different from the ones they were taught by their parents because of the inherent qualities of the content of the new options. At times people look at the evidence, but often they try to judge a variant insofar that it is consistent and reconcilable with other beliefs they hold. They are convinced by new facts (or at times try to ignore them, as in Benabou 2008) or by new and persuasive theories. Thus, for example, Darwinism, which cast a new light on the evolution of species, had deep (and unintended) consequences for the cultural beliefs of certain groups. It was judged on the basis of its merit, but for a large number of people it clashed with other beliefs they held and was thus rejected. Marxism was another new item on the cultural menu of the second half of the nineteenth century, which persuaded many people to change their beliefs on the basis of the new cultural variant's inherent logic and its ability to fit the facts and allow people to interpret their environment.

But how do people exactly assess content? Why do some people choose to become Marxists or believe the germ theory of disease and others do not? Some knowledge and cultural beliefs are *tight*, which is to say, they are supported by a preponderance of easy-to-evaluate evidence so that there is little to choose from.[19] Few people in the twenty-first century hold on to the Ptolemaic universe, believe that smoking tobacco is safe, or think that a collectivist economic regime will bring about economic prosperity. But in many cases, when knowledge is not tight or when it is more complex to evaluate, beliefs may not become fixed in the population. This often leads to unpredictable distributions: few Americans believe that the earth is flat and that infectious diseases are caused by miasmas, but the theory of evolution is another matter.[20] Unless there is a relatively obvious and straightforward

---

[19] As I have argued elsewhere (e.g., Mokyr 2002, 6), it matters little whether the cultural variant chosen is in some definable sense "correct." What does matter, however, is whether it is "effective." By that I mean that it is consistent with other objectives that this society has. Thus if society prefers health over sickness, as seems plausible, then medical theories that imply techniques that actually make people better would be more likely to be chosen. The historical difficulty is, however, that evaluating the effectiveness of techniques, especially in medicine, may be quite difficult without large databases and the ability to analyze them.

[20] A 2009 Gallop Poll reported that 39 percent of Americans believed in the theory of evolution whereas 25 percent did not, and 36 percent had no opinion. The proportion of believers in evolution rose, as would be expected, with education and declined with the frequency

way of evaluating a cultural belief, people prefer to choose cultural variants that are consistent with their other beliefs and form a coherent whole. Cognitive science has shown that here is a built-in tendency to filter out information and ideas that in some way contradict strongly held beliefs and stereotypes (Henrich 2001). As noted, cultural variants tend to be subject to pleiotropic effects, that is, adjacent beliefs tend to occur together. We observe that cultural beliefs occur in clusters: those Americans who hold on to evangelical religion also tend to think that widespread gun ownership is desirable, that abortion and narcotics should be illegal, that marriage should be confined to heterosexual couples, that the Bible should be taken literally, and object to large-scale federal redistribution policies, although logically these beliefs are not all obviously connected.

Direct bias: A central feature of all social learning is that society appoints cultural authorities who have great influence on others' cultural beliefs.[21] Such authorities are especially important in religious contexts (priests), but are just as central in modern society, in which "experts" such as scientists, physicians, and others become central in helping others decide what is true, safe, effective, and moral. One reason is that complex social and physical processes are hard for laymen to comprehend, yet they may be essential to underpin certain important cultural beliefs. Subtle statistical models and sophisticated experimentation may be needed to discriminate between important conclusions about, say, the effects of nutrition or the causes of crime. Especially in the subset of cultural beliefs that I have referred to as "useful knowledge," that underpin production techniques in use, authorities and trusted experts are indispensable because such knowledge can operate effectively only if there is a fine subdivision of knowledge through specialization. They are an example of the "one-to-many" transmission (Seki and Ihara 2012).

The authority-driven, choice-based social learning process requires society to solve two major problems. The first is the question who appoints such authorities, who monitors their reliability, and who appoints the appointers and the monitors. The second is the problem that if authority is too powerful and too entrenched, it may establish an *orthodoxy*, that is, it may act to reduce and possibly eliminate its own contestability and thus

---

of church attendance. See http://www.gallup.com/poll/114544/darwin-birthday-believe-evolution.aspx (accessed July 5, 2010).

[21] Greif (2011) provides a special case of this in what he calls "moral authorities" who are assigned to decide what is morally appropriate. This example generalizes to a host of other cultural dimensions: medical authorities make diagnoses, educational authorities set school curricula, and leading scientists determine what is appropriate science.

crystallize and make further progress through innovation increasingly hard. It is a hallmark of societies that are open and culturally dynamic that all authorities are contestable. We may define successful *cultural entrepreneurs* as people who successfully contest and overthrow existing authorities and create a new competing variant that catches on among a substantial subset of society. Every society has in every generation men and women whose ideas are radically novel and, if accepted by a sufficiently large group, would change the cultural landscape in this society: this is one way of thinking about Martin Luther and Charles Darwin. Rapid cultural change occurs when a successful cultural entrepreneur either persuades existing authorities to adopt the innovation or overthrows them and becomes an authority him or herself.

Rhetorical bias: A bias can be imparted through persuasion, in which some charismatic and persuasive individual is simply very good at convincing others of the correctness of his or her views. Cultural entrepreneurs in many cases are successful not just on the basis of the message itself but also on the *framing* of their beliefs or theories. Historically, such persuasion often occurred through the disciples or epigones of cultural entrepreneurs. The doctrines of Marx were spread by such influential followers as Engels, Lenin, and Mao Zedong, whose own cultural innovations were comparatively marginal, those of Keynes famously by John Hicks and Alvin Hansen, among others. The cultural variants that emerged as the result of this dissemination process were often modified and altered by apostles and interpreters: Marxism did not always follow what Marx wrote, any more than Calvinism was wholly described by Calvin.[22] Rhetorical techniques are of course important here: commercials and propaganda campaigns are rhetorically-sophisticated attempts to persuade people of certain cultural variants (they can be beliefs, values, or preferences) on the basis of form as much as or more than content.

Model-based bias: The beliefs of people who are "role models" or appear worth imitating create a model that others follow because these traits are correlated with other features that are deemed desirable. Individuals (or groups) observe cultural elements of the most successful members of society and adopt their preferences and beliefs. Successful movie or sports stars are used to sponsor or endorse certain products or behaviors in the hope that their irrelevant but desirable qualities will induce others to

---

[22] As Landes (2000, 11) remarks in his discussion of Calvinism, its original "hard belief in predestination did not last more than a generation or two (it is not the kind of dogma that has lasting appeal)." One might even be tempted to add that the belief in predestination was doomed from the start.

adopt their apparent preferences or cultural beliefs. Such biases are a good illustration of the importance of framing effects in choice-based cultural evolution.

Frequency dependence: Individuals will often choose their cultural beliefs by simply determining what the majority of people in the relevant set around them believe. The logic of this bias is in part to save on information costs and in part to avoid the possible social sanction implied by differing from the majority. This conformism bias would tend to create homogenization, if it worked only in one direction. But there could be perverse frequency dependence through "rebellious" or deliberate nonconformist behavior, if such behavior is not penalized too severely. Indeed, in some models in which almost everyone conforms, it can be profitable to rebel. In the Bisin andVerdier framework, frequency bias is built in, because parents can choose only between socializing their children themselves or having them socialized by a randomly chosen other individual in society. Parents may prefer to choose an educator who will resemble their values, but because of agency problems, a higher chance of transmission "errors" is introduced. Moreover, children will be subject to conformist biases when in contact with peers. The economic logic of frequency dependence is similar to direct bias: in making cultural choices and learning of new cultural variants, people are trying to save information costs, and thus the importance of frequency bias depends on the costs of ascertaining the characteristics of the cultural feature in question.

As to the perverse frequency dependence: such individuals presumably are the populations from which many cultural entrepreneurs originate. Institutions differ in the way they treat cultural deviants, from burning heretics and banishing innovators, to a free-wheeling live-and-let-live mentality. In that sense, of course, cultural choices are reflexive: one important cultural value is whether to tolerate other (possibly heterodox) values and to give new cultural elements a fair chance to compete in the market places for ideas and values. A belief in cultural (including religious) tolerance can especially be of great economic value when it is relatively rare; it allows an economy to attract and absorb religious refugees who tend to be creative and networked. The willingness of seventeenth-century Netherlands and the United States in more recent centuries to accept Jews and dissenting Christians contributed a great deal to their economies, especially in high-skilled manufacturing and financial services.[23]

---

[23] In Industrial Revolution Britain, where de facto religious tolerance had been part of society after 1660, small religious groups such as Huguenots and Quakers played disproportionate large roles in the economy (Mokyr 2009, 114, 362).

Rationalization bias: One of the ways in which cultural change can take place or be resisted is through the existence of a historically given set of institutions, thus creating feedback from institutions to culture. There is an inherent tendency to internalize existing social norms and socially-mandated rules (Greif 2011). Suppose there is a law or social norm, such as a proscription on intimate relations with close relatives, that penalizes a certain action. Such penalties may make the action eventually seem undesirable *just* because there is a penalty associated with it. This might happen in an attempt to rationalize the institution (if it is punished, there must be a reason for it) or it may happen during the socialization by parents imbuing their children a sense of "sin" in some action that was punishable. What was once forbidden now becomes taboo. Some people tend to eat according to strict table manners even when they eat alone simply because they have internalized the rule of holding the knife with the right hand and a fork with the left. Yet the internalization of institutions and norms into preferences is probably evolutionarily unstable and can easily be "invaded" by a mutant, unless it is supported by some deeper ethical belief or other knowledge.[24] Thus people eating by themselves may drop their formal table manners but still wash their hands before eating for hygiene reasons.

Coercion bias: In a highly authoritarian or coercive society, cultural beliefs can be changed by force. Of course, one could never force people to *believe* certain propositions, only make them behave in ways they would not otherwise, that is, make them pretend as if they accepted the culture of the coercive authority. This can create preference falsification and what Greif and Tadelis have called crypto-morality.[25] On the whole, such schemes are unstable and can lead to sudden collapses, such as the fall of totalitarian states and the sharp decline of the ideologies that supported them. But political rulers can control and manipulate oblique and horizontal transmission mechanisms (schools, churches, media, spontaneous meetings) and thus try to influence beliefs and enforce what could be called political socialization. The historical evidence that this actually works at the level of values, based on the evidence of political revolutions, from the French to the Russian to the Iranian, is rather mixed. But clearly, schools and military service can reproduce certain elements of socialization such as a willingness to

---

[24] An example would be the Jewish dietary laws. Jews who grew up eschewing pork do often not like eating pork even when they have given up on the observance of other rules. Yet unless one were to discover a good medical reason to not eat pork, eventually more and more non-kosher Jews will overcome this reluctance.

[25] Kuran (1987, 1997); Greif and Tadelis (2010).

accept punctuality, discipline, temperance, and a belief in virtuousness of obedience, hard work, and new technology.

Salient events bias: Dramatic and traumatic events can have a discontinuous effect on culture through powerful framing effects. Catastrophes such as the Black Death, the Holocaust, or 9/11 changed ideology and beliefs through the powerful challenge such events can exert on existing beliefs.[26] Areas where such events are especially important are political ideology and social "values" that pertain to the role of the state. Major and dramatic failures of the free market will create more support for a more regulated and managed economy, as happened in the industrialized West in the 1930s. Major failures of a managed economy such as the former Soviet bloc will increase support for a free market economy both in affected areas and those competing with them.

4. Culture and Growth

How exactly does this kind of framework help us understand economic history, that is how does culture affect economic growth and change? There are three separate mechanisms that should, in principle, be kept apart.

The first and most obvious is that cultural beliefs are a critical variable in fostering *cooperation* and thus *exchange*. Trust, as has been pointed out many times, is a central transactions-cost-reducing device, and thus makes exchange at arm's length easier and cheaper and affects the economy through Smithian growth (Fukuyama 1996; Zak and Knack 2001). Related to trust is loyalty, which mitigates principal-agent problems and reduces opportunistic behavior. Public-mindedness, or *asabiya* in Ibn Khaldun's famous formulation, is another cultural element related to cooperation: the willingness to avoid free riding and contribute to a collective good despite the incentive that each individual has to shirk is a third element. Economic performance, no matter how we look at it, needs a certain level of cooperation and cannot accommodate an economy that consists entirely of extremely selfish free riders; principal agent issues and monitoring costs are just too pervasive (Seabright 2010).

---

[26] Less traumatic but salient events can have similar effects on cultural beliefs and eventually on institutions. Two examples are the Great London Smog of December 1952, which sufficiently changed views of environmental pollution to lead to a slew of environmental legislation, and the Three Mile Island accident in the United States in 1979, which changed the public perception of the cost-benefit calculus of nuclear power in the United States and effectively ended the construction of new reactors.

Ideology is a mechanism by which society overcomes free-rider problems, as North pointed out as early as 1981 (North 1981, 31). Such public-mindedness includes the willingness to punish defectors, even if that comes at a personal price. The cultural elements that account for trust and loyalty tend to be frequency-dependent; anyone who observes that most others are trusting, loyal, and public-minded are more likely to be so themselves, and also be willing to penalize a few deviants who try to take advantage. The seminal work of Greif on the Maghribi traders is perhaps the best illustration of this kind of historical phenomenon, but there are many other examples.[27] Much less explored by economic historians, but of equal interest, is the importance of religion. Many religions postulated an omniscient and moral God who meted out justice to those who did not play by the rules and exhibited opportunistic behavior. Shariff et al. (2009) postulate that cultural evolution favored a belief in a committed omniscient deity who cared about cooperative behavior and would punish individuals who displayed opportunistic behavior. This faith, they believe, led to a significant growth in cooperative behavior in societies where monitoring costs tended to be high and punishing defectors was difficult. It suggests altruistic behavior and an adherence to certain fairness norms even toward strangers.[28] There is some experimental data to back this up, but the historical evidence here is not all that unambiguous. It might be added that strong religious beliefs also contributed to the resolution of asymmetric information situations, as they were an element in trying to elicit truth-telling from participants by making witnesses swear a holy oath, with a strong implication of severe divine punishment if broken.

A second obvious nexus between culture and growth is through *individual virtues*, on which quite a lot has been written lately by economists representing very different viewpoints (McCloskey 2006 and 2010; Doepke and Zilibotti 2007), but much of this literature goes back to Max Weber

---

[27] Janet Tai Landa, for instance, has demonstrated such networks could enforce contracts among ethnically homogeneous middleman groups such as Chinese immigrants outside China (Landa 1981, 1995).

[28] The argument is basically that in any non-cooperative setting it is costly to punish free riders, while the benefits are shared with non-punishers and thus create an externality and making cooperative outcomes more difficult to attain. Religious beliefs, by postulating an external punisher with low or zero cost of monitoring and punishing, would help solve this problem. This implies that religious societies, in which such beliefs were prevalent, would have higher inclusive fitness. Moreover, even if people were unsure about the existence of this supernatural punishing agency, it would be rational for them to stick to Pascal's wager and behave as if they believed in it. See for instance Johnson and Kruger (2004) and Johnson (2009).

and his views on the connection between individual morality and economic behavior. Virtues that are viewed as crucial for economic performance are frugality (important, obviously, to capital formation), industriousness (determining labor input and effort), temperance (which affects productivity), and charitableness (which helps reduce the fear of risk-taking). Of special interest here is a cultural propensity toward education and human capital, an emphasis on child quality, some of which is driven by religion (Botticini and Eckstein 2011; Becker and Wößmann 2009). None of those "virtues" were guarantees of growth: education could be quite sterile or even counterproductive, charitableness could lead to moral hazard, and excess frugality to lack of demand. But clearly a potential connection exists. Another important cultural feature that affects economic growth is an individualist versus a collectivist culture, which has been applied to British exceptionalism in a stimulating book by Alan MacFarlane (1991) and to economic growth in general in recent work by economists (Gorodnichenko and Roland 2011). What also surely matters is whether values are such as to appreciate and reward effort and talent rather than ancestry, identity, and political connections. Another value, with a more ambiguous effect of economic performance, is a preference for a more compassionate and egalitarian society, or whether "equal opportunity" matters more than "equal outcome" and the redistribution implied by these policies.

A third nexus between culture and economic performance, and the one I shall focus on here, operates through the attitude toward "useful knowledge" – that is, the part of culture that concerns the understanding and exploitation of the physical environment. The systematic exploitation of natural regularities and phenomena is the essence of technology, and the willingness and ability to do so are very much part of culture. Economic progress through technological creativity is deeply affected by the cultural background of the advance of technology – that is, which elements in society's beliefs and values are conducive to continuous technological progress and eventually brought about the great historical discontinuity of the eighteenth century.

There is more than one element at play here. One cultural variant in much of European culture that has not received its full due is the willingness of Europeans to adopt foreign ideas and techniques (Mokyr 1990, 186–189). This in no way is to deny European xenophobia, arrogance, and barbarism toward non-Europeans. But the odd historical phenomenon is that despite the obvious contempt Europeans had for foreign cultures, they had few qualms about adopting their ideas and useful knowledge when these suited their goals. This was already quite visible in the Middle Ages and the relation between European culture and that of the Islamic world. The philosopher Ibn Rushd (Averroes) and the physician Ibn Sina (Avicenna) had a vast influence in the medieval West, and Europeans never felt the slightest shame in naming the revolutionary arithmetic system they adopted after 1200 "Arabic numerals" (even if they were not) or consuming beverages with alcohol (the word derived from the Arabic *Al Kohl*) in them. The eagerness to adopt foreign ideas and technology became a veritable torrent after 1500, when the Europeans realized that there was a huge treasure of techniques, plants, and animals to exploit in the foreign lands they visited and then invaded. They often named these techniques and goods after their believed place of origin, from chinaware to turkeys. While such behavior sounds natural and normal to a modern observer, it is striking how much more difficult other societies before 1900 found it to adopt Western ideas and techniques. There is clearly a cultural element here, a pragmatic recognition that one can usefully distinguish between the character and religion of foreigners, which may be seen as repugnant, and their techniques and knowledge, which can be usefully adopted and adapted. But other factors played a role, above all the relentless competition between European polities at every level, which had accustomed them to imitate techniques from neighbors they had no liking for, and may have led them to expect that if they did not adopt an advantageous innovation from outside the European States System, some rival would gain an advantage. Of course, I do not mean to imply that non-European cultures were entirely incapable of adopting such foreign techniques. In the nineteenth century, the Islamic world made half-hearted attempts to reform and try to import the palpably successful techniques working in Europe. But apart from Meiji Japan, before 1914 few wholly succeeded.

An equally interesting cultural trait in European culture is reflected in Europeans' degree of respect toward the knowledge and values of earlier generations. To what extent were tradition and continuity valued for their own sake, and to which extent does a society suffer from a subconscious inferiority complex relative to its ancestors? The degree to which a society is "backward-looking-with-respect" is an interesting variable and goes a long way toward explaining its willingness to commit to and invest in progress. The iron fist of the past in many cases placed a powerful constraint on what societies could do in terms of intellectual and technological innovation. The most powerful example may be the odd economic history of European Jews.[29] The proposition that the "truth" had been revealed to earlier

---

[29] Despite their huge advantage in literacy and human capital for many centuries, Jews played an almost imperceptible role in the history of science and technology before and during the early Industrial Revolution. There were a few exceptions to this rule, such as Jacob ben

generations and that all that was left was to exegesize and interpret the writings of ancient authorities had both a religious and a secular component. The religious component was the belief that God had revealed the truth to a founder of the religion or his followers, but would not do so on a continuing basis. The secular component was one of awe and admiration for the wise men who wrote in the past, and a sense of inferiority of the current generation. Overcoming such respect has proven a major stumbling block for progress not just in Judaism but also in Confucian China and the Islamic world. To be sure, in almost all past societies there was a built-in tendency to resist innovation and protect the status quo and incumbency in the name of tradition. Moreover, a fair amount of innovation was always possible within the constraints of an existing canon, but the threat of being accused of heresy and apostasy remained a reality in many societies. The tolerance for heterodox ideas and deviant notions, and the willingness of institutions to allow them to contest existing cultural variants is a key ingredient of economic change (Mokyr 2002 ch. 6).

Our own age has largely shed its respect for the knowledge of previous generations, although the admiration for novelty coexists (uneasily) with the beliefs of large groups who still cling to the literalness of ancient texts. In the nineteenth and twentieth centuries, rapid rates of technological and scientific change established a disdain for the knowledge of previous generations. The equation that newer equals better applied in many areas. Authority and literalness fell into disrepute, especially in the secular twentieth-century West. It is now taken as axiomatic.[30] This struggle was fought and won in Europe even before the Enlightenment could clear the rest of the cultural grounds for the construction of a more progressive economy.

Immanuel (Bonet) Lates, physician to the late fifteenth century popes and the inventor of an important instrument to measure astronomical altitudes. Jews were re-admitted into Britain after 1656, and it stands to reason that if more of them had had mechanical interests, more of them would have found their way to Britain where the atmosphere was conducive to inventors in the second half of the eighteenth century – as did many other Continental engineers. After they shook off their obsession with the writing of past generations during the Jewish *haskala* or enlightenment, the share of Jews among leading scientists and inventors rose steeply. Among the more notable names are those of the physical chemist Fritz Haber, inventor of the Haber-Bosch process, arguably one of the most important inventions of all time; Lazar L. Zamenhof, the inventor of Esperanto; Paul Ehrlich, the originator of modern immunology; flight pioneer Otto Lilienthal; Theodore von Kármán, the father of supersonic flight; László Bíró, the inventor of the ballpoint pen, and many others. But in the annals of the Industrial Revolution, Jews are hard to find.

[30] It is telling that in many disciplines of science and technology, practitioners and experts have very little knowledge of or respect for the "wisdom of earlier generations." In recent decades that has come to include economics.

Another important value that mattered directly to economic performance was what could be called the *hierarchy of social values*: which activities or characteristics conveyed dignity and social prestige and were correlated with what their social environment would regard as "success?" How did one attain the approbation and respect of one's relevant social circle? Among the historically important criteria we may count in no obvious order, ancestry, military, and physical prowess, learning and wisdom, political power, creativity (literary, artistic), piousness, wealth, and administrative ability. An economist interested in growth might ask where in all this do commerce and artisanal skills figure? Clearly the place of "wealth" in this cultural ranking must matter to incentivize people in their career-choices and efforts? Insofar that innovation is driven by a desire to earn a profit, or to gain material resources in some other way, the social prestige or "dignity" (to use McCloskey's term) of wealth accumulation would support innovation. This combination is the foundation of modern capitalism, as every observer since Marx has maintained.

The inescapable fact is that by this criterion the track record of almost any society is at best mixed. The culture that views the life of a leisured landed gentleman as the summum of human existence survived far beyond what its putative medieval military functions could ever justify. The disdain and mockery of writers such as Molière notwithstanding, successful people with money tried to buy themselves and their children out of a productive lifestyle, what Braudel (1973, p. 726) has called the "treason of the bourgeoisie." This so-called treason is, perhaps, less surprising at closer examination. Given the physical vicissitudes and risks of productive life in earlier times, it was quite widely believed that wisdom, literature, and art were largely produced and supported by a leisurely class. Only small pockets of the world such as the Netherlands in its Golden Age proved that the opposite could be equally the case. All the same, and despite many setbacks, wealth made in productive pursuits became slowly more acceptable as a signal of personal achievement and success.[31] Here, too, the evidence suggests rather sudden changes in the century before the Industrial Revolution. As Weber and others have pointed out, religion became more friendly toward commerce and industry and "accorded high esteem to the manual

---

[31] The idea of "gentleman" acquired over time a connotation of someone respectable and reliable, a person of honor who could be trusted and thus would refrain from opportunistic behavior. Such a reputation was of course invaluable for anyone running a business, and thus, in an ironic twist of history, the ideal of gentleman slowly turned from an unproductive drone to a wealth-creating and useful citizen (McCloskey 2006, 294–296). For details, see Mokyr (2009).

arts" (Webster 1975, 325). In contemporary America, of course, income and economic status has achieved a status that is probably unique; elsewhere wealth, while never quite as despised as some would have us believe, was often an intermediate product to buy other forms of cultural status such as nobility, political power, social prestige, or the salvation of the soul.

5. The Cultural Roots of the Industrial Enlightenment

Any story about the historical origins of economic growth must start with the British Industrial Revolution. As I have argued at length, the Industrial Revolution depended for its success and sustainability on the prior existence of a series of diverse but connected cultural changes that in the absence of a better term I have called the Industrial Enlightenment. But as Gregory Clark (2007, 183) has pointed out, looking for the Enlightenment as an explanation of the Industrial Revolution just pushes the question back one stage: whence the Enlightenment? How did it happen that the culture of a critical group of educated Europeans changed in ways that favored modern science and technological progress?

If there is anything economists have persuaded themselves of in the area of economic growth it is that innovation will thrive in the correct institutional environment. Cultural change, much like most innovation that takes place in competitive environments, is often associated with cultural entrepreneurs. I defined cultural entrepreneurs as people who become influential to the point where they change the culture of a sufficiently large number of others to affect their behavior and eventually institutions in significant ways. Their influence operates through many of the transmission biases noted in section 3. The interaction of a gifted and lucky cultural entrepreneur with a suitable and fertile environment creates such changes. In that sense, cultural entrepreneurs are no different from the standard innovator-businessmen model of entrepreneurship so widely used by economists. Entrepreneurs "drive history" mostly in the limited sense that they take advantage of opportunities created by an environment larger and stronger than themselves. Yet this does not mean that such individuals do not matter. A fertile soil in which no seeds are planted will remain barren. Why do some societies spawn such entrepreneurs and others do not, and why are cultural entrepreneurs sometimes successful, and what determines their success?

What explains the growing success of cultural entrepreneurs in the European environment after 1500? The first was the ability to overcome the resistance of reactionary elements. Many societies, including imperial China and medieval Europe, cracked down on innovators who could have threatened the status quo. After 1500 or so, the environment in Europe made it increasingly difficult for reactionary regimes to suppress "heretics" – the lack of coordination and absence of agreement on who was a heretic and what was heresy between the splintered European polities made it all but impossible for any ruler to suppress new ideas; the initiator of the new cultural variant would simply pack up his suitcases and move across the boundaries, seeking the protection of a rival ruler. Luther and the pugnacious but influential physician Paracelsus were among the more notable early examples of cultural entrepreneurs who took advantage of this coordination problem, but there were many others in the decades between the Reformation and the end of the religious wars in 1648 who took advantage of this peculiar system (Mokyr 2006, 2007). In many cases, political hostility between the European powers led to one ruler protecting the cultural gadflies that irritated his enemies.[32] By the eighteenth century, the impotence of European states to suppress intellectual innovators had become part of common knowledge, and most rulers had for all practical purposes given up persecuting heretics.[33] Modern writers on the topic, following eighteenth-century writers, feel that the competition between rulers in the state system constrained them in their tax policy and forced them to have more respect for the property rights of their citizens.[34] But in the long term, their inability to

[32] One example was Tommasso Campanella (1568–1639), an Italian monk who studied astronomy, astrology, and occult philosophy and like many others became skeptical of the Aristotelian orthodoxy. Accused from an early age of heresy by the Inquisition, his ability to play one power against another in fragmented Italy ran out when he was sentenced to life imprisonment in 1599 (for anti-Spanish activity rather than for heresy) and spent twenty-seven years in a Neapolitan jail. However, his conditions there were sufficiently benign that he could write seven books in jail, including a pamphlet defending Galileo during his first trial in 1616. He could accomplish this in part because the Emperor Rudolf, Duke Maximilian of Bavaria, and other Catholic notables were exerting influence to protect him. In the end, he was released from jail through the intervention of the Pope Urban VIII, but then got in trouble again. He had succeeded, however, to endear himself to the French authorities (anxious to embarrass the Spanish), and through the intervention of the French ambassador he made it out of Italy to France, where he was honored by the court of Louis XIII and eventually accepted even by the suspicious Cardinal Richelieu and died in Paris (Headley 1997, 117–127).

[33] This is illustrated by the careers of heterodox Enlightenment writers like Rousseau and Helvétius. Their work annoyed the authorities, but after short exiles, they were allowed to return to France. More striking is the history of the atheist gadfly Julien La Mettrie, whose heretical works first forced him to take refuge in Leiden, but even there his hedonism so annoyed his hosts that he was forced to leave for Berlin, where Frederick the Great delighted in his often outrageous opinions.

[34] E. L. Jones (1981), in his classic work on the rise of Europe has referred to the "States System," an idea that has caught on and become quite influential, although it was expressed in somewhat different terms already by eighteenth century writers, including Hume and

suppress dissent and heterodoxy, due to the inherent coordination failures implied by political fragmentation, may have been equally important. The typical European intellectual innovator in this age was footloose, moving easily from court to court and from town to town. Erasmus, Descartes, Grotius, Huygens, Leibnitz, and many others were international superstars, and people in positions of power and wealth competed among themselves to attract them.[35]

The other environmental factor that created opportunities for cultural entrepreneurship in this age was the emergence of a unified intellectual market, in which ideas were aimed at a transnational European educated elite, allowing people access to a larger constituency and thus covering the fixed costs of research and writing by catering to a larger market. The emergence of a "Republic of Letters" in which natural philosophers, mathematicians, experimentalists, and alchemists communicated with one another by letter and the printed word, and in which they learned to play by the rules of open science, was an essential step toward avoiding the kind of intellectual atomization that may have thwarted cultural entrepreneurs in other highly fragmented political systems.[36] The emergence of the Republic of Letters depended on technological factors as well: the printing press and the growth of a continent-wide postal system in the sixteenth century. This unique European combination – political fragmentation within an

---

Gibbon. The basic model looks at the various political entities ("islands" in Jones's simile) in Europe in a fashion similar to the competitive model in economics; this competition had salutary effects on the European societies because states competed for tax bases and the best citizens, and could not afford to alienate them (North 1981, 27, 138; for a formal model, see Karayalçin 2008). This meant that governments ended up (most of the time) treating their most successful and creative citizens with respect, taxed them with some restraint, and often followed active industrial policies, sponsoring technological transfer from more advanced nations, attracting skilled craftsmen, financing manufacturing enterprises, and protecting their industries with tariffs.

[35] An extreme case was Jan Amos Comenius (Komensky) (1592–1670), one of the leading scholars of his age, who was early in life persuaded by the writings of Francis Bacon that the "millennium" could be achieved by advances in natural philosophy and applied his belief in progress in educational reform. A Czech Protestant, he fled his native Moravia in the early years of the Thirty Years' War and settled in Poland in 1620. He was invited by another early Baconian, Samuel Hartlib, to settle in Britain, but once again had to flee because of the British Civil War. Via Sweden and Hungary he ended up back in Poland, but chased away by the outbreak of war, he escaped to Amsterdam in 1657, where he lived the rest of his life. Like many seventeenth-century rebels and original thinkers, he took strong religious positions which often got him in trouble, but he survived repeatedly by fleeing in time, losing his family and his books in the process. Among other honors, he was invited to become president of the newly founded Harvard College (Spinka 1943, 53, 84).

[36] For more details, see Mokyr (2011–2012).

intellectually unified market – created, in that sense, the best of all possible combinations in the premodern environment.

A further important element in the success of cultural entrepreneurs was their ability to recruit effective disciples and epigones to spread their gospel. As already noted, cultural change often works in widening concentric circles, by apostles who spread the gospel of the master, at times more effectively than the master him or herself. This was especially important during the Reformation, when Lutheranism was spread by followers of Luther such as Philipp Melanchton and Calvinism by men such as Guido de Bres and John Knox. Newton's revolution in physics spread through the work of many scholars, among them in Britain John T. Desaguliers, the Dutchmen Willem s'Gravesande and Herman Boerhaave, and in France Voltaire (helped by Mme du Châtelet). Some cultural entrepreneurs were not invariably great communicators themselves except through their writings, but a few effective disciples would provide additional rhetorical bias. An example is Adam Smith, an effective teacher but not nearly as effective as his successor Dugald Stewart.[37]

Finally, there is historical materialism. In its extreme form, this view denies any independent role for individuals in cultural dynamics. Culture is wholly determined, in this view, by economic or class interests, and cultural entrepreneurs are mere agents of forces stronger than themselves and have no independent effect on the outcome. Did new cultural variants in the centuries before the Industrial Revolution spread as a response to the needs of an economic elite? Were the rise of a mechanical world-view, a belief in the efficacy of useful knowledge to promote material welfare, and a strong push to diffuse the findings of natural philosophy among those who could make practical use of it all determined by the rise of a new urban bourgeoisie? If this were taken literally to be the case, cultural entrepreneurs would not matter at all; in the absence of Luther and Calvin, the Reformation would still have taken place, and Calvinism would have still existed, invented by another person and under a different name. The extreme version is almost as unacceptable as its complete opposite, which attributes *everything* to the agency of exceptional individuals.

---

[37] Dugald Stewart was a student of Thomas Reid and Adam Smith, and later Professor of Moral Philosophy at Edinburgh. Among his students were the later prime ministers John Russell and Lord Palmerston as well as other major Whig figures such as Lord Brougham and Henry Cockburn. His lectures turned Smith's thought into the fountainhead of all economic theory. Stewart "made the book [*Wealth Of Nations*] virtually Holy Scripture to generations of Edinburgh-educated thinkers, economists, and politicians who in turn spread its influence to Oxford, Cambridge, London, and the rest of the English-speaking world" (Herman 2001, 229–230; see also Rothschild 2001).

Again, an evolutionary metaphor may be of help. A mutation will spread in a favorable environment and die out in an unfavorable one; but the pre-existence of such an environment does not guarantee that a new and adaptive cultural variant will actually emerge, much less will it determine fully what its phenotype will be like. Moreover, the adaptiveness of cultural variants always seems more obvious ex post than ex ante. Did the rise of commercial capitalism and an urban bourgeoisie require a religious reform? The outcomes of the struggle between Protestantism and Catholicism, for instance, are not consistent with a view that predicts that one of them was more fit to a particular environment; historical contingency largely determined the outcomes that made the Southern Netherlands, Bohemia, and Bavaria Catholic, and the Northern Netherlands and Prussia Protestant. This is not to say, of course, that economic conditions have no effect on whether a cultural variant will succeed or not; they are part of the environment in which cultural variants compete. Given the multitude of transmission biases, however, there is no predicting which variant will prevail.

How did modern, technology-based economic growth begin in the West? A cultural explanation of such economic change would require a changing set of relevant beliefs among social groups that mattered for technological change. It should be stressed from the outset that for this kind of growth to take place, what mattered was the belief of a limited subset of society, not some measure of median or modal beliefs. It was the beliefs of an educated elite, people of learning who not only were literate but in fact read, wrote, computed, observed, experimented and were well-networked with others much like them. These groups involved scientists, astrologers, engineers, alchemists, merchants, skilled artisans, literary types, and politicians. The culture of other members of the social elite, such as aristocrats, mattered as well, if only because others would want to imitate them. Richard Baxter in England helped forge a new and more favorable attitude toward material culture and production.[38] A new set of beliefs about the social role of useful knowledge and its implications emerged among these groups after 1650,

---

[38] It may seem odd for an economic historian to point to a Puritan theologian as an important figure in the economic development of the West, but Baxter's influence on both sides of the Atlantic in the eighteenth century was huge, and Max Weber regarded him as the author who "stands out above many other writers on Puritan ethics, both because of his eminently practical and realistic attitude, and, at the same time, because of the universal recognition accorded to his works" (Weber [1905] 1938, 155). His idea of the glorification of God through "good works" focused on hard work and those works that were "good materially."

most heavily concentrated in Britain, but spilling over to the rest of Western Europe and, with some delay, becoming part of a new cultural milieu. The importance of these beliefs has been argued with great vigor by Margaret C. Jacob (1997, 2000; Jacob and Stewart, 2004).

Much of the literature written by historians and historical sociologists on economically relevant cultural change in Britain has focused on the impact of Puritanism on the rise of modern science, although many of the key figures were not Puritans. The literature on Puritanism and the rise of science is large and was inspired by the work of Robert K. Merton as its focal point, although by his own admission, Merton was not the first to propose a connection between seventeenth-century religion in Britain and the rise of a "modern science" there (Merton 1973; [1938], 2001).[39] The hypothesis of a strong causal link between Puritanism as a source of modern science has been criticized heavily, although Merton was quite cautious not to claim more for his thesis than the evidence could bear (Shapin 1988; Cohen 1990). What is widely agreed on is that Puritan thought, its claims to hark back to the Early Church notwithstanding, helped clear the way for more "modern" ways of thinking about the "canon" of the past and liberate European culture from the dead hand of classical authorities (Webster 1975).

Elizabethan England in some ways was still strongly committed to the classical canon.[40] By the early seventeenth century, one can see how European intellectuals were increasingly coming to terms with their break with classical science and philosophy. The English physician and physicist William Gilbert in his *De Magnete* (1600), a widely admired and pioneering work in its time, dismissed Ptolemy's astronomy as "now believed only by idiots" and proclaimed that the only avenue to truth was experiment and observation, not the authority of Greek sages (Jones 1961 [1936], 17). Attacks on Aristotle became more common and less bashful throughout Europe.[41] A full-scale, century-long battle erupted between progressive

---

[39] The most striking and erudite work to appear prior to Merton's was that by Richard Foster Jones ([1936] 1961).

[40] In the fourteenth century, Oxford had a rule that any master who deviated from Aristotle's *Organon* would be fined 5 shillings per deviation (Devlin 2000, 58). This rule was still on the books when Giordano Bruno visited Oxford in 1583.

[41] In 1536, Petrus Ramus, a French intellectual, submitted an MA thesis with the title "Quaecumque ab Aristotele dicta essent, commentitia esse," the translation of which is somewhat in dispute but roughly meaning "whatsoever Aristotle has said is false (or confused)." Francis Bacon, in his *New Organon,* had nothing but scorn for the "schoolmen" who had incorporated "the contentious and thorny philosophy of Aristotle, more than was fit with the body of religion" (Bacon [1620] 1999, 124).

thinkers, who became increasingly confident in the capabilities of their generation, and those who clung to the notion that all that was valuable in human civilization had been produced by the great authorities of classical antiquity.

The seventeenth-century debate between "ancients" and "moderns" may seem like a storm in a teacup to modern eyes, but was quite serious at the time (Levine 1981, 73). It concerned, again, the issue of "respect toward earlier sages." Were modern scholars and authors nothing but midgets standing on the shoulders of giants, or were they giants themselves? The debate reflected a watershed in cultural evolution that had been two centuries or more in the making. Many of the scholars who rose to prominence in the mid-seventeenth century accepted the critical attitude toward received authority. "Whatever the schoolmen may talk," wrote one of them, "yet Aristotle's Works are not necessarily true and he himself hath by sufficient Arguments proved himself to be liable to error.... Learning is Increased by new Experiments and new Discoveries... we have the advantage of more time than they had and knowledge is the daughter of time" (John Wilkins, in his *Discourse Concerning a New Planet,* [1648], 1684) Earlier, George Hakewill's *Apologie* (1627) argued against the prevalent view of "decay" that held that human capabilities were declining over time. Pascal, in his pre-Jansenist and more progressive days, noted that it would be unjust to show the "ancients" more respect than they had shown to those who had preceded them (Bury 1955, 68), a logical point entirely missed by Jewish rabbinical theologians.[42]

The notion that their own generation was superior to anything that had come before spread among the British writers of the age, including the work of the (non-Puritan) clergyman Joseph Glanvill (1636–1680), who wrote a famous book entitled *Plus ultra, or, The Progress and Advancement of Knowledge since the Days of Aristotle* (1668) in which he proudly listed area by area the advances that science had made since antiquity, much of which he ascribed to the work of the Royal Society and its members. He noted with some exuberance that "a ground of high expectation from Experimental Philosophy is given, by the happy genius of this present Age... and that a ground of expecting considerable things from Experimental Philosophy is

---

[42] Auguste Comte noted that "the idea of continuous progress had no scientific consistency, or public regard, till after the memorable controversy at the beginning of the last [i.e., eighteenth] century about the general comparison of the ancients and the moderns... that solemn discussion constitutes a ripe event in the history of the human mind which thus, for the first time, declared that it had made an irreversible advance" (Comte 1856, 441).

given by those things which have been found out by illiterate tradesmen or lighted by chance."[43]

Progress, the "moderns" realized, was inevitable not only because knowledge was cumulative but also because the tools of research had been improved. Galen had no microscope, Ptolemy no telescope, Archimedes no algebra or calculus. More than anything, however, it was realized, knowledge was cumulative. People living in the present know more than those who came before them because earlier knowledge had been transmitted to them. Much of the battle of the books, of course, was about taste, and an argument whether one would prefer Shakespeare to Sophocles or Milton to Virgil seems otiose today. However, dismissing R. F. Jones as "whiggish" because he felt sympathy for those who thought that there were good grounds to prefer Galileo to Archimedes or Harvey to Galen seems unproductive as well. One of the debaters, the linguist and biographer William Wotton (1666–1727), indeed made the crucial distinction between areas that were cumulative (such as science and technology) and those that were not (such as rhetoric). But his debate with one of the last of the "ancients," William Temple, marks the rearguard action of a battle that had been fought and won for two centuries: from that point on it was beyond any question that a reference to Aristotle or any other author in the canon, from the Bible down, would not be regarded as sufficient evidence.[44]

Not all authors of the late seventeenth and eighteenth century subscribed to a belief that progress was possible or even likely, and doubters such as Thomas Hobbes never quite bought into it. As late as 1704, the conservative Jonathan Swift, who wrote a famous satirical essay on the battle of the ancients and moderns, concluded that "we cannot learn to which side Victory fell." By that time, however, most intellectuals regarded the debate as over. The Enlightenment ensured that by the end of the eighteenth century any interest in the debate itself had waned. There was still respect for classical civilization, and the children of the elite were taught its language and literature; but nobody serious confused it with

---

[43] Glanvill would not be counted as "enlightened" by our standards – he staunchly defended the existence of witches and spirits and wrote a book vehemently attacking those who doubted their existence.

[44] The late-seventeenth-century "Battle of the Books" was in fact a rearguard action that shows how strong the position of the "moderns" had become. In the words of one scholar, "to sample a few of Temple's [William Temple, one of Wotton's main opponents] opinions about ancients and moderns gives one a sense of the genteel arrogance the Enlightenment had to put up with and overcome.... Temple served up a pastiche of pseudo-intellectual commonplaces" (Traugott 1994, 504–505).

a substitute for the useful knowledge that was needed to advance material conditions.

The obvious corollary of the "triumph of the moderns" was a growing belief in the possibility of progress. Studies about the *History of the Idea of Progress*, starting from Bury's seminal book ([1932], 1955), have without exception pointed to the Age of Enlightenment as the age in which the idea of progress came to dominate much of Western thought. In the market for ideas that evolved in the seventeenth century, the relevant idea that triumphed was that history does not move in endless cycles, nor is it a stationary process. History has a unit root. It trends in a particular direction even if progress is punctuated by temporary reversals or *ricorsi* as Vico termed them. The idea of progress is logically equivalent to an implied disrespect of previous generations. As Carl Becker noted in his classic work written in the early 1930s, "a Philosopher could not grasp the modern idea of progress... until he was willing to abandon ancestor worship, until he analyzed away his inferiority complex toward the past, and realized that his own generation was superior to any yet known" (Becker [1932], 2003, 131). Seventeenth-century Europe already shows quite a few signs of a belief in progress, starting with Bacon and Descartes themselves and their disciples.[45] By the time of Condorcet, this had become commonplace. To be sure, a prevalent belief in progress is neither a necessary nor a sufficient condition for actual progress to occur, but it is plausible that progress is more likely when a pivotal elite is committed to the idea.

The idea of progress, then, consisted of three separate components. The first was that history showed an upward trend of improving culture, art, literature, and knowledge. The second was a belief that this trend was likely to continue in the future. The third was a set of recommendations of how to bring it about, which involved of course some kind of model on what the engine behind social progress really was. It was not just a British idea: quite a few Continental writers came up with very similar views, and in fact it was brought to a rather feverish and wildly optimistic crescendo late in the eighteenth century by writers such as Turgot and Condorcet. The belief

---

[45] Among those who believed strongly in the progressiveness of human knowledge was the French author Bernard LeBovier Fontenelle (1657–1757). In 1688, Fontenelle published a small essay titled *Digression sur les anciens et les modernes* in which he postulated that scientific progress, and the economic progress that will go with it, were not just possible but in fact inevitable. He noted that in how in his age a truth (*justesse*) ruled that had been hitherto unknown, and predicted that this would in the future go much further, and that one day the current generation would be "ancients" and that it would be fair and reasonable for posterity to outdo them.

in progress in Britain was less ecstatic and more pragmatic than on the Continent. Spadafora (1990, 17) aptly defines the social climate in Britain as "confidence without complacency." Knowledge was the key to progress, and as long as it would grow, the material condition of the human race would as well. As Erasmus Darwin wrote in 1784, the "common heap of knowledge . . . will never cease to accumulate so long as the human footstep is seen upon the earth" (cited by Musson and Robinson 1969, 192). It was, however, one thing to have faith in the eventual occurrence of progress and quite another to bring it about; yet that is precisely what the many national and local "improving societies" founded in Britain intended.[46]

6. Cultural Entrepreneurs and the Industrial Revolution

Ever since Tolstoy, it has been fashionable to dismiss the impact of individuals on history by mocking the "intellectual prowess and persuasive capabilities of a few men" and stressing cultural change as "a confluence of available ideas" although one is left wondering where such influential ideas might have come from in the first place.[47] Yet while the impact of cultural entrepreneurs cannot be understood on their merits alone, they provide useful focal points to understand how and why deep cultural changes could take place. We may think of them as the proverbial canary in a coal mine: their success is an indication that in some way society is ready for some kind of change in its beliefs. They also illustrate the contingent component of history in general. None of this implies, of course, that we can prove

---

[46] Among the major organizations set up with explicit and conscious purpose to improve society, the Society of Arts (established in 1754) was meant to enhance "such Productions, Inventions or Improvements as shall tend to the employing of the Poor and the Increase of Trade." The Act of Founding the British Museum of 1753 stated similarly that the museum was meant to bring about "advancement and improvement" in useful knowledge (cited by Spadafora 1990, 79). The Royal Institution, established in 1799 by Count Rumford, similarly described its purpose as "the speedy and general diffusion of all new and useful improvements in whatever quarter of the world they may originate, and teaching the application of scientific discoveries to the improvements of arts and manufactures in this country and to the increase in domestic comfort and convenience" (Bence Jones 1871, 121).

[47] The quote is from Lowengard (2006). Tolstoy famously advocated in *War and Peace* that "to study the laws of history we must completely change the subject of our observation, must leave aside kings, ministers, and generals, and the common, infinitesimally small elements by which the masses are moved." The problem is that the masses need to be coordinated, and that such coordinators are not just pawn of deeper historical forces, but also have agency themselves. When that agency becomes important to the outcome, we may say that history is at a bifurcation point or at a "critical juncture" (Acemoglu and Robinson 2012) and that fairly small events may set the process on a different trajectory.

beyond a reasonable doubt that history would have been dramatically different without the actions of these entrepreneurs. We simply do not know for sure. Adam Smith, Marx, and Keynes were very much products of a certain economic environment and would not have succeeded had they written their works in a different time. But were they inevitable products of their environment?

The changes that were critical to the success of the cultural variants prevalent in eighteenth-century Britain (and much of the rest of Western Europe) were heavily influenced by two cultural entrepreneurs whose influence on late seventeenth- and eighteenth-century European elite culture was decisive: Francis Bacon and Isaac Newton (Mokyr 2013).[48] While both men were English, their influence penetrated into the Continent as well. They were helped by a large number of followers and epigones who interpreted and extended their work and thinking, and thus were instrumental in introducing a set of cultural changes among Europe's thin educated layer that turned out to be crucial to subsequent economic development. Their respective influences reinforced and complemented one another. As Jacob (1997, 33) has argued, by the late seventeenth century, Baconianism was in part subsumed in Newtonianism.

Francis Bacon's intellectual influence in his own lifetime was limited, but fairly soon after his death in 1626, scientists and intellectuals began to express the impact his work had on their thinking. Puritans and non-Puritans alike expressed their debt to him. Charles Webster, in his magnum opus, states that among Puritans, Bacon's writings "came to attain almost scriptural authority" (1975, 335). Following his death, his disciples banded together in the so-called Hartlib Circle, in which the Prussian immigrant Samuel Hartlib (1600–1662), who arrived in England two years after Bacon's death, occupied a central role. Hartlib was prototypical follower, a highly effective "intelligencer" in the terminology of the time, not an original thinker, but highly effective in organizing an intellectual elite into following a coherent program.[49] He was an inveterate correspondent and instrumental

---

[48] Bacon, Newton, and Locke were Thomas Jefferson's list of "the greatest men who ever lived."

[49] The term was first applied to him by John Winthrop, governor of Massachusetts. Webster (1970, 3) sees him as the one who undertook the Baconian ideal of organizing Europe's intellectuals in a "noble and generous fraternity" – obviously an early version of the eighteenth-century Republic of Letters. One of his main projects was his "Office of Address and Correspondency," a kind of virtual Solomon's House in which useful knowledge was circulated and distributed by means of epistolary networks, a precursor of the basic Enlightenment project to reduce access costs and enhance the dissemination of scientific and technological knowledge.

in disseminating scientific writing in a wide array of applied fields, ranging from medicine to horticulture.[50] He and his friend John Dury (1596–1680) followed Bacon in the judgment of the value of knowledge in its degree of "usefulness."

But what was it about Bacon's vision that so grabbed the imagination and beliefs of educated people (mostly after his death)? The cultural sea change that Bacon and the Baconians brought about was the revision of the agenda of research and the growing conviction that science should serve the purpose of economic progress. In one famous aphorism (81) in his *Novum Organum* (1620), Bacon summarized his view about the agenda of science: "The true and lawful goal of the sciences is simply this, that human life be enriched by new discoveries and powers." He fully realized that this was an elite culture and continues: "The Great majority have no feeling for this. . . . But every now and then it does happen that and exceptionally intelligent and ambitious craftsman applies himself to a new invention and as a rule ruins himself in the process." Another twentieth-century scholar has put it well: "The story of Francis Bacon as that of a life devoted to a great idea . . . commonplace today, but in his day it was a novelty. It is simply that knowledge ought to bear fruit in works, that science ought to be applicable to industry, that men ought to organize themselves as a sacred duty to improve and transform the conditions of life" (Farrington [1949], 1979, 3). This idea became one of the founding principles of the Royal Society, which in its first years consistently claimed that its research would be heavily focused on improving technology. Thomas Sprat, in his *History of the Royal Society*, proclaimed that "Philosophy will attain perfection when either Mechanic Labourers shall have philosophical heads, or the Philosophers shall have Mechanical Hands" (Sprat 1667, 397).[51] This idea, too, was powerfully expressed by Bacon in his writings, and quoted over and over again by his followers. In his early *In Praise of Knowledge* (1592) Bacon indicated that some of those claims could be dismissed as the self-serving rhetoric of intellectuals seeking patronage and intended to endear the Royal Society to the authorities or (some) rich patrons, but there can be little doubt that many of its original members genuinely believed in the

---

[50] Hartlib was particularly interested in bee-keeping, both as an interesting agricultural pursuit and because he saw the symbolism of bees pollinating flowers analogous to men of learning spreading information to increase the productivity of the economy.

[51] It was widely observed that this was far from a reality in this era; half a century after Sprat, Mandeville still noted that "they are very seldom the same sort of people, those that invent Arts and Improvements in them, and those that enquire into the Reason of Things" ([1724] 1755, 121).

Baconian message. It should be added that the message was, of course, not unique to Bacon. Descartes, in his *Discourse,* declares that he believed that the notions of physics would make it possible to discover principles that would turn humans into the lords and possessors of nature and to invent "an infinity of devices which should make it possible to enjoy the fruit of the earth" and especially to preserve human health (Descartes [1637], 1965, 50).[52]

Part of Bacon's message was that science should be empirical and experimental. Many seventeenth-century Puritans regarded experimental science, or as they called it, "experimental philosophy," not just as the key to scientific progress but also with a deep ethical sentiment: this was, from many points, of view, an example of "good works."[53] In this way we see a nice example of cultural epistasis: on the one hand, the belief that experimental science held the key to the advance of useful knowledge, on the other the notion that by carrying out experimental investigations one could get somehow closer to understanding the deity.[54] These two cultural elements jointly implied a flourishing of scientific experimentation, in search of the natural regularities that would allow people to control nature "for the Glory of the Creator and relief of Man's estate" as Bacon put it in his *Advancement of Learning* ([1623], 1996, pp. 147–48).

Bacon's inductive methodology, its limitations notwithstanding, was enormously influential, especially in areas in which the discovery of obvious underlying mechanisms was beyond the power of the scientists of the age. Organizing what was known about natural regularities in accessible ways, it was hoped, would make the knowledge more intelligible and potentially more useful. For instance, the first chemical affinity table was put together by Étienne Geoffroy in 1718, and while Geoffroy claimed to be inspired by Newton, his emphasis was not on the understanding of chemical facts but on ordering the "brute phenomena themselves" as Dear (2006, 42) put it. Botany and zoology were treated in the same way: by cataloging and

---

[52] Descartes's influence waned, however, in the eighteenth century as that of Bacon increased, and so his success as a cultural entrepreneur was more limited. Cf. Gay (1969), 145–50.

[53] Charles Webster (1975, 333) remarks that the collaboration between Baconian philosophers and "enlightened craftsmen" was built upon the hope of preparing a technological revolution, a prospect that at the time may have appeared absurdly utopian. In due time, however, it is exactly this cooperation that became the cornerstone of the Industrial Revolution and the origin of modern growth in Europe (Mokyr 2002, 2009).

[54] Robert Boyle, one of the most dominating figures in British science of the second half of the seventeenth century, was a deeply committed follower of Bacon, wholly committed to an experimental approach to science, and yet he was a deeply religious man, a lay theologian, for whom science was a way to practice his religion (Wojcik 1997).

classifying, it was hoped, some patterns and regularities would emerge. In the absence of a clear concept of evolution to say nothing of more advanced concepts of physiology, many skeptics such as the great French botanist George-Louis Leclerc, Count of Buffon, thought such a project foolhardy, yet Linnaeus and his many disciples persisted in what became a central project of Enlightenment science.

Isaac Newton's role as a cultural entrepreneur was quite different but no less powerful. Jacob, the foremost proponent of the centrality of a "Newtonian Enlightenment" has argued that Newtonianism was key to a number of mechanical adaptations, but in fact it is not easy to show how the Newtonian science *directly* led to any specific inventions. Newton was more interested in motion than in heat, and yet it is the latter that turned to be crucial to most developments in power and materials. Mechanical science, as developed by Galileo and Newton, was initially of little direct help to the mechanical advances in the textile industry. Differential calculus, Newton's most practical invention, did become more useful to some engineers in the second half of the eighteenth century, but it is not easy to assess its exact role in technological progress.[55] If Newton had a role to play in the Industrial Revolution, it was through his impact as a cultural entrepreneur. He was an unlikely candidate for that position, as Keynes pointed out in his posthumous lecture on "Newton, the Man" (Keynes, 1946).

What, then, was the significance of Newton for the cultural changes that prepared the ground for the Industrial Enlightenment? Clearly, Newton's influence can be attributed in large part to "content bias" (his work was convincing because it rang true to those who could understand it) and direct bias (his followers were men of substantial authority and scientific prestige). His disciples and epigones, both in Britain and on the Continent, were rhetorically gifted and often in positions of influence and power. But there was also some model-based bias: young scientists and mathematicians all knew about his fame and fortune, and the social prestige of a career in science would never be the same. Newton illustrated the enormous prestige that a truly successful scientist could attain in a society that began to value useful knowledge. He was knighted, elected to Parliament, and became quite wealthy. He was surrounded by admiring students (most notably Richard Bentley, Samuel Clarke, and William Whiston), and was on close terms with all the leading intellectuals and scientists of his age, unless he

---

[55] The best-known application of calculus was to hydraulics, but the French mathematician Antoine Parent famously erred in his computation of the maximum useful effect that a waterwheel could draw from the force of a stream.

had quarreled with them. Hans Sloane, Newton's successor as president of the Royal Society, basked in the prestige of his predecessor to elevate the prominence of natural history. Newton thus completed what the Puritans had started: to raise the social standing of scientists and researchers as people who should be respected and supported because their work was destined to become the primum mobile of social progress, and Newton had shown once and for all that this was feasible.

But there were also cultural spillovers. His work enormously boosted the confidence of the "moderns" as opposed to the "ancients" – his new interpretation of the universe was almost at once recognized to overthrow what little there was left of ancient cosmology and physics, and vindicated the many authors who had been pleading against a sense of inferiority of their own age. Moreover, he was deeply integrated in a *European* as opposed to an *English* academic sphere and regarded quite early on as an international scientific superstar, the most successful and brilliant citizen of the Republic of Letters. Despite the innovativeness of his theories, his main scientific fights were not with those who disagreed with him on essential matters, but priority disputes (Hooke) or access to data (Flamsteed). His religious views were heterodox, but there is no evidence that these stood in the way of his celebrity and powerful patronage positions he occupied after 1687.

Newton's combination of his formidable mathematical and analytical skills with his continuous reliance on empirical and experimental data was a shining example that lesser scientists could only hope to mimic. The classical canon had been largely based on logic and authority; Bacon had wanted to supplement it with the collection of facts and data that, somehow, would then fall into place. In the end, he felt, one should always prefer principles gained by induction from observation and experiment (Iliffe 2003, 272). This is, of course, precisely what Newton did. He never claimed to understand *the causes of* the principles he discovered, only that they were universal and intelligible. The implication was that once nature was intelligible, it could be manipulated, controlled, and applied to human needs. The concept of a mechanical universe in which the regularities were wholly predictable and deterministic, although in the air for a long time, was given an enormous boost by Newton's work. Anyone who believed in the feasibility and desirability of progress found this message congenial.

Applications of Newton's model of knowledge were attempted in other fields, with mixed results. His excursions into chemistry in the famous "query 31" at the very end of the third edition of his *Optics*, for instance, included a discursion about chemical affinity that later inspired other chemists, including the aforementioned Geoffroy, to compile the first tables of chemical affinities (Brock 1992, 76). In the same query, Newton conjectured that his scientific method may even be able to "enlarge the bounds of moral philosophy" (Newton 1719, 381). The Dutch physician Herman Boerhaave, who taught medicine, chemistry, and botany at Leiden between 1709 and 1738 ascribed to Newtonian principles to explain the human body in terms of gravitation and attraction (Dobbs and Jacob 1995, 85).[56] Newton's impact on economics, especially Adam Smith, has also recently been emphasized (Montes 2008). His impact on the physical sciences was, a fortiori, enormous.

Yet, as I noted above, the apostles and epigones of every cultural entrepreneur adapt and alter the original message, and Newton was no exception. Dobbs and Jacob (1995, 61) stress that Newton was not a Newtonian. He showed little taste in his lifetime for applications, and unlike his nemesis Robert Hooke, invented little worth mentioning. Most of his epigones, too, were not famous for large technological advances, although John T. Desaguliers experimented a great deal with electricity without making any breakthroughs of note.[57]

The connection between the Scientific Revolution and the Industrial Revolution was more subtle. It is true that some of Newton's followers were able to demonstrate his principles using mechanical devices. But, as Cardwell (1972) and others have noted, the dispute between the Newton measure of force (momentum, or mass times velocity) and the Huygens-Leibniz notion of vis-viva (mass times velocity squared) was not altogether in Newton's favor, as the vis-viva concept was more useful to engineers interested in "work," duty, and efficiency. The confusing dispute regarding which of the two concepts was to be preferred illustrates that Newton's work left a lot for the future and that concepts such as momentum, force, work, power, and torque had not been fully worked out until late in the eighteenth century (Home 2002, 361).

---

[56] Boerhaave (1668–1738) serves as another classic example of the kind of epigone that is instrumental in disseminating the ideas of the true cultural entrepreneurs, in his case Descartes and Newton. Enormously famous and renowned in his own days, his original contributions were few and middling, yet he helped spread the main cultural beliefs of the Enlightenment, not only in his own country but throughout Europe.

[57] Jacob (1997) has expressed this view most eloquently. It is true that the career and work of Jean T. Desaguliers exemplifies the positive effect of Newtonianism in Britain, focusing on the practical and useful application of the new mechanical science, but during Desaguliers's life (1683–1744), nor during that of other similarly-minded Newtonians such as James Jurin (1684–1750), no Industrial Revolution took place.

But what Newton did was to produce the crashing crescendo to a century in which natural philosophers had worked to raise the social prestige of "useful knowledge" as both socially beneficial and personally virtuous. Such a transformation was essential if useful knowledge – science, technology, medicine – were to play the transformative roles in history they did. But he also changed the methodological premises of how useful knowledge was constructed. In Newton's work the emphasis is on mathematics and instrumentality, not on explaining the deep causes of things (Dear 2006, 37–38). Perhaps the most important contribution that Newton's work made to the Industrial Enlightenment was the elegance and completeness with which he explained phenomena and regularities that had puzzled people for centuries. The point was not just that his equations, which explained celestial motions as well as provided a theoretical basis for much that had been known before on the motions of earthly bodies and the behavior of light, provided a world of order and logic. It was also the Baconian ideal of understanding nature through observation and experiment and thus its control seemed so much closer. In the age of Enlightenment, Newton became the epitome of the potential of human rationality, and, as Peter Gay (1969, 130) has put it, "In the deification of Newton, the Enlightenment of the philosophes and the age of Enlightenment were at one." Deification, of course, was the fate of many of the truly successful cultural entrepreneurs – from Jesus to Marx.

The world was operating through mechanical principles that were intelligible, despite its seemingly chaotic nature. Newton's work filled other scholars with hope that areas such as farming, medicine, chemistry, electricity, materials, and even the "science of man" would soon be similarly reduced to well-understood elegant laws. Yet the economic effects were not immediate, because Newtonianism and the world view it implied needed to filter down to the practical people with a proclivity toward improvement; the development of public science, a central part of the Industrial Enlightenment, was therefore an integral part of the technological developments of the later eighteenth century (Jacob and Stewart 2004). The importance of Newton for subsequent developments is also in the change in the function of religion that his work implied. There is a deep irony in this that is hard to miss. Newton was a deeply religious man, for whom his findings affirmed to his mind the ever-presence of a wise deity who had created a world of knowable regularities.[58] But Newtonian mechanical

---

[58] While it surely is far-fetched to see in his Arianist (and thus heretical) convictions a driving force for his science, his Christian faith affirmed and supported his scientific

philosophy did not need a personal God, and it is telling that many of his Enlightenment followers, above all Voltaire, could uncouple his scientific works from his faith and adopt the former without paying much attention to the latter.[59] Enlightenment science often coexisted with religion, but it needed it less than the Puritan scientists did in the mid seventeenth century. Indeed, for the Puritans and for many other seventeenth-century natural philosophers, experimental science and the creation and dissemination of useful knowledge was a form of worship.

7. Conclusions

With the growing consensus that Northean institutions are the central story in explaining differences in economic performance (Acemoglu and Robinson 2012) the issue of why some economies somehow develop "better" institutions and what it is exactly that these institutions do to make an economy develop faster, has become paramount. The emphasis in the literature so far has been on market-supporting institutions and the growth of cooperation and trust as social norms, as well as on the historical roots of the development of political factors behind the evolution of constraints on the executives and low levels of predatory behavior, rent-seeking, and redistribution. I have highlighted another much-neglected factor, namely attitudes toward science and technology. "Attitudes" are of course a component of something much larger we call "culture." In the end, economists cannot avoid the concept, although they may not have a comparative advantage in analyzing it. For an economy to create the technical advances that enabled it to make the huge leap of modern growth, it needed a *culture of innovation*, one in which new and sometimes radical ideas were respected and encouraged, heterodoxy and contestability were valued, and novelty tested, compared, and diffused if found to be superior by some criteria to what was there before.

An evolutionary approach toward culture helps us understand why certain cultural variants may become dominant in the population. This approach relies on the idea of "biases" proposed by models of cultural evolution, which explain why individuals change the cultural traits they receive

---

work. He could do this by developing eclectic and idiosyncratic religious beliefs that were designed to be consistent with his scientific insights. He ignored the problems that his mechanical theory posed for cosmogenesis and ostensibly adhered to the literal biblical text (Snobelen 1999).

[59] Voltaire regarded Newton practically in religious terms, regarding himself as Newton's apostle and admitted that Newton was the "God to whom I sacrifice" (Feingold 2004).

vertically (through genes or socialization) from their elders and adopt others. Second, despite the understandable reluctance of scholars to attribute aggregate outcomes to the deeds of specific individuals, the activities of cultural entrepreneurs often played a major role in persuading large numbers of people to accept a set of beliefs different from their parents. It is hard to argue that any specific cultural entrepreneur was genuinely indispensable; surely if Newton had not been born, the Age of Enlightenment could have picked another idol to use as a model of the triumph of the human mind. Nobody would argue that had it not been for Newton or Bacon or another dozen hall-of-famers, Europe's economic history would have resembled Somalia's or Afghanistan's. But it is exactly the European environment that allowed such talents to flourish and enabled them to have the influence they had that makes their impact worth noting. Studying cultural entrepreneurs as focal points for cultural change may be helpful in understanding the Industrial Enlightenment, the Industrial Revolution, and in the end much of the economic history of the world in the past quarter millennium.

Acknowledgments

Some of the material in this chapter is adapted from my *The Cultural Roots of the Modern Economy* (2014) and related papers. I am grateful to Avner Greif, Eric Jones, and Deirdre McCloskey for comments on an earlier draft that led to substantial improvements.

9

What Really Happened During the Glorious Revolution?

Steven C. A. Pincus and James A. Robinson

1. Introduction

"In many vital matters the reign of William the Third marked a dividing line between ancient and modern ways," observed the financial journalist W. A. Steel in the pages of *Macmillan's Magazine* in the late nineteenth century. It was in that reign, he noted, that the English "gave a parliamentary basis to the monarchy, established the power of the House of Commons, and originated the idea of a homogeneous cabinet and a responsible ministry, laying thus the foundations of our political liberty." The English lay the foundations for future economic growth during that reign as well, one illustration of which was "the clear understanding and steady prudence of the men who established a system of banking which in its leading features has seen little essential change from that time to the present."[1] In the view of this confident late Victorian, the Glorious Revolution had started the process that would make Britain into the first modern nation.

This account of the decisive and innovative nature of the Glorious Revolution has long been disputed by specialists in both political and economic history. Scholars across the ideological and methodological spectrum have chimed in with a single voice. The Revolution of 1688, they all claim, was an act of recovery and conservation rather than one of innovation. The purpose of the Revolution of 1688–1689, argues J. R. Jones, "was restorative and conservationist." The revolutionaries in England, he affirms, "did not aim, like the dominant revolutionaries in France a century later, at transforming government, the law, society, and changing the status of all individuals who composed the nation." John Morrill proclaims that "the Sensible Revolution

---

[1] William Anderson Steel. 1894. "The Founders of the Bank of England." *Macmillan's Magazine*, 70(417): 184.

of 1688–89 was a conservative revolution." 1688–1689 "was a 'glorious revolution' – in the seventeenth century sense of that word," concurs Jonathan Scott, "because at last it restored, and secured, after a century of troubles, what remained salvageable of the Elizabethan church and state." Hugh Trevor-Roper notes that because the Revolution "was essentially defensive, the product of determined resistance to innovation, it too was necessarily conservative."[2] Harry Dickinson remarks that "the latest works on the Glorious Revolution agree that it was a conservative settlement." "Most scholars have reached a consensus," chimes in Kathleen Wilson, "that the Revolution was largely an episode in patrician politics, unrelentingly 'conservationist' in ideological, political and social effect."[3]

This notion that the Revolution of 1688 was conservative, that it did little to change either the political arrangements or the economic trajectory of England, is widely accepted by economic historians as well. Gregory Clark suggests that the fact that interest rates did not fall discontinuously after 1688 demonstrates that "secure private property rights existed in England at least as early as 1600." In fact, he argues that the increase in taxation after 1688 meant that "The Glorious Revolution had an immediate negative effect" on economic growth and that none of the political events of the seventeenth century had any impact on total factor productivity.[4] Others, such as Nathan Sussman and Yishay Yafeh, follow Clark in seeing the interest rate evidence as demonstrating that the Glorious Revolution had no impact on either financial development or the economy, and Stephen Quinn has argued that government borrowing after 1688 even drove up interest rates, thus discouraging private investment.[5] The idea that the Glorious

---

[2] J. R. Jones, "The Revolution in Context," in *Liberty Secured? Britain Before and After 1688*, ed. J. R. Jones (Stanford: Stanford University Press, 1992), 12; John Morrill, "The Sensible Revolution," in *The Anglo-Dutch Moment*, ed. Jonathan Israel (New York: Cambridge University Press, 1991), 103; Jonathan Scott, *Algernon Sidney and the Restoration Crisis, 1677–1683* (New York: Cambridge University Press, 1991), 27; Trevor-Roper, *Counter-Reformation to Glorious Revolution* (Chicago: University of Chicago Press, 1992), 246.

[3] Howard Nenner, "Introduction," in *Politics and the Political Imagination in Later Stuart Britain*, ed. Howard Nenner (Rochester, NY: University of Rochester Press, 1997), 1; H. T. Dickinson, "The Eighteenth Century Debate on the 'Glorious Revolution,'" *History* 61 (1976): 29; Kathleen Wilson, "A Dissident Legacy; Eighteenth Century Popular Politics and the Glorious Revolution," in *Liberty Secured? Britain Before and After 1688*, ed. J. R. Jones (Stanford: Stanford University Press, 1992), 299.

[4] Gregory Clark, "Political Foundations of Modern Economic Growth: England, 1540–1800," *Journal of Interdisciplinary History* 26(4): 565. Gregory Clark, *A Farewell to Alms* (Princeton: Princeton University Press, 2007), 149, 241–242.

[5] Nathan Sussman and Yishay Yafeh, "Institutional Reforms, Financial Development and Sovereign Debt: Britain 1690–1790," *Journal of Economic History* 66(4): 906–935. Stephen

Revolution made government financial policy more credible has been dismissed by Anne Murphy who insists that "the financial promises of the post-Glorious Revolution government were no more credible than those of previous Stuart monarchs."[6] The latest interpretation of the British Industrial Revolution by Robert Allen is similarly dismissive of the role of 1688. Allen addresses the view that it was "the Glorious Revolution of 1688 that consolidated parliamentary ascendancy, limited royal prerogatives and secured private property... supposedly... [creating] a favorable climate for investment that made the Industrial Revolution possible." But he concludes that this view has "some weaknesses." Interest rates, he notes, did not fall immediately after 1688, suggesting that there was no real change in the financial environment, that property rights had long been secure and that taxes rose, which was bad for incentives. Allen also points out the lack of a mechanism leading from 1688 to the industrial revolution – or as he puts it, "It was a long stretch from the excise tax on beer... to Watt's invention of the separate condenser."[7]

In the midst of this emerging consensus that the Revolution of 1688 mattered little, Douglass North and Barry Weingast published their pathbreaking "Constitutions and Commitment" essay in the pages of the *Journal of Economic History*. In many ways North and Weingast were reviving the late-nineteenth-century interpretation espoused by Steel and many Whig radicals before him. North and Weingast, however, added a good deal. Whereas the older story insisted that there were fundamental changes, North and Weingast offer an account of why these changes took place, and they provided a new mechanism linking these changes to subsequent economic growth. They argued that "institutions played a necessary role in making possible economic growth and political freedom."[8]

In this essay we revisit North and Weingast's argument and the evidence supporting it. We argue that North and Weingast were correct in their belief that the Revolution of 1688 was a decisive turning point in the political and economic history of England (and later Britain).[9] However, we suggest that

---

Quinn, "The Glorious Revolution's Effect on English Private Finance: A Microhistory, 1680–1705," *Journal of Economic History* 61(3): 593–615.

[6] Anne L. Murphy, The Origins of English Financial Markets: Investment and Speculation Before the South Sea Bubble (Cambridge: Cambridge University Press, 2009), 5.

[7] Robert C. Allen, *The British Industrial Revolution in Global Perspective* (Cambridge: Cambridge University Press, 2009), 5.

[8] Douglass C. North and Barry R. Weingast, "Constitutions and Commitment: The Evolution of Institutions Governing Public Choice in Seventeenth-Century England," *Journal of Economic History* 49(4): 831.

[9] We make no detailed attempt to defend this point here although we do suggest what we believe are some of the most significant elements of a convincing story: See also Daron

the causal account provided by North and Weingast is not substantiated by what actually happened in the wake of the revolution. They characterized the Glorious Revolution as a change in the de jure institutions, alternatively "formal" institutions, specifically emphasizing how this constrained the future actions of the king. In fact, the Revolution Settlement actually established very few new de jure rules or rights. Its only clear innovative characteristic – the exclusion of Catholics from the throne – appears to have had very few long-term political or economic implications. Nevertheless, important institutional changes did take place. Rather than being de jure, the most significant of these were de facto, alternatively "informal," in the sense that they emerged in the context of a large change in the English political equilibrium that they greatly helped to consolidate and reinforce. This was important for the economy, but for different reasons than those proposed by North and Weingast.

2. North and Weingast's Argument

What then were the institutional innovations that in North and Weingast's view led to a transformation in England's political and economic fortunes? They start with the premise that the key impediment to economic success in the early modern period was that monarchies faced a commitment problem. Although it would have been advantageous for property rights to be secure, monarchs could not commit themselves to respect property rights. This severely undermined people's incentives to invest. The inability to commit caused inefficiencies in a variety of contexts. For instance, the monarch often needed to borrow to finance wars, but could not because he could not commit to repay those who lent him money. This commitment problem could potentially have been solved in different ways. North and Weingast (1989, 804) note,

A ruler can establish such commitment in two ways. One is by setting a precedent of "responsible behavior," appearing to be committed to a set of rules that he or she will consistently enforce. The second is by being constrained to obey a set of rules that do not permit leeway for violating commitments. We have very seldom observed the former.... The latter story is, however, the one we tell.

For North and Weingast, behavioral changes without institutional constraints are extremely unlikely to solve the commitment problem.

The view that North and Weingast develop is that the Glorious Revolution represented a change in institutions that "altered the incentives of

Acemoglu and James A. Robinson, *Why Nations Fail: The Origins of Power, Prosperity and Poverty* (New York: Crown, 2012).

government actors in a manner desired by the winners of the Revolution" (804). By changing the "rules of the game" that determined the costs and benefits of different actions by the king, the Glorious Revolution solved the problem of credibility because after 1688, it was either not feasible or not desirable for the king to renege on commitments. The Revolution of 1688 led to a "fundamental redesign of the fiscal and governmental institutions," which was mostly motivated by a desire to gain "control over the exercise of arbitrary and confiscatory power by the Crown" (804). The "Revolution settlement," North and Weingast claim, "restructured the society's political institutions." The Revolution, they imply, did not rely on a ruler "appearing to be committed to a set of rules that he or she will consistently enforce" (804) – that is, virtuous behavior – but rather "constrained" the ruler "to obey a set of rules that do not permit leeway for violating commitments" (804).

More specifically North and Weingast emphasize three "main features of the institutional revolution." The first is parliamentary supremacy and a "permanent role for Parliament" (816) and a situation where "the Crown no longer called or disbanded Parliament at its discretion alone." Second, Parliament gained a central role in financial matters with the crown kept on a short leash and Parliament being granted "the never-before-held right to audit how the government had expended its funds" (816). Third, royal prerogative powers "were substantially curtailed and subordinated to the common law, and the prerogative courts (which allowed the Crown to enforce its proclamations) were abolished" (816). In addition the "independence of the judiciary from the Crown was assured" with judges no longer serving "at the king's pleasure" (816).

North and Weingast go on to emphasize that these new rules were self-enforcing because of a credible threat of removal of any monarch who violated them. They point out that "the conditions which would 'trigger' this threat were laid out in the Revolution Settlement, and shortly afterwards the Declaration of Rights" (816). They also note that at the same time, the revolution did not create the opposite problem of parliamentary tyranny because "the institutional structure that evolved after 1688 did not provide incentives for Parliament to replace the Crown and itself engage in similarly 'irresponsible' behavior" (804). In essence a balance of power emerged.

These new institutions served to "limit economic intervention and allow private rights and markets to prevail in large segments of the economy" (808). They had many ramifications, for instance, they "significantly raised the predictability of government" (819).

3. What Really Happened?

Did the Revolution Settlement of 1689 instantiate the institutional changes that North and Weingast have stipulated? Did the Revolution Settlement guarantee parliamentary supremacy, allow Parliament for the first time to audit governmental spending, establish the supremacy of the common law, offer a new credible threat of removal against the king for malfeasance, and significantly raise the predictability of government?

Consider first parliamentary supremacy. Contemporaries and subsequent commentators have all noted that from 1689 onward, Parliament has met every year. "We were" by 1700, recalled the Whig bishop of Salisbury Gilbert Burnet, "become already more than half a commonwealth; since the government was plainly in the House of Commons, who met since once a year, and as long as they thought fit."[10] Julian Hoppit notes that "the Glorious revolution marked a sea change in the meetings of parliament."[11] "After 1689 there were sessions every year without fail," Mark Knights points out, "and each session lasted longer, averaging 112 days, almost double the Restoration figure." And the post-revolutionary parliament had a much larger set of legislative achievements. The average parliamentary session between 1689 and 1714 passed more than twice the number of statutes than had sessions before the accession of William and Mary.[12]

Profound as this change was, it is difficult to maintain, as North and Weingast have, that new institutions contained within the Revolution Settlement constrained the crown to call Parliament more regularly let alone annually. The Declaration of Rights, that document so central to the Revolution Settlement, merely stipulated that "Parliaments ought to be held frequently and suffered to sit."[13] Even this was no new development, as many contemporary commentators were well aware. In Edward III's reign, for example, Parliament had passed a statute that called for Parliament to "be holden every year, or oftener if need be."[14] At the time of the Revolution, one Whig recalled in the 1730s, it was not judged "necessary, to the security and preservation of the subjects' liberty" to insist on annual

---

[10] Gilbert Burnet, *History of His Own Time* (Edinburgh: Hamilton, Balfour and Neild, 1753), Vol. IV, 359.

[11] Julian Hoppit, "Patterns of Parliamentary Legislation, 1660–1800," *The Historical Journal* 39(1): 113.

[12] Mark Knights, *Representation and Misrepresentation in Later Stuart Britain* (Oxford: Oxford University Press, 2005), 12.

[13] Journal of the House of Commons, 7 February 1689, Vol. 10, 22.

[14] Archibald Hutcheson, A Speech Made in the House of Commons, on Tuesday the 24th of April 1716 (London: J. Baker and T. Warner, 1716), 3–4.

parliaments, much less elections every year or three years."[15] In the bill of rights, concurred Archibald Hutcheson two decades earlier, "among that long catalogue of grievances which precede the said declaration, there is not the least mention made of want of frequent elections, but only that parliament ought to be free."[16]

The Revolution Settlement was no more innovative with respect to financial accountability. The 1624 Subsidy Act had included a financial oversight clause that was triggered in 1625. The Long Parliament successfully implemented a variety of forms of financial oversight, establishing the Committee of Accounts in 1644. After the restoration of the monarchy in 1660, Charles II was forced to accept a new commission of accounts in 1667 that was explicitly modeled on the 1644 commission. After 1688, the government chose – but was not required to – provide the House of Commons with an annual estimate of its expenditures, though the Commons did create a statutory commission of accounts in 1691.[17]

There was also no new legislation enjoining the supremacy of the common law at the revolution. Again the Declaration of Rights did proclaim that "the commission for creating the late court of Commissioners for Ecclesiastical Causes, and all other commissions and courts of like nature, are illegal and pernicious."[18] But this was merely a restatement of old law. Parliamentary legislation in 1641 had eliminated the Courts of Star Chamber and High Commission, forbidding the future creation of prerogative courts.[19] The Revolution Settlement, in the view of its more fervent defenders, had not created new legislative constraints upon the crown. What had changed was Parliament's ability to enforce already existing laws. The English had long

---

[15] An Address to the Free-Holders of Great-Britain (London: J. Roberts, 1734), 46.

[16] Hutcheson, *Speech*, 1716, p. 7; Clayton Roberts, "The Constitutional Significance of the Financial Settlement of 1690," *Historical Journal* 20(1): 69. Roberts argues that no acts passed by Parliament in 1689 guaranteed frequent parliaments: It was the need for money.

[17] This paragraph relies on: Paul Seaward, "Parliament and the Idea of Accountability in Early Modern Britain," in *Realities of Representation: State-Building in Early Modern Europe and European America*, ed. Maija Jansson (Basingstoke: Palgrave Macmillan, 2007), 45–62; J. A. Downie, "The Commission of Public Accounts and the Formation of the Country Party," *English Historical Review* 91(358): 33–51; Clifford B. Anderson, "Ministerial Responsibility in the 1620s," *Journal of Modern History* 34(4): 381–389.

[18] Journal of the House of Commons, February 7, 1689, Vol. 10, 22.

[19] Angus McInnes, "When Was the English Revolution?," *History* 67(221): 381–383. McInnes's article emphasizes the minimal effect of much legislation passed between 1640–1660. He insists that the later Stuart kings were able to evade the legal restrictions that remained, but he does not deny that the prerogative courts were outlawed.

held many "ancient liberties," recalled Colley Cibber who had taken up arms in 1688, but they did not have "a real being, before the Revolution."[20]

Naturally James II's dramatic political demise in the winter of 1688–1689 did provide a warning to future monarchs. But for English kings this was a refresher course, not a new lesson. James II's father, Charles I, had not only lost his throne, but his head on January 30, 1649, for his alleged malfeasance in office. James II's brother, Charles II, had faced innumerable rebellions and a real threat of civil war in 1678–1681. And, of course, English political upheavals in the fifteenth century, so lovingly described in William Shakespeare's history plays, surely did not teach kings they were invincible. James II's deposition was indeed a stern warning. But it was hardly a new warning.

Far from making government more predictable, the Revolution of 1688 instantiated one of the most intensely polarized and unstable periods in English and then British history. The revolution gave birth to the rage of party. "Whig and Tory are as of old implacable," commented the poet and diplomat Matthew Prior in the 1690s.[21] "The heats and animosities grow everyday higher in England," William Blathwayt wrote to his fellow Whig George Stepney, "parties very much animated against one another."[22] The British were "a nation so divided into parties," wrote the politically enigmatic former paymaster of the queen's forces James Brydges in 1714, "that no one is allowed any good quality by the opposite side."[23] Party divisions cut deeply into British society. Party politics was not a game played only by a rarefied metropolitan elite. "If an Englishman considers the great ferment into which our political world is thrown at present, and how intensely it is heated in all its parts," the Whig journalist and future secretary of state Joseph Addison suggested in 1711, "he cannot suppose it will cool again in less than three hundred years."[24] Robert Molesworth thought that the party divisions accentuated after the revolution would "last as long amongst us as those of Guelf and Gibelline did in

---

[20] Colley Cibber, *An Apology for the Life of Colley Cibber* (London: R. and J. Dodsley, 1756) 4th ed., vol. I, 50.

[21] Matthew Prior (London) to earl of Manchester, November 13, 1699, Beinecke, OSB MSS fc 37/2/67.

[22] William Blathwayt (Breda) to George Stepney, July 21, 1701, Beinecke OSB MSS 2/Box 2/Folder 32; William Blathwayt (Dieren) to George Stepney, August 26, 1701, Beinecke, OSB MSS 2/ Box 2/Folder 33.

[23] James Brydges to Nicholas Philpott, September 29, 1714, HEH, ST 57/11, 10.

[24] *Spectator* 2(101) June 26, 1711: 11; *Spectator* 2(112) July 9, 1711: 167; *Spectator* 2(126) July 25, 1711: 250. All quotations from the 1758 Tonson edition.

Italy."[25] "A man is no sooner in England, he cannot set his foot over the border," agreed Daniel Defoe in his *Review*, "but he falls a party-making, a dividing, a caballing."[26] "The people of England, unhappily divided in their notions and in their politics," chimed in the Church of England cleric Arthur Ashley Sykes, "that all and every step approved by one side is for that very reason disapproved by the other."[27] "The general division of the British nation is into Whigs and Tories," concluded Addison, "there being very few, if any, who stand neuters in the dispute, without ranging themselves under one of these denominations."[28]

These party conflicts were not the staid, or ritualized contests of twenty-first-century industrial democracies. "It is most certain that no nation under heaven is so unhappy by means of our intestine quarrels and divisions," asserted one English pamphleteer reflecting on a plethora of comment by European observers, "we hate one another, and are ready to cut one another's throats."[29] This was no hyperbole, no rhetorical flourish. George Smalridge, the Tory Bishop of Bristol, thought there was "no other way of deciding the present quarrel between the parties" than by "a Civil War."[30] In fact, far from making government more stable and predictable, the revolution ushered in an age of remarkable instability. There were aborted rebellions in 1692, 1694, 1696, 1704, 1708, and 1722, and an all-out civil war in 1715. Even when elections generated relatively peaceful ministerial changes the financial markets took a beating. When the Tories took office in 1710, for example, Whig financiers refused to offer loans to the new government, setting off an international financial crisis.[31] The result was that foreign governments and domestic investors alike learned to be wary of radical policy shifts after each and every British election. The effect of party strife was not predictability but its opposite. "Our inconsistency in the pursuit of schemes," concluded Joseph Addison, "has as bad an influence on our domestic as on our foreign affairs."[32]

---

[25] Robert Molesworth, *The Principles of a Real Whig* (London: J. Williams, 1775), 6. This is a reprint of a 1711 work.

[26] Daniel Defoe, *Review* 4(136), December 25, 1707: 541.

[27] Arthur Ashley Sykes, *The Suspension of the Triennial Bill* (London: James Knapton, 1716), 22.

[28] *The Free-Holder* 19, February 24, 1716: 107; *The Free-Holder* 54, June 25, 1716: 379.

[29] An Epistle to a Whig Member of Parliament (London: J. Roberts, 1716), 7.

[30] George Smalridge Bishop of Bristol to Sir Roger Mostyn, October 8, 1715, Leicestershire Record Office, DG7/Box 4950/Bundle 24.

[31] David Stasavage, *Public Debt and the Birth of the Democratic State* (Cambridge: Cambridge University Press, 2003), 124.

[32] Jospeh Addison, *The Free-Holder* 25, March 15, 1716: 179.

While North and Weingast were right to insist on a radical change in English political behavior after 1688 – contemporaries echo their views that something profound had indeed changed – the mechanisms they have highlighted cannot have been the cause. Nothing in the Declaration of Rights or in the Revolution Settlement of 1689 specified that Parliament meet every year, created a new method for Parliament to audit royal spending, provided new guarantees for the supremacy of common law courts, or provided new credible threats of removal against miscreant rulers. Nor did the settlement instantiate more stable or predictable governments. The causes of England's revolutionary transformation must be sought elsewhere.

4. Evidence of Change

While North and Weingast may incorrectly specify the mechanisms generating England's remarkable economic and political transformation in the late seventeenth century, they are right to believe that something changed. Upon reviewing a range of economic statistics from the seventeenth century, Sir Robert Walpole's economic advisor John Crookshanks concluded that after the revolution, "the trade and interest of England had more security and encouragement than in all the preceding reigns." There was, he said, "a Masterly Genius presiding for the advantage of England."[33] The most obvious and most easily documented changes are in the political and legislative arena. We have already mentioned one very significant change – after 1688, Parliament met every year. Figure 9.1 illustrates the significance of this by plotting the number of days per year between 1660 and 1715. Though early on after the Restoration Charles II did summon Parliament, and Parliament sat frequently at very contentious times like the exclusion crisis of the late 1670s, the picture shows a distinct structural change after 1688. Figure 9.2, using data compiled by Julian Hoppit, shows another very significant innovation after 1688, a rapid acceleration in the volume of legislation that Parliament produced. This legislation dealt with many things that were important for the economy. For example, soon after the Glorious Revolution the first Calico Act (1701) was passed to protect the English textile industries. Other important legislation had the consequence of allowing large reorganizations of property rights that greatly facilitated not just the rational use of farm land via enclosures but also sped up the construction of infrastructure, particularly the spread of canals and turnpike roads.

---

[33] John Crookshanks (Twickenham) to Robert Walpole, August 17, 1724, Cambridge University Library, CH (H) Correspondence 1161.

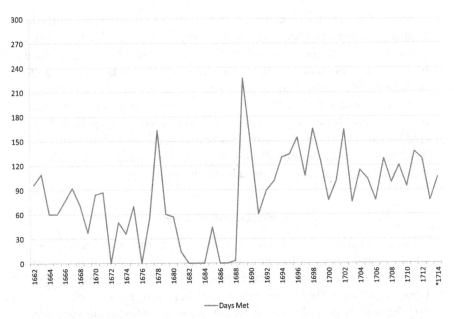

Figure 9.1. Number of days per-year that the House of Commons met, 1660–1715. *Source:* Author's calculations from the *Journal of the House of Commons*.

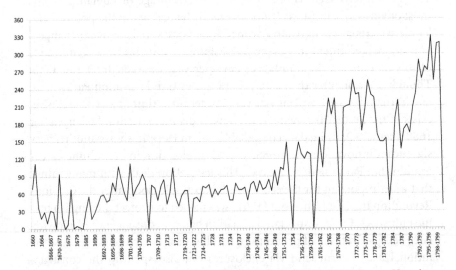

Figure 9.2. Amount of parliamentary legislation per year, 1660–1798. *Source:* Hoppitt, Julian. "Patterns of Parliamentary Legislation, 1660–1800." *The Historical Journal*, 39(1): 109–131.

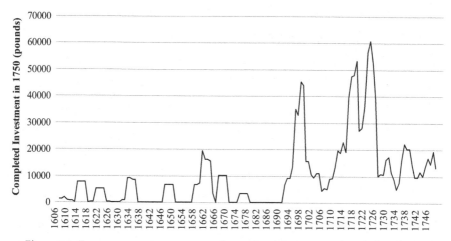

Figure 9.3. Four-year moving average of completed investment in road and river improvements, 1607–1749. *Source:* Dan Bogart. "Did the Glorious Revolution Contribute to the Transport Revolution? Evidence from Investment in Roads and Rivers," Forthcoming. *Economic History Review.*

Figure 9.3 uses data put together by Dan Bogart and illustrates that the increase in transportation legislation after 1688 did not just result in spilt ink. It also resulted in a rapid expansion of the transportation network.[34]

After the revolution, Parliament, for the first time, became a primarily legislative body. This gave a very different dynamic to policy making. One way of seeing this is the escalation of petitioning after 1688. Figure 9.4, based on information compiled from the Journal of the House of Commons, shows part of this. This figure records petitions received by the House per year and within all petitions identifies how many of them had some political economy content. We count a petition as having had political economic content if it concerned anything relating to the economic well-being of the country, including petitions from any professional groups (brewers, weavers) merchant petitions, petitions over land and transportation – building a harbor or road, and into the eighteenth century, payment of army arrears. Many petitions focused on the economy, for example, attacks on monopolies took

[34] On the volume of legislation see Julian Hoppitt, "Patterns of Parliamentary Legislation, 1660–1800," *The Historical Journal* 39(1): 109–131; on transportation see Dan Bogart, "Did the Glorious Revolution Contribute to the Transport Revolution? Evidence from Investment in Roads and Rivers," *Economic History Review* 64(4): 1073–1112; for evidence on the reorganization of property rights see Dan Bogart and Gary Richardson "Property Rights and Parliament in Industrializing Britain," *Journal of Law & Economics* 54(2): 241–274; see also Rick Szostak, *The Role of Transportation in the Industrial Revolution* (Montreal: McGill-Queen's University Press, 1991) for this argument.

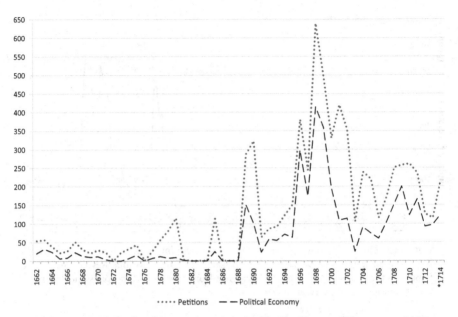

Figure 9.4. Number of petitions per-year received by the House of Commons, 1660–1715. *Source:* Author's calculations from the *Journal of the House of Commons.*

place via intense petitioning campaigns, and Parliament was responsive to these campaigns.[35] The figure shows vividly the take-off in petitioning after 1688 reflecting the new locus of authority and decision making in British politics.

Critics of the thesis that the Glorious Revolution was an important change have focused on the two areas that North and Weingast themselves emphasized. The first is the stability of property rights and the second the interest rate evidence. We largely agree that 1688 did not change the security of property rights. The earl of Nottingham, no Jacobite, pointed out that "the liberties and property of the subject were as little infringed in the reign

---

[35] On the role of petitions in the attack on the Royal Africa Company see William Pettigrew, "Free to Enslave: Politics and the Escalation of Britain's Transatlantic Slave Trade, 1688–1714," *William and Mary Quarterly,* 3rd series, 64(1): 3–38; for a more general statement of the importance of petitioning and parliamentary sovereignty for economic policy see William Pettigrew, "Some Under-Appreciated Connections Between Constitutional Change and National Economic Growth in England, 1660–1720," Unpublished; the responsiveness of the state is argued in Lee Davidson, Tim Hitchcock, Tim Keirn, and Robert B. Shoemaker, "Introduction: The Reactive State: English Governance and Society, 1689–1750," in *Stilling the Grumbling Hive,* ed. Lee Davidson et al. (New York: Palgrave Macmillan, 1992).

of King James as is in any other since the conquest except only in matters of religion" and in the arena of secular property little had changed since 1688.[36] But the fact that property rights were secure did not mean that economic policy was such as to promote economic growth. With respect to the interest rate evidence we believe that North and Weingast were themselves mistaken in pointing to falling interest rates as a key implication of their view. They deduced this hypothesis from the idea that default risk would reduce the supply of loans at any given interest rate, thus tending to increase the equilibrium interest rate relative to a situation with lower risk of default. However, the financial world of Charles II and James II was not one characterized by a competitive market where the interest rate changed to equilibrate the supply and demand for loans. Copious evidence in fact suggests that credit was rationed to the Stuart kings, because there was indeed a severe risk that they would default. With credit rationing the interest rate does not move to clear the market for loans. In financial terms what 1688 did was to relax this rationing of credit, but such relaxation should not show up in terms of lower interest rates but rather greater quantities of loans. That this was indeed the case is illustrated by Figure 9.5. That figure shows that while the Stuart kings were able to issue little debt, the monarchy after 1688 was able to borrow extensively. We believe therefore that the interest rate evidence is a red herring. A final telling piece of evidence that things changed after 1688 is represented in Figure 9.6 which shows government tax receipts per capita between 1490 and 1815. This figure shows the rapid expansion of the English/British state after the Glorious Revolution. The idea that the revolution was "conservative" or "restorative" cannot be reconciled with this evidence of such a structural change in fiscal policy and the size of the state, as of course it cannot be reconciled with the structural shift in the meeting of Parliament and the outpouring of new legislation.

5. Why Things Changed

Why did these changes happen? Why did English men and women turn to Parliament as a source of redress so much more frequently after 1688? Why did Parliament legislate with so much more frequency after 1688? Why did Parliament sit twice as long on average after 1688?

The answer, we suggest, was not that the English parliamentary classes agreed to "some credible restrictions on the state's ability to manipulate

---

[36] Earl of Nottingham, "Jacobitism," ca. 1715, Leicestershire Record Office, DG7/Box 4960/ P.P. 149.

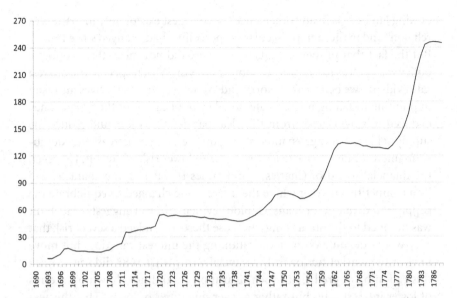

Figure 9.5. Total outstanding government debt (millions of pounds), 1690–1788. *Source:* Mitchell, Brian R. 1988. *British Historical Statistics.* Cambridge: Cambridge University Press.

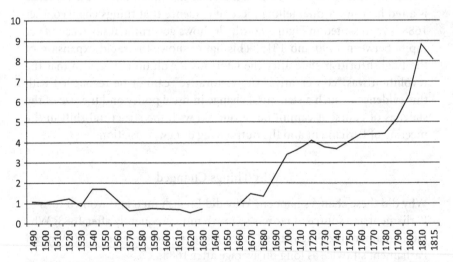

Figure 9.6. Total revenue per capita in England, 1490–1815 (in constant prices of 1451–75) (nine-year moving average). *Source:* O'Brien, Patrick K. and P. A. Hunt. 1999. "England 1485–1815," in Richard Bonney ed. *The Rise of the Fiscal State in Europe, 1200–1815.* Oxford: Oxford University Press. Data available at: http://esfdb.websites.bta .com/table.aspx?resourceid=11287.

economic rules to the advantage of itself and its constituents." The English did not in the wake of the Revolution agree to "limit economic intervention" (North and Weingast, 808). Instead, the changes after 1688 were caused by two interrelated factors. Most fundamentally, the Glorious Revolution did lead to a significant shift in power and authority to Parliament. This change set in motion a set of de facto institutional changes with very important consequences. These included parliamentary sovereignty and changed the locus of decision making with respect to both economic and foreign policy. Nevertheless, these changes in themselves would not have amounted to what they did without the rise of the Whig Party and the fact that it, and not the Tory Party, dominated the newly empowered Parliament.

To understand what went on and what didn't go on during and after the Revolution of 1688 it is crucial to put it in the context of the entire way the political equilibrium was changing in England during this period. After two decades of remarkable economic growth in the later seventeenth century, England was becoming a more dynamic, more urban, and more commercial society. The Venetian Resident Alberti reported in the 1670s "That the City of London has never had so much trade as now." John Houghton, in his new economically oriented periodical noted, "We have increased more in trade" since 1665 "than it is possible any nation has done in like space." This impression of substantial late-seventeenth-century English economic growth was confirmed by more statistically minded contemporaries as well as later scholars.[37]

---

[37] This is substantiated in chapter 3 of Steven Pincus, *The First Modern Revolution* (New Haven: Yale University Press, 2009); Daron Acemoglu, Simon Johnson, and James A. Robinson, "The Rise of Europe: Atlantic Trade, Institutional Change, and Economic Growth," *American Economic Review* 95(3): 546–579. D. C. Coleman, *Economy of England*, 92, 135, 200–201; Douglass C. North and Robert Paul Thomas, *The Rise of the Western World: A New Economic History* (Cambridge: Cambridge University Press, 1973), 109, 113, 118; Jan de Vries, *The Economy of Europe in an Age of Crisis* (Cambridge: Cambridge University Press, 1976), 17, 244–254; E. A. Wrigley, *Poverty, Progress and Population* (Cambridge: Cambridge University Press, 2004), 44–67; Clay, *Economic Expansion*, 1: 3. From the 1630s England's population remained steady at around 5 million people. Francois Crouzet, *A History of the European Economy* (Charlottesville: University Press of Virginia, 2001), 74; Alberti to Doge and Senate, 29 March 1675, CSPV, 380; Alberti to Doge and Senate, 23 November 1674, CSPV, 313–314; John Houghton, *A Collection of Letters*, April 27, 1682, 49; John Houghton, *England's Great Happiness*, 1677, 20; Abstract of a Representation of the General State of Trade, December 23, 1697, HEH, EL 9874, 1; Report of the Board of Trade, December 23, 1697, BL, Sloane 2902, f. 171v; W. E. Minchinton has claimed that "the Restoration was the economic exit from medievalism and the period 1660–1688 a period of commercial expansion": W. E. Minchinton, ed., *The Growth of Overseas Trade in the Seventeenth and Eighteenth Centuries* (London: Methuen & Co., 1969), 11.

The newly dynamic economy shifted the social balance. Manufacturers, urban dwellers, and colonial traders became much more wealthy. Most thought that as England became a nation of tradesmen and shopkeepers, there had been a shift of political power. John Aubrey was convinced that "the balance of the government [is] quite altered, and put into the hands of the common people." Dr. Charles Aldworth, a fellow of the ill-fated Magdalen College, confided to his commonplace book that recently "the commons" had "got the riches of the nation in their hands by trade" and had thus become "a match both for Kings and Lords." James II's friend and loyal supporter Sir Edward Hales knew that as a result of "the great increase in trade since Henry VIIIth's time," the English people had achieved "an equality of riches" and therefore power. Sir Henry Capel argued in Parliament that political trust was placed where "there is most property," and to him it was clear that "the property of England was in the Commons." Significantly, this was the conclusion of memorandum circulated widely in James II's court in 1685. "Trade and negotiation has infected the whole kingdom, and no man disdains to marry or mix with it," the author of the memorandum contended, "by this means the very genius of the people is altered, and it will in the end be the interest of the crown to proportion its maxims of power suitable to this new nature come among us." A variety of arithmetical calculations proved unequivocally that "trade is much the over-balance of the wealth of the nation, and consequently must influence the power for good or ill."[38] A large proportion of those who enjoyed this newfound political power were Whigs. The Whig Party, formed in 1679–1680, demonstrated its newfound political might in its sophisticated campaign to exclude the Duke of York, the future James II, from the throne. So powerful had they become, that many thought England was on the brink of civil war in 1681. On the eve of the revolution, then, rapid social change had altered the balance of property and therefore the political equilibrium in England.

James II responded dynamically to the changing sociology of power. He decided to shift the economic basis of royal power. Whereas previous English monarchs had based their authority on being the largest landowners

---

[38] Houghton, *England's Great Happiness*, 1677, 19; Guy Miege, *New State of England* (London: H. C., 1691), 2: 229; John Aubrey, *Wiltshire Collections*, c. 1670, John Edward Jackson, ed. (Devizes: Wiltshire Archaeological and Natural History Society, 1862), 9; Dr. Charles Aldworth, Commonplace Book, Essex RO, D/Dby Z56; Sir Edward Hales, "Treatise on Government," 1692, AWA, Old Brotherhood Papers, Book III/258; Sir Henry Capel, December 2, 1689, Grey, 9: 469; Barnes, *Memoirs*, Longstaffe, 213; "An Essay on the Interest of the Crown in the American Plantations," 1685, BL, Add. 47131, ff. 24–25.

in England, James realized this was an increasingly fragile economic foundation. James decided that England's economic future lay in the East and West Indies. This overseas element was crucial because the scope for unilaterally increasing taxation – on a class whose rents were steadily declining – within England was limited. To increase taxes without the consent of Parliament was impossible. Though James sought to pack Parliament with his supporters to pass his religious legislation, he aimed to secure a permanent increase in his revenue by expanding and rationalizing England's overseas empire. He created the Dominions of New England and the West Indies and sought, with the aid of the director of the East India Company, Josiah Child, to create a dominion of India based in Bombay. This new territorial empire, he believed, would allow him to split up the world with his French cousin Louis XIV. Louis XIV would rule over Europe, while James would have an English overseas empire. This new empire would fill James II's coffers with a minimum of parliamentary oversight. It was both the domestic and imperial projects that the revolutionaries cut short in 1688.

The immediate proximate outcome of the Glorious Revolution was that James's programs of absolutism both at home and abroad failed. William and Mary abandoned James II's grand plans to build a self-financing centralized empire. However, William and Mary were not constrained to abandon James II's grand imperial vision by the Bill of Rights or any other statutory element of the Revolution Settlement. Nothing in the Revolution Settlement stipulated the demise of the Dominions of New England or the West Indies; nothing demanded that Josiah Child's plans for a vast territorial empire in India be abandoned.

William and Mary also surrendered the right to collect customs for life. Since the reign of Henry IV, English kings had been granted the customs income for life on their accession. James II started to collect the customs before being granted it and announced "That some might possibly suggest that it were better to feed and supply him from time to time only, out of their inclination to frequent Parliaments; but that, would be but a very improper Method to take with him."[39] Persuaded by James II's promises not to alter the constitution in church and state, both Commons and Lords went along with it. In 1689, attitudes had changed. William wanted the customs for life, but he only got it for four years.

Another interesting example of William and Mary's tacit surrender of rights comes from reduced use of the royal prerogative. Though the

---

[39] E. A. Reitan, "From Revenue to Civil List, 1689–1702: The Revolutionary Settlement and the 'Mixed and Balanced' Constitution," *The Historical Journal* 13(4): 572.

monarchy had lost the prerogative courts in the 1640s this had not stopped Charles II and James II using the royal prerogative to establish the Ecclesiastical Commission. And both sons of Charles I had also intervened in the judiciary to remove judges whose decisions they did not like. Yet William did not. Consider the seminal case of *Nightingale v. Bridges* in 1689 where Justice Holt ruled that overseas trading monopolies could not be created by the royal prerogative but only by Parliament.[40] This was a significant blow to the power of the monarchy, but William did nothing.

Why did these changes occur? Why did William (and Mary) accede to demands that James II had refused? The answer cannot simply lie in the personality of William III. William was no closet republican. In fact, he had come to come to power in the United Provinces in 1672 after a wave of popular antirepublican riots. He emerged as the Stadholder, or political leader, of the United Provinces, only after the republican leaders John and Cornelius De Witt had been publicly lynched by Orangist (monarchist) mobs. William was, like his uncle James II, a Stuart with every reason to want a strong monarchy.

Scholars have treated the evident increase in parliamentary authority as a nonproblem. Some have argued that in the wake of the revolution, the parliamentary classes agreed to keep the king poor and this was the basis of Parliament's supremacy. Others have asserted that the English commitment to war after 1688 made parliamentary dominance inevitable.

Clayton Roberts has most forcefully developed the view that parliamentary power was based on keeping the monarchy short of money even in peacetime. Contemporaries certainly made similar arguments. For example, while the new monarchs "pressed" to have the customs settled for life, "it was taken up as a general maxim, that a revenue for a certain and short term, was the best security that the nation could have for frequent parliaments."[41] This was no retrospective rationalization. A wide variety of members of Parliament agreed, in the wake of James II's successful efforts to create an absolutist imperial state, that keeping the king "poor" was the best way to "necessitate him to call frequent parliaments."[42] Yet Roberts's own figures demonstrate that the only reason that William's revenues fell short of his expenditures was because he had allowed the Hearth Tax to be abolished in March of 1689 and because of a fall in customs revenues

---

[40] Steven Pincus, *The First Modern Revolution* (New Haven: Yale University Press, 2009), 385.

[41] Burnet, *History*, 1753, vol. 4, 61.

[42] *Some Remarks Upon Government* (London, 1689), 19.

created by the outbreak of war with France.[43] So William's financial straits were self-inflicted.

The view that warfare was the most significant determinant of parliamentary sovereignty after 1688 has many advocates. Jennifer Carter sums up this perspective: "In the 1690's the circumstances of the war gave Parliament an unexpected advantage over the Crown because the government needed money, and the political climate suggested to members of Parliament that they impose various limits on the powers of the Crown not contemplated in 1689."[44] In essence this view is that the desire of William III to conduct a large-scale war with France meant that he had to call Parliament every year in order that they pass a supply bill. It was this that empowered Parliament and allowed it to introduce such innovations as auditing the king's accounts.

Neither of these views is entirely satisfactory. Why did William agree to the abolition of the Hearth Tax that had brought James II an income of £200,000 a year? William himself told Sir George Savile the Marquis of Halifax that those who had persuaded him to give up the Hearth Tax wanted a commonwealth, something William himself clearly did not want.[45] Why did he commit himself to fighting a war that would significantly constrain his freedom of action? English kings had fought wars for centuries without diminishing their powers. Louis XIV was not forced by the Nine Years' War or the War of the Spanish Succession to cede much of his political authority. Why did the Nine Years' War and the War of the Spanish Succession have radically different political effects in England? The answer to these questions is to be found in the party politics of the later seventeenth and eighteenth centuries.

While many Whigs and Tories agreed in late 1688 to put an end to James II's absolutist imperialism, they had radically different visions of what to put in its place. The Tories wanted to dismantle the English fiscal-military state that had been growing by leaps and bounds since the 1640s. The Whigs wanted a big and interventionist state that would serve the interests of the new urban and manufacturing classes. The Whigs, in other words, wanted a state run by themselves and in their interests rather than an absolutist state. The Whigs, like most revolutionaries, wanted to capture the state. On most

---

[43] Clayton Roberts, "The Constitutional Significance of the Financial Settlement of 1690," *The Historical Journal* 20(1): 59–76.

[44] Jennifer Carter, "The Revolution and the Constitution," in *Britain After the Glorious Revolution*, ed. Geoffrey Holmes (London: St. Martin's Press, 1969), 55.

[45] H. C. Foxcroft, Life and Letters of Sir George Savile, Bart., First Marquis of Halifax (London: Longmans, Green, and Co., 1898), 2: 225.

issues, William III's sympathies were with the Tories. But William's highest priority was to limit the growing power of Louis XIV. Only the Whigs were willing and able to provide William the resources necessary to fight the world's greatest power.

From the outset, the Whigs had wanted to go to war with France. The party began to coalesce in the later 1670s, in part, to compel Charles II to go to war with Louis XIV. Andrew Marvell, John Locke, Algernon Sidney, William Lord Russell, and the first earl of Shaftesbury – the first generation of Whig politicians – had all been passionate Francophobes. Louis XIV, the Whigs believed, was trying to achieve a universal monarchy. He was trying to become a world hegemon. Central to Louis XIV's strategy, they argued, was to take over the world's trade. This was why Jean-Baptiste Colbert had done so much to jump-start French industry. This was why the French had established high tariff barriers to exclude English manufactures from much of Europe. In order to make his subjects "sole merchants of all trades," Louis XIV placed "all manner of discouragements upon all foreign factories and merchants by difficulty in their dispatches, delays in point of justice, subjecting them to foreign duties and seizures, not suffering them to be factors in the French or any other nation but their own, and in case of death to have their estates seized as aliens." The net effect of these measures was predictably devastating for English merchants. England, which continued to import French luxury items without the large protectionist imposts that Louis XIV placed on English goods, began to run up a huge trade deficit. The result was "that in few years (if some timely expedient be not applied) all the money of this nation will be drawn into France." The conclusion was inescapable: "the French doth deal far more unkindly with us than the Dutch."[46]

---

[46] The French Intrigues Discovered (London: R. Baldwin, 1681), 5–6, 15; Slingsby Bethel, Observations on the Letter Written to Sir Thomas Osborne (London: J. B., 1673), 11, 19; Popery and Tyranny: Or, The Present State of France (London, 1679), 13; Slingsby Bethel, An Account of the French Usurpation Upon the Trade of England (London, 1679), 6; Englands Glory By the Benefit of Wool Manufactured Therein, from the Farmer to the Merchant; and the Evil Consequences of its Exportation Unmanufactured (London: T. M., 1669), 8; The Reply of W. C. (1685), 3–4, 6–7, 9–10; The Ancient Trades Decayed, Repaired Again (London: T. N., 1678), 14–15. See also: Joseph Hill, The Interest of these United Provinces (Middelburg: T. Berry, 1673), sig. N4v; Francois de Lisola, The Buckler of State and Justice Against the Designs Manifestly Discovered of the Universal Monarchy, Under the Vain Pretext of the Queen of France Her Pretension (London: Richard Royston, 1673), 13; A Relation of the French King's Late Expedition into the Spanish Netherlands (London: John Starkey, 1669), sig. A3r; "Marquis de Fresno's Memorial," December 20, 1673, HEH, EL 8457; Roger Coke, A Discourse of Trade (London: H. Brome, 1670), sig. B1v; A Free Conference Touching the Present State of England Both at Home and Abroad

War against France was a central aim of the revolutionaries and William had, since the 1670s, led the European struggle against Louis XIV. Even before William and his entourage had reached London in December 1688 – even before it was clear that William and Mary would be offered the crown – English men and women throughout the nation were convinced that they would finally go to war against France, that they would finally engage in the struggle against the aspiring universal monarch Louis XIV. The news of the revolution "will be most of all menacing in France," thought Sir Robert Southwell, "all our thunderbolts will light there besides what may fall from the rest of Europe. They have great desolations and inhumanities to account for and it looks as if Heaven were now disposed to send an avenger." "This sudden revolution of affairs," the Levant Company informed Sir William Trumbull, "may occasion a speedy breech with France." The Dutch Ambassador Van Citters learned that "the City in the next Parliament will very strongly insist upon a war with France." The directors of the East India Company reported in early December 1688 that "war against France" was "the most general inclination of the English Protestants of all qualities and degrees." John Locke thought that no one in England "can sleep" until "they see the nation settled in a regular way of acting and putting itself in a posture of defense and support of the common interest of Europe."[47]

Not all wars needed to be so expensive. Not all wars required a financial revolution to finance them. But, the Whigs argued, a war against the world's greatest power required remarkable sacrifices. Such a war required new sorts of taxes and new sorts of financial instruments that could tap into the new wealth generated by the remarkable economic advances of the later seventeenth century. The Whigs maintained that the war was necessary whatever the cost. Sir John Lowther could not but admit the "extraordinary

(London: Richard Royston, 1678), 48–49; Edmund Ludlow, "A Voyce," Bodleian, Eng. Hist. C487, 1052; The Emperour and the Empire Betray'd (London: B. M., 1681), 68, 71–72; Whig polemic drew heavily on a pan-European literature: Hubert Gillot, Le Regne de Louis XIV et l'Opinion Publique en Allemagne (Nancy: A. Crepin-Leblond, 1914); P. J. W. Van Malssen, Louis XIV d'Apres les pamphlets Repandus en Hollande (Amsterdam: H. J. Paris, [1937]).

47   Sir Robert Southwell (Kingsweston) to Ormonde, December 14, 1688, Victoria and Albert Museum, Forster and Dyce Collection, F.47A.41, no. 28 (foliation illegible); Levant Company to Sir William Trumbull, December 14, 1688, BL, Trumbull MSS Misc 26, un-foliated (since recatalogued); Van Citters (London) to States General, November 30/December 10, 1688, BL, Add 34510, f. 192v; EIC to General and Council at Bombay, December 5, 1688, IOL, E/3/91, f. 297r; Locke to Edward Clarke, January 29, 1689, De Beer, *Correspondence*, 3: 546; Locke (Whitehall) to Charles Mordaunt, February 21, 1689, De Beer, *Correspondence*, 3: 575–576. See also: London Newsletter, December 28, 1688, HRC, Pforzheimer/Box 10/Folder 5.

charge" of the war, but he pointed out this was because England had never before gone to war "with so potent a prince as the French King." "I have always been of opinion that the French king is the most likely to trouble England," the ancient Whig William Sacheverell testified, "and I doubt not but gentlemen will give a million in trade" to support the war effort. The Gloucestershire Whig and former political exile Sir John Guise responded to Tory complaints about the cost of the war by insisting in November 1691 that "when I voted for the war against France, I was in earnest, and I have not abated since the war." "The taxes indeed fall heavy upon everybody," wrote Anne Pye, whose husband Sir Robert Pye had taken up arms in the parliamentary cause and again in the revolutionary cause in 1688, "but considering the slavery we are freed from, I wonder people complain." "We must do anything rather than be slaves to the French," argued succinctly the Whiggish absentee Barbados planter Edward Littleton.[48]

The Whig war strategy was an expensive one. They believed that the only way to defeat Louis XIV, to put an end to his aspirations for world hegemony, was to defeat him on land in Europe and at sea. To defeat Louis XIV, who had an army of more than 200,000 men at his disposal, required an unprecedented exertion from the English state. It required a financial revolution. The Whigs felt the only way to meet the costs would be to support growth in the manufacturing sector. This was why the Whigs insisted upon the repeal of the Hearth Tax – a tax that hit the manufacturing sector the hardest. This was why the Whigs created the Bank of England against stiff Tory opposition. The Bank of England, as opposed to the Tory Land Bank, was designed not only to provide loans to the government to support the war, but also to provide low-interest loans to manufacturers.[49]

---

[48] Sir John Lowther, March 31, 1690, Grey, 10: 23; William Sacheverell, March 22, 1690, Grey, 10: 6; Sir John Guise, November 19, 1691, Grey, 10: 176; Anne Pye to Abigail Harley, June 14, 1689, BL, Add 70014, f. 232r; Edward Littleton, *A Project of a Descent Upon France* (London: Richard Baldwin, 1691), 24. Littleton produced two other Whiggish pamphlets on the war: *Descent Upon France Considered* (London: Richard Baldwin, 1693) and *Management of the Present War Against France Consider'd* (London: R. Clavel et al., 1690). Abigail Swingen has highlighted the Whiggish aspects of his famous *Groans of the Plantations*: Abigail Swingen, *The Politics of Labor and the Origins of the British Empire, 1650–1720* (University of Chicago Dissertation, 2007), 2: 271. See also: *A Remonstrance and Protestation of All the Good Protestants . . . with Reflections Thereupon* (London: Randall Taylor, 1689), p. 15; *Advice to English Protestants* (London: J. D. for Awnsham Churchill, 1689), 22; *The Fate of France* (London: Richard Baldwin, 1690), sig. A2v.

[49] On party politics and the establishment of the bank, see Alice Wolfram and Steven Pincus, "A Proactive State? The Land Bank, Investment and Party Politics in the 1690s," in *Regulating the British Economy*, ed. Perry Gauci (Burlington VT: Ashgate, 2011).

The Tories, by contrast, wanted a very different kind of war. While they detested the Francophilic policies of James II, they did not feel as threatened as the Whigs by Louis XIV's project to dominate Europe. Perhaps because they were less dependent on European markets for their livelihoods, the Tories wanted a short and cheap war that would have as its fundamental aim the prevention of a Jacobite restoration. For Tories the war was always about defending the regime change in the British Isles. The struggle on the continent was a peripheral concern. So, for Tories like Colonel John Granville, it was clear that "of your enemies, your chiefest, [is] King James." Unsurprisingly, given this assessment, Tories were always far more interested in the course of the struggle in Scotland and Ireland than in the European war with Louis XIV.[50]

Tories quickly seized on the immense cost of the war and the massive interruption in English trade. The Nine Years' War was in fact larger than any previous English military commitment. The army ballooned to almost double what it had been under James II, and the naval forces were much more numerous as well. In all, England had on average more than 115,000 men in arms during the Nine Years' War. The average military expenditure was almost £5.5 million, or about 74 percent of the annual state budget. The average annual tax revenue during the war was about double what it had been before 1689. These kinds of numbers made Tories and their political allies quick to insist that the country could simply not afford a massive continental war. "If you make not an end of the war this year," insisted one of the most prominent Tories, Sir John Trevor, in November 1689, "I know not how we can supply another." "I do believe that we cannot supply the war above a year longer," chimed in the ancient and quirky William Garraway, who had once again fallen in line with the Tories. The diehard Tory Sir Edward Seymour told the House of Commons that it was "mistaken" to believe that "England was in a condition to carry on the war for themselves and the confederates."[51]

For Tories, the remedy was increasingly clear: England should sever its continental commitments and adopt a blue-water policy. Such a strategy, the Tories argued, would be much less expensive, would allow England to

---

[50] Colonel John Granville, April 29, 1690, Grey, 10: 96; Sir Thomas Clarges, May 1, 1690, Grey, 10: 107; Roger Morrice Entering Book, April 27, 1689, DWL, 31 Q, 546–547; Roger Morrice, Entering Book, June 8, 1689, DWL 31 Q, 568; *A Smith and Cutler's Plain Dialogue about Whig and Tory* (London, 1690), 1.

[51] John Brewer, *Sinews of Power*, 29–40, 89; Sir John Trevor, November 2, 1689, Grey, 9: 393; William Garraway, November 2, 1689, Grey, 9: 392; Sir Edward Seymour, November 2, 1689, Grey, 9: 390.

protect its trade, and would obviate the necessity of relying on untrustworthy and perfidious allies. Sir Thomas Clarges had long insisted that "the strength of England consists in our navy." In the 1690s Clarges continued to defend a blue-water strategy in the war against France. By sending "all our force into Flanders" where Louis XIV was "irresistible," the only outcome would be to "ruin England." "The most natural way" for England to fight the war, Clarges suggested, was "by sea." The English should become "masters of America" rather than dominant in Europe. "As we are an island," Clarges pointed out, "if the French have all the seventeen provinces [of the Dutch Republic and the Spanish Netherlands], and we are superior at sea, we may still be safe." England's "security," agreed Sir Edward Seymour, was "to be found only in the fleet." The new Tory ally Robert Harley agreed "that the sea must be our first care, or else we are all prisoners to our island." Sir Richard Temple, who was a committed Tory after 1689, believed passionately that "it imports this monarchy to have a vigorous militia at sea both for defense, offense and commerce." A land army, he thought, was unnecessary for England. Instead of alliances and conquests on the continent, Temple argued, "the enlargement of trade and Dominion of the Sea ought to be the proper object of our Empire." Tory advocates of a blue-water strategy had coalesced around the notion "that England is not much concerned in the general fate of Europe," "that the sea which divides us from the rest of the world is our safeguard against all dangers from abroad," and "that when we engage in any foreign war, it is not so much for our preservation, as to make a show of our power."[52]

The Tories consistently initiated a series of legislative projects to make it difficult to finance the war. In 1693, for example, the Tories penned a bill, the Triennial Bill, to guarantee that parliamentary elections would be held at least once every three years. Although scholars have usually assumed that this was part and parcel of the Whig agenda, it was not. The Whigs wanted Parliament to meet frequently both because that would make it easier for Parliament to obstruct an arbitrary king and because frequent meetings made it much easier to pass social and economic legislation, legislation that would facilitate economic development. "It is not in the frequent elections

---

[52] Sir Thomas Clarges, November 16, 1685, Grey, 8: 366; DWL, 31 T III, 17; Sir Thomas Clarges, November 19, 1691, Grey, 10: 177; Sir Thomas Clarges, November 21, 1692, Grey, 10: 264; Sir Edward Seymour, November 21, 1692, Grey, 10: 271; [Robert] Harley, November 21, 1692, Grey, 10: 268; Sir Richard Temple, "An Essay Upon Government," Bodleian, MS Eng. Hist. c. 201, ff. 6–7, 13; *A Letter Written to One of the Members of Parliament* (London, 1692), 2. The author is summarizing the position to criticize it; Charles Leslie, *Delenda Carthago*, 1695, 1.

of Parliament, but in their frequent sitting, that our safety consists," one Whig pamphleteer put it pithily.[53] Tories introduced the bill into the House of Commons in 1693 and eventually forced it through because they believed no member of Parliament who had to face the electorate with any regularity would vote for new taxes. At the very least, frequent changes of administration would make it difficult to undertake any grand and expensive projects. Frequent elections meant smaller government.[54]

The Tories were not satisfied with the Triennial Bill. From 1691, the Commission of Accounts – meant to inquire into the finances of the war – took on an increasingly Tory character. The reasons were obvious: The Tories were interested in limiting government expenditure on the war.[55] In 1696 the Tories sought to limit the war effort by destroying the Bank of England. Harley and Foley, the same men behind the Triennial Bill and the Commission of Public Accounts, brought in a bill to create the Land Bank and destroy the Bank of England.

Despite Tory victories in a variety of skirmishes, the Whigs determined the direction of English (and then British) policy in the decades following the revolution. Whig ministers directed the war efforts in the Nine Years War' and the War of the Spanish Succession. Whig institutions – the bank, the Land Tax, the new East India Company, the Duke of Marlborough's army – provided the essential infrastructure for the war effort. Whig financiers

---

[53] *An Epistle to a Whig Member of Parliament* (London: J. Roberts, 1716), 17; Arthur Ashley Sykes, *The Suspension of the Triennial Bill* (London: James Knapton, 1716), 5.

[54] The architects of the triennial bill were Tories Robert Harley and Paul Foley, with substantial support from the Tory earl of Nottingham. The Tories spoke against repeal in 1716, whereas the Whigs advocated repeal. Robert Harley, January 28, 1693, Narcissus Luttrell's Diary, January 28, 1693, All Souls College, MS 158b, p. 309; Sir Joihn Lowther of Lowther, January 28, 1693, Luttrell's Diary, January 28, 1693, ASC, MS 158b, p. 310; Sir Thomas Clarges, January 28, 1693, Luttrell's Diary, ASC, MS 158b, p. 310; Paul Foley, January 28, 1693, Luttrell's Diary, ASC, MS 158b, p. 310; Robert Harley, February 9, 1693, Luttrell's Diary, ASC, MS 158b, p. 344; Narciss Luttrell's Diary, March 14, 1693, ASC, MS 158b, p. 439; *Exeter Mercury or Weekly Intelligencer*, April 17, 1716, issue 60: 4; Daniel Defoe, *Some Considerations on a Law for Triennial Parliaments* (London: J. Baker and T. Warner, 1716), 12; *The Alteration of the Triennial Act Considered* (London: R. Burleigh, 1716), 4; Walter Moyle to Horace Walpole, April 20, 1716, *Memoirs of Sir Robert Walpole* (London: T Cadell, 1798), vol. 2: 62; *An Address to the Free-Holders of Great-Britain* (London: J. Roberts, 1734), 46–47. Whigs from the first claimed that the triennial bill was a Jacobite plot to put an end to the war: Lord Falkland, February 9, 1693, Luttrell's Diary, ASC, MS 158b, p. 346; Sir Charles Sedley, February 9, 1693, Luttrell's Diary, ASC, MS 158b, p. 344.

[55] Angus McInnes, *Robert Harley, Puritan Politician* (London: Gollancz, 1970) 44; Downie, "Commission of Public Accounts," 33–51. Downie and McInnes disagree as to when the commission became a political tool. But what Downie sees as a coalition opposed to war spending is what we and others see as the basis of the new Tory party.

provided loans at key moments. All of this had profound, indeed revolutionary, social consequences. Tories were convinced that the Whigs were the party of social revolution. Whigs supported the war, they believed, in large part because its escalating costs and increasingly punishing taxes were destroying the landed interest.[56] At the time of the revolution, St. John later recalled, "the moneyed interest was not yet a rival able to cope with the landed interest, either in the nation or in Parliament." All that had now changed, St. John informed Orrery in 1709, because "we have now been twenty years engaged in the most expensive wars that Europe ever saw." "The whole burden of this charge," St. John was sure, was paid by "the landed interest during the whole time." The result was that "a new interest has been created out of their fortunes and a sort of property which was not known twenty years ago, is now increased to be almost equal to the *Terra Firma* of our island." According to St. John, "the landed men are become poor and dispirited."[57] Tory "lands" had paid for the Whig wars, complained *The Examiner*.[58] "Power, which according to the old maxim was used to follow the land, is now gone over to money." "If the war continues some years longer" warned the authors of this Tory newspaper, "a landed man will be little better than a farmer at rack-rent to the army, and to the public funds."[59] This was not, in the Tory estimation, an unintended consequence of the Nine Years' War and the War of the Spanish Succession. The cries for "supporting a common cause against France, reducing her exorbitant power, and poising that of Europe in the public balance" were "specious pretences" of the Whigs to allow them to pile "taxes upon taxes, and debts upon debts" so that "a small number of families" could gain "immense wealth." "In order to fasten wealthy people to the New Government" the Whigs, according to *The Examiner*, had "proposed these pernicious

---

[56] The landed interest was, of course, in large part an ideological construct; see Julian Hoppit, "The Landed Interest and the National Interest, 1660–1800," in *Parliaments, Nations and Identitties in Britain and Ireland, 1660–1850*, ed. Hoppit (Manchester: Manchester University Press, 2003), 84.

[57] Henry St. John, Viscount Bolingbroke, *Letters on the Study and Use of History* (London: A. Millar, 1752), Letter 8, 267–268, 382–383; Henry St. John (Bucklebury) to Orrery, July 9, 1709, Bodleian, Eng. Misc. e. 180, ff. 4–5. While I agree on many issues with Isaac Kramnick, I dissent from his view that Bolingbroke's thought was shaped by the credit crisis of 1710 and the later South Sea Bubble. Bolingbroke's social critique was already manifest. Kramnick, *Bolingbroke and His Circle* (Cambridge, MA: Harvard University Press, 1968), 63–64. Dickinson is surely right to read this letter as expressing "the views of the Tory squires." H. T. Dickinson, *Bolingbroke* (London: Constable, 1970), 69.

[58] *The Examiner*, 4(1) August 24, 1710.

[59] *The Examiner*, 14(1) October 26–November 2, 1710.

expedients of borrowing money by vast premiums, and at exorbitant interest."[60]

The Whig war strategy had succeeded in turning the British social world upside down. "The effects of frequent parliaments and of long wars," Henry St. John mourned, was "the departing from our old constitution and from our true interest."[61] The authors of *The Examiner* later drew a verbal picture of the social revolution that had taken place. "Our streets," they complained, "are crowded with so many gay upstarts" that they "outshine our quality in furniture and equipage. Our English gentry with the antiquated bodies and virtues of our forefathers, are perfectly lost in a blaze of meteors." This was bad enough. But Britain's natural rulers not only faced competition in the world of the beaux monde. They also risked being replaced. "We have seen footmen removed from behind the coach into the inside, and the livery left off for the laced coat," observed the authors of *The Examiner* chillingly. "Princes have been made out of pages, chancellors out of clerks, and the white staff and blue ribbon bestowed as playthings upon the lackey and by-blow."[62] No wonder the Whigs had "a rage of warring."[63]

The Tories wanted a cheap war that would make the state unnecessary. They hoped to fight a sea war that would pay for itself. By the early eighteenth century, the Tories thought that seizing a territorial foothold in South America and access to the fabulous wealth of the South American silver and gold mines, would allow them to pay off the war debt and make further increases in state finance unnecessary. Britain could once again be governed by a landed elite supported by a territorial empire. The Whig war strategy, by contrast, required a large redistributive state. The Whigs wanted to stop French expansionism. But they hoped to do that by prying open European and Spanish American markets for British manufactured goods. They were happy to spend and spend to defeat the French, especially as the expenditures would help to support new and burgeoning British industries.[64]

---

[60] Bolingbroke, *Letters on the Study and Use of History*, 1752, Letter 8, 341–342; *The Examiner*, 6(1), August 31–September 7, 1710; *The Examiner*, 14(2), October 26–November 2, 1710.

[61] Henry St. John (Whitehall) to Orrery, June 12, 1711, Bodleian, MS. Eng. Misc. e. 180, f. 85r. He later elaborated that "the state is become, under ancient and known forms, a new and undefinable monster, composed of a king without monarchical splendor, a senate of nobles without aristocratical independency, and a senate of commons without democratical freedom." *Letters on the Study and Use of History*, 1752, Letter 8, 387.

[62] *The Examiner*, 3(15) January 9–12, 1713: 2.

[63] Bolingbroke, *Letters on the Study and Use of History*, 1752, Letter 8, 381–382.

[64] These points are substantiated at greater length in Steve Pincus, "The Pivot of Empire: the Sir John Neale Lecture," in *Rethinking the British Empire in the Augustan Age* ed. Jason Peacey (forthcoming).

Had the Tories dominated politics in the decades after the revolution, English (then British) state and society would have looked very different. Both Whigs and Tories, it is true, were interested in making sure that no future James IIs could come to power. Both Whigs and Tories agreed to put an end to the possibility of royal arbitrary government. But the Tories would not have fought a series of incredibly expensive wars against France. The Tories would not have created the Bank of England, an institution that provided crucial loans to new manufacturing initiatives. The Tories would not have wanted a standing parliament that could legislate over such a wide swath of social and economic life. The Tories would not have passed the series of turnpike acts, for example, that did so much to improve Britain's economic infrastructure. The Tories, in effect, would have created – or tried to create – a vast territorial empire with a remarkably small state. That this did not happen, that the Whigs were able to seize the political initiative after 1688, had a great deal to do with the shifts that had already taken place in the sociology of power prior to 1688.

These arguments suggest that the right way to think of the Glorious Revolution is of a series of interlinked institutional changes that took place in the broader context of a reorientation of the political equilibrium of England. The conflict stopped in its tracks the absolutist project that had started with Charles II and intensified with James II, but it did not do only this. It did not simply recreate a status quo ante or constrain future kings from doing the sort of thing that Charles and James had tried to do. Rather, it led to a permanent increase the in the power and authority of Parliament. Some, like Lois Schwoerer, would argue that this increased power was manifested in the change in the oath of office the king had to make and in the fact that Parliament had changed the order of succession, both part of the de jure process that generated the Declaration of Rights.[65] Such a view would be consonant with that stressed by North and Weingast. But we have argued that it is very difficult to tie any of the significant changes to any clauses of the Declaration or subsequent Bill of Rights. The Glorious Revolution was not significant because it was a change in the de jure rules, but it was important in helping to cement a change in the distribution of power in the country. We have shown that this change was manifested in many ways, via William not trying to assume the collection of customs for life, in the reduced use of the royal prerogative and in the adoption of policies, such as the repeal of the Hearth Tax, which William clearly did not like.

---

[65] Lois G. Schwoerer *The Declaration of Rights, 1689* (Baltimore: Johns Hopkins University Press, 1981).

This change had very significant consequences for institutions. The emergence of parliamentary sovereignty changed the way that economic and foreign policy was made. Policy now responded to different interests both inside and outside Parliament. In 1678 Parliament had tried to make Charles II go to war. It failed. In March and April of 1689 an address to the House of Commons urged William to go to war before he wanted to. William tried to suppress the address, but Parliament now got its way.

What enforced this de facto institutional change? It is possible that the key role here was played by the threat of revolution "off the equilibrium path," but we have argued that this seems too blunt a tool to have really worked and anyway had long been present. The Revolution Settlement did not define what constituted a violation sufficiently egregious to warrant revolt and didn't even create a mechanism by which Parliament could constitute itself if the king failed to call it. William vetoed laws and even prorogued Parliament when it looked like it might pass legislation he didn't like. Why didn't that trigger revolt? An alternative hypothesis about what made these changes self-enforcing is the juxtaposition of William's need for financial resources and the intensified warfare England embarked on after 1688. But as we have argued neither the financial argument nor war on their own seem sufficient to explain the changes. Moreover, neither mechanism would have operated without the shift in authority to Parliament which after 1688 induced William to abolish the Hearth Tax and called the shots on foreign policy, including the decision to initiate war. These mechanisms also would not have operated without the dominance of the Whig Party, which wanted an expensive war and greatly expanded role for the state. Nevertheless, the exact nature of the changes that made the new set of institutions self-enforcing needs a great deal of further research.

6. Conclusions

In this paper we have argued that contrary to the consensus view of political and economic historians, North and Weingast were correct to emphasize the importance of the Glorious Revolution as a significant institutional change. They were right that this represented part of a dramatic shift in the political equilibrium of England (then Britain). What they have described imprecisely was the nature of this shift and the mechanisms via which it transformed the economy. We have argued that the shift was not one of rewriting the de jure rules of the game, as they characterized it, but was rather a change in the distribution of power in favor of Parliament that had important consequences for de facto institutions. An important component of these changes flowed from the fact that Parliament came to be dominated by the newly dynamic manufacturing middle classes. However, the importance of this change for future economic growth did not stem from the fact that it established a credible commitment to property rights. We agree with other scholars that although the Stuart monarchs had attempted to intervene in the economy and judiciary, there was not a sufficiently broad threat to property rights to hold back investment or innovation.[66] We also believe that the revolution was important not because it led to a balance of power between the legislature and executive or because it led to stability or a small state but because the new political equilibrium featured parliamentary sovereignty and Parliament was to be dominated by the Whig Party for the coming decades. This had several momentous consequences. The first set flowed from parliamentary dominance itself with the consequent switch in the nexus of authority. This led to very significant policy changes because party political ministries, rather than the king's private advisors, now initiated policy. Because party ministries depended on public support to stay in power, they were necessarily more responsive to public pressure. After 1688 party politicians rather than the king set the economic agenda. The second set emanated from the Whig dominance because it meant that the economic program of the Whigs began to be implemented. That program was intentionally designed to accelerate growth of the manufacturing sector.

Acknowledgments

This paper was written for Douglass North's ninetieth birthday celebration. We would like to thank Doug, Daron Acemoglu, Stanley Engerman, Joel Mokyr, and Barry Weingast for their comments and suggestions. We are grateful to Dan Bogart, Julian Hoppit, and David Stasavage for providing us with their data and to María Angélica Bautista and Leslie Thiebert for their superb research assistance.

---

[66] A caveat to this argument though is that had James II succeeded in his attempt to build an absolutist state, property rights might have become a lot less secure.

10

The Grand Experiment That Wasn't?

New Institutional Economics and the Postcommunist Experience*

Scott Gehlbach and Edmund J. Malesky

Within the academy, the collapse of communism was greeted with optimism that the "natural experiment" underway in Eastern Europe and the former Soviet Union would put to rest long-running debates about the origins and consequences of various institutions stressed by Douglass North and other new institutionalists. With the advantage of hindsight, this optimism appears to have been somewhat misplaced. Identification of causal effects has proven difficult, and few debates have been definitively resolved. Scholars who hoped to identify the effect of constitutions have progressively pushed back the causal apparatus, such that today the emphasis is as much on the precommunist experience as on the postcommunist transition. At the same time, the advent of new data and a change in focus to within country institutions have begun to pay dividends for the study of another key institution: property rights at the level of the firm. In the pages that follow, we trace this evolution of the literature, showing how the study of transition has responded and contributed to our understanding of key political and economic institutions.

1. A Natural Experiment?

Before the first Soviet tank withdrew across an East European border and the last Trabant rolled off a dusty East German production line, a wave of anticipation swept the social sciences. As everyday observers, scholars watched history unfold with the anxious hope that the Cold War was drawing to a close. As academics, however, there was another, more immediate reason to celebrate the fall of the Berlin Wall and the collapse of the Soviet Union: the promise of a large-scale, country-level experiment in political and economic change.

It is sometimes said that social scientists have natural-science envy. This may be true. But the attraction is not the rigor of the scientific method or the mathematical modeling. We have plenty of both. For many, it is instead the elegance of the randomized medical trial, the parsimony of the vacuum chamber – the confidence that one can actually isolate and test a causal theory. Although laboratory experiments play a central role in behavioral economics and psychology, and field experiments are becoming increasingly common in development economics and political economy, there are many important topics that are simply off-limits to randomized control trials. It would be clearly unethical (not to mention impractical), for instance, to randomly sow civil war across countries in order to observe its socioeconomic consequences.

Unfortunately, many of the concerns of those interested in the New Institutional Economics identified with Douglass North and others fall into this category. By the time we observe institutions, they have often existed for decades or centuries, enmeshed in complex feedback loops that make it extremely difficult to isolate origins, causes, and effects. Moreover, institutions are not the only determinants of economic performance: Geographic and economic endowments, for example, also play a role, often in interaction with institutions. How do we disentangle the impact of institutions from the role played by other factors, and what drives institutional change? Even when we can identify the unique origin of a particular institution, its very selection may represent the negotiation between actors with an eye toward its future consequences. In these cases, should the institution be credited for economic outcomes, or would another institution have accomplished the same goals, given the bargaining power and goals of the actors who constructed it?

And then it happened. Beginning in 1989, the hammer and sickle came crashing down in the Eastern Bloc, with twenty-seven newly formed countries emerging from the wreckage. Each would transition from its communist past, meaning it would simultaneously choose new sets of economic and political institutions. Because students of transition were there at the creation, we would be able to observe, in our lifetimes, the choice, crystallization, and impact of these institutions. Nina Bandelj described the rare opportunity to observe institutional creation: "Social scientists rarely come across a natural experiment setting that allows them to examine the conditions under which a market comes into existence de novo" (Bandelj 2004, 3). Similarly, Jeffrey Checkel expressed the excitement over the promise of a relatively controlled environment: "The revolutions in Eastern Europe and the dissolution of the USSR . . . present a golden opportunity – a theorist's dream – to control better for the independent effect of the different variables" (Checkel 1993, 297).

They were not alone. A Google Scholar search of "natural experiment" and "former Soviet Union" today yields more than 1,200 academic books and articles, including work by some of the most prominent names in economics, sociology, psychology, and even the natural sciences. Among the purported experiments available for study are those that examine key arguments from the New Institutional Economics, not least of which is the centrality of property rights to economic growth (North and Thomas 1973). Heading an ambitious project that began in cooperation with the late William Riker, for example, David Weimer welcomed the "extraordinary 'natural experiment' for comparative study on a grand scale of the political economy of property rights" (Weimer 1997, xv). With twenty-seven transition countries unwinding years of state ownership and central planning, fundamental decisions needed to be made about ownership and defense of private property. Weimer's research team saw a unique opportunity to observe how these decisions affected business investment and economic growth. Among the project's many contributions were investigations into the process of privatization and the creation of property rights anew (Frye 1997), the origins of credible commitments to protect the property of citizens and investors (Diermeier, Ericson, Frye, and Lewis 1997; Weingast 1997), the role of political organizations such as legislatures in defining and defending property rights (Kiernan and Bell 1997) and the interaction between property rights and contracting institutions (Ericson 1997).

Others aimed even more broadly, targeting the fundamental relationship between economic and political institutions and GDP growth (Wolf 1999; Fidrmuc 2001; Pomfret 2003; Krammer 2008; Eicher and Schrieber 2010). Paakkonen (2008, 2) summarized the key assumption behind the enterprise:

The troublesome simultaneity of human capital and institutions is more or less controlled, since the level of human capital in the beginning of transition was high and roughly at the same levels across the countries. Yet we witness markable [sic] differences in the growth performance, not explained by the differences in the initial human capital.

Some scholars used the term "natural experiment" more metaphorically than literally, as a close examination of the quote from Weimer demonstrates. Moreover, there were some notable early contributions that stressed the importance of historical legacies for post communist outcomes, including the design of privatization policies (Stark 1992; Earle, Frydman, and Rapaczynski 1993). Nonetheless, the general optimism that the collapse of communism could teach us something about institutions had much to do with the belief that the postcommunist experience approximated conditions of a controlled laboratory experiment: "what [communism] left behind was, in institutional terms, a tabula rasa" (Elster, Offe, and Preuss 2000, 25).

Heightening this sense of opportunity was a contemporaneous development in the social sciences: the publication in 1990 of Douglass North's *Institutions, Institutional Change, and Economic Performance* (North 1990a). Although North's work was already well-known among many economists and political scientists, for numerous scholars this landmark text clarified the questions of transition. (An admittedly conservative Google Scholar search of "Douglass North" and "postcommunism" yields nearly 1,000 hits.) The determinants of economic performance included not only formal but informal institutions, including culture, beliefs, and other topics hitherto relegated to the "softer" social sciences. Politics and economics were intertwined. Transition was therefore not merely a question of economic and political liberalization, but a "process of large-scale institutional change" (Dewatripont and Roland 1996).

Moreover, the fact of institutional change could not be taken for granted, even with the collapse of the Berlin Wall. As North (1990a, 37) wrote,

Even the Russian Revolution, perhaps the most complete formal transformation of a society we know, cannot be completely understood without exploring the survival and persistence of many informal constraints.

Surely the same was true of the velvet revolutions of 1989 and the disintegration of Soviet communism in 1991.

In this chapter, we track the research agenda that grew out of the East European and post-Soviet experience. We ask: What has postcommunism taught us about institutions, institutional change, and economic performance? Rather than an exhaustive survey of the literature, we focus on two institutions central to the New Institutional Economics and the postcommunist transition: constitutions and private property. In both cases, we show that although the heuristic of the natural experiment was appealing, in practice it has often proved misleading. Countries and firms started the postcommunist transition with extremely different baselines, so that very little was actually held constant across units in the switch to market-based economic systems; institutions were selected based on initial conditions that often had independent effects on outcomes; and institutions and outcomes have interacted repeatedly over time. As a result, much of the optimism over what seemed like an unparalleled opportunity to resolve long-standing debates has been lost.

Nevertheless, some progress has been made, especially as new data have become available and attention has shifted to within-country studies, where more heterogeneity can be held constant. Moreover, the postcommunist experience has generated more than its share of anomalous behavior, and we have learned something about institutions in attempting to explain these outcomes. As we will show, the more vigorously we push to explain post-communist outcomes, the more we are forced to confront and understand the full spectrum of issues raised by Douglass North over the course of his career. Indeed, one might argue that this is the primary contribution to the social sciences of the transition experience: to illustrate that we cannot understand social outcomes without understanding the process of institutional change.

2. The Constitution Experiment

The postcommunist transformation was (at the very least) a "dual transition," with simultaneous change in both political and economic institutions. From a Northean perspective, the key insight was that these transitions were not separable. Modern economic growth is tied to the existence of political constitutions that encourage investment and the development of markets (North and Weingast 1989; Weingast 1993, 1995). One of the great questions of the early transition era followed directly from this understanding: Which constitutional arrangements were most likely to lead to economic reform and long-term growth?

The debate over constitutional arrangements had its roots in a well-developed literature in comparative politics, much of it based on the Latin American and East Asian experience. Following the literature, we focus on two key features of constitutions: form of government and electoral system.[1]

With respect to form of government, there was strong disagreement among scholars as to whether presidential or parliamentary systems were better able to generate democratic stability and economic growth (Lijphart 1992; Stepan and Skach 1993; Linz 1994). One group argued that strong presidencies, defined as those with few constraints placed on them by other institutions, could undersupply public goods and therefore undermine political stability in developing states (e.g., Linz and Valenzuela 1994;

---

[1] Some of these arguments have been subsequently worked out formally; see, for example, Persson and Tabellini (2000).

Przeworski et al. 1996). By contrast, other scholars emphasized the ability of citizens in presidential systems to identify the particular actors responsible for policy decisions, thereby providing presidencies with greater transparency and accountability (Shugart and Carey 1992, 42–46), which could generate better public-goods provision and stability.

The debate over electoral systems echoed that over form of government, with a contrast drawn between systems that offer greater representation and those that provide more accountability. Because proportional-representation systems more precisely translate parties' vote shares into parliamentary seat shares, they facilitate the greatest spectrum of policy views in the legislature (Lijphart 1984, 1994; Huber and Powell 1994; Powell and Vanberg 2000), providing greater opportunities to exploit policy trade-offs when designing reforms and offering additional checks on opportunistic behavior. On the other hand, majoritarian systems promote greater accountability. Voters can identify the policymaker responsible for particular policies, and if s/he does not do their bidding, they can vote him or her out in the next election (Carey and Hix 2009).

The debate over constitutional arrangements in Eastern Europe and the former Soviet Union drew on these broader arguments in the literature. Echoing North and Weingast, one group of scholars held that constitutions that bound the hands of the executives were necessary for economic reform. This "credible commitment school," best exemplified by the work of Jon Elster (1993, 1997; Elster, Offe, and Preuss 2000), favored strong legislatures and proportional-representational systems, as these features were most likely to tie the hands of policymakers and force legislative compromise. Thus, the goal of constitutions is to prevent self-dealing by politicians or revisions of existing law and contractual commitments (Elster 1993), a feature that Weingast (1993) termed "negative constitutionalism." Elster (1992) conjectured that among postcommunist states, those with weaker executive powers were more likely to achieve successful economic reform and growth. Stephan Haggard (1997) made this point explicitly, suggesting that the higher number of veto players in parliamentary regimes implies a limited ability to renege on commitments to reform.

A second group of scholars, which Hellman (1996) referred to as the "stopgap constitutionalists," contended that transition required strong executive power in the short-term. Foremost among the advocates of this approach was Stephen Holmes (1993a, 1993b, 1993c, 1995). As Przeworski (1991) noted (though he himself was not an advocate of a strong presidency), output was expected to follow a "J-curve" during the transition period, with short-term declines balanced against long-term growth. Economic reform therefore required that the government be isolated from electoral pressure as unemployment and the subsequent pain of economic dislocation rose.

The stopgap constitutionalists made two recommendations. First, they argued for an interim period before binding constitutions were enacted to allow policymakers maximum insulation from political pressure and flexibility in responding to societal demands. The classic example of this approach is Poland, which operated for five years under a "Little Constitution." Second, scholars argued for especially strong executives, who could presumably drive through economic reforms in the face of entrenched interests and creatively identify compromises between contending groups. To demonstrate this point, Holmes cited the example of the Russian reformer Yegor Gaidar, whom he suggested would never have risen to the premiership in a parliamentary system, and whose achievements would not have been so far-reaching had he not been able to hide behind Yeltsin's charisma (Holmes 1993c, 125).[2]

Early Evidence

Both proponents of binding constraints and super-presidentialism looked to the postcommunist experiment as an opportunity to test and presumably find support for their respective theories. On the eve of transition, Jon Elster (1991, 449), a key participant, wrote hopefully of the opportunity:

Under these conditions, the constitution-making processes in Eastern Europe amount to a gigantic natural experiment. The countries in question present an optimal degree of diversity for comparative analysis: they are neither too similar nor too different. The focus of comparison is twofold. On the one hand, one can examine the processes of constitution-making. On the other hand, one can study and compare the outcome of these processes.

In a well-known article drawing on data from the transition period, Joel Hellman (1996) seemed to resolve the debate, offering the first empirical data from the transition experience to test the two competing theories. Using a measure of progress in economic reform from the EBRD as his dependent variable, Hellman demonstrated that economic reform was not impacted directly by when or if a new constitution was implemented. Yet he did find significant evidence that higher levels of executive power (operationalized by the number of constraints on executive decision making) were negatively correlated with progress in economic reform, and that the negative effects

---

[2] The debate between these two camps can be understood as a question of emphasis – whether ex post or ex ante political constraints are more important. See, for instance, Dewatripont and Roland (1992, 1995).

were stronger in those countries that postponed writing new constitutions. This seemed to be a victory for the credible-commitment school.

In a related contribution, Hellman (1998) argued that the case for a strong presidency was based on a fundamental misunderstanding of transition dynamics. Not all citizens suffered from early, partial reforms. Rather, the initial benefits of transition were often captured by interest groups, who could then use their newfound economic power to block further reform. The poster children for these winners were the Russian oligarchs, who used enormous economic resources acquired through privatization to subsequently block trade liberalization and other policies that would have reduced their rents (Aslund 1995). Hellman presented evidence that this outcome was less likely in states with parliamentary systems, as such constitutions tended to promote coalition governments and offered more constraints on executive power.

Hellman's early finding that postcommunist states with more veto players not only had fewer reform reversals but implemented more reform to begin with has held up over time, with Frye and Mansfield (2003) fleshing out the result for the specific case of trade policy. Figure 10.1 depicts the basic relationship, which is robust to the inclusion of numerous controls. Given the strong theoretical prior that reform should be less likely with numerous veto players (Tsebelis 2002), this stands as a key finding of the transition experience. Gehlbach and Malesky (2010) formalize Hellman's logic, showing that the ability of special interests to lobby for inefficient policies may be reduced when veto players are numerous; intuitively, the larger the number of veto players, the more actors that special interests must pay off. When "partial reform" is inefficient, as in postcommunist countries, this implies a greater likelihood of full reform.[3]

Contamination of the Experimental Setting

Notwithstanding the strong association between constitutional choice and economic-reform outcomes, early contributions to the study of constitutions in the transition setting raised more questions than they answered. Credible commitment theorists, stopgap constitutionalists, and even Hellman sidestepped the important question of how particular democratic institutions had come into being in the first place. There was little exploration of a critical Northean concern: Why do some states choose the "right"

---

[3] Gehlbach and Malesky (2010) test the predictions of their model using panel data from postcommunist countries, employing various strategies to control for the possible endogeneity of veto players to economic reform.

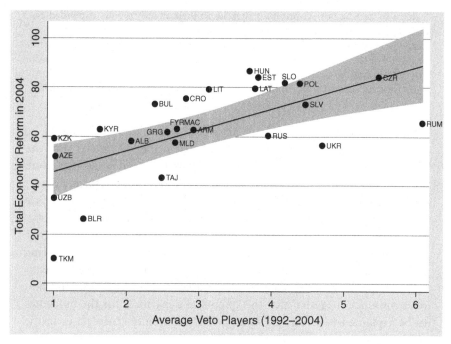

Figure 10.1. Bivariate relationship between average veto players and economic reform in 2004. Veto players is the CHECKS measure from the Database of Political Institutions (Beck et al. 2001). Economic reform is the EBRD Average Transition Indicator, rescaled to take values from 0 to 100.

institutions, whereas others do not? North himself quoted William Riker in expressing his skepticism that one could easily identify the effect of constitutions on outcomes (North 1990, 60):

> The question is: Does constitutional structure cause a political condition and a state of public opinion or does the political condition and the state of public opinion cause the constitutional structure? This at first sounds like the chicken and egg problem in which there is no causal direction; but I think that usually there is a cause and that constitutional forms are typically derivative. (Riker 1976, 13)

At the very onset of the transition era, a spirited debate took place in the *Slavic Review* that pitted Valerie Bunce, a specialist on Eastern Europe and the former Soviet Union, against Philippe Schmitter and Terry Karl, experts on Europe and Latin America, respectively. Schmitter and Karl (1994, 177) had offered up the transition countries as a test case for evaluating theories of transition from authoritarianism that had emerged from the Latin American and Southern European experience, claiming:

Indeed, by adding post-communist regimes to their already greatly expanded case base, transitologists and consolidologists might even be able to bring the powerful instrumentarium of social statistics to bear on the study of contemporary democratization. For the first time, they could manipulate equations where the variables did not outnumber the cases and they could test their tentative conclusions in cultural and historical contexts quite different from those which generated them in the first place.

Bunce resisted in a piece comically titled "Should Transitologists be Grounded?" (Bunce 1995), pointing out that while she agreed with the idea that similar experiences should be compared across regions, there were a number of reasons to suspect that Eastern Europe and the former Soviet Union offered less-than-ideal test cases. Bunce made two points that are critical for understanding the utility of the natural-experiment heuristic. First, she argued that there was considerable heterogeneity across countries that would be very difficult to hold constant in any empirical study, referring to "the sheer magnitude of diversity in the region and its correlation with religious, political, socio-economic and spatial markers" (126). Second, and related, Bunce suggested that the "points of departure" for the outcomes to be explained were very different across the twenty-seven states in the region.[4]

These concerns become apparent when we take stock of the numerous contributions that claim to exploit the postcommunist "natural experiment." In many cases, different scholars hold constant and problematize the same variable. For example, tests of the impact of institutions on economic growth and investment typically assume that we can treat the distribution of "institutions" (sometimes more accurately described as governance or economic reform) as exogenous. On the other hand, as discussed above, scholars such as Elster (1991) and Weimer (1997) believe the natural experiment is the selection of those institutions in the first place.

If Elster and Weimer are correct, we cannot possibly consider "institutions to growth" analyses as natural experiments, as the setting violates the assumption of as-if randomness that defines such research designs (e.g., Acemoglu 2005; Dunning 2005). Once we know the factors that undergird institutional choice, such as the preferences and relative strength of actors at the bargaining table, we must consider the possibility that these

---

[4] Consider, for example, the size of the informal sector (i.e., economic actors who neither pay taxes nor take advantage of certain public services), a key outcome of institutional design in the postcommunist setting. One cannot equate the growth of the informal economy with its size later in the transition period (Johnson, Kaufmann, and Shleifer 1997) if some countries started out with more informal activity than others (Alexeev and Pyle 2003).

same factors are responsible for economic performance. Geddes (1995), for example, argues that countries choosing parliamentary systems already had a high level of societal consensus in support of economic reform prior to choosing institutions. Of course, those seeking to understand institutional choice have an analogous problem: Why do regimes at the start of the reform process differ in the preferences and bargaining power of key political actors?

The selection of electoral systems can be similarly influenced by the underlying goals and power of political actors (Benoit 2007). Benoit and Hayden (2004) explore the evolution of Poland's electoral system, demonstrating that in each of five major episodes of electoral reform, party voting over electoral rules was determined by expectations of how electoral systems would translate into seat shares. In a related study, Bryon Moraski (2006) shows that regional politicians in Russia were able to accurately forecast the types of electoral rules that would best serve their interests, and that they selected electoral systems based on these forecasts (regional outsiders favored proportional representation, whereas old-regime politicians opposed it).

That the selection of institutions is nonrandom is neatly illustrated by Kopstein and Reilly (2000), who demonstrate that a simple measure of geographic distance from Vienna or Berlin is more strongly correlated with economic reform than is Hellman's careful measure of executive strength, implying that legacy and geography (including the possibility of EU accession) shape institutions and choices.

As the saying goes, "There are turtles all the way down." In other words, each causal factor is itself the result of a deeper cause. Experiments are designed to short-circuit these causal chains, following an intervention from its origin to the resulting effect. The so-called "natural experiment" from communism, however, did not break these long-run causal chains, randomly distributing institutions across the region. Rather, the collapse of Soviet communism appears simply to have mediated the long-run historical trajectory.

Institutional Legacies
As the endogeneity of institutions in transition became evident, researchers chose to focus on the evolution of institutions themselves. For scholars working in this tradition, it is not coincidental that the states that built constitutions with strong legislatures were the leading economic reformers, as both institutional development and reform are likely correlated with various unobserved characteristics.

The starting point for much of this analysis is Steven Fish's observation that the first postcommunist elections are strongly correlated with future reform trajectories (Fish 1998). Fish argued that a strong turnout for reformists in the initial elections led to three secondary effects: radical economic reform programs, reformation or marginalization of the old communists, and the emergence of noncommunist politicians. Fish tested this argument with cross-country data, finding that the initial election outcome outperformed various other potential determinants of reform progress, including religious tradition and level of economic development.

In an oft-cited piece, Kitschelt (2003) criticized such "tournaments of variables" that included factors at different conceptual distances from what the authors were trying to explain, thereby allowing proximate explanations such as initial election outcomes to obscure the effect of deeper determinants. From this perspective, the real cause of economic reform can only be discovered if we ask why initial election results varied so much across postcommunist countries.

Darden and Grzymala-Busse (2006) provide an answer to this question, arguing that school curricula at the initial moment of mass literacy shaped values and beliefs in subsequent generations in ways that can be traced to policy preferences at the onset of the postcommunist period. In particular, where mass literacy was first achieved through curricula with nationalist content (i.e., those describing the precommunist heritage of the regime), subsequent anticommunist convictions tended to be stronger. As a result, the seat share of noncommunist factions in the first postcommunist election was greater in countries that had precommunist literacy campaigns. These countries, the authors argue, were especially good candidates for the creation of democratic institutions and market economies.

Darden and Grzymala-Busse's study exposes the role of beliefs in institutional change, a central theme in Douglass North's more recent work (see especially North 2005). This theme has been taken up by other scholars. Herrera (2005), for example, has shown in a study of Russian sovereignty movements that regional activism is determined by subjective beliefs about relative economic position rather than by objective economic conditions. Similarly, Darden (2009) traces the evolution of economic institutions to the beliefs of political elites of how best to bring about economic growth. Of course, ideas change over time, a pattern demonstrated by Aligica and Evans (2009) and their colleagues at Collegium Budapest, who have set about documenting the paradigm change in the social sciences (particularly economics) prior to and after economic reform.

The concern with nationalism in Darden and Grzymala-Busse's work is also present in the work of Frye (2010), who presents a novel approach to identifying the effect of political institutions on economic reform. In Frye's theory, nationalist sentiment in the communist era determines the degree of political polarization in the transition period, but the degree of democracy determines the impact of polarization on reform choices. In particular, polarization between liberal and ex-communist factions generates ambiguity over future policy, which reduces the anticipated returns to investment for businesses and entrepreneurs. Democracy augments this effect, as political competition increases the likelihood of a change in government.

Other notable work on legacies has shown that the sources of today's political and economic institutions extend back further still, to the experience with democracy in the interwar period (Pop-Eleches 2007) and pre–World War I empires that eventually gave in to today's nation-states (Grosjean 2010). What helps these pieces stand apart is that they provide a causal pathway by which a temporally distant variable (e.g., the timing of mass literacy) can affect contemporary outcomes of interest (e.g., the evolution of political and economic institutions).

Conclusions

Looking back on the literature on macro-political institutions in postcommunist countries, one might say that the field has finally caught up with Douglass North. What began as a spirited debate over the impact of constitutions on economic reform quickly gave way to a realization that the constitutions themselves were subject to nonrandom selection. The causal apparatus has been progressively pushed back, to the point where the literature today is as likely to credit nineteenth-century empires as postcommunist policies for economic growth. Along the way, scholars have gained an appreciation for the role of ideas in economic change, with decisions about political and economic institutions rooted in beliefs about the way the world works.

In principle, one could go two directions from here. First, in the spirit of much modern empirical political economy (e.g., Acemoglu, Johnson, and Robinson 2001, 2002), one might exploit what we have learned about the long-run determinants of political institutions to identify their effects, thus returning to the research program established at the start of the transition period. In practice, this is more difficult than it sounds, as the typical analysis includes more than one potentially endogenous variable, and the various long-term determinants often seem to run through similar channels (Gehlbach and Malesky 2010). With very few exceptions (e.g., Frye 2010), there has been little work of this sort.

The second option is to continue to focus on the long-term determinants of institutional change. This is largely the direction the field has gone, which strikes us as a positive development. Given that we know so little about the evolution of institutions, a sustained research program along these lines has the potential to tell us much that we do not know. Of course, the more we learn about the sources of institutions, the better we will be able to identify their effects, so this direction is complementary to the first.

3. The Property Rights Experiment

As political constitutions were being rewritten in the early 1990s in Eastern Europe and the former Soviet Union, an equally momentous change was taking place at the level of the firm. Across the postcommunist world, programs of mass privatization were transferring ownership of state-owned enterprises, large and small, to private economic actors. What impact this ultimately had on property rights and firm behavior is a second great question of transition.

At some level, there was less initial uncertainty about the ownership experiment than there was about the constitution experiment. Growth rates had been declining for years in the socialist bloc, as intensive (total factor productivity) growth failed to replace extensive (factor) growth (Kornai 1992). The inefficiencies of state ownership were well-documented – such concepts as the soft budget constraint (Kornai 1986; Dewatripont and Maskin 1995) and the ratchet effect (Berliner 1952; Weitzman 1980; Freixas, Guesnerie, and Tirole 1985) had long since passed into general usage. Few doubted the superiority of a system of private property rights.

What was contested was how to transition from the current system to a "private property regime" (Frydman and Rapaczynski 1994), where private property would predominate and the state would support the rights of private owners. To some extent, the debate merely echoed larger questions about the appropriate insulation of reformers (see above) and speed of reform (see Earle and Gehlbach 2003 for a review). In addition, however, there were specific issues of privatization policy design: whether to privatize to domestic or foreign owners, whether to allocate shares through vouchers or auctions, whether to grant special privileges to owners and managers of the enterprise, and so forth.[5] These decisions were potentially consequential not only for their direct impact on corporate governance and thus firm performance, but because the initial distribution of property rights could

---

[5] Roland (2000) provides a typology. For a discussion of how these debates played out on the ground, see Boycko, Shleifer, and Vishny (1995), Shleifer and Treisman (2000), and Appel (2004).

affect the lobbying power of economic actors and thus the general shape of postcommunist political economies (Sonin 2003; Hoff and Stiglitz 2004). (For the most part, these debates concerned the transformation of existing firms rather than entry of new firms; see, for example, Fischer and Gelb [1991]. We return to the issue of entry in this chapter.

From the perspective of the firm, the key questions at the beginning of the transition period thus related to how rather than whether ownership should be transferred to private actors. There was, moreover, reason to think that these questions could be answered. Unlike earlier privatizations in Western Europe and Latin America, programs to transfer ownership rights in postcommunist countries involved thousands of firms, not dozens. Moreover, the diversity of methods possible in principle was matched in practice: voucher giveaways to outsiders in Czechoslovakia, voucher giveaways to insiders in Russia, sales to foreigners in Hungary, and so forth.[6]

Identifying Privatization Effects

In retrospect, of course, the obvious problem in evaluating different theories of privatization was that firms were not randomly selected for privatization. This greatly complicated the task of identifying the effects of ownership on firm performance, and thus of comparing outcomes across different privatization methods. But this did not prevent the emergence of numerous empirical studies of privatization, some of which dealt with the selection issue more explicitly than others. By the early 2000s, there had been sufficient work to take stock. Two comprehensive surveys of the empirical literature came to similar conclusions (Megginson and Netter 2001; Djankov and Murrell 2002). In general, privatization is associated with improved productivity and other measures of firm performance. The effects are more pronounced when firms are privatized to outsiders, who are more inclined to undertake restructuring, and especially when privatization involved sales to foreigners. Concentrated ownership is better than diffuse ownership.[7]

In important respects, these conclusions mirrored the expectations of much work on privatization-policy design. But a new puzzle emerged from these initial empirical studies: The positive estimated effect of privatization did not extend to all countries where it was undertaken. As with many other elements of transition performance, Eastern Europe seemed to outperform the former Soviet Union. Although differences in the allocation of shares

---

[6] For a comprehensive description, see Frydman, Rapaczynski, and Earle (1993a, b) and Earle et al. (1994).

[7] For somewhat later reviews, see Guriev and Megginson (2007) and Estrin et al. (2009).

could have directly accounted for some of the variation – insider privatization in Russia was subject to particular criticism – the effect of owner type itself varied across countries.

Moreover, the results were consistent with strong evidence that the business environment was systematically less friendly to private enterprise in the former Soviet Union (Frye and Shleifer 1997; European Bank for Reconstruction and Development 1999). Social science had changed in the first decade of transition, with a renewed emphasis on institutions, due in no small part to the publication in 1990 of North's *Institutions, Institutional Change and Economic Performance*. The strong suspicion was that institutional variation was responsible for the sharp divergence in privatization performance across countries. At this juncture, however, there were few studies that directly measured the impact of institutions on performance, leading the authors of one of the surveys to term institutions the "elusive determinant" (Djankov and Murrell 2002, 779).

In any event, the data used in these early studies of privatization – typically cross sections, with state-owned enterprises in one sector sometimes compared to privatized firms in another – were generally not of sufficient quality to convince skeptics of the empirical patterns that had emerged. There was reason to suspect that governments had chosen more productive firms, or firms whose productivity was growing more quickly, for privatization. The mere existence of a positive correlation between privatization status and productivity was no evidence of a causal effect. Moreover, even where identification issues at the firm level had been addressed in a more or less convincing fashion, there remained the problem of identifying the institutions responsible for observed variation in privatization effectiveness. Most estimates of privatization effects were country-level, there were relatively few countries with comparable firm-level data, and cross-country inference had its own inference problems.

There the problem might have stood. Mass privatization was one of the great social experiments of recent decades, yet it was not a natural experiment. Early empirical work had uncovered some striking regularities, but given fundamental inference problems, a passive reader of the literature could be excused for falling back on prior beliefs. Finally, as a student suggested to one of us, transition was over – it was time to move on to other topics.

Fortunately for the study of institutions, not everyone tired of transition so quickly. Years of effort finally paid off in datasets worthy of the questions being asked of them – some of the best firm-level data in the world today come from postcommunist countries. Armed with long panels and able to compare ownership across firms in the same sector, scholars were able to employ various program-evaluation techniques (including models with firm-specific trends, as described below) to more convincingly identify privatization effects (in particular, see Brown, Earle, and Telegdy 2006, 2010). The new studies upheld some previous results, overturned others, and raised new questions.[8]

Most important for the study of institutions, however, the basic question of cross-country variation in privatization effectiveness persisted. The estimates in Brown, Earle, and Telegdy (2010) suggest that privatization to domestic owners resulted in an increase in multifactor productivity of 14 percent to 24 percent in Romania, 5 percent to 15 percent in Hungary, and 2 percent to 4 percent in Ukraine, versus a decrease in productivity of 3 percent to 5 percent in Russia. (The ranges here reflect differences based on whether the specification incorporates firm-specific time trends or only firm fixed effects.) To some extent, this reflects the basic East-West divide that characterized progress in reform more generally, though few would have argued that Romania was a more radical reformer than Hungary, or Ukraine than Russia.

Explaining Privatization Effects

Of course, if cross-country inference is difficult with twenty-five or so observations, it may be hopeless with four. The new data presented a way out of this cul-de-sac. Unlike earlier studies, which tended to be based on surveys of firms in a relatively small number of regions in any particular country, the industrial-census data used in the more recent literature are comprehensive with respect to regional coverage. With more than 250,000 firm-year observations in the Russian data, for example, it is possible to estimate privatization effects for nearly every one of Russia's approximately eighty regions.[9] Within-country comparison of the resulting estimates can hold constant the macroeconomic environment and other confounding variables while taking advantage of substantial institutional heterogeneity across regions.

---

[8] One striking finding, documented in Brown, Earle, and Telegdy (2010), is that privatization tends not to reduce employment – increased scale generally compensates for increased productivity.

[9] Russia's federal system includes semiautonomous regions located within larger regions. Moreover, there has been some consolidation of regions in recent years. For both reasons, counts of regions vary from study to study.

Brown, Earle, and Gehlbach (2009) present a methodological framework for such studies. Starting with firm-level data, their estimating equation is

$$x_{jt} = f(k_{jt}, l_{jt}) + Y\gamma + w_t\alpha_j + F_{jt}\phi + D_{jt}I\vartheta + D_{jt}R\delta + n_{jt}, \quad (1)$$

where j indexes firms and t indexes time periods. The variable x_{jt} is output, f is a vector of industry-specific production functions, k_{jt} is capital stock, l_{jt} is employment, Y is a vector of industry-year interaction dummies, w_t is a vector of aggregate time variables, and F_{jt} is an indicator of whether the firm was foreign-owned at the end of year $t - 1$. (With relatively few foreign privatizations in the dataset, the effect of foreign ownership is assumed to be constant across regions.) The variable D_{jt} is an indicator for domestic private ownership, I is a vector of industry dummies, and R is a vector of region dummies; the interaction of industry dummies with the domestic-privatization indicator controls for variation across regions in industrial composition. Selection bias is corrected for by defining $w_t \equiv (1, t)$, which implies a model with firm fixed effects and firm-specific trends. Brown, Earle, and Telegdy (2006) show that once these two idiosyncratic factors are taken into account, there is no statistically significant difference in the behavior of preprivatization productivity across privatized and state-owned firms.

Estimation of Equation 1 produces region-level estimates of the effect of domestic privatization on firm productivity. In the second step of their two-step procedure, Brown, Earle, and Gehlbach then estimate

$$\hat{\delta}_r = Z_r\mu + \varepsilon_r, \quad (2)$$

where $\hat{\delta}_r$ are the first-stage estimates of the region-level effect of domestic privatization on multifactor productivity and Z_r is a vector of regional characteristics.[10] Identification rests on finding regional characteristics that are plausibly exogenous to privatization performance.

Although still in its infancy, this approach holds the potential to identify institutional determinants of variation in privatization performance. Figure 10.2 illustrates pooled estimates of regional privatization effects for Russia and Ukraine. Two features stand out. First, the country-level estimates in Brown, Earle, and Telegdy (2006) mask enormous variation across regions in the estimated effect of domestic privatization on firm

[10] A potential complication in estimating this equation is that the precision of first-stage estimates of δ_r is generally greater in regions with more firm-year observations, implying that ε_r has smaller variance in such regions. Brown, Earle, and Gehlbach (2009) show that their results are robust to second-stage estimation by FGLS, using an estimator first suggested by Hanushek (1974).

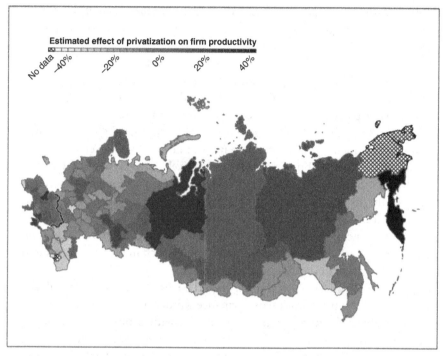

Figure 10.2. Estimated effect of domestic privatization on firm productivity from firm-level regression with firm fixed effects and firm-specific time trends, Russia and Ukraine. Estimates control for country-sector privatization effects.

productivity. The regional estimates vary from a reduction in productivity of 40 percent to an increase of 40 percent. Second, this variation appears to be systematic. With exceptions, regions with positive (negative) estimated privatization effects are generally located next to other regions with positive (negative) estimated effects. To the extent that institutional and other characteristics are distributed smoothly across regions, this suggests that underlying factors may be driving the effect of privatization on firm performance.

Brown, Earle, and Gehlbach (2009) focus on one such characteristic: the ability of the state to provide a supportive business environment to privatized firms. Notwithstanding the often high levels of social spending in postcommunist countries, the public administrations of postcommunist states are in fact not large by world standards (Schiavo-Campo, de Tommaso, and Mukherjee 1997; Brym and Gimpelson 2004). This was especially true during the first decade of transition, as the vacuum left by party bureaucracies was not quickly filled by civil servants. Together with the liberalization of economic activity, this often meant a failure of the state to provide basic regulatory functions (Frye 2000; Grzymala-Busse and Jones Luong 2002).

In this context, the size of regional public administrations is potentially consequential for the postcommunist business environment. Many basic regulatory functions, including licensing and the control of energy tariffs, are at least partially under the control of regional bureaucracies. Brown, Earle, and Gehlbach (2009) present evidence that firms spend less time and money obtaining permits and pay fewer kickbacks to government officials where regional bureaucracies are relatively large – the ability of any individual bureaucrat to hold up a firm may be smaller when there are more officials to whom firms can appeal (Shleifer and Vishny 1993). This may be consequential for private (as opposed to state-owned) enterprises, which in principle have the greatest incentive to engage in restructuring and other activities that increase productivity, but which in practice may find it difficult to do so in the absence of a supportive state.

Consistent with this theoretical perspective, Brown, Earle, and Gehlbach (2009) find that privatization performance is much more effective in regions with relatively large regional bureaucracies, with a one-standard deviation increase in public-administration employment associated with a 9-percentage-point increase in the estimated effect of privatization on firm productivity. Their identification strategy rests in part on the fact that the size of regional bureaucracies appears to be historically determined, driven by development priorities during the communist era.[11] Although there was substantial growth in public administrations during the transition period, this trend is almost completely secular: The relative size of bureaucracies changed very little from year to year. While one should be cautious about generalizing this result in the absence of empirical evidence from other contexts, it does suggest that the size of the state apparatus may be an important determinant of how the state interacts with private economic actors.

Two other recent papers adopt a similar research design to explore the impact of institutions on firm performance. The first of these, Earle and Gehlbach (2012), generalizes the methodology of Brown, Earle, and Gehlbach (2009) to estimate region-year privatization effects, this time in Ukraine. These estimates in hand, Gehlbach and Earle then explore the consequences of the relative performance of privatized firms of a particular

---

[11] Brown, Earle, and Gehlbach (2009) also exploit scale economies in public administration to develop instruments based on regional population density and the number of subregional jurisdictions.

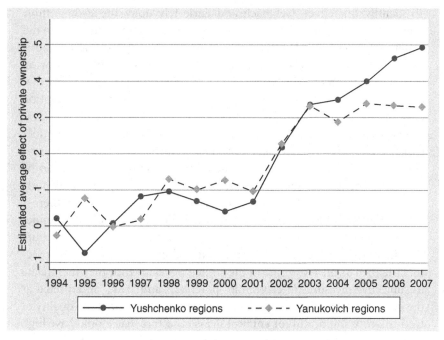

Figure 10.3. Average effect of privatization on firm productivity, by year.

moment of institutional change, Ukraine's 2004 Orange Revolution. Ukraine is a country with generally few constraints on opportunistic behavior by office holders, implying that property rights are dependent on connections to the current governing elite; echoing an earlier period of English history, "ownership rights var[y] with the power of the lord" (North, Wallis, and Weingast 2009, 157). The Orange Revolution disrupted these connections for a large class of business owners concentrated in regions supportive of Viktor Yanukovich, the chosen successor of President Leonid Kuchma and eventual loser in 2004's presidential elections. Mass "reprivatization" of previously privatized enterprises, although ultimately not carried out, was seriously debated after the seizure of power by Viktor Yushchenko and his Orange coalition partners. Consideration of this policy, which was seen as a serious assault on private property rights, has been blamed for the collapse in growth in 2005 (Aslund 2005).

Consistent with this interpretation, Gehlbach and Earle show that the relative performance of privatized enterprises in regions supportive of Yanukovich declined following the Orange Revolution, relative to similar regions supportive of Yushchenko. Figure 10.3 illustrates the result.

To identify this effect, Gehlbach and Earle rely upon the strong ethnic character of voting in Ukraine's 2004 presidential election: Yushchenko did better in regions with few Russians. Controlling for industrial composition, which might be related to a region's "Russianness" through historical patterns of settlement and development, there is little reason to think that changes in the performance of privatized firms after the Orange Revolution depend directly on ethnicity.

The second paper, by Bruno, Bytchkova, and Estrin (2008), examines entry of new firms rather than transformation of existing firms. Generally neglected at the beginning of the transition, entry has proved to be an important part of the restructuring of the enterprise sector in post-communist countries. As with privatization performance, however, there is substantial variation in entry rates across and within countries. In a manner similar to Rajan and Zingales (1998), Bruno, Bytchkova, and Estrin measure the difference across regions from the "natural" entry rate in particular sectors (defined as the entry rate in the United States), which they then relate to subjective measures of economic "potential" and "risk," interpreted as the quality of local institutions. Their primary finding is that the quality of institutions is important for entry of firms in sectors that should have high entry rates, but that it matters little when entry is expected to be minimal. Although they cannot completely rule out reverse causation, they argue that any such effect is likely to be minimal, given that their institutional measures are defined for the region as a whole, whereas relative entry rates are estimated at the level of region-sector.

Conclusions

As this brief overview illustrates, the primary challenge in such work is identifying plausibly exogenous variation in institutions at the subnational level. Although qualitatively the same problem as that confronting cross-country studies, there is reason to believe that it may be easier to address these issues in within-country studies, which hold a great deal of heterogeneity constant. This approach does leave certain questions aside (e.g., the impact of macroeconomic environment on privatization performance), but it seems particularly well-suited to exploring the effect of political institutions on the emergence of private property rights. Data and research design have finally caught up with one of the big questions of transition.

Work to date on these issues has examined only a narrow range of institutional features and outcomes. One missing piece of the puzzle is variation across sectors rather than regions in the effect of privatization on firm performance. Although the region-level estimates discussed above control for sector-specific privatization effects, explaining these differences has not been a priority of existing research. Yet survey evidence suggests that governments in post-Soviet countries (though not those in Eastern Europe, for reasons connected to the initial creation of tax systems in the early transition period) disproportionately protect sectors that are important sources of tax revenue (Gehlbach 2008), consistent with North and Thomas's argument that "the fiscal needs of government may induce the protection of certain property rights which hinder rather than promote growth" (North and Thomas 1973, 8). Thus, we might expect privatization effects to be different in sectors that are important to the state for revenue or other reasons.

For a reader of Douglass North, it is also striking that the role of beliefs is at best implicit in existing studies. Support for revising privatization is far stronger in Ukraine and Russia than in Hungary and Romania (Denisova et al. 2009), with much support for this policy the apparent consequence of beliefs that state-owned enterprises work better (Denisova et al. 2010). As the results from Ukraine discussed above illustrate, fear that privatization may be revised can negatively affect the performance of privatized firms, which in turn could reinforce beliefs that private ownership is ineffective. Understanding such equilibrium effects should be a high priority for future research.

4. The Grand Experiment

For scholars working on the postcommunist transition during the 1990s, Douglas North's *Institutions, Institutional Change, and Economic Performance* was arguably one of two works that helped to set the intellectual agenda. The other was Janos Kornai's *The Socialist System* (Kornai 1992). Released nearly contemporaneously, the books shared more than space on a shelf of recent publications. Each transcended traditional disciplinary boundaries to argue for the importance of understanding the interrelationship of economics, politics, and social norms. Each suggested that more intellectual energy should be directed at examining the institutions that underpin economic systems, not just the policies and outcomes that are their visible manifestation.

Like North, Kornai argued that mere changes in policy were insufficient to improve economic performance. That had been tried repeatedly in the communist bloc: market socialism in Hungary, self-management in Yugoslavia, Jaruzelski's decentralizing reforms in Poland, glasnost and perestroika in the Soviet Union. Without fail, the results were disappointing, often exacerbating rather than solving such chronic problems as widespread shortages and the production of inferior consumer goods. Given strong complementarities among elements of the socialist system, only wholesale change in the underlying institutions could fundamentally reorient the political economies of the region.

The problem, as Douglas North has repeatedly demonstrated, is that we know very little about what facilitates the emergence of institutions conducive to sustained economic growth. Expectations early in the transition period that the postcommunist experience would provide a definitive answer to this question proved too grand. Far from a natural experiment, the transformation of institutions in Eastern Europe and the Soviet Union was more like a poorly constructed science-fair project, with multiple treatments, none randomly assigned. Although much has been learned despite these difficulties – we have a better sense of the historical determinants of constitutions, we know much more about the impact of privatization on firm performance – at this juncture the advance in knowledge seems unequal to the scale of the transition itself.

For the truth is that something remarkable was achieved, especially in the western half of the postcommunist world. Writing a decade and a half after the collapse of the Berlin Wall, Kornai documented the uniqueness of the transition in Central Eastern Europe (Kornai 2006). Both political and economic institutions have changed fundamentally, with greater competition in each sphere. This change was largely nonviolent, it was not coerced by a foreign power, and it occurred during a short period of time. None of the other "great transformations" combined all of these elements – not the advent of modernity in Europe, not the changes in China after Mao, and certainly not Lenin and Stalin's transformation of Russia.

From the perspective of North, Wallis, and Weingast (2009), if not yet "open-access orders," with free and mutually reinforcing entry of organizations into the economic and political spheres, some postcommunist countries are at least on the "doorstep." Just as interesting, there is enormous variation within as well as across countries in the nature of political and economic institutions. This variation, and the advent of new data that take advantage of the scale of the postcommunist experience, hold the promise of further insights into the nature of institutions and institutional change.

Even where the transformation was disappointing (if not, in retrospect, surprising), the collapse of socialism has taught us something about the "natural state" that characterizes most countries, with restricted entry of political and economic organizations. Russia and most other post-Soviet republics have returned to the main flow of human history (Shleifer and

Treisman 2000; Treisman 2010). On this journey, political and economic actors have often behaved in ways that appear puzzling, at least from the perspective of theory developed to explain open-access societies. In broadening our conceptual frameworks to incorporate these anomalies, we learn something about the institutions that govern the vast majority of the world's population.

The postcommunist experience thus represents a grand experiment, if not a natural one. The questions of transition are the questions that Douglas North has taught us to ask: What institutions are conducive to economic growth, and how do they emerge? For those willing to explore what is increasingly political and economic history, this is the golden age of the study of transition.

Acknowledgments

For helpful comments, we thank the editors, participants in the conference on "The Legacy and Work of Douglass C. North: Understanding Institutions and Development Economics," members of the Postcommunist Politics Workshop at UW–Madison, John Earle, and three anonymous referees. Tricia Olsen graciously provided research assistance.

11

Using Economic Experiments to Measure Informal Institutions

Pamela Jakiela

1. Introduction

In many developing countries, formal legal institutions play a minimal role in the lives of most citizens, particularly those living in rural areas. Many states do not have the capacity to protect property rights and enforce contracts consistently; for example, many African governments have struggled to project power outside their national capitals in the post-independence period (Herbst 2000). Even when state capacity is present, laws are not always enforced. In such contexts, the informal rules of the game may be more salient determinants of economic outcomes than formal laws and regulations. However, the amorphous nature of social norms and conventions makes them substantially more difficult to analyze than legal or government institutions. From a development perspective, the gradual evolution of norms makes it difficult to distinguish between those informal institutions that facilitate growth and modernization from those that result from economic progress.

In this essay, I explore the potential for using economic experiments to study informal institutions. North (1990a) defines institutions broadly, as "the humanly devised constraints that shape human interaction." Though legal institutions – for example, written constitutions – are devised intentionally and explicitly, many constraints on human interaction evolve organically without ever being formally codified. The set of all "humanly devised constraints" can thus be partitioned into explicit legal institutions and informal institutions, which are "conventions, norms of behavior, and self imposed codes of conduct" and the enforcement mechanisms associated with these norms (North 1995). By this definition, the set of informal institutions comprises both internalized preferences over the outcomes of human interactions which shape individual behavior even in the absence of social enforcement mechanisms and social conventions, which occur in equilibrium.[1] Individual preferences include the desire to adhere to internalized moral codes of fairness or correct behavior – for instance, when individuals feel an innate desire to give to worthy charitable causes or an aversion to excessive inequality. Agents may also have a preference for punishing the antisocial actions of others, even at a cost to themselves.

An obstacle to understanding how informal institutions differ across cultures is the impossibility of observing behavior out of equilibrium, which makes it difficult to disentangle individual preferences from individual beliefs about others' strategies and the economic environment. In particular, it is hard to tease apart the moral component of preferences – trustworthiness, respect for property rights, egalitarianism, and so forth – from strategic considerations arising from the repeated nature of social interactions. That patterns of behavior differ across cultures is apparent. What is not immediately apparent is whether such differences result from differences in preferences both for subjectively defined good behavior and for punishing violators of standards of good behavior or whether the differences are simply different feasible Nash equilibria in the repeated game of human social interaction.

Economic experiments allow us to study interpersonal interactions with no possible social or reputational repercussions. They can be used to measure "internally enforced standards of conduct" in disparate societies and groups and to separate these revealed preferences from social mechanisms of norm enforcement (North 1990a, 40). Thus, experiments allow us to disentangle the internal and external components of informal institutions and measure individual preferences and values, such as altruistic preferences that are difficult to capture in survey data.

In this essay, I discuss the use of economic experiments to measure internalized informal institutions, by which I mean the component of informal institutions that results from the specific preferences of a population and not the (potentially arbitrary) selection of one of many equilibria. Section 2 describes the main experimental economic tools that have been used to measure individual preferences for fairness and differences in internalized fairness norms across societies. Section 3 summarizes the key findings from cross-cultural experiments. Section 4 explores variation in individual

---

[1] Throughout the essay, we use the term "preferences" in the economic sense, as a complete and transitive ordering over potential final outcomes or payouts. Young (1998) defines a "convention" as "equilibrium behavior in a game played repeatedly by many different individuals in society, where the behaviors are widely known to be customary."

fairness preferences within a single, specific culture. Here, I test the hypothesis that the correlations between societal characteristics and individual choices in experiments that have been documented across cultures also exist within a single specific culture. To do this, I present new results from dictator games conducted in rural, agricultural areas of western Kenya, highlighting the relationship between access to roads, and consequently markets, and individual decisions in the laboratory environment. After discussing the robustness of these findings and possible alternative interpretations, I conclude with Section 5.

2. The Experimental Approach to Measuring Informal Institutions

Studying individual decisions in controlled laboratory environment allows researchers to separate the internalized component of informal institutions from externally imposed social-enforcement mechanisms. Within the lab, individuals can interact in anonymous, one-shot settings; strategic and reputational considerations can be effectively shut down. Hence, lab experiments can be used to measure aspects of informal institutions that are effectively internalized and manifest as individual revealed preferences – for example, a taste for fairness or for egalitarian payout distributions.

The vast majority of cross-cultural experimental research has focused on four simple experiments designed to measure altruism and reciprocity: dictator, ultimatum, trust, and public goods games. These four games have been conducted all over the world, with subject populations ranging from university students in the United States and Europe to hunter-gatherers in Tanzania and Papua New Guinea (cf. Camerer 2003; Henrich et al. 2004).[2] The robust conclusion of all experimental studies is that human behavior is almost never consistent with the "standard" model of self-interest: Across a range of contexts, many individuals are willing to reduce their own payout s to help or cooperate with others. However, variation in play points to the diversity in preferences for fairness both within and across human societies. For example, Roth et al. (1991) conducted ultimatum games in four wealthy populations – Israel, Japan, the United States, and Yugoslavia – and reported significant, though relatively small, cross-cultural differences in individual behavior. Examining a far wider range of societies, including some extremely

---

[2] See Henrich et al. (2010b) for an overview of the ways in which subjects in Western university experimental labs are not representative of humanity in general.

primitive peoples, Henrich et al. (2010) report far more dramatic cultural differences.[3]

Dictator, ultimatum, trust, and public goods games are all designed to measure the tendency for humans to be generous and cooperative and to punish noncooperation, in anonymous one-shot interactions. Thus, the experiments all seek to measure aspects of individual social preferences,[4] which characterize an individual's willingness to trade off personal gain and perceived moral rectitude or fairness (Levitt and List 2007).

In dictator games, one player is allocated a sum of money, and that player decides how to divide that money between him or herself and another player (Forsythe et al. 1994). Games are anonymous, so subjects never learn the identity of the sender (or receiver) with whom they have been matched. Hence, dictator games provide a measure of generalized altruism unconfounded by strategic or reputational concerns and have been used to measure the strength of egalitarian norms within and across societies (cf. Cappelen et al. 2007; Barr et al. 2009).

If dictators were self-interested money-maximizers, they would clearly allocate nothing to other players. In practice, subjects in dictator games in university experimental labs typically allocate an average of 20 to 30 percent of the budget to the other player, and the vast majority of dictators transfer a positive amount (Camerer 2003; Engel 2011).

Ultimatum games are similar to dictator games, except that the responder is given a choice between accepting the proposer's offered division of the budget or rejecting it, in which case both parties receive nothing (Güth et al. 1982). As with dictator games, the subgame perfect Nash equilibrium among self-interested players is clear: Proposers allocate as little as possible to responders, who prefer any positive amount to leaving the game empty-handed. In practice, rejections of low offers are common in most, but not all, societies; anticipating this, proposers generally offer responders a substantial fraction of the budget (Camerer 2003).

Dictator games measure internal constraints on behavior directly, since an internally enforced moral standard is the only reason to rein in unobservable selfish behavior. In contrast, ultimatum experiments cannot be used to measure internalized norms of generosity: In an ultimatum game,

---

[3] For evidence on heterogeneity in social preferences within societies, see Cappelen et al. (2007), Fisman et al. (2007), Fisman et al. (2009).

[4] Agents have social preferences if the consumption or welfare of another individual enters into their utility function.

the willingness to share may demonstrate altruism but may also be motivated by the fear of having a proposal rejected. Thus, the key deviation from the standard model demonstrated by individual choices in ultimatum games is the willingness of responders to turn down unequal offers. Ultimatum games measure negative reciprocity, the willingness to punish unacceptably selfish behavior at a cost to oneself. A measure of the strength of such enforcement mechanisms is the minimum acceptable offer (MAO), the smallest fraction of the budget responders are willing to accept. When the MAO is zero, responder behavior is consistent with the standard model of pure self-interest.

A third variety of simple experiments used to measure internalized norms is the trust game (Berg et al. 1995). In trust games, one player – the "sender" or "trustor" – is allocated an amount of money, X. The sender chooses an amount $Y = X$ to send to a second player, the "trustee." The money sent by the trustor is multiplied by a factor $\lambda > 1$ such that the trustee receives 3Y. The trustee then chooses an amount $Z = 3Y$ to send back to the trustor. Hence the sender's total payout is $X - Y + Z$, and the trustee's payout is $3Y - Z$. Giving by trustees demonstrates positive reciprocity – the willingness to reward kindness with kindness at expense to oneself. Within trust games, this is often referred to as "trustworthiness." Overall, the evidence that trustees are more generous than players in dictator games is limited (Cox 2004). Moreover, trust is often a bad investment: The expected return on sending money is typically close to zero and often negative (Berg et al. 1995; Ashraf et al. 2006).

A final experimental measure of individual social preferences is the public goods game. In public goods games, players are randomly assigned to groups of size $n = 2$. Players are each endowed with a budget, m, that they divide between a private account and a public account. Each token that an individual allocates to the public account is multiplied by a factor η, where $1 < \eta < n$. Public goods games are often repeated and can include the possibility of punishment; at the end of each round, players in punishment treatments are allowed to pay an amount c to reduce the payout to another player by γc. In a typical public goods game, contributions to the public account are common. Contribution levels tend to decline over time in the absence of punishment. However, when opportunities to sanction uncooperative behavior are available, high levels of giving to the public account are observed throughout most games (Fehr and Gächter 2002).

The four types of experiments described above are the most commonly used lab experimental measures of individual social preferences underlying informal institutions. They are not, however, the only options available.

First, variants of these basic designs that have been introduced in university lab settings are often suitable for use in the field to measure social norms and individual values. For instance, Henrich et al. (2010) include the third party punishment game proposed by Fehr and Fischbacher (2004). Many authors use original variants of the basic experimental designs that have been modified to explore specific development questions (Jakiela et al. 2010). Finally, new experiments can be designed for the specific purpose of exploring informal institutions in poor communities. See, for example, Barr and Genicot (2008) on risk-pooling and Goldberg (2011) and Jakiela et al. (2010) on sharing norms.

3. Using Experiments to Measure Differences across Societies

Early cross-cultural experiments focused on replicating experiments in controlled laboratory environments in multiple industrialized countries. For example, Roth et al. (1991) conducted identical ultimatum games in Israel, Japan, Slovenia, and the United States; Croson and Buchan (1999) ran trust games in China, Japan, South Korea, and the United States. Both studies noticed relatively minor differences in behavior across cultures. Ashraf et al. (2006) conducted identical trust games in Russia, South Africa, and the United States. They noted that non-white South Africans invest significantly less than Russians, Americans, and white South Africans, though they do not return significantly less than other groups when assigned the role of trustee.

Henrich et al. (2010) explored cross-cultural variation in dictator and ultimatum game play across a wider range of development levels. They conducted dictator and ultimatum games in fifteen societies, ranging from the Hadza hunter-gatherers of Tanzania to wage workers in Ghana and the United States.[5] Mean offers within the dictator game ranged from 26 percent of the budget among the Hadza hunter-gathers of Tanzania to 47 percent of the budget among both wage workers in rural Missouri and the Sanquianga, a sedentary fishing population in Colombia (Barr et al. 2009); mean offers in the ultimatum games were strikingly similar, ranging from 26 to 48 percent of the budget. Comparing behavior across societies, the authors noticed a strong association between giving in both dictator and ultimatum games and the average level of market integration measured by the share of household calories purchased, rather than grown, hunted, or gathered,

---

[5] They also conduct third-party punishment games, which are not discussed here. Earlier waves of the project are documented in Henrich et al. (2004).

averaged across all households from a given society (Henrich et al. 2010). They argue that the association between market integration and dictator game giving is evidence that markets lead to the emergence of shared norms of cooperation and fairness, rather than self-interest:

> The efficiency of market exchange involving infrequent or anonymous transactions improves with an increasingly shared set of motivations and expectations related to trust, fairness, and cooperation. This lowers transaction costs, raises the frequency of successful transactions, and increases long-term rewards. (Henrich et al. 2010)

How should we reconcile this striking empirical pattern with the conventional wisdom that markets promote self-interest? One interpretation is that markets clarify the concept of ownership, thereby constraining acts of self-interest in settings where agents do not have clear property rights.[6] This suggests that market integration is positively correlated with self-interest in settings where the dictator has a clear claim to the budget. We return to this point in Section 4.

The same set of authors also explore the enforcement side of informal institutions using the ultimatum game (Henrich et al. 2006; Henrich et al. 2010). The range of offers observed in the ultimatum games is strikingly similar to that seen in the dictator games, and the correlation between the average dictator game offer and the average ultimatum game offer is 0.775. Not surprisingly, market integration is also strongly associated with ultimatum-game giving. Of course, this giving may be motivated either by altruism or by a fear of rejection. To explore internalized norms of enforcement and specifically the willingness to reject unequal offers, the authors examine variation in the average minimum acceptable offer across societies. MAOs range from 0.06 among both the Yasawa people of Fiji and the Kenyan Samburu to 0.38 among the Kenyan Gusii. Interestingly, the correlation between the MAO and the mean offer at the society level is quite low – only 0.161 – suggesting that both internal and external enforcement of fairness norms are important determinants of behavior in ultimatum games.

Henrich et al. (2010) argue that punishing unfair or uncooperative behavior by strangers is critical in large populations, and indeed they noticed a strong correlation between community size and MAO. Interestingly, they also report that hyper-fair offers of more than 50 percent of the budget are

---

[6] Clearly, there is ambiguity about property rights in experiments only in the sense that the dictator was chosen at random and has no "natural" claim to ownership (Locke 1980[1690]); if property rights are characterized as "control rights" following Grossman and Hart (1986), then the dictator holds unambiguous property rights.

rejected in many societies. The tendency to do so appears to be correlated with the level of giving observed in the dictator game: the only societies in which hyper-fair offers are never rejected are those with the lowest average levels of dictator game giving. This suggests that dictators who share a large fraction of their budgets may be motivated by an aversion to inequality, which would also lead them to reject overly generous ultimatum game offers that create uneven distributions of income.

Hermann et al. (2008) also document a willingness to punish generosity among university students in Asia, Europe, the Middle East, and North America. They conduct repeated public goods games in fifteen industrialized countries. Subjects in a number of countries are observed punishing those making relatively large contributions to the public good, though these punishments are often in retaliation (for previous punishment of low contributions). The authors use data from the World Values Survey to examine the association between behavior in the experiment and country-level norms of civic participation and respect for formal institutions. In particular, they regress the prevalence of "antisocial punishment" within the experiment on an index of responses to questions about whether tax evasion, fare dodging, and illegitimate benefits claims are ever justified. They noticed that respect for the rule of law is negatively and significantly related to the frequency of antisocial punishment.

Though these cross-cultural patterns are striking, they raise as many questions about the evolution of informal institutions as they answer. In particular, although several studies discuss plausible mechanisms of cultural change, none report empirical evidence of a causal link. More broadly, the focus on cross-society comparisons means that observed differences may be due to variation in the genetic makeup of a population, its history and political culture, its ecological and economic environment, and formal institutions themselves.

4. How Informal Institutions Evolve within Societies

How do cross-cultural differences arise? If market integration or any other factor is causally related to differences in informal institutions across societies, we would also expect to observe similar correlation within societies. Moreover, evidence from a single society is more likely to convincingly demonstrate causal relationship: Differences between societies result from the interplay of a variety of complex geographic and historical factors; it is often not feasible to disentangle such factors empirically. Within a community, ceteris paribus assumptions can be more reasonable, both because individual differences can be controlled for directly and because it is some-times possible to exploit exogenous variation in causal factors of interest.

To illustrate the potential for exploring variation in informal cultural norms within a society, I test Henrich et al.'s (2010) hypothesis that mar-ket integration is related to giving in experiments using data from dictator games I conducted in seven rural communities in western Kenya in 2007. The experiments were designed to compare the willingness to share earned and unearned income in rural villages. The experimental design builds on numerous studies in university labs which suggest that dictators are less gen-erous with earned income than with the unearned income typically used in experiments (Hoffman et al. 1994; Cherry et al. 2002). Fahr and Irlenbusch (2000) term this increase in entitlement that results from earning the budget an "earned property right." Prior to my experiments, this disparity had not been documented in a non-undergraduate population; and I noticed only weak evidence of earned property rights in rural Kenya.[7]

I conducted dictator games that differed in terms of the source of the dictator's budget. In luck treatments, dictators rolled a twenty-sided die to determine the size of their budgets. In effort treatments, dictators were paid a piece rate for completing a simple but tedious task collecting a specific type of dried bean from a bucket containing a variety of types. The luck treatments allow us to test the hypothesis that market integration is associated with greater generosity in a standard dictator game, where neither player has a strong claim to the budget. The effort treatments allow for consideration of the relationship between market integration and generosity when income is earned and, consequently, ownership claims are clearer.

Experimental sessions took place in Busia District, a poor, predominantly rural area in western Kenya. Each experimental session took place in a different community.[8] A total of 272 subjects participated across all sessions. Table 11.1 provides summary statistics on the participants. The median subject is a twenty-seven-year-old married man with less than eight years of formal education. Less than half the subjects (48.5 percent) completed primary school, and only 14.3 percent completed secondary. The education level for the sample is therefore slightly below the average for the region: According to the 2008 round of the Kenya Demographic and Health Survey, 59.3 percent of males and 53.9 percent of females in rural Western Province completed primary school, and 19.6 percent of males and 16.7 percent of females completed secondary. Almost all subjects (95.7) percent are involved

---

[7] Additional results are reported in Jakiela (2011).

[8] A detailed description of the experimental protocol is provided in (Jakiela 2011). Experi-mental instructions are available on the author's Web site.

Table 11.1. *Summary statistics*

Variable	Mean	S.D.	Median	N
Female	0.404	0.492	0	272
Married	0.697	0.460	1	271
Household size	5.871	2.448	5	271
Age	27.325	5.286	27	271
Completed primary school	0.485	0.501	0	272
Completed secondary school	0.143	0.351	0	272
Farm household	0.956	0.206	1	272
Luhya ethnic group	0.665	0.473	1	272
Teso ethnic group	0.283	0.451	0	272
Luo ethnic group	0.037	0.189	0	272
Christian	0.974	0.159	1	272
Community groups	2.011	1.674	2	272
Trusts neighbors and kin	0.750	0.434	1	272
Trusts strangers	0.408	0.492	0	272
Near paved road	0.452	0.499	0	272

in subsistence agriculture, and many also engage in other labor market activities. The median subject is a Christian who belongs to the Luhya ethnic group, a Bantu-speaking people who form the second largest ethnic group in Kenya and the majority group in Western Province. Of the subjects in the sample, 66.5 percent are Luhya, and all but four of the remaining subjects are either Teso or Luo, two locally significant minorities. Subjects participate in an average of 2.0 community groups, the most popular being rotating savings and credit associations (ROSCAs), bible study groups, and women's groups. Seventy-five percent of subjects claim to trust their neighbors and family completely or somewhat, but only 40.8 percent trust people they've just met.

Table 11.2 reports summary statistics on experiment outcomes in the luck and effort treatments. The main outcome variable, *DG Offer*, is the fraction of the budget allocated by dictators to their partners within

Table 11.2. *Dictator game outcomes*

Outcome	Luck treatments	Effort treatments
Partner share	0.265 (0.194)	0.244 (0.190)
Partner share zero	0.151 (0.359)	0.171 (0.377)
Partner share half	0.161 (0.367)	0.152 (0.359)

Standard errors in parentheses.

the experiment. In my sample, dictators allocate their partners an average of 26.5 percent of the budget in the luck treatments and 24.4 percent of the budget in the effort treatments. Thus, although subjects allocate less of their budget to others when the money being divided is earned, the effect is quite small. However, a t-test of the equality of the means across treatments does reject the null hypothesis (p-value < 0.001). There is a similar, small but significant, difference across treatments in the likelihood that a dictator keeps the entire budget to herself: Subjects do so 15.1 percent of the time in the luck treatments and 17.1 percent of the time in the effort treatments. Differences in the likelihood of allocating one's partner exactly half the budget also move in the same direction, but they are not statistically significant.

My goal is to examine the relationship between market integration and individual choices in the dictator game. As a proxy for market integration, I look at whether or not a community is located on a paved road. This measure differs from that used by Henrich et al. (2010): They calculate the proportion of a household's total calories that were purchased. Unfortunately, their measure requires extremely detailed data that is unavailable to me ex post. To my knowledge, proximity to roads has not yet been used as a proxy for market exposure in the experimental literature; however, the relationship between access to paved roads and market integration has long been recognized (cf. Fafchamps 1992; Goletti et al. 1995). Though proximity to roads is quite likely to be correlated with market exposure, roads are an imperfect measure because they may also be correlated with other factors. We explore possible channels of impact and alternative interpretations further below.

Figure 11.1 presents histograms of the share of the total budget dictators allocated to their partners in the luck and effort dictator game treatments, disaggregated by proximity to the road. All four distributions are bimodal, with significant spikes at zero and 50 percent of the total budget. Looking first at the luck treatments, the pattern observed across societies is also evident within this particular society: Subjects in communities that are not on the paved road allocate their partners half the budget 11.4 percent of the time, while those near the paved road split the budget evenly 23.9 percent of the time. However, the pattern is reversed in the effort treatments, where dictators in communities located on a road are less likely to split the budget evenly, doing so 11.0 percent of the time as opposed to 19.4 percent of the time in more remote areas.

To test the robustness of this finding and explore potential demographic confounds, I estimate the association between living near a paved road and

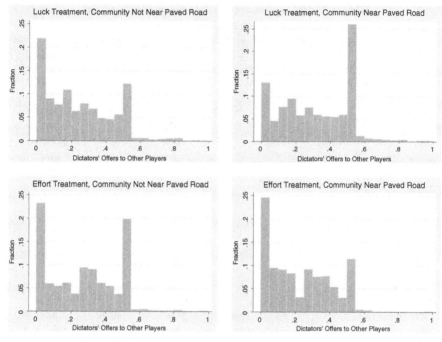

Figure 11.1

giving in the dictator game in a regression framework. I estimate the OLS regression

$$DGOffer_{i,b} = \alpha + \beta\, Paved_i + \zeta\, Budget + \gamma X_i + \varepsilon_{ib}, \qquad (1)$$

where $DGOffer_{i,b}$ is the fraction of the budget that subject i allocates to the other player at budget size b,[9] $Paved_i$ is an indicator for residing in a community located on the paved road, *Budget* is a control for the size of the budget, X_i is a vector of individual controls such as gender and education level, and ε_{ib} is a mean-zero error term. Standard errors are clustered at the subject level in all specifications.

In the OLS regression with only budget size controls, the coefficient on *Paved*$_i$s positive and significant in the luck treatments (Column 1, Table 11.3). The point estimate suggests that being in a community located near the road increases the amount allocated to one's partner by 7.1 percentage

---

[9] The strategy method was used to record individual decisions within the experiment, so all subjects indicated their preferred division of a series of feasible budgets.

Table 11.3. *OLS regressions of DG offer on proximity to road*

Dependent Variable = DG Offer Treatment:	Luck (1)	Luck (2)	Effort (3)	Effort (4)
Community on paved road	0.071**	0.080**	− 0.041*	− 0.046*
	(0.033)	(0.033)	(0.024)	(0.024)
Female	*	− 0.006	*	− 0.025
		(0.031)		(0.026)
Age	*	0.002	*	0.001
		(0.004)		(0.003)
Married	*	− 0.06	*	0.044
		(0.043)		(0.03)
Completed primary school	*	0.024	*	0.017
		(0.037)		(0.027)
Completed secondary school	*	− 0.023	*	0.046
		(0.048)		(0.047)
Teso	*	0.044	*	− 0.029
		(0.041)		(0.025)
Other ethnic group	*	0.063	*	− 0.082*
		(0.054)		(0.045)
Observations	2140	2140	4946	4886
R^2	0.041	0.064	0.04	0.079
Budget controls	Yes	Yes	Yes	Yes
Constant	Yes	Yes	Yes	Yes

Coefficients significantly nonzero at .99 (***), .95 (**) and .90 (*) confidence levels. Standard errors clustered at the player level in all specifications.

points, relative to a base level of $DGOffer_{i,b}$ of approximately 31 percent of the budget. Including controls for gender, marital status, educational attainment, and ethnic group increases the coefficient estimate for the indicator to 8.0 percentage points. The coefficient is significantly different from zero at the 95 percent confidence level in both specifications.

As the histograms suggest, the pattern is reversed in the effort treatments. OLS regressions of giving in the effort dictator games with and without controls are reported in Columns 3 and 4, respectively (Table 11.3). Here, the coefficient on Paved is consistently negative and significant at the 90 percent confidence level. Including the controls has little impact on the estimated coefficient magnitude: The point estimate is 0.41 without controls and 0.42 when they are included. Thus, the association between proximity to a paved road and giving in dictator games appears context-specific and disappears once entitlements within the experiment become less ambiguous.

An important question is whether market integration impacts the proportion of subjects who behave in a self-interested manner or, alternatively, induces those sharing a positive amount to give more (or less). Figure 11.1 suggests that proximity to a paved road may shift dictators to (or away from) the particularly salient 50–50 split of the budget. To test these hypotheses, I estimate Probit regressions of the likelihood of allocating the other player nothing (Table 11.4, Panel A) and exactly one half of the budget (Table 11.4, Panel B). Probit regressions of the indicator for giving nothing to the other player do not suggest a significant association with proximity to a paved road in either the luck or effort treatments.

The coefficient estimate for the indicator is negative but insignificant in all specifications (Table 11.4). Thus, my proxy for market exposure does not appear to influence the probability of behaving in a strictly self-interested manner. In contrast, proximity to a paved road is strongly associated with the likelihood of allocating the other player exactly half the budget. In luck treatments, the indicator is positive and statistically significant with and without controls; it is negative and significant in the effort treatments. The coefficient estimate indicates that being in a community on the paved road is associated with a 13.5 percent increase in the probability of splitting the budget evenly in the luck treatments, but a 9.2 percentage point decrease in the likelihood of doing so in the effort treatments.

Thus far, I have replicated and extended Henrich et al.'s (2010) cross-society findings within a single cultural environment. As in their work, my proxy for market exposure is positively and significantly associated with giving in standard dictator games. However, I noticed that the market integration proxy is negatively and significantly associated with DG giving when dictators earn the budget they divide. This is consistent with the interpretation that markets induce generous behavior when entitlement claims are ambiguous but do not lead to greater altruism in all contexts. My results also suggest that these associations between proximity to a paved road and DG giving are not driven by significant differences in the proportion of strictly self-interested subjects; rather, the patterns suggest that those who share a positive amount use a different calculus when determining how much to allocate the other player.

One concern about my results is that proximity to the paved road may be correlated with characteristics other than market integration. In fact, this critique extends beyond the present research to all studies, including the results presented in Henrich et al. (2010), which explore associations between variables without a credible source of exogenous variation in the independent variable of interest. For example, while Henrich et al. (2010)

Table 11.4. *Probit regressions of DG giving on proximity to road*

Treatment:	Luck (1)	Luck (2)	Effort (3)	Effort (4)
Panel A: Dependent Variable = DG Offer Zero				
Community on paved road	− 0.3.14	− 0.373	− 0.156	− 0.156
	(0.265)	(0.265)	(0.174)	(0.178)
Female	*	0.198	*	0.069
		(0.233)		(0.195)
Age	*	− 0.016	*	− 0.01
		(0.026)		(0.019)
Married	*	0.477	*	− 0.034
		(0.349)		(0.223)
Completed primary school	*	0.039	*	0.3*
		(0.273)		(0.178)
Completed secondary school	*	− 0.054	*	− 0.696**
		(0.373)		(0.298)
Teso	*	− 0.578*	*	0.171
		(0.348)		(0.178)
Other ethnic group	*	− 1.323***	*	0.51
		(0.458)		(0.369)
Observations	2140	2140	4946	4886
Pseudo R^2	0.015	0.055	0.003	0.032
Panel B: Dependent Variable – DG Offer Exactly Half				
Community on paved road	0.497**	0.579**	− 0.373**	− 0.426**
	(0.225)	(0.234)	(0.175)	(0.183)
Female	*	− 0.001	*	0.12
		(0.231)		(0.188)
Age	*	0.043*	*	0.006
		(0.025)		(0.018)
Married	*	− 0.392	*	0.181
		(0.288)		(0.204)
Completed primary school	*	0.335	*	0.201
		(0.274)		(0.197)
Completed secondary school	*	− 0.193	*	− 0.027
		(0.31)		(0.381)
Teso	*	0.227	*	− 0.149
		(0.309)		(0.19)
Other ethnic group	*	− 0.45	*	− 0.31
		(0.291)		(0.369)
Observations	2140	2140	4946	4886
Pseudo R^2	0.032	0.06	0.049	0.062
Budget controls	Yes	Yes	Yes	Yes
Constant	Yes	Yes	Yes	Yes

Coefficients significantly nonzero at .99 (***), .95 (**) and .90 (*) confidence levels. Standard errors clustered at the player level in all specifications.

Table 11.5. *OLS regressions of individual characteristics on proximity to road*

Outcome:	Primary school	Secondary school	Household farms	Community groups	Trust index
	(1)	(2)	(3)	(4)	
Community on	0.007	0.012	− 0.033	0.28	0.162*
paved road	(0.061)	(0.043)	(0.025)	(0.2)	(0.09)
Female	0.029	0.009	− 0.003	0.283	− 0.106
	(0.062)	(0.043)	(0.026)	(0.209)	(0.09)
Age	− 0.008	− 0.009*	0.003	0.068**	0.009
	(0.006)	(0.005)	(0.002)	(0.02)	(0.009)
Constant	0.699**	0.373***	0.883***	− 0.089	0.882**
	(0.165)	(0.13)	(0.065)	(0.553)	(0.248)
Observations	271	271	271	271	271
R^2	0.009	0.018	0.014	0.061	0.023

Coefficients significantly nonzero at .99 (***), .95 (**) and .90 (*) confidence levels. Standard errors clustered at the player level in all specifications.

control for age, sex, education, income, wealth, household size, and community size, it is impossible to control for, or even measure, all possible confounds. Market integration may be correlated with community group participation, numeracy, comprehension of the structure of the experiment, a desire to conform to the experimenter's expectations, access to credit, and unobserved innate abilities (such as cognitive ability), all of which may have an impact on behavior within the dictator game. Moreover, the correlation between exposure to markets and giving in the dictator game can never tell us whether markets lead to greater generosity or markets arose in those locations initially characterized by altruism and interpersonal trust.

Thus, the aim of this paper is not to make a causal case, but to document the cross-cultural associations observed in previous work within an individual society. However, in an attempt to shed some light on the possible mechanisms underlying the observed association between my proxy for market exposure, proximity to a paved road, and behavior within the dictator game, I present the results of a series of regressions on individual characteristics on the Paved indicator, controlling for age and gender. Results are presented in Table 11.5. The outcomes I consider are completion of primary school, completion of secondary school, whether a household farms, the number of community groups to which a subject belongs, and an index of trust, which combines answers to questions on whether one trusts one's neighbors, one's family, and people one is meeting for the first time.

Unsurprisingly, the point estimate suggests that those living near a road are slightly less likely to farm (Table 11.5, Column 3); however, this result is not significant. More interestingly, those near roads are not significantly more likely to complete primary or secondary school than other subjects, and both estimated coefficients, while positive, are quite small (Table 11.5, Columns 1 and 2). This absence of an impact on education is particularly intriguing since, as we discuss in more detail below, education is often seen as one of the primary drivers of modernization and the adoption of market and science oriented values (Inkeles 1969). Proximity to the paved road is positively correlated with both participation in community groups and the trust index, though only the later result is statistically significant, and then only at the 90 percent confidence level (Table 11.5, Columns 4 and 5). Though only suggestive, these results suggest that my proxy variable is likely correlated with various forms of social capital. However, whether this represents a confound associated with my proxy for market exposure or a potential causal pathway underlying both my results and those of others is an open question.

5. Conclusions

The evidence presented here demonstrates the use of experimental economic methods to measure the self-imposed codes of conduct underlying informal institutions, and the variation in these preferences for fairness within and across societies. Specifically, I have shown that giving in dictator games is significantly associated with market integration, or some factor correlated with it, in rural western Kenya, just as it is when one looks across cultures around the world. However, I have not yet provided a satisfactory answer to the question of causal identification. Very little work to date has done so. One exception is Jakiela et al. (2010). That paper, like this one, explores variation in individual social preferences in rural Kenya. In that case, we exploit the exogenous variation in success in primary school, the result of a randomized trial of a scholarship program for girls in western Kenya. Social scientists have long hypothesized that formal schooling is causally related to the emergence of "modern" values, and empirical studies demonstrate a robust correlation (cf. Inkeles 1969). We show that random assignment to the scholarship treatment group is a strong predictor of performance on the Kenyan primary school leaving exam, allowing us to use an instrumental variables approach to estimate the impact of academic achievement on social preferences. We recruit a sample of girls from the treatment and control groups in the scholarship program to participate in a variant of the effort dictator game treatments described above that allow dictators to take from other players' earnings. We noticed that academic success is causally related to respect for earned property rights in the economic experiments.

The study is one of the first to exploit exogenous variation in field experiments to isolate the causal mechanisms of cultural change. Di Tella et al. (2007) use a natural experiment to create exogenous variation in property rights and estimate the impact of land ownership on individual beliefs. Studies such as these, which focus on the micro-level to demonstrate how informal institutions change over time, are the next step to understanding how to identify and strengthen the types of informal institutions that promote development. Equally importantly, these studies translate some of the fundamental insights of Douglass North into the empirical language of modern development economics. Just as the work of Acemoglu et al. (2001) brought a new focus on institutions to the literature on economic growth, empirical micro-level studies of the correlates and determinants of values and internalized constraints on behavior can shed light on the links between behavioral economics, informal institutions, and economic development.

12

Experimental Evidence on the Workings of
Democratic Institutions

Pedro Dal Bó

1. Introduction

Much research in economics studies the link between institutions and economic performance (see North 1981; La Porta et al. 1998; Acemoglu, Johnson, and Robinson 2001; and Easterly and Levine 2003, among others). Douglass C. North's work has significantly contributed to our understanding of the determinants of institutions and their effect on economic performance. I follow here the definition of institutions in North (1981): "Institutions are a set of rules, compliance procedures, and moral and ethical behavioral norms designed to constrain the behavior of individuals" (201–202), with a focus on formal institutions.

In this chapter, I summarize experimental evidence on the determinants of institutional change in democratic environments and its effect on behavior. Experimental economics has much to contribute to the study of institutions (their effects and determinants) as it allows researchers to circumvent the usual threats to identification that arise with naturally occurring data. It is possible, for example, to exogenously vary plausible determinants of efficient institutional change and identify their impact.

The main question I address in this chapter is when do people choose to establish efficient institutions (institutions that give members of society incentives to take actions that are socially desirable)? I summarize previous experimental literature that uncovered important elements behind the failure to establish efficient institutions. These elements include coordination problems, perceived and real heterogeneity as to which efficient institution is best for each subject, and uncertainty about the effects of the alternative institutions. In addition, I present novel experimental results supporting a hypothesis put forward by North (1990a) regarding one of the possible determinants of efficient institutional change: citizens' understanding of reality. I show that subjects with a more limited strategic understanding of the environment (but with the same information) are less likely to demand efficient institutions.

In this chapter, I also describe a recent literature showing that democracy may affect behavior and economic performance not only through its effect on institutional choice (and the incentives faced by citizens) but also directly by making citizens more prosocial.

There is an extensive and fascinating experimental literature on political economy that is not reviewed in this chapter given the focus here on democratic institutional change and the direct effect of democracy.[1]

2. Democratic Institutions and Social Dilemmas

North (1990a) discusses the conditions needed for political markets to lead to efficient institutions. He stresses, first, the importance of people having a correct understanding of reality so that they can understand the impact of different regulations and institutions, and second, the importance of equal access to decision making: "The institutional structure most favorable to approximating such conditions is the modern democratic society with universal suffrage" (109).

A series of different experiments have studied the choice of institutions in democratic settings. These experiments are different in many dimensions but share a central question: How likely are democracies to choose efficient institutions, regulations, and policies?

Simple Experiment on Voting to Overcome a Social Dilemma
North (1990) discusses reasons democracies may fail to fulfill their potential with respect to institutional choice. First, citizens may fail to fully understand reality. This could be either due to the lack of information on the part of the voters or their lacking a correct model to predict the impact of different institutions on behavior and welfare. Second, elected representatives may not have incentives to make decisions following the desires of their constituencies. While much of the literature has focused on the latter

---

[1] See for example the experimental literature on voter turnout (Schram and Sonnemans 1996; Goeree and Holt 2005; Grosser and Schram 2006; Levine and Palfrey 2007; Gerber, Green, and Larimer 2008) and the experimental literature on voting behavior, information aggregation and efficiency of voting rules (Morton and Williams 1999; Hung and Plott 2001; Casella, Gelman, and Palfrey 2006; Battaglini, Morton, and Palfrey 2007; Casella, Palfrey, and Riezman 2008; Battaglini, Morton, and Palfrey 2010; Casella 2011; Esponda and Vespa 2010).

Table 12.1. *Stage game payoffs*

Own action	Other's action	
	C	D
C	10	50
D	30	70

problem (see Barro 1973 and Ferejohn 1986 among others), less is known about the former problem. Even if agency issues and other issues that can lead to inefficient policies (e.g., Alesina and Drazen 1991; Fernandez and Rodrik 1991) were absent, could still be the case that people may fail to choose efficient institutions? How sensitive is the institutional decision to the understanding citizens have of reality?

I discuss results from a simple experiment designed to answer these questions. In this experiment, subjects were anonymously divided into groups of ten to participate in two-person prisoners' dilemma games with random matching between games. In the prisoners' dilemma game, each subject chooses simultaneously between C (cooperate) or D (defect).[2] The payoffs depend on both actions as shown in Table 12.1. Regardless the action of the other subject, each subject earns more points if he or she chooses D. The unique Nash equilibrium of the game (if subjects care only about points) is for both subjects to choose D. This is an inefficient outcome as mutual cooperation results in higher payoffs for both subjects.

After ten rounds of playing the prisoners' dilemma game, subjects were given the possibility of eliminating one of the two actions by plurality. Each subject voted on whether to keep all actions, eliminate D, or eliminate C. After voting, the subject participated in ten more rounds depending on the decision made by plurality. To study the effect of subjects' understanding of the game on voting decisions, I modified the presentation of the game to the subjects. In half the sessions, the computer screen showed the payoff matrix with the subject's action as rows and the partner's actions as columns. Feedback about the outcome was also provided by highlighting the chosen row and column. In the other half of the sessions, the payoffs were not displayed as a matrix, and feedback did not stress the behavior of the partner by highlighting his or her behavior in the matrix (this behavior was still reported). Figure 12.1 shows a screenshot of each treatment (payoffs are set in cents).

---

[2] For neutrality, in the experiments the actions C and D were called 2 and 1 respectively. For convenience of the reader, I use here the usual names, C and D.

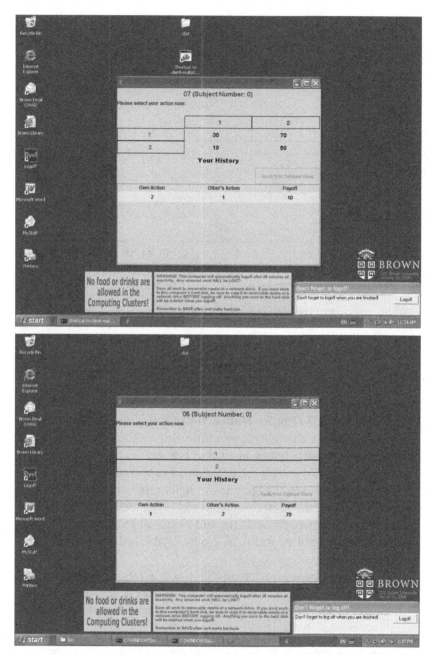

Figure 12.1. Multistage screens for "See Matrix" and "Do Not See Matrix"

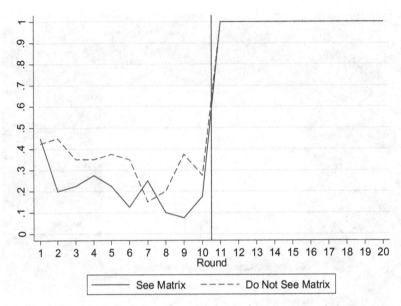

Figure 12.2. Evolution of cooperation in democracy experiment

I hypothesize that not showing the game as a matrix may diminish sub-jects' understanding of the structure of the game and the likely effect of modifying the game by eliminating a strategy. I called these two treatments "See Matrix" and "Do Not See Matrix" treatments, respectively.

The participants were eighty Brown University or RISD undergraduates.[3] Half the subjects participated in each of the treatments. As Figure 12.2 shows, in the first ten rounds the evolution of cooperation is consistent to what has been found in the literature: a significant cooperation rate that decreases with experience (see Andreoni and Miller 1993; and Dal Bó 2005 among others). Between rounds ten and eleven all groups voted in favor of eliminating D. In other words, all groups established an institution that leads to efficiency.

However, the aggregate result hides differences in voting across treatments (see Figure 12.3). In both treatments, 12.5 percent of the subjects voted to eliminate C. Of the subjects who saw the matrix, 75 percent voted to

---

[3] Subjects were recruited through the Brown University Social Science Experimental Lab-oratory and interacted anonymously through computers using the Multistage (Caltech-UCLA) software in a computer lab at Brown.

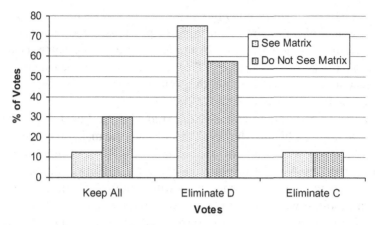

Figure 12.3. Distribution of votes in democracy experiment

eliminate D against 57 percent of those who did not see the matrix. This suggests that changing the way in which the information was displayed had a large effect on the voting decisions of the subjects but not in the outcomes.[4]

The difference in voting behavior is consistent with the idea that seeing the payoff matrix helps the subjects understand how their payoff depends not only on their own action but also on the action of their partners, and how eliminating D would affect their payoff. In particular, seeing the matrix may have helped them understand the two ways in which eliminating D would affect their payoff: negatively (reducing the subject's own set of possible actions) or positively (forcing all subjects to cooperate).

However, the median voter in this experiment always voted to eliminate D, leading to an efficient evolution of institutions. Does this mean that people will always choose efficient institutions? Or are there elements related to the underlying game or the voting mechanisms that can lead to inefficient institutions? A series of previous experimental papers have addressed these questions. Most of these papers are not integrated into a single literature. I will attempt to integrate them here.

---

[4] Personal characteristics of the subjects like whether they were economics majors, year in college, their (self-reported) math and verbal SAT scores (a measure of cognitive ability), and their actions in a beauty contest game (a measure of strategic sophistication) had no significant impact on voting decisions.

More Evidence on Voting and Efficiency

One element of the environment from the previous experiment that may facilitate the evolution of efficient institutions is that the effect of the changes considered was easy to predict.[5] That is, if D is eliminated there is no uncertainty about the outcome of the game. In real life, it is unlikely that an institutional change can have such a clear effect.

Dal Bó, Foster, and Putterman (2010) studied institutional choice under a case of more ambiguity (however, this was not the main objective of the paper, which is discussed in the next section). In this experiment, subjects were anonymously divided into groups of four subjects to participate in two-person prisoners' dilemma games with random matching. After ten rounds, subjects were given the opportunity to impose a fine on unilateral defection by majority.[6] This fine converted the prisoners' dilemma game into a coordination game. In the resulting game, both mutual defection and mutual cooperation are equilibria (of course, only the latter is efficient). The fact that the institutional change did not eliminate defection from the game but only changed payoffs to make mutual cooperation a possible equilibrium may better approximate a realistic feature of regulation: that it may pay to follow the regulation only if others are following it as well (think about speeding on the road).

In this game, the subjects' opinion on whether imposing the fine would be beneficial or not depended on their beliefs about others' response to the fine. Contrary to the previous experiment, there was no clear theoretical prediction of how subjects would vote. If they expected to coordinate on cooperation, they should vote for the fine; otherwise, they could vote against it.

Dal Bó, Foster, and Putterman (2010) found that 54 percent of the subjects voted in favor of the fine, and 46 percent voted against it, out of a total of 424 subjects. Almost half of the subjects voted against an institution that could lead to efficiency in equilibrium. Moreover, the researchers found that voting for the fine was positively correlated with cognitive ability (as

[5] Carpenter (2000) previously considered institutional choice (but not through voting) in an environment in which the effect is easy to predict. In that experiment, subjects played in pairs. One subject had to propose which game out of five to play in pairs. Four of the games were prisoners' dilemma games, and a fifth one was a game in which the symmetric efficient outcome was a Nash equilibrium. The other player could accept the proposal or not (in which case they played one of the prisoners' dilemma games). Thirty out of the thirty-five proposals were to play the game that was not a prisoners' dilemma game, and all but three of these offers were accepted.

[6] The voting stage was complicated by the fact that the computer server could choose to disregard the votes. However, this does not change the incentives to vote in any particular way.

measured by self reported SAT math scores) and strategic ability, measured by behavior in a beauty contest game.[7] They found no significant effects of class in college, pursuing an economics degree, or political ideology.[8]

This result suggests that a large proportion of people may be reluctant to vote for an institution that may lead to efficiency if the efficient outcome is not guaranteed. In these two experiments there was only one policy that could lead to efficiency. More than one policy option can lead to inefficiency as there could be a coordination problem between voters on which policy to support, and this could delay efficiency. Walker et al. (2000) studied this issue in the context of a common-pool resources (CPR) game. Each player in the game decided on an amount to extract from a common pool; the cost of extracting depended on the total extraction by all players.[9] This game is a social dilemma game in which the Nash equilibrium is to extract more than is socially optimal.

In that experiment, groups of seven players participated in ten rounds of the CPR game. After that, players participated in ten more rounds of a modified CPR game with two stages. In the first stage each player proposed a vector of extractions (one number for each player) and then all players voted on all proposals. The authors considered two voting rules: majority and unanimity. If one proposal won, the second stage of the game implemented that vector of extractions. If no proposal won, then the players participated in a normal CPR game.

Under unanimity rule there is a unique sub-game perfect equilibrium of the game if we do not consider weakly dominated strategies. In this equilibrium someone proposes that each player extracts the same socially optimal amount. This level of extraction is lower than the equilibrium level of extraction without institutions and results in greater payoffs.

Under majority there is a multiplicity of equilibria. In addition to the symmetric socially optimal level of extraction, there are several proposals that let only four of the seven players extract resources from the common-pool. Given such a minimum winning coalition, players would choose a level of extraction to maximize their own sum of payoffs. This results in a

---

[7] See Bosch-Domènech et al. (2002) and references therein for a detailed description of beauty contest games and the role of levels of strategic reasoning to explain behavior in these games.

[8] Putterman, Tyran, and Kamei (2010) studied voting on formal sanctions in linear public goods games. They found that a large majority of groups learn to impose sanctions that make contributions reach optimal levels. Moreover, Putterman, Tyran, and Kamei show that voting is influenced by cooperative inclination and ideology.

[9] Note that the common pool is replenished after every period. This is not a dynamic game.

total sum of payoffs that is greater than in the equilibrium without institutions but lower than under the symmetrical socially optimal extraction. Since there are thirty-five possible minimum coalitions, there is a large number of possible equilibria. This multiplicity could decrease the probability that players can agree in a policy to reduce extraction from the common pool.

Walker et al. (2000) studied nine groups under majority rule and four groups under unanimity rule. Under majority rule, only five out of nine groups (56 percent) managed to impose restrictions on extraction from the common pool. Under unanimity rule, 75 percent, or three out of four groups, were able to impose restrictions. While this difference is not statistically significant (p-value of 0.55), it suggests that subjects may be more likely to agree on a restriction under unanimity rule as it eliminates coordination problems that arise from the multiplicity of minimum winning coalitions.[10]

Consistent with this idea is the difference in the type of restrictions chosen by the groups under the two voting rules. In the last round under majority rule, 60 percent of the restrictions were of the minimum winning coalition type, and 40 percent were of the symmetric type. Under unanimity, all restrictions were of the symmetric type. This difference was significant, at the 10 percent level. There is also a difference in the number of distinct proposals under both rules. In the last round, under majority rule there was an average of 4.11 distinct proposals while under unanimity there were only 1.25 distinct proposals. This difference is significant at the 1 percent level.

But the failure to impose restrictions on extractions is not only due to the multiplicity of optimal minimum coalitions. In fact, a substantial number of proposals involve suboptimal extraction levels. From the data reported in Walker et al. (2000), we can calculate that in the last round under majority rule, 19 percent of the proposals involved minimum winning coalitions with inefficient extraction rates, and 6 percent of the proposals involved symmetric suboptimal rates. For unanimity, 14 percent of the proposals involved symmetric suboptimal rates. That is, in an environment in which there was no real disagreement on the fundamentals of the game, some subjects disagreed on what they considered optimal extraction for a minimum winning coalition or all players. This disagreement increased the

---

[10] The p-values reported here regarding Walker et al. (2000) are of my own calculation using the Wald test considering one observation per group.

number of distinct proposals and reduced the chance of any restrictions being imposed.[11]

A clear example is provided by the only group that was not able to impose restrictions in the last round under unanimity. In this last round, two subjects in this group proposed that all subjects extract six tokens, while the other subjects proposed to extract seven tokens (the optimal symmetric amount). This difference in what was considered optimal by different subjects resulted in the group not imposing any restrictions on extractions.

If perceived differences in interests may decrease the chances that a group may democratically choose restrictions to solve a social dilemma, real differences may too. Margreiter, Sutter, and Dittrich (2005) studied CPR games as in Walker et al. (2000) with the difference that players were not necessarily homogenous. In groups of six players, half the subjects had a high cost and half a low cost. As before, subjects proposed a vector of extraction and then voted. The authors considered only majority rule. They compared behavior in groups with heterogeneous costs with sessions with a homogenous cost set between the high and low cost of the heterogeneous cost groups. They find that heterogeneous groups relative to homogenous groups have a larger number of distinct proposals, a lower number of accepted proposals and, as a result, a higher average number of extractions and lower payoffs (all these differences are statistically significant at the 5 percent level).

Kroll, Cherry, and Shogren (2007) presented evidence from majority voting on vectors of contributions in a linear public goods game. They found that groups that were able to vote on binding vectors of contributions reached significantly higher levels of contributions than groups that could not. Yet not all groups made the most of the opportunity to create efficient institutions in equilibrium.

Ertan, Page, and Putterman (2009) studied a linear public goods game with the possibility of post-contribution punishments. They showed that efficiency was greater when only low contributors could be punished. Ertan et al. then studied an environment in which subjects could choose whether to allow punishment of all contributors, low contributors only, or high contributors only. They showed that subjects learn to allow punishments of low contributors only. Noussair and Tan (2011) show that this learning may

---

[11] One could argue that the number of suboptimal proposals does not matter if subjects focus only on optimal proposals. However, the data shows that a similar percentage of subjects also tend to vote for suboptimal proposals.

be hampered by heterogeneity in the productivity of contributions across subjects.

Two recent papers study environments in which subjects choose independently whether to participate in an institution that may eliminate or reduce free-riding among its members. In Kosfeld, Okada, and Riedl (2009) the institution had members contribute all their endowments to a linear public goods game. In Hamman, Weber, and Woon (2011), the institution is the delegation of contribution decisions to one of the members. In both studies, subjects who did not belong to the contribution could still enjoy the public good. Kosfeld, Okada, and Riedl (2009) found that many subjects chose to participate in the institution, increasing contributions and welfare. However, they did not make the most of the opportunity as many subjects chose not to remain in the institution if some other subjects chose to free ride. Hamman, Weber, and Woon (2011) showed that most subjects chose not to participate of the institution unless they were able to communicate with other subjects.

The previous experiments considered social dilemmas that did not depend on past behavior. However, there are many social dilemmas for which dynamic elements are of importance. Battaglini, Nunnari, and Palfrey (2009) studied the effect of voting institutions on the dynamics of public goods investments. They studied theoretically the dynamic accumulation of durable public goods depending on whether players made contribution decisions independently or through a binding voting procedure (each round one of the players proposed a level of public good investment and transfers across players, and that proposal passed if it received the majority of votes). In theory, the level of investment without voting is below that with voting, and investment under the latter is lower than the socially optimal one.[12] With voting there is lower investment than socially optimal due to the fact that minimum willing coalitions do not consider the interest of players outside of the coalition.

The authors brought their model to the lab and found that behavior was consistent with the main predictions from the model. The voting institution resulted in an increase in investment in the public good and an increase in earnings but, as expected, these increases were not large enough to reach efficiency. However, the authors found that proposals tended to deviate from those predicted by theory: they tended to give some transfers to a larger set of players than was predicted. While these proposals are not necessary

---

[12] In the solution of the model the authors focus on the Markov perfect equilibrium (MPE) concept.

symmetric, they are reminiscent of the higher than expected presence of symmetric proposals under majority rule in Walker et al. (2000).

Another paper that considers voting in a dynamic game is Bischoff (2007). This paper considers a dynamic CPR game where there is a recommended level of extraction and a probability of detecting deviations from this recommended level (detected deviators earn zero that period). The experimental data shows that when subjects could vote on the recommended level of extraction and the probability of detection, performance was worse than when they could not vote. While the reasons for this are not clear, the author concludes that "This result contradicts elementary economic reasoning and cast doubt on the ability of individuals to predict correctly the impact of change and thus their capability to apply institutional change to resolve social dilemma situations" (35).

How able are humans in using institutional change to solve social dilemma situations? Table 12.2 summarizes the results from the series of experiments described in this section involving voting and for which the needed information is available. The table shows the basic characteristics of the experiment in each paper: the basic game being played, the dimension of institutional improvements that were allowed, and whether the symmetric efficient outcome could be reached in equilibrium with institutional change. The table also shows whether allowing for institutional changes through voting resulted in an increase in earnings and a measure of efficiency gain that can be compared across experiments: the increase in earnings due to voting relative to the increase that would arise if subjects would reach the efficient outcome.

While voting results in an increase in payoffs in the large majority of experiments, there is large variation in the efficiency gain. In many cases, subjects are far from making the most of the opportunities provided by institutional change. The average increase in payoffs is only 25 percent of the possible increase.

Among the experiments reported in Table 12.2, the effect of allowing for institutional changes depended on whether the changes could make the symmetric efficient outcome an equilibrium. When efficiency could be reached in equilibrium, the efficiency gain was 64 percent. That is, when institutional changes can lead to improvements in equilibrium, subjects use this opportunity to some degree but not fully across the experiments reviewed here. On the contrary, when efficiency could not be reached in equilibrium, the possibility of institutional change actually leads to a decrease in efficiency of 50 percent. The difference between these two effects is statistically significant at the 10 percent level. This difference underscores the fact that

Table 12.2. *The effect of voting to overcome social dilemmas*

Paper	Basic game	Voting on	Symmetric efficiency in equilibrium	Increase in earnings	Efficiency gain
This chapter	PD	Eliminate C or D	YES	YES	100%
Kroll, Cherry, and Shogren (2007)	VCM	Contribution vectors	YES	YES	82%
Carpenter (2000)	PD	Fine on DC, subsidy on CD	YES	YES	79%
Putterman, Tyran, and Kamei (2010)	VCM	Fine	YES	YES	72%
Margreiter, Sutter, and Dittrich (2005)	CPR	Extraction vectors	YES	YES	67%
Homogeneous					
Walker et al. (2000) Majority	CPR	Extraction vectors	YES	YES	63%
Walker et al. (2000) Unnanimity	CPR	Extraction vectors	YES	YES	55%
Margreiter, Sutter, and Dittrich (2005)	CPR	Extraction vectors	YES	YES	43%
Heterogeneous					
Sutter, Haigner, and Kocher (2010)	VCM	Punishments or rewards	NO	YES	34%
Dal Bó, Foster, and Putterman (2010)	PD	Fine on DC	YES	YES	14%
Kamei (2010)	VCM	Fine	NO	YES	6%
Bischoff (2007) No Communication	Dynamic CPR	Extraction and detection	NO	NO	−64%
Bischoff (2007) Communication	Dynamic CPR	Extraction and detection	NO	NO	−175%
Average					29%

Note: Efficiency gain = (Payoff when voting − Payoff when not voting)/(Efficient payoff − Payoff when not voting).

providing material incentives to align personal incentives with group goals is important for institutions to be effective. If the set of institutions available to citizens cannot eliminate the difference between personal incentives and group goals, it is unlikely that democratic choice among the available institutions will have much impact on payoffs.

While the previous literature has uncovered other important elements behind the failure of subjects to set up efficient institutions (such as coordination problems, perceived and real heterogeneity of interests, and uncertainty about the effect of reforms), more research is needed on the determinants of efficient institutional improvements. I believe that in particular it is important to understand how subjects' perceptions and understanding of the game and their personal characteristics affect the demand for institutional reform.

3. The Direct Effect of Democracy

The previous section reviewed experiments studying how subjects democratically choose institutions so as to affect behavior. In this section I review experiments showing that democratic choice may affect behavior itself, in addition to the effect through the choice of incentives.

The idea that democracy may have a direct effect on behavior goes at least back to Tocqueville (1838): "It is not always feasible to consult the whole people, either directly or indirectly, in the formation of the law; but it cannot be denied that, when such a measure is possible, the authority of the law is much augmented. This popular origin, which impairs the excellence and wisdom of legislation, contributes prodigiously to increase its power." Other political scientists have also put forward the related idea that political participation may be itself beneficial (see Pateman 1970; Thomson 1970; and Finkel 1985).[13]

In economics, there is a long literature providing evidence consistent with the idea that democracy may have a direct effect on behavior. For example,

---

[13] This idea is also related to the idea of procedural justice in social psychology (see for example Thibaut and Walker 1975; Folger 1977; Lind and Tyler 1988; and Kees van den Bos 1999) and the idea of procedural utility in economics (Frey, Benz, and Stutzer 2004). On the related literature comparing endogenous and exogenous games see Van Huyck, Battalio, and Beil (1993), Crawford and Broseta (1998), Bohnet and Kübler (2005), Potters, Sefton, and Vesterlund (2005), Charness, Fréchette, and Qin (2007), and Lazear, Malmendier, and Weber (2006). Relatedly, Olken (2010) studied the effect of direct democracy relative to representative democracy in the provision of public goods. He found greater satisfaction under direct democracy even when there were little differences in the provision of public goods.

Bardhan (2000) shows that farmers are more likely to follow irrigation rules that they have themselves chosen. Frey (1998) finds lower tax evasion in Swiss cantons with greater political participation. At the level of the firms there is evidence showing that worker participation in decisions may have a positive effect in productivity (see Levine and Tyson 1990; Bonin, Jones, and Putterman 1993; and Black and Lynch 2001). Several experiments show that punishments and rewards in public good games have greater impact on contributions when they are allowed democratically (see Tyran and Feld 2006; Ertan, Page, and Putterman 2009; and Sutter, Haigner, and Kocher 2010).

   While the evidence provided by this literature is consistent with the existence of a direct effect of democracy, it does not necessarily prove that such an effect exists due to three possible identification issues. First, societies or groups with democratic institutions may differ from societies or groups without those institutions (endogenous democracy). For example, Swiss cantons with great democratic participation may differ from cantons with low democratic participation. The former may have a more civic-minded citizenry, which may directly affect tax evasion.[14] Second, democratic societies or groups may choose different institutions or policies (policy choice). For example, farmers may choose better irrigation rules and therefore be less likely to violate them. As such, it is important to precisely control for the type of policies or institutions being imposed. Third, democratic choice allows groups with different characteristics to choose different policies (selection into policy). This selection into policies would exist when there is democratic choice and not when institutions or policies are chosen from outside, making the detection of a direct effect of democracy difficult. For example, the extra effect of rewards and punishments on contributions when they are allowed democratically found by Sutter, Haigner, and Kocher (2010) could be due to unobservable characteristics affecting both how groups vote and their response to rewards and punishments. Dal Bó, Foster, and Putterman (2010) present results from an experiment designed to overcome these three identification hurdles and test for the existence of a direct effect of democracy.

Identifying the Direct Effect of Democracy

In each experimental session in Dal Bó, Foster, and Putterman (2010), subjects participated anonymously through computers. Subjects were randomly divided into groups of four for the entire session. Each session consisted of

---

[14] Wallis (2013) discusses other endogeneity problems in the study of institutions in the field.

Table 12.3. *Stage game payoffs in Dal Bó, Foster, and Putterman (2010)*

Initial payoffs			Modified payoffs		
	Other's action			Other's action	
Own action	C	D	Own action	C	D
C	50	10	C	50	10
D	60	40	D	48	40

two parts. In part 1, subjects played ten rounds of the prisoner's dilemma game in Table 12.3 (initial payoffs). After each round subjects were randomly rematched with another subject in their group for the next round. In part 2 of the experiment the subjects played ten rounds as in part 1, but the payoffs could be modified at the beginning of this part to the payoffs in Table 12.3 (modified payoffs). The modification of payoffs consisted of imposing a tax on unilateral defection. Whereas under the initial payoffs the unique Nash equilibrium is mutual defection, under the modified payoffs both mutual defection and mutual cooperation are Nash equilibria.

Whether the payoffs were modified was determined following the procedure shown in Figure 12.4. First, subjects voted on whether to modify payoffs. Second, the computer randomly chose whether to consider the votes in each group. If the computer considered the votes, then the majority

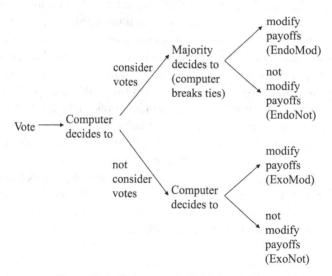

Figure 12.4. Voting stage in Dal Bó et al. (2010)

won, and in the case of a tie, the computer broke the tie. If the computer did not consider the votes in a group, it randomly chose whether to modify payoffs or not in that group. The subjects' computer screens informed them whether the computer randomly chose to consider the votes and whether payoffs were modified. The subjects did not learn the exact distribution of votes, including whether the computer needed to break a tie.

As shown in Figure 12.4, there are four possible outcomes of the voting stage: endogenous modification (EndoMod), endogenous nonmodification (EndoNot), exogenous modification (ExoMod) and exogenous nonmodification (ExoNot), where Endo denotes that the votes of the group were considered, Exo denotes that the votes were not considered, and Mod denotes that payoffs were modified. Not denotes that payoffs were not modified. For example, if the votes were considered and subjects voted to modify payoffs, the group ends with the outcome EndoMod.

After the voting stage, the subjects played ten more rounds with other subjects in their group, with the payoff matrix depending on the results from the voting stage.

After the ten rounds in part 2, the subjects answered a series of questions including questions regarding personal characteristics such as academic major, class, math and verbal SAT scores, and political philosophy. Finally, the subjects participated in a "beauty contest" game (in order to measure their strategic sophistication).

This design overcomes the three identification hurdles previously mentioned: endogenous democracy, policy choice, and selection into policy. As democracy is exogenously determined there is no problem with democratic groups being different than no democratic groups. This solves the problem of endogenous democracy. In addition, the implemented payoff matrix (that is the policy) is perfectly observed. This allows us to control perfectly for the policy that subjects face. This solves the problem of policy choice. The last hurdle is the problem of selection into policy (the fact that subjects who vote to modify payoffs are likely to behave differently from subjects who vote not to modify payoffs). How the design allow us to solve this last problem of identification will be clear in the next paragraphs.

Table 12.4 presents data from the experiment showing the existence of a direct effect of democracy. To underscore the contribution of the paper, I will first provide a comparison that suggests the existence of a direct effect of democracy but fails to pass the last identification hurdle: selection into policy.

Note that 72 percent of the subjects under EndoMod cooperated in round 11, whereas only 50 percent of subjects cooperated under ExoMod. Because

Table 12.4. *The effect of the democracy – Dal Bó et al. (2010)*

	Panel A: Number of observations			
	Consider votes		Not consider votes	
Vote for modify	Modify (EndoMod)	Not modify (EndoNot)	Modify (ExoMod)	Not modify (ExoNot)
No	17	55	31	26
Yes	55	25	33	34
Total	72	80	64	60

	Panel B: Cooperation percentage in round 11			
	Consider votes		Not consider votes	
Vote for modify	Modify (EndoMod)	Not modify (EndoNot)	Modify (ExoMod)	Not modify (ExoNot)
No	41.18	14.55	41.94	3.85
Yes	81.82	24.00	57.58	23.53
Total	72.22	17.50	50.00	15.00

the source of democracy is exogenous and we are comparing behavior under exactly the same policy (modified payoffs), the first two identification hurdles (endogenous democracy and policy choice) are not a problem here. However, from panel A in Table 12.4, note that EndoMod groups tend to have a majority of subjects who voted for modification (55 compared to 72), while ExoMod groups had a similar number of subjects voting for modification and against modification (33 compared to 31). Therefore, this comparison fails to control for selection into policy. Groups that chose to modify payoffs are on average different than groups that had the modification imposed on them in the number of Yes and No voters, and thus they are not comparable.

To overcome this last identification hurdle, selection into policy, Dal Bó, Foster, and Putterman (2010) compared behavior in EndoMod and ExoMod controlling by the vote of the subject. In such a way, we can compare subjects who voted in the same way (and therefore are comparable) in the two treatments. For subjects who voted to modified payoffs, we find a rate of cooperation of 82 percent when the modification is democratic, relative to a rate of 58 percent when the modification is imposed from the outside. This difference is statistically significant at the 1 percent level. This shows that for subjects who voted for modification there is a direct effect of democracy.

There is no effect, however, for subjects who voted to stay in the prisoners' dilemma.

The authors present a decomposition of the total effect of modifying payoffs into a selection effect, an exogenous treatment effect, and the direct effect of democracy: the difference between the exogenous and endogenous treatment. They find that of the total effect, 8 percent is due to the selection effect, 66 percent due to the exogenous treatment effect, and 26 percent due to the direct effect of democracy.[15] These magnitudes stress the importance of the direct effect of democracy: It is more than three times the selection effect and more than 40 percent of the exogenous treatment effect.

Exploring Mechanisms behind the Direct Effect of Democracy

Why did subjects who modified payoffs democratically cooperate more than those under exogenously modified payoffs? It could be that knowing about the democratic modification provides information about the votes of the other subjects (there must be a total of at least two votes in favor of modification) and this information affects behavior. Knowing that a majority voted yes may affect the subjects' expectations about which equilibrium is more likely. We call this the information hypothesis: The direct effect of democracy is not really direct but operates by affecting the information that subjects have about the other subjects in their group. An alternative hypothesis is that the effect measured by Dal Bó, Foster, and Putterman (2010) was not due to differences in information.

Dal Bó, Foster, and Putterman (2010) provide data from additional sessions that show that the effect is not due to information. In these additional sessions, subjects under exogenous modification were informed whether

---

[15] The total effect is the difference in cooperation rates between ExoMod and EndoNot, and it can be calculated from Table 12.4 as follows: TE = 72.22 − 17.50 = 54.72. The selection effect is the change in cooperation rates if we keep the cooperation rates of Yes and No voters as in ExoMod but change their prevalence to that in EndoMod. The selection effect can be calculated from Table 12.4 as follows: SE = (17/72 − 55/80)14.55 + (55/72 − 25/80)24 = 4.27. The exogenous treatment effect is the difference in cooperation rates between ExoMod and ExoNot with the prevalence of Yes and No voters as in EndoMod. From Table 12.4, ExoTrE = (17/72)(41.94 − 3.85) + (55/72)(57.58 − 23.53) = 36. The endogenous treatment effect is the difference of cooperation rates between EndoMod and ExoMod with prevalence of Yes and No voters as in EndoMod. From Table 12.4, EndoTrE = (17/72)(41.18 − 14.55) + (55/72)(81.82 − 24) = 50.45. The direct effect of democracy is the difference between the endogenous and exogenous treatment effect: DE = 14.45. The percentages in the text come from comparing the selection effect, exogenous treatment effect and the direct effect to the total effect.

Table 12.5. *The effect of democracy controlling for information – Dal Bó et al. (2010) modified payoffs*

	Panel A: Number of observations			
	Original sessions		Additional sessions	
	Consider votes		Not consider votes Vote share	
Vote for modify	Yes (EndoMod)	No (ExoMod)	≥ 2 (ExoModH)	≤ 2 (ExoModL)
No	17	31	20	38
Yes	55	33	56	14
Total	72	64	76	52
	Panel B: Cooperation percentage in round 11			
Vote for modify	(EndoMod)	(ExoMod)	(ExoModH)	(ExoModL)
No	41.18	41.94	35.00	23.68
Yes	81.82	57.58	62.50	64.29
Total	72.22	50.00	55.26	34.62

there were at most two or at least two votes in favor of modification. This gives them the same information about votes that subjects obtain under democracy. These two additional treatments are denoted ExoModH and ExoModL in Table 12.5.

As shown in Table 12.5, 82 percent of subjects who voted for modification under endogenous modification cooperated in round 11, whereas only 63 percent cooperated under exogenous modification under the same information (at least two votes in favor of modification). This difference is statistically significant at the 5 percent level.

Moreover, the information about votes have no significant effect on the cooperation rate under exogenous modification (58 percent for no information, 63 percent for at least two votes in favor of modification, and 64 percent for at most two votes in favor of modification).

In conclusion, Dal Bó, Foster, and Putterman (2010) find that the direct effect of democracy cannot be explained by differences in information. It appears that democracy directly affects subjects' behavior. This may be due to democracy strengthening cooperative social norms or operating as a coordination device. More research is needed to disentangle the two possibilities.

Table 12.6. *The spillover effect of democracy – Kamei (2010) average contribution under modified payoffs*

	Endo-Exo		Exo-Exo
Vote for modify	Endo	Exo	Exo
No-No	7.35	7.65	5.84
Yes-Yes	16.55	15.73	12.05

The Spillover Effect of Democracy

Kamei (2010) shows that the direct effect of democracy can spillover from democratic environments to other environments. That is, a person participating in a democratic decision may also behave in a more prosocial manner in nondemocratic environments. This has implications for our understanding on how democratic participation can foster cooperative behavior in a society or organization. In this experiment, subjects could vote to modify the payoffs from a linear public goods game to reduce the benefits of investing in the individual account. This reduction, however, was not enough to change the unique Nash equilibrium under monetary payoffs: It was still a best response to contribute nothing to the public account. Subjects voted and participated in two public goods games with two different partners. Some subjects faced exogenously modified payoffs in both games (that is, votes were not considered in both games; these subjects are called Exo-Exo) while other subjects had their votes considered in one group but not the other (these subjects are called Endo-Exo).

Table 12.6 reports, for groups with modified payoffs, the average contribution of the subjects as a function of whether votes were considered or not for both No-No and Yes-Yes voters.[16] As in Dal Bó, Foster, and Putterman (2010), it is important to compare behavior of subjects that voted in the same way so as to control for selection into policy.

Yes-Yes voters contributed more in groups under exogenous modification if in the other group they faced and endogenous modification than if they faced an exogenous modification in both groups (15.73 versus 12.05 contribution points over a total of 20 possible points – significant at the 5 percent level). This difference shows that when subjects had their votes considered in one group, they increased their contribution in the other group as well. There are no significant differences for subjects who voted not to modify

---

[16] No-No (Yes-Yes) voters are those that voted against (for) the modification of payoffs for both groups.

payoffs, so the spillover effect is limited to subjects who wanted to modify payoffs.[17]

Note that the data from Table 12.6 also allows us to measure the direct effect of democracy. For Yes-Yes voters, contributions in groups with a democratic modification were significantly greater than those from subjects who did not participate in any democratic group (16.55 versus 12.05 – significant at the 1% percent level). This is interesting because, contrary to the case in Dal Bó, Foster, and Putterman (2010), in this experiment the modification of payoffs does not affect the set of equilibria under the assumption of material payoffs. As such the fact that democracy affects behavior is more surprising.

Finally, the results from Kamei (2010) have implications for the set of identification strategies available to measure the direct effect of democracy. While Dal Bó, Foster, and Putterman (2010) controlled by individual vote so as to avoid selection into policy effects while comparing behavior across people, an alternative would be to have the same subject participate in one democratic group and one nondemocratic group. In this way, personal characteristics could be controlled for while calculating the effect of democracy on behavior. The spillover effect found by Kamei (2010) suggests that this identification strategy may fail to measure the direct effect of democracy appropriately as the subject behavior in the nondemocratic group is affected by the participation in the democratic group.

4. Conclusions

An important feature of society is the possible tension between the incentives faced by each of its members and society as a whole. This tension may result in inefficient outcomes. One way in which societies may solve this tension is by using the power of the state to establish institutions (for example, regulations and policies) that would align the incentives of individuals with the goals of society. One important issue, then, is to study to what degree citizens would vote to impose these institutions. Studying these issues with naturally occurring data is difficult not only due to the usual endogeneity concerns but also due to the fact that it may be difficult to determine what outcomes and institutions are efficient. However, this can be done in experiments where the researcher has full control over the environment.

---

[17] This is consistent with the fact that the direct effect of democracy in Dal Bó, Foster, and Putterman (2010) is limited to voters in favor of modification.

In this chapter I summarized a series of experiments showing that subjects do not always make the most of the opportunity to set up institutions that would lead to efficient behavior. While this literature has identified important factors behind this result, I believe that more research is needed to better understand the determinants of efficient institutions.

I end the chapter by summarizing the recent literature on the direct effect of democracy. This literature shows that democratic institutions may have an effect on behavior not only through the choice of policies and regulations that affect incentives and thus behavior – that is, there is a direct effect of democracy. This effect has been shown not to depend on the information revealed through voting. Moreover, this effect spills over from democratic to nondemocratic environments.

Acknowledgments

I thank Anna Aizer, Ernesto Dal Bó, Andrew Foster and Louis Putterman for many productive discussion and comments. I also thank CASSEL (UCLA) and SSEL (Caltech) for the Multistage software, Omar Ahmed for adapting it to experiments discussed in this paper, and James Campbell, Bruno García, and Jonathan Rodean for experimental and research assistance. Part of this work was supported by grant number 0720753 from the National Science Foundation. Any opinions, findings, and conclusions or recommendations expressed in this material are those of the author and do not necessarily reflect the views of the National Science Foundation.

References

Acemoglu, Daron. 2005. "Constitutions, Politics and Economics: A Review Essay on Persson and Tabellini's 'The Economic Effects of Constitutions'." *Journal of Economic Literature*, 43(4): 1025–1048.

Acemoglu, Daron, and James A. Robinson. 2006. "De Facto Political Power and Institutional Persistence." *American Economic Review*, 96(2): 325–330.

Acemoglu, Daron, and James A. Robinson. 2012. *Why Nations Fail: The Origins of Power, Prosperity, and Poverty*. New York: Crown Publishers.

Acemoglu, Daron, Simon Johnson, and James A. Robinson. 2001. "The Colonial Origins of Comparative Development: An Empirical Investigation." *American Economic Review*, 91(5): 1369–1401.

Acemoglu, Daron, Simon Johnson, and James A. Robinson. 2002. "Reversal of Fortune: Geography and Institutions in the Making of the Modern World Income Distribution." *Quarterly Journal of Economics*, 117: 1231–1294.

Acemoglu, Daron, Simon Johnson, and James A. Robinson. 2005a. "Institutions as the Fundamental Cause of Long-Run Growth." In *Handbook of Economic Growth*, ed. Aghion and Durlauf, New York: North Holland.

Acemoglu, Daron, Simon Johnson, and James A. Robinson. 2005b. "The Rise of Europe: Atlantic Trade, Institutional Change, and Economic Growth." *American Economic Review*, 95(3): 546–579.

Acheson, James M., James A. Wilson, and Robert S. Steneck. 1998. "Managing Chaotic Fisheries." In *Linking Social and Ecological Systems: Management Practices and Social Mechanisms for Building Resilience*, ed. Fikret Berkes and Carl Folke, 390–413. New York: Cambridge University Press.

Agrawal, Arun. 1994. "Rules, Rule Making, and Rule Breaking: Examining the Fit between Rule Systems and Resource Use." In *Rules, Games, and Common-Pool Resources*, ed. Elinor Ostrom, Roy Gardner, and James Walker, 267–282. Ann Arbor: University of Michigan Press.

Agrawal, Arun, and Gautam N. Yadama. 1997. "How Do Local Institutions Mediate Market and Population Pressures on Resources? Forest Panchayats in Kumaon, India." *Development and Change*, 28(3): 435–465.

Akerlof, G. A. (1970). "The Market for 'Lemons': Quality Uncertainty and the Market Mechanism." *The Quarterly Journal of Economics*, 84(3): 488–500.

Alberts, Susan, Chris Warshaw, and Barry R. Weingast. 2011. "Democratization and Countermajoritarian Institutions: The Role of Power and Constitutional Design in Self-Enforcing Democracy." Working Paper, Hoover Institution, Stanford University.

Alberts, Susan, Chris Warshaw, and Barry R. Weingast. 2012. "Democratization and Countermajoritarian Institutions: The Role of Power and Constitutional Design In Self-Enforcing Democracy." In Comparative Constitutional Design, ed. Tom Ginsburg, New York: Cambridge University Press.

Alchian, Armen A. 1965. "Some Economics of Property Rights." *Il Politico*, 30(4): 816–819.

Alchian, Armen, and Harold Demsetz. 1973. "The Property Rights Paradigm." *Journal of Economic History*, 33(1): 16–27.

Alesina, Alberto, and George-Marios Angeletos. 2003. "Fairness and Redistribution: US versus Europe." Mimeo, Harvard University.

Alesina, Alberto, and Allan Drazen. 1991. "Why Are Stabilizations Delayed?" *American Economic Review*, 81(5): 1170–1188.

Alexeev, Michael, and William Pyle. 2003. "A Note on Measuring the Unofficial Economy in the Former Soviet Republics." *Economics of Transition*, 11(1): 153–175.

Aligica, Paul Dragos, and Anthony Evans. 2009. *The Neoliberal Revolution in Eastern Europe: Economic Ideas in the Transition from Communism*. London: Edward Elger.

Allen, Douglas. 2012. *The Institutional Revolution*. Chicago: University of Chicago Press.

Allen, Robert C. 2009. *The British Industrial Revolution in Global Perspective*. Cambridge: Cambridge University Press.

Anderson, Clifford B. 1962. "Ministerial Responsibility in the 1620s." *Journal of Modern History*, 34(4): 381–389.

Anderson, Lee G. 1986. *The Economics of Fisheries Management*. Baltimore, MD: Johns Hopkins University Press.

Anderson, Lee G. 1995. "Privatizing Open Access Fisheries: Individual Transferable Quotas." In *The Handbook of Environmental Economics*, ed. Daniel W. Bromley, 453–474. Oxford: Blackwell.

Andreoni, James, and John H. Miller. 1993. "Rational Cooperation in the Finitely Repeated Prisoner's Dilemma: Experimental Evidence." *Economic Journal*, 103(4): 570–585.

Appel, Hilary. 2004. New Capitalist Order: Privatization and Ideology in Russia and Eastern Europe. Pittsburgh, PA: University of Pittsburgh Press.

Arrow, Kenneth J. 1951. *Social Choice and Individual Values*. New York: Wiley.

Arrow, Kenneth. 1971. "Political and Economic Evaluation of Social Effects and Externalities." In *Frontiers of Quantitative Economics*, ed. M. D. Intriligator, 3–23. Amsterdam: North Holland.

Arruñada, Benito. 2003. "Property Enforcement as Organized Consent." *Journal of Law, Economics and Organization*, 19: 401–444.

Arruñada, Benito. 2011a. "Organizational Foundations of the Land Registry." *Registradores de España*, 58(January–February): 84–86.

Arruñada, Benito. 2011b. "Property Titling and Conveyancing." In *Research Handbook on the Economics of Property Law, Research Handbooks in Law and Economics Series*, ed. Kenneth Ayotte and Henry E. Smith, 237–256. (Series editors: Richard Posner and Francesco Parisi.) Cheltenham, UK: Edward Elgar.

Arthur, W. B. 1994. *Increasing Returns and Path Dependence in the Economy*. Ann Arbor: University of Michigan Press.

Ashraf, Nava, Iris Bohnet, and Nikita Piankov, 2006. "Decomposing Trust and Trustworthiness." *Experimental Economics*, 9: 193–208.

Aslund, Anders. 1995. *How Russia Became a Market Economy*. Washington, DC: Brookings Institution.

Aslund, Anders. 2005. "The Economic Policy of Ukraine after the Orange Revolution." *Eurasian Geography and Economics*, 46(5): 327–353.

Bacon, Francis. 1620 [1999]. *Selected Philosophical Works*, ed. Rose-Mary Sargemt. Indianapolis: Hackett Publishing.

Bacon, Francis. 1996 [1623]. *The Advancement of Learning*. Repr. in *Francis Bacon: the Major Works*. Oxford World Classics, Oxford University Press. World Classics: Oxford University Press.

Bandelj, Nina. 2004. "Institutional Foundations of Economic Transformation in Central and Eastern Europe (1990–2000)." Working Paper 04–14, Center for the Study of Democracy, University of California, Irvine.

Banerjee, Abhijit, and Esther Duflo. 2006. "The Economic Lives of the Poor." *Journal of Economic Perspectives*, 21(1): 141–168.

Bardhan, Pranab. 2000. "Irrigation and Cooperation: An Empirical Analysis of 48 Irrigation Communities in South India." *Economic Development and Cultural Change*, 48(4): 847–865.

Barr, Abigail, and Garance Genicot. 2008. "Risk Pooling, Commitment and Information: An Experimental Test." *Journal of the European Economic Association*, 6(6): 1151–1185.

Barr, Abigail, Chris Wallace, Jean Ensminger, Joseph Henrich, Clark Barrett, Alexander Bolyanatz, Juan Camilo Cardenas, Michael Gurven, Edwins Gwako, Carolyn Lesorogol, Frank Marlowe, Richard McElreath, David Tracer, and John Ziker. 2009. "Homo Æqualis: A Cross-Society Experimental Analysis of Three Bargaining Games," University of Oxford Department of Economics, Discussion Paper Series 422.

Barro, Robert J. 1973. "The Control of Politicians: An Economic Model." *Public Choice*, 14(1): 19–42.

Barzel, Yoram. 1989 [1997]. *Economic Analysis of Property Rights: Political Economy of Institutions and Decisions*. Cambridge and New York: Cambridge University Press.

Basu, Kaushik. 2000. *Prelude to Political Economy: A Study of the Social and Political Foundations of Economics*. New York: Oxford University Press.

Bates, Robert H. 1981. *Markets and States in Tropical Africa*. Berkeley and Los Angeles: University of California Press.

Bates, Robert H. 1983. *Essays on the Political Economy of Rural Africa*. Cambridge: Cambridge University Press.

Bates, Robert H. 1989. *Beyond the Miracle of the Market: The Political Economy of Agrarian Development in Kenya*. New York: Cambridge University Press.

Battaglini, Marco, Rebecca Morton, and Thomas Palfrey. 2007. "Efficiency, Equity, and Timing of Voting Mechanisms." *American Political Science Review*, 101(3): 409–424.

Battaglini, Marco, Rebecca Morton, and Thomas Palfrey. 2010. "The Swing Voter's Curse in the Laboratory." *Review of Economic Studies*, 77(1): 61–89.

Battaglini, Marco, Salvatore Nunnari, and Thomas R. Palfrey. 2009. "Political Institutions and the Dynamics of Public Investment." Mimeo, Princeton University.

Beck, Thorsten, George Clarke, Alberto Groffi, Philip Keefer, and Patrick Walsh. 2001. "New Tools in Comparative Political Economy: The Database of Political Institutions." *World Bank Economic Review,* 15(1): 165–176.

Becker, Carl L. 1932. *The Heavenly City of the Eighteenth-Century Philosophers.* New Haven and London: Yale University Press.

Becker, G. S. 1981. *A Treatise on the Family.* Cambridge MA: Harvard University Press.

Becker, Gary, and H. Gregg Lewis. 1973. "On the Interaction between the Quantity and Quality of Children." *Journal of Political Economy,* 81(2): 279–288.

Becker, George. 1984. "Pietism and Science: a Critique of Robert K. Merton's Hypothesis." *American Journal of Sociology,* 89(5): 1065–1090.

Becker, Sascha O., and Ludger Wößmann. 2009. "Was Weber Wrong? A Human Capital Theory of Protestant Economic History." *Quarterly Journal of Economics,* 124(2): 531–596.

Benabou, Roland, and Efe Ok. 2001. "Social Mobility and the Demand for Redistribution: The POUM Hypothesis." *Quarterly Journal of Economics,* 116(2): 447–487.

Benabou, Roland, and Jean Tirole. 2006. "Belief in a Just World and Redistributive Politics." *Quarterly Journal of Economics,* 121(2): 699–746.

Benabou, Roland. 2008. "Ideology (Joseph Schumpeter Lecture)." *Journal of the European Economic Association,* 6(2–3): 321–352.

Benjamin, Paul, Wai Fung Lam, Elinor Ostrom, and Ganesh Shivakoti. 1994. *Institutions, Incentives, and Irrigation in Nepal. Decentralization: Finance & Management Project Report.* Burlington, VT: Associates in Rural Development.

Benoit, Kenneth, and Jacqueline Hayden. 2004. "Institutional Change and Persistence: The Evolution of Poland's Electoral Systems, 1989–2001." *Journal of Politics,* 66(2): 396–427.

Benoit, Kenneth. 2007. "Electoral Rules as Political Consequences: Explaining the Origins and Change of Electoral Institutions." *Annual Review of Political Science,* 10: 363–390.

Benson, Bruce. 1989. "The Spontaneous Evolution of Commercial Law." *Southern Economic Journal,* 55(3): 644–661.

Berg, Joyce E., John Dickhaut, and Kevin McCabe. 1995. "Trust, Reciprocity, and Social History." *Games and Economic Behavior,* 10(1) 122–142.

Berliner, Joseph. 1952. "The Informal Organization of the Soviet Firm." *Quarterly Journal of Economics,* 66: 342–365.

Berman, Harold. 1983. *Law and Revolution: The Formation of Western Legal Tradition.* Cambridge MA: Harvard University Press.

Besley, Timothy, and Maitreesh Ghatak. 2010. "Property Rights and Economic Development." In *Handbook of Development Economics,* vol. IV, ed. M. Rosenzweig and D. Rodrik, New York: North Holland.

Besley, Timothy. 1995. "Property Rights and Investments Incentives: Theory and Evidence from Ghana." *Journal of Political Economy,* 103(5): 903–922.

Binmore, Kenneth. G. 1994. *Game Theory and the Social Contract: Playing Fair.* Cambridge, MA: MIT Press.

Binmore, Kenneth G. 1998. *Game Theory and the Social Contract: Just Playing.* Cambridge, MA: MIT Press.

Binswanger, Hans, and Mark Rosenzweig. 1986. "Behavioural and Material Determinants of Production Relations in Agriculture." *Journal of Development Studies,* 22(3): 503–539.

Bischoff, Ivo. 2007. "Institutional Choice versus Communication in Social Dilemmas – An Experimental Approach." *Journal of Economic Behavior & Organization*, 62: 20–36.

Bisin, Alberto and Thierry Verdier. 1998. "On the Cultural Transmission of Preferences for Social Status." *Journal of Public Economics*, 70: 75–97.

Bisin, Alberto and Thierry Verdier. 2001. "The Economics of Cultural Transmission and the Dynamics of Preferences." *Journal of Economic Theory*, 97: 298–319.

Black, Sandra E., and Lisa M. Lynch. 2001. "How to Compete: the Impact of Workplace Practices and Information Technology on Productivity." *Review of Economic and Statistics*, 83(3): 434–445.

Blomquist, William. 1992. *Dividing the Waters: Governing Groundwater in Southern California*. San Francisco: ICS Press.

Bogart, Dan. 2013. "Did the Glorious Revolution Contribute to the Transport Revolution? Evidence from Investment in Roads and Rivers." *Economic History Review*, forthcoming.

Bogart Dan, and Gary Richardson. 2013. "Property Rights and Parliament in Industrializing Britain." *Journal of Law & Economics*, forthcoming.

Bohnet, Iris and Dorothea Kübler. 2005. "Compensating the Cooperators: Is Sorting in the Prisoner's Dilemma Possible?" *Journal of Economic Behavior and Organization*, 56: 61–76.

Bonin, John P., Derek C. Jones, and Louis Putterman. 1993. "Theoretical and Empirical Research on Producers' Cooperatives: Will Ever the Twain Meet?" *Journal of Economic Literature*, 31(3): 1290–1320.

Bosch-Domènech, Antoni, José G. Montalvo, Rosemarie Nagel and Albert Satorra. 2002. "One, Two, (Three), Infinity, . . . : Newspaper and Lab Beauty-Contest Experiments." *American Economic Review*, 92(5): 1687–1701.

Botticini, Maristella, and Zvi Eckstein. 2012. *The Chosen Few: How Education Shaped Jewish History*. Princeton: Princeton University Press.

Bowles, Samuel. 2004. *Microeconomics: Behavior, Institutions, and Evolution*. Princeton: Princeton University Press.

Bowles, Samuel, and Herbert Gintis. 2009. "Beyond Enlightened Self-Interest: Social Norms, Other-Regarding Preferences, and Cooperative Behavior." In *Games, Groups, and the Global Good*, ed. Simon Levin and Dorrecht Heidelberg. London, New York: Springers.

Boycko, Maxim, Andrei Shleifer, and Robert W. Vishny. 1995. *Privatizing Russia*. Cambridge, MA: MIT Press.

Boyd, Robert., Herbert Gintis, and Samuel Bowles. 2010. "Coordinated Punishment of Defectors Sustains Cooperation and Can Proliferate When Rare." *Science* 328: 617–620.

Boyd, Robert, and Peter J. Richerson. 1985. *Culture and the Evolutionary Process*. Chicago: University of Chicago Press.

Boyd, Robert and Peter J. Richerson. 2005. *The Origins and Evolution of Cultures*. Oxford and New York: Oxford University Press.

Boyd, Robert, Samuel Bowles, Colin Camerer, Ernst Fehr, Herbert Gintis, and Richard McElreath. 2004. "Overview and Synthesis." In *Foundations of Human Sociality: Economic Experiments and Ethnographic Evidence from Fifteen Small-Scale Societies*, ed. Joseph Henrich, Robert Boyd, Samuel Bowles, Colin Camerer, Ernst Fehr, and Herbert Gintis, 8–54. Oxford: Oxford University Press.

Boyd, Robert, Samuel Bowles, Colin Camerer, Ernst Fehr, Herbert Gintis, and Richard McElreath, Steven Heine, and Ara Norenzayan. 2010. "The Weirdest People in the World?" *Behavioral and Brain Sciences*, 33(2/3): 1–75.

Braudel, Fernand. 1967. *Capitalism and Material Life*. New York: Harper.

Braudel, Fernand. 1973. *The Mediterranean and the Mediterranean World in the Age of Philip II*. 2nd ed. New York: Harper Collins.

Braudel, F. 1992. *The Structures of Everyday Life*. Berkeley: University of California Press.

Brewer, John. 1990. *Sinews of Power: War, Money and the English State, 1688–1783*, Cambridge, MA: Harvard University Press.

Brock, William H. 1992. *The Norton History of Chemistry*. New York: W. W. Norton.

Brousseau, Eric and Jean-Michel Glachant (eds.). 2008. *New Institutional Economics: A Guidebook*. Cambridge: Cambridge University Press.

Brown, J. David, John S. Earle, and Almos Telegdy. 2006. "The Productivity Effects of Privatization: Longitudinal Estimates from Hungary, Romania, Russia, and Ukraine." *Journal of Political Economy*, 114(1): 61–99.

Brown, J. David, John S. Earle, and Almos Telegdy. 2010. "Employment and Wage Effects of Privatisation: Evidence from Hungary, Romania, Russia, and Ukraine." *Economic Journal*, 120(545): 683–708.

Brown, J. David, John S. Earle, and Scott Gehlbach. 2009. "Helping Hand or Grabbing Hand? State Bureaucracy and Privatization Effectiveness." *American Political Science Review*, 103(2): 264–283.

Bruhl, Aaron-Andrew P. 2010. "Burying the 'Continuing Body' Theory of the Senate." *Iowa Law Review*, 1410.

Bruno, Randolph Luca, Matria Bytchkova, and Saul Estrin. 2008. "Institutional Determinants of New Firm Entry in Russia: A Cross Regional Analysis." IZA Discussion Paper 3724.

Bryce, James. 1901. *Studies in History and Jurisprudence*. New York: Oxford University Press.

Brym, Robert J., and Vladimir Gimpelson. 2004. "The Size, Composition, and Dynamics of the Russian State Bureaucracy in the 1990s." *Slavic Review*, 63(1): 90–112.

Buchanan, James. 1975. "A Contractarian Paradigm for Applying Economic Theory." *American Economic Review*, 65(5): 225–230.

Buchanan, James, and Gordon Tullock. 1962. *The Calculus of Consent: Logical Foundations of Constitutional Democracy*. Ann Arbor: Michigan University Press.

Bunce, Valerie. 1995. "Should Transitologists Be Grounded?" *Slavic Review*, 54(1): 111–127.

Burnet, Gilbert. 1753. *History of His Own Time*. Vol. IV. Edinburgh: Hamilton, Balfour and Neild.

Bury, J. B. [1932] 1955. *The Idea of Progress: an Inquiry into its Growth and Origin*. New York: Dover Publications.

Calvert, Randall. 1995. "Rational Actors, Equilibrium, and Social Institutions." In *Explaining Social Institutions*, ed. Knight, Jack and Itai Sened, 57–95. Ann Arbor: University of Michigan Press.

Camerer, Colin. 2003. *Behavioral Game Theory*. Princeton, NJ: Princeton University Press.

Campbell, Donald T. 1969. "Reforms as Experiments." *American Psychologist*, 24(4): 409–429.

Campbell, Donald T. 1975a. "'Degrees of Freedom' and the Case Study." *Comparative Political Studies*, 8(2): 178–193.

Campbell, Donald T. 1975b. "On the Conflicts between Biological and Social Evolution and between Psychology and Moral Tradition." *American Psychologist*, 30(11): 1103–1126.

Cappelen, Alexander W., Astri Drange Hole, Erik O. Sorensen, and Bertil Tungodden. 2007. "The Pluralism of Fairness Ideals: An Experimental Approach." *American Economic Review*, 97(3), 818–827.

Cardwell, Donald S. L. 1972. *Turning Points in Western Technology*. New York: Neale Watson, Science History Publications.

Carey, John, and Simon Hix. 2009. "The Electoral Sweet Spot: Low-Magnitude Proportional Electoral Systems." Presented at the Annual Meeting of the American Political Science Association.

Carpenter, Jeffrey P. 2000. "Negotiation in the Commons: Incorporating Field and Experimental Evidence into a Theory of Local Collective Action." *Journal of Institutional and Theoretical Economics*, 156: 661–683.

Carter, Jennifer. 1969. "The Revolution and the Constitution." In *Britain After the Glorious Revolution*, ed. Geoffrey Holmes. London: St. Martin's Press.

Casella, Alessandra. 2011. "Agenda Control as a Cheap Talk Game: Theory and Experiments with Storable Votes." *Games and Economic Behavior*, 72(1): 46–76.

Casella, Alessandra, Andrew Gelman, and Thomas R. Palfrey. 2006. "An Experimental Study of Storable Votes." *Games and Economics Behavior*, 57(1): 123–154.

Casella, Alessandra, Thomas R. Palfrey, and Raymon Riezman. 2008. "Minorities and Storable Votes." *Quarterly Journal of Political Science*, 3(2): 165–200.

Cavalli-Sforza, Luigi L., and Feldman, M. W. 1981. *Cultural Transmission and Evolution: A Quantitative Approach*. Princeton: Princeton University Press.

Charness, Gary, Guillaume R. Fréchette, and Cheng-Zhong Qin. 2007. "Endogenous Transfers in the Prisoner's Dilemma Game: An Experimental Test of Cooperation and Coordination." *Games and Economic Behavior*, 60(2): 287–306.

Checkel, Jeffrey T. 1993. "Ideas, Institutions, and the Gorbachev Foreign Policy Revolution." *World Politics*, 45(2): 271–300.

Cherry, Todd L., Peter Frykblom, and Jason F. Shogren. 2002. "Hardnose the Dictator." *American Economic Review*, 92(4): 1218–1221.

Cheung, Steven N. S. 1969. "Transaction Costs, Risk Aversion, and the Choice of Contractual Arrangements." *Journal of Law and Economics*, 13(1): 23–42.

Cheung, Steven N. S. 1973. "The Fable of the Bees: An Economic Investigation." *Journal of Law and Economics*, 16(1): 11–33.

Cheung, Steven N. S. 1983. "The Contractual Nature of the Firm." *Journal of Law and Economics*, 26(1): 1–21.

Chris Wallace, Jean Ensminger, Joseph Henrich, Clark Barrett, Alexander Bolyanatz, Juan Camilo Cardenas, Michael Gurven, Edwins Gwako, Carolyn Lesorogol, Frank Marlowe, Richard McElreath, David Tracer, and John Ziker. 2009. "Homo Aequalis: A Cross-Society Experimental Analysis of Three Bargaining Games," University of Oxford Department of Economics Discussion Paper Series 422 2009.

Cibber, Colley. 1756. *An Apology for the Life of Colley Cibber*. 4th ed. Vol. I. London: R. and J. Dodsley.

Clark, Andy. 1997. Being There: Putting Brain, Body, and World Together Again. Cambridge, MA: MIT Press.

Clark, Gregory. 1996. "Political Foundations of Modern Economic Growth: England, 1540–1800." *Journal of Interdisciplinary History*, 26(4): 563–588.

Clark, Gregory. 2007. *A Farewell to Alms*. Princeton: Princeton University Press.

Coase, Ronald H. 1959. "The Federal Communications Commission." *The Journal of Law and Economics*, 2: 1–40.

Coase, Ronald H. 1960. "The Problem of Social Cost." *The Journal of Law and Economics* 3: 1–44.

Coase, Ronald H.1988a. *The Firm, the Market and the Law*. Chicago: The University of Chicago Press.

Coase, Ronald H. 1988b. "The Nature of the Firm", Originally Published in *Economia*, 4 (16) November 1937, In *The Foundations of the New Institutional Economics*, ed. Claude Ménard. Cheltenham, UK and Brookfield, VT: Edward Elgar: 51–70.

Coase, Ronald H. 1992. "The Institutional Structure of Production." *The American Economic Review*, 82(4): 713–719.

Cohen, Bernard I. 1990. "Introduction: the Impact of the Merton Thesis." In *Puritanism and the Rise of Modern Science*, ed. Bernard I. Cohen. New Brunswick: Rutgers University Press: 1–111.

Coleman, James. 1990. *Foundations of Social Theory*. Cambridge: Harvard University Press.

Commons, John R. 1932. "The Problem of Coordinating Law, Economics, and Ethics." *Wisconsin Law Review*, 8: 3–26.

Comte, Auguste. 1856. *Social Physics from the Positive Philosophy*. New York: Calvin Blanchard.

Cooter, R. 1998. "Expressive Law and Economics." The Journal of Legal Studies 27, 585–608.

Copes, Parzival. 1986. "A Critical Review of the Individual Quota as a Device in Fisheries Management." *Land Economics*, 62(3): 278–291.

Cox, James C. 2004. "How to Identify Trust and Reciprocity." *Games and Economic Behavior*, 46: 260–281.

Cox, Gary W., Douglass C. North, and Barry R. Weingast. 2013. "The Violence Trap: A Political-Economic Approach to the Problems of Development." Working Paper, Hoover Institution, Stanford University, August 2013.

Crawford, Sue E., and Elinor Ostrom. 1995. "A Grammar of Institutions." *American Political Science Review*, 89: 582–600.

Crawford, Sue E., and Elinor Ostrom. 2005. "A Grammar of Institutions." In *Understanding Institutional Diversity*, ed. Elinor Ostrom, 137–174. Princeton: Princeton University Press.

Crawford, Vincent P., and H. Haller. 1990. Learning How to Cooperate: Optimal Play in Repeated Coordination Games. *Econometrica*, 58: 571–595.

Crawford, Vincent P., and Bruno Broseta. 1998. "What Price Competition? The Efficiency-Enhancing Effect of Auctioning the Right to Play." *American Economic Review*, 88(1): 198–225.

Croson, Rachel, and Nancy Buchan. 1999. "Gender and Culture: International Experimental Evidence from Trust Games." *American Economic Review*, 89(2): 386–391.

Crouzet, Francois. 2001. *A History of the European Economy*. Charlottesville: University Press of Virginia.

Dal Bó, Pedro. 2005. "Cooperation Under the Shadow of the Future: Experimental Evidence from Infinitely Repeated Games." *American Economic Review*, 95(5): 1591–1604.

Dal Bó, Pedro, Andrew Foster, and Louis Putterman. 2010. "Institutions and Behavior: Experimental Evidence on the Effects of Democracy." *American Economic Review*, 100(5): 2205–2220.

D'Alembert, Jean Le Ronde. [1751] 1995. *Preliminary Discourse to the Encyclopedia*, ed. Richard N. Schwab. Chicago: University of Chicago Press.

Darden, Keith. 2009. *Economic Liberalism and Its Rivals: The Formation of International Institutions Among the Post-Soviet States*. New York: Cambridge University Press.

Darden, Keith, and Anna Grzymala-Busse. 2006. "The Great Divide: Literacy, Nationalism, and the Communist Collapse." *World Politics*, 59(1): 83–115.

Darwin, Charles. 1859/1871. *The Origin of Species and Descent of Man and Selection in Relation to Sex*. New York: Modern Library.

Davidson, Lee, Tim Hitchcock, Tim Keirn, and Robert B. Shoemaker. 1992. "Introduction: The Reactive State: English Governance and Society, 1689–1750." In *Stilling the Grumbling Hive*, ed. Lee Davidson et al. New York: Palgrave Macmillan.

Davis, Lance E., and Douglass C. North. 1971. *Institutional Change and American Economic Growth*. Cambridge, UK: Cambridge University Press.

De Roover, Raymond. 1963. "The Organization of Trade." In *Cambridge Economic History of Europe*. Vol. III, ed. E. E. Rich, Edward Miller, and M. M. Postan. Cambridge: Cambridge University Press.

De Soto, Hernando. 2000. *The Mystery of Capital: Why Capitalism Triumphs in the West and Fails Everywhere Else*. New York: Basic Books.

De Vries, Jan. 1976. *The Economy of Europe in an Age of Crisis*. Cambridge: Cambridge University Press.

Dear, Peter. 2006. *The Intelligibility of Nature: How Science makes Sense of the World*. Chicago: University of Chicago Press.

Deininger, Klaus. 2003. *Land Policies for Growth and Poverty Reduction*. Washington D.C.: World Bank and Oxford University Press.

Deininger, Klaus, and Gershon Feder. 2009. "Land Registration, Governance, and Development: Evidence and Implications for Policy." *The World Bank Research Observer*, 24(2): 233–266.

Dell, Melissa. 2010. "The Persistent Effects of Peru's Mining Mita." *Econometrica*, 78(6): 1863–1903.

Demsetz, Harold. 1967. "Toward a Theory of Property Rights." *American Economic Review*, 57: 347–359.

Demsetz, Harold. 1982. *Economic, Legal, and Political Dimensions of Competition*. Amsterdam: North Holland.

Denisova, Irina, Markus Eller, Timothy Frye, and Ekaterina V. Zhuravskaya. 2009. "Who Wants to Revise Privatization? The Complementarity of Market Skills and Institutions." *American Political Science Review*, 103(2): 284–304.

Denisova, Irina, Markus Eller, Timothy Frye, and Ekaterina V. Zhuravskaya. 2010. "Everyone Hates Privatization, But Why? Survey Evidence from 28 Post-Communist Countries." Mimeo.

Denzau, Arthur, and Douglass North. 1994. "Shared Mental Models: Ideologies and Institutions." *Kyklos*, 47(1): 3–31.

Descartes, René. [1637] 1965. *Discourse on Method, Optics, Geometry, and Meteorology.* Translated by Paul J. Olscamp. Indianapolis: Hackett Publishing.

Deschler, Lewis. 1975. *Deschler's Procedure inn the U.S. House of Representatives*, Washington, D.C.: U.S. Government Printing Office.

Devlin, Keith. 2000. *The Language of Mathematics: Making the Invisible Visible.* New York: Henry Holt.

Dewatripont, Mathias, and Eric Maskin. 1995. "Credit and Efficiency in Centralized and Decentralized Economies." *Review of Economic Studies*, 62: 541–556.

Dewatripont, Mathias, and Gérard Roland. 1992. "Economic Reform and Dynamic Political Constraints." *Review of Economic Studies*, 59(4):703–730.

Dewatripont, Mathias, and Gérard Roland. 1995. "The Design of Reform Packages Under Uncertainty." *American Economic Review*, 85(5): 1207–1223.

Dewatripont, Mathias, and Gérard Roland. 1996. "Transition as a Process of Large-Scale Institutional Change." *Economics of Transition*, 4(1): 1–30.

Di Tella, Rafael, Sebastián Galiani, and Ernesto Schargrodsky. 2007. "The Formation of Beliefs: Evidence from the Allocation of Land Titles to Squatters." *Quarterly Journal of Economics* 122: 209–241.

Dickinson, Harry T. 1970. *Bolingbroke.* London: Constable.

Dickinson, Harry T. 1976. "The Eighteenth Century Debate on the 'Glorious Revolution.'" *History*, 61: 29.

Diermeier, D., Ericson, J., Frye, T., and Lewis, S. 1997. Credibility and Commitment: The Case of Property Rights. In *The Political Economy of Property Rights*, ed. D. Weimer, 20–42. Cambridge: Cambridge University Press.

Dixit, A. K. 2004. Lawlessness and Economics: Alternative Modes of Governance. New York: Oxford University Press.

Djankov, Simeon, and Peter Murrell. 2002. "Enterprise Restructuring in Transition: A Quantitative Survey." *Journal of Economic Literature*, 40(3): 739–792.

Do, Quy-Toan, and Lakshmi Iyer. 2008. "Land Titling and Rural Transition in Vietnam." *Economic Development and Cultural Change*, 56: 531–579.

Dobbs, Betty Jo Teeter, and Jacob, Margaret C. 1995. *Newton and the Culture of Newtonianism.* New York: Humanity Books.

Doepke, Matthias, and Zilibotti, Fabrizio. 2008. "Occupational Choice and the Spirit of Capitalism." *Quarterly Journal of Economics*, 123(2): 747–793.

Dollinger, Philippe. 1970. *The German Hansa.* Stanford: Stanford University Press.

Doran, Michael. 2010. "The Closed Rule." Georgetown University Law Center.

Downie, J. A. 1976. "The Commission of Public Accounts and the Formation of the Country Party." *English Historical Review*, XCI(358): 33–51.

Dunning, Thad. 2005. "Improving Causal Inference: Strengths and Limitations of Natural Experiments." *Political Research Quarterly*, 61(2): 282–293.

Durlauf, Steven. 2002: "On the Empirics of Social Capital." *The Economic Journal*, 112(483): 459–479.

Dworkin, Ronald. 1986. *Law's Empire.* Cambridge, MA: Harvard University Press.

Earle, John S., and Scott Gehlbach. 2003. "A Spoonful of Sugar: Privatization and Popular Support for Reform in the Czech Republic." *Economics and Politics*, 15(1): 1–32.

Earle, John S., and Scott Gehlbach. 2012. "The Productivity Consequences of Political Turnover: Firm-Level Evidence from Ukraine." Mimeo.

Earle, John S., Roman Frydman, and Andrzej Rapaczynski, eds. 1993. *Privatization in the Transition to a Market Economy: Studies of Preconditions and Policies in Eastern Europe.* New York: St. Martin's Press.

Earle, John S., Roman Frydman, Andrzej Rapaczynski, and Joel Turkewitz. 1994. *Small Privatization: The Transformation of Retail Trade and Consumer Services in the Czech Republic, Hungary, and Poland.* Budapest: CEU Press.

Easterly, William. 2002. *The Elusive Quest for Growth. Economists' Adventures and Misadventures in the Tropics.* Cambridge, MA: MIT Press.

Easterly, William, and Ross Levine. 2003. "Tropics, Germs, and Crops: How Endowments Influence Economics Development." *Journal of Monetary Economics,* 50(1): 3–39.

Eggertsson, Thrainn. 1990. *Economic Behavior and Institutions.* Cambridge: Cambridge University Press.

Eicher, Theo, and Till Schrieber. 2010. "Structural Policies and Growth: Time Series Evidence from a Natural Experiment." *Journal of Development Economics,* 91: 169–179.

Elkins, Zachary, Tom Ginsburg, and James Melton. 2008. *The Endurance of National Constitutions.* Cambridge: Cambridge University Press.

Ellickson, Robert. 1991. *Order Without Law: How Neighbors Settle Disputes.* Cambridge: Harvard University Press.

Elster, Jon. 1979. *Ulysses and the Sirens.* New York, Cambridge University Press.

Elster, Jon. 1991. "Constitutionalism in Eastern Europe: An Introduction." *University of Chicago Law Review,* 58(2): 447–482.

Elster, Jon. 1992. "Making Sense of Constitution-Making." *East European Constitutional Review,* 1: 15.

Elster, Jon. 1993. "Bargaining Over the Presidency." *East European Constitutional Review,* 2(4): 95–98.

Elster, Jon. 1997. "Afterward: The Making of Postcommunist Presidencies." In *Postcommunist Presidencies,* ed. Raymond Taras. New York: Cambridge University Press.

Elster, Jon. 2000. *Ulysses Unbound.* New York: Cambridge University Press.

Elster, Jon, Claus Offe, and Ulrich K. Preuss. 2000. *Institutional Design in Post-Communist Societies: Rebuilding the Ship at Sea.* New York: Cambridge University Press.

Engel, Christoph. 2011. "Dictator Games: A Meta Study." *Experimental Economics,* 14: 583–610.

Engerman, Stanley L., and Kenneth L. Sokoloff. 2002. Factor Endowments, Inequality, and Paths of Development Among New World Economies, *Economia,* 3: 41–109.

Engerman, Stanley L., and Kenneth L. Sokoloff. 2005a. The Evolution of Suffrage Institutions in the New World. *Journal of Economic History,* 65: 891–921.

Engerman, Stanley L., and Kenneth L. Sokoloff. 2005b. Institutional and Non-Institutional Explanations of Economic Differences. In *Handbook of New Institutional Economics,* ed. Ménard and Shirley. Dordrecht, Netherlands: Springers.

Engerman, Stanley L., and Kenneth L. Sokoloff. 2008. Institutions in Political and Economic Development: Theory, History, and Findings. *Annual Review of Political Science,* 11: 119–135.

Epstein, Lee, and Jack Knight. 1998. *The Choices Justices Make.* Washington, DC: CQ Press.

Epstein, Richard A. 1985. *Takings: Private Property and the Power of Eminent Domain.* Cambridge: Harvard University Press.

Ericson, Joel M. 1997. "Private Firms, City Government, and Arbitration: Enforcing Economic Legality in St. Petersburg." In *The Political Economy of Property Rights: Institutional Change and Credibility in the Reform of Centrally Planned Economies*, ed. David L Weimer, 150–178. New York: Cambridge University Press.

Ertan, Arhan S., Talbot Page, and Louis Putterman. 2009. "Who to Punish? Individual Decisions and Majority Rule in Mitigating the Free-Rider Problem?" *European Economic Review*, 53(5): 495–511.

Eskridge, William N. Jr. 1991. "Overriding Supreme Court Statutory Interpretation Decisions." *Yale Law Journal*, 101: 331–455.

Eskridge, William N. Jr., and John Ferejohn. 1992. "The Article I, Section 7 Game," *Geo. Law J.* (February) 80: 523–564.

Esponda, Ignacio, and Emanuel I. Vespa. 2010. "Pivotal Voting in the Laboratory." Mimeo, New York University.

Estrin, Saul, Jan Hanousek, Evžen Kočenda, and Jan Svejnar. 2009. "The Effects of Privatization and Ownership in Transition Economies." *Journal of Economic Literature*, 47(3): 699–728.

European Bank for Reconstruction and Development. 1999. *Transition Report 1999: Ten Years of Transition*. London: EBRD.

Fafchamps, Marcel. 1992. "Cash Crop Production, Food Price Volatility, and Rural Market Integration in the Third World." *American Journal of Agricultural Economics*, 74(1): 90–99.

Fahr, René, and Bernd Irlenbusch. 2000. "Fairness as a Constraint on Trust in Reciprocity: Earned Property Rights in a Reciprocal Exchange Experiment." *Economics Letters*, 66(3), 275–282.

Faragher, John Mack. 1993. *Daniel Boone: Life and Legend of an American Pioneer*. New York: Henry Holt and Company.

Farrell, Joseph, and Matthew Rabin. 1996. "Cheap Talk." *Journal of Economic Perspectives* 10, 103–118.

Farrington, Benjamin. 1979. *Francis Bacon: Philosopher of Industrial Science*. New York: Farrar, Straus and Giroux.

Fearon, James D. 2006. "Why Use Elections to Allocate Power?" Paper presented at the annual meetings of the American Political Science Association.

Feder, Gerschon, Tongroj Onchan, Yongyuth Chalamwong, and Chira Hongladarom. 1988. *Land Policies and Farm Productivity in Thailand*. Baltimore: Johns Hopkins University Press.

Fehr, Ernst, and Simon Gächter. 2002. "Altruistic Punishment in Humans." *Nature*, 415: 137–140.

Fehr, Ernst, Simon Gächter, and Urs Fischbacher. 2004. "Third-Party Punishment and Social Norms." *Evolution and Human Behavior*, 25: 63–87.

Feifer, George. 1964. *Justice in Moscow*. New York: Simon and Schuster.

Feingold, Mordechai. 2004. *The Newtonian Moment: Isaac Newton and the Making of Modern Culture*. New York: Oxford University Press.

Feller, Daniel. 1984. *The Public Lands and Jacksonian Politics*. Madison: University of Wisconsin Press.

Ferejohn, John. 1986. "Incumbent Performance and Electoral Control." *Public Choice*, 50(1–3): 5–25.

Fernandez, Raquel, and Dani Rodrik. 1991. "Resistance to Reform: Status Quo Bias in the Presence of Individual-Specific Uncertainty." *American Economic Review* 81: 1146–1155.

Fernández-González, Álvaro, and Bruce Aylward. 1999. "Participation, Pluralism and Polycentrism: Reflections on Watershed Management in Costa Rica." *Unasylva* 50(199): 52–59.

Fidrmuc, Jan. 2001. "Democracy in Transition Economies: Grease or Sand in the Wheels of Growth?" *EIB Papers*, 6(20): 24–40.

Field, Erica. 2003. "Fertility Responses to Land Titling: The Roles of Ownership Security and the Distribution of Household Assets." Unpublished mimeo, Harvard University.

Field, Erica. 2005. "Property Rights and Investment in Urban Slums," *Journal of the European Economic Association*, 3(2–3): 279–290.

Field, Erica. 2007: "Entitled to Work: Urban Property Rights and Labor Supply in Peru." *Quarterly Journal of Economics*, 122(4): 1561–1602.

Field, Erica, and Maximo Torero. 2003. "Do Property Titles Increase Credit Access among the Urban Poor? Evidence from a Nationwide Titling Program in Peru." Unpublished mimeo, Princeton University.

Filmer, Sir Robert. 1680 [1991]. *Patriarcha*. In *Patriarcha and other Writings*, ed. Johann P. Sommerville, Cambridge: Cambridge University Press.

Finkel, Steven E. 1985. "Reciprocal Effects of Participation and Political Efficacy: A Panel Analysis." *American Journal of Political Science*, 29(4): 891–913.

Finnis, J. 2009. "Natural Law Theories." *Stanford Encyclopedia of Philosophy*. Stanford: Stanford University Press.

Fischer, Stanley, and Alan Gelb. 1991. "The Process of Socialist Economic Transformation." *Journal of Economic Perspectives*, 5(4): 91–105.

Fish, M. Steven. 1998. "The Determinants of Economic Reform in the Post-Communist World." *East European Politics and Societies*, 12(1): 31–78.

Fisman, Raymond, Shachar Kariv, and Daniel Markovits. 2007. "Individual Preferences for Giving." *American Economic Review*, 97(5): 1858–1876.

Folger, Robert. 1977. "Distributive and Procedural Justice: Combined Impact of 'Voice' and Improvement on Experienced Inequity." *Journal of Personality and Social Psychology*, 35(2): 108–119.

Follett, Mary Parker. 1902. *The Speaker of the House of Representatives*. New York: Longmans, Green. Reprinted by Burt Franklin Reprints, 1974.

Forsythe, Robert, Joel Horowitz, N. S. Savin, and Martin Sefton. 1994. "Fairness in Simple Bargaining Games." *Games and Economic Behavior*, 6(3): 347–369.

Fortmann, Louise, and John W. Bruce, eds. 1988. *Whose Trees? Proprietary Dimensions of Forestry*. Boulder, CO: Westview Press.

Freixas, Xavier, Roger Guesnerie, and Jean Tirole. 1985. "Planning under Incomplete Information and the Ratchet Effect." *Review of Economic Studies*, 52(2): 179–191.

French, R. R. 2002. *The Golden Yoke: The Legal Cosmology of Buddhist Tibet*. Ithaca: Snow Lion Publications.

Frey, Bruno S. 1998. "Institutions and Morale: the Crowding-out Effect." In *Economics, Values, and Organization*, ed. Avner Ben-Ner and Louis Putterman. Cambridge: Cambridge University Press.

Frey, Bruno S., Matthias Benz, and Alois Stutzer. 2004. "Introducing Procedural Utility: Not Only What, but Also How Matters." *Journal of Institutional and Theoretical Economics*, 160(3): 377–401.

Friedman, Barry. 2001. "Modeling Judicial Review." Mimeo, NYU School of Law.

Friedman, David. 1979. "Private Creation and Enforcement of Law: A Historical Case." *Journal of Legal Studies*, 8: 399–415.

Frydman, Roman, and Andzrej Rapaczynski. 1994. *Privatization in Eastern Europe: Is the State Withering Away?* Budapest: CEU Press.

Frydman, Roman, Andrzej Rapaczynski, and John S. Earle. 1993a. *The Privatization Process in Central Europe*. London: CEU Press.

Frydman, Roman, Andrzej Rapaczynski, and John S. Earle. 1993b. *The Privatization Process in Russia, Ukraine, and the Baltic States*. London: CEU Press.

Frye, Timothy. 1997. "Russian Privatization and the Limits of Credible Commitment." In *The Political Economy of Property Rights: Institutional Change and Credibility in the Reform of Centrally Planned Economies*, ed. David L Weimer. New York: Cambridge University Press.

Frye, Timothy M. 2000. *Brokers and Bureaucrats: Building Market Institutions in Russia*. Ann Arbor: University of Michigan Press.

Frye, Timothy M. 2010. *Building States and Markets After Communism: The Perils of Polarized Democracy*. New York: Cambridge University Press.

Frye, Timothy M, and Andrei Shleifer. 1997. "The Invisible Hand and the Grabbing Hand." *American Economic Review*, 87(2): 354–358.

Frye, Timothy M, and Edward D. Mansfield. 2003. "Fragmenting Protection: The Political Economy of Trade Policy in the Post-Communist World." *British Journal of Political Science*, 33: 635–657.

Fukuyama, Francis. 1996. *Trust: The Social Virtues and The Creation of Prosperity*. New York: Penguin Books.

Fuller, L. 1964. *The Morality of Law*. New Haven: Yale University Press.

Furubotn, Eirik G., and Rudolf Richter. 1991. *The New Institutional Economics*. College Station: Texas A&M University Press.

Furubotn, Eirik G., and Rudolf Richter.1997. *Institutions and Economic Theory: The Contribution of the New Institutional Economics*. Ann Arbor: The University of Michigan Press.

Gadgil, Madhav, Fikret Berkes, and Carl Folke. 1993. "Indigenous Knowledge for Biodiversity Conservation." *Ambio*, 22: 151–156.

Galiani, Sebastian, and Ernesto Schargrodsky. 2004. "Effects of Land Titling on Child Health." *Economics and Human Biology*, 2(3): 353–372.

Galiani, Sebastian, and Ernesto Schargrodsky. 2010. "Property Rights for the Poor: Effects of Land Titling." *Journal of Public Economics*, 94: 700–729.

Galiani, Sebastian and Ernesto Schargrodsky. 2012. "Land Property Rights and Resource Allocation." *Journal of Law and Economics*, 54: 329–345.

Galor, Oded, and Moav, Omer. 2002. "Natural Selection and the Origins of Economic Growth." *Quarterly Journal of Economics*, 117(4): 1133–1191.

Gates, Paul Wallace. 1968. *History of Public Land Law Development*. Washington, D.C.: GPO.

Gay, Peter.1969. *The Enlightenment. Vol. 2: The Science of Freedom*. New York: Norton.

Geddes, Barbara. 1995. "A Comparative Perspective on the Leninist Legacy in Eastern Europe." *Comparative Political Studies*, 28: 239–274.

Gehlbach, Scott. 2008. *Representation through Taxation: Revenue, Politics, and Development in Postcommunist States.* New York: Cambridge University Press.

Gehlbach, Scott, and Edmund J. Malesky. 2010. "The Contribution of Veto Players to Economic Reform." *Journal of Politics*, 72(4): 957–975.

Gely, Rafael, and Pablo T. Spiller. 1992. "The Political Economy of Supreme Court Constitutional Decisions: The Case of Roosevelt's Court Packing Plan." *International Review of Law and Economics*, 12: 45–67.

Gerber, Alan, Donald P. Green, and Christopher W. Larimer. 2008. "Social Pressure and Voter Turnout: Evidence from a Large-Scale Field Experiment." *American Political Science Review*, 102(1): 33–48.

Gilligan, T., and K. Krehbiel. 1987. "Collective Decision-Making and Standing Committees: An Informational Rationale for Restrictive Amendment Procedures." *Journal of Law, Economics, & Organization*, 3(2): 287–337.

Glaeser, E. L., and Andrei, Shleifer. 2002. "Legal Origins." *Quarterly Journal of Economics*, 117: 393–406.

Glaeser, E. L., David Laibson, and Bruce Sacerdote. 2002. "An Economic Approach to Social Capital." *Economic Journal*, 112(483): 437–458.

Glanvill, Joseph. 1668. *Plus Ultra, or, The Progress and Advancement of Knowledge Since the Days of Aristotle.* London: James Collins.

Goeree, Jacob K., and Charles A. Holt. 2005. "An Explanation of Anomalous Behavior in Models of Political Participation." *American Political Science Review*, 99(2): 201–213.

Gold, Martin B. 2008. *Senate Procedure and Practice.* 2nd ed. Lanham, MD: Rowland & Littlefield.

Goldberg, Jessica. 2011. "The Lesser of Two Evils: The Roles of Impatience and Selfishness in Consumption Decisions." Mimeo, University of Maryland.

Goletti, Francesco, Raisuddin Ahmed, and Naser Farid. 1995. "Structural Determinants of Market Integration: the Case of Rice Markets in Bangladesh." *Developing Economies*, 33(2), 185–202.

Gorodnichenko, Yuriy, and Roland, Gerard. 2011. "Culture, Institutions and the Wealth of Nations." Unpublished working paper. University of California, Berkeley.

Gould, Stephen J. 1989. *Wonderful Life: The Burgess Shale and the Nature of History.* New York: W. W. Norton.

Grantham, George. 2007. "Review of Eric L. Jones, Cultures Merging." *Journal of Economic History*, 67(4): 1086–1088.

Greif, Avner. 1994. "Cultural Beliefs and the Organization of Society: a Historical and Theoretical Reflection on Collectivist and Individualist Societies." *Journal of Political Economy*, 102(5): 912–950.

Greif, Avner. 2005. "Commitment, Coercion and Markets: The Nature and Dynamics of Institutions Supporting Exchange." In *Handbook of New Institutional Economics*, ed. Ménard, C. and M. Shirley. Dorrecht, Heidelberg, London, New York: Springers.

Greif, Avner. 2006. *Institutions and the Path to the Modern Economy: Lessons from Medieval Trade.* Cambridge: Cambridge University Press.

Greif, Avner. 2011. "Integrating Culture in Institutional Analysis: the Case of Morality." Unpublished manuscript, Stanford University.

Greif, Avner, and David Laitin. 2004. "A Theory of Endogenous Institutional Change." *American Political Science Review*, 98(4): 14–48.

Greif, Avner, and Steven Tadelis. 2010. "A Theory of Moral Persistence: Crypto-Morality and Political Legitimacy." *Journal of Comparative Economics*, 38(3): 229–244.

Grosjean, Pauline. 2011. "Long Term Institutional Persistence: Ottoman Rule and Financial Development in the Regions of Europe." *Journal of Comparative Economics*, 39: 1–16.

Grosser, Jens, and Arthur Schram. 2006. "Neighborhood Information Exchange and Voter Paraticipation: An Experimental Study." *American Political Science Review*, 100(2): 235–248.

Grossman, Sanford J., and Oliver D. Hart. 1986. "The Costs and Benefits of Ownership: A Theory of Vertical and Lateral Integration." *Journal of Political Economy*, 94(4): 691–719.

Grubb, Farley. 2011. "U.S. Land Policy: Founding Choices and Outcomes, 1781–1802." In *Founding Choices: American Economic Policy in the 1790s*, ed. Douglass Irwin and Richard Sylla, 259–290. Chicago: University of Chicago Press and NBER.

Grzymala-Busse, Anna, and Pauline Jones Luong. 2002. "Reconceptualizing the State: Lessons from Post-Communism." *Politics and Society*, 30(4): 529–554.

Guiso, Luigi, Paola Sapienza, and Luigi Zingales. 2006. "Does Culture Affect Economic Outcomes?" *The Journal of Economic Perspectives*, 20(2): 23–48.

Guiso, Luigi, Paola Sapienza, and Luigi Zingales. 2008. "Long-Term Persistence." NBER Working Papers, #14278.

Guriev, Sergei, and William L. Megginson. 2007. "Privatization: What Have We Learned?" In *Beyond Transition. Proceedings of the 18th ABCDE*, ed. Francois Bourguignon and Boris Pleskovic. Washington, DC: World Bank.

Güth, Werner, Rolf Schmittberger, and Bernd Schwarze. 1982. "An Experimental Analysis of Ultimatum Bargaining." *Journal of Economic Behavior and Organization*, 4(3), 367–388.

Hadfield, Gillian K. and Stephen Macedo. 2012. "Rational Reasonableness: Toward a Positive Theory of Public Reason." *Law and Ethics of Human Rights*, 6(1): 6–46.

Hadfield, Gillian K., and Barry R. Weingast. 2012. "What is Law? A Coordination Model of the Characteristics of Legal Order." *Journal of Legal Analysis*, 4(1): 1–44.

Hadfield, Gillian K., and Barry R. Weingast. 2013a. "Law without the State: Legal Attributes and the Coordination of Decentralized Collective Punishment." *Journal of Law and Courts*, 1(1): 1–32.

Hadfield, Gillian K., and Barry R. Weingast. 2013b. "Microfoundations of the Rule of Law." *Annual Review of Political Science* (forthcoming).

Haggard, Stephan. 1997. "Democratic Institutions, Economic Policy and Development." In *Institutions and Economic Development*, ed. Christopher Clague. Baltimore, MD: Johns Hopkins Press.

Hakewill, George. 1627. *An Apologie of the Power and Providence of God in the Government of the World*. Oxford: Printed by John Lichfield and William Turner.

Hamman, John R., Roberto A. Weber, and Jonathan Woon. 2011. "An Experimental Investigation of Electoral Delegation and the Provision of Public Goods." *American Journal of Political Science*, 55(4): 737–751.

Hamilton, Alexander, John Jay, and James Madison. 1788 [n.d.]. *The Federalist Papers*. New York: Modern Library.

Hanushek, Eric A. 1974. "Efficient Estimators for Regressing Regression Coefficients." *The American Statistician*, 28(2): 66–67.

Hardin, Garrett. 1968. "The Tragedy of the Commons." *Science*, 162(3859): 1243–1248.

Hardin, Russell. 1989. "Why a Constitution?" In *The Federalist Papers and the New Institutionalism*, ed. Bernard Grofman and Donald Wittman. New York: Agathon Press.

Hardin, Russell. 2006. "Constitutionalism." In *Oxford Handbook of Political Economy*, ed. Barry R. Weingast and Donald Wittman. New York: Oxford University Press.

Harré, Rom. 1974. "Some Remarks on 'Rule' as a Scientific Concept." In *Understanding Other Persons*, ed. Theodore Mischel, 143–184. Oxford: Basil Blackwell.

Harris, John Janet Hunger, and Colin M. Lewis, eds. 1995. *The New Institutional Economics and Third World Development*. New York: Routledge.

Hartog, Hendrik. 1983. *Public Property and Private Power: The Corporation of the City of New York in American Law, 1730–1870*. Ithaca, NY: Cornell University Press.

Hayek, Friedrich A. 1960. *The Constitution of Liberty*. Chicago: University of Chicago Press.

Headley, John M. 1997. *Tommaso Campanella and the Transformation of the World*. Princeton, NJ: Princeton University Press.

Hellman, Joel S. 1996. "Constitutions and Economic Reform in the Postcommunist Transitions." *East European Constitutional Review*, 5(1): 46–56.

Hellman, Joel S. 1998. "Winners Take All: The Politics of Partial Reform in Postcommunist Transitions." *World Politics*, 50(2): 203–234.

Henrich, Joseph. 2001. "Cultural Transmission & the Diffusion of Innovation." *American Anthropologist*, 103: 992–1013.

Henrich, Joseph, Robert Boyd, Samuel Bowles, Colin Camerer, Ernst Fehr, Herbert Gintis, and Richard McElreath. 2004. "Overview and Synthesis," in Joseph Henrich, Robert Boyd, Samuel Bowles, Colin Camerer, Ernst Fehr, and Herbert Gintis, eds., *Foundations of Human Sociality: Economic Experiments and Ethnographic Evidence from Fifteen Small-Scale Societies*, Oxford: Oxford University Press.

Henrich, Joseph, Richard McElreath, Abigail Barr, Jean Ensminger, Clark Barrett, Alexander Bolyanatz, Juan Camilo Cardenas, Michael Gurven, Edwins Gwako, Natalie Henrich, Carolyn Lesorogol, Frank Marlowe, David Tracer, and John Ziker. 2006. "Costly Punishment Across Human Societies." *Science*, 312(5781): 1767–1770.

Henrich, Joseph, Jean Ensminger, Richard McElreath, Abigail Barr, Clark Barrett, Alexander Bolyanatz, Juan Camilo Cardenas, Michael Gurven, Edwins Gwako, Natalie Henrich, Carolyn Lesorogol, Frank Marlowe, David Tracer, and John Ziker. 2010. "Markets, Religion, Community Size, and the Evolution of Fairness and Punishment." *Science*, 327(5972): 1480–1484.

Herbst, Jeffrey. 2000. *States and Power in Africa: Comparative Lessons in Authority and Control*. Princeton, NJ: Princeton University Press.

Herman, Arthur. 2001. *How the Scots Invented the Modern World*. New York: Crown.

Hermann, Benedikt, Christian Thoni, and Simon Gachter. 2008. "Antisocial Punishment Across Societies." *Science*, 319(5868): 1362–1367.

Herrera, Yoshiko. 2005. *Imagined Economies: The Sources of Russian Regionalism*. New York: Cambridge University Press.

Hobbes, Thomas. 1651 [1991]. *Leviathan*, ed. Richard Tuck. Cambridge: Cambridge University Press.

Hoff, Karla, and Joseph E. Stiglitz. 2004. "After the Big Bang? Obstacles to the Emergence of the Rule of Law in Post Communist Societies." *American Economic Review*, 94(3): 753–763.

Hoffman, Elizabeth, Kevin McCabe, Keith Shachat, and Vernon Smith. 1994. "Preferences, Property Rights and Anonymity in Bargaining Games." *Games and Economic Behavior*, 7(3), 346–380.

Hofstadter, Richard. 1969. *The Idea of a Party System: The Rise of Legitimate Opposition in the United States, 1780–1840*. Berkeley: University of California Press.

Holland, John H. 1995. *Hidden Order: How Adaptation Builds Complexity*. Reading, MA: Addison-Wesley.

Holmes, Stephen. 1993a. "Back to the Drawing Board." *East European Constitutional Review*, 2(1): 21–25.

Holmes, Stephen. 1993b. "The Postcommunist Presidency." *East European Constitutional Review*, 2(4):36–39.

Holmes, Stephen. 1993c. "Superpresidentialism and its Problems." *East European Constitutional Review*, 2(4): 123–126.

Holmes, Stephen. 1995. "Conceptions of Democracy in the Draft Constitutions of Post-Communist Countries." In *Markets, States, and Democracy: The Political Economy of Post-Communist Transformation*, ed. Beverly Crawford. Boulder, CO: Westview Press.

Home, R.W. "Mechanics and Experimental Physics." In *The Cambridge History of Science, Vol. 4: Eighteenth-century Science*. Cambridge: Cambridge University Press: 354–374.

Hong, Lu, and Scott E. Page. 2001. "Problem Solving by Heterogeneous Agents." *Journal of Economic Theory*, 97: 123–163.

Hoppitt, Julian. 1996. "Patterns of Parliamentary Legislation, 1660–1800." *The Historical Journal*, 39(1): 109–131.

Huber, John, and G. Bingham Powell. 1994. "Congruence Between Citizens and Policymakers in Two Visions of Democracy." *World Politics*, 46(3): 291–326.

Hughes, Jonathan R. T. 1976. *Social Control in the Colonial Economy*. Charlottesville: University of Virginia Press.

Hughes, Jonathan R. T. 1977. "What Difference Did the Beginning Make?" *American Economic Review*, 67(1): 15–20.

Hume, David. 1739–1740. *A Treatise of Human Nature*, ed. David Fate Norton and Mary J. Norton. New York: Oxford University Press.

Hung, Angela A., and Charles R. Plott. 2001. "Information Cascades: Replication and an Extension to Majority Rule and Conformity-Rewarding Institutions." *American Economic Review*, 91(5): 1508–1520.

Huntington, Samuel P. 1968. *Political Order in Changing Societies*. New Haven and London: Yale University Press.

Iliffe, Rob. 2003. "Philosophy of Science." In *The Cambridge History of Science*, Vol. 4: Eighteenth-Century Science, 267–284. Cambridge: Cambridge University Press.

Inkeles, Alex. 1969. "Making Men Modern: On the Causes and Consequences of Individual Change in Six Developing Countries." *American Journal of Sociology*, 75(2): 208–225.

InterAmerican Development Bank. 2003. *Modernization of the State, Strategy Document*. Washington, D.C.: InterAmerican Development Bank.

International Monetary Fund. 2003. *World Economic Outlook, April 2003: Institutions and Growth*. Washington, D.C.: International Monetary Fund.

International Monetary Fund. 2005. World Economic Outlook, September 2005: Building Institutions. Washington, D.C.: International Monetary Fund.

Jacob, Francois. 1977. "Evolution and Tinkering." *Science,* 196(4295): 1161–1166.

Jacob, Margaret C. 1997. *Scientific Culture and the Making of the Industrial West.* 2nd ed. New York: Oxford University Press.

Jacob, Margaret C. 2000. "Commerce, Industry, and the Laws of Newtonian Science: Weber Revisited and Revised." *Canadian Journal of History,* 35(2): 275–292.

Jacob, Margaret C., and Larry Stewart. 2004. *Practical Matter: Newton's Science in the Service of Industry and Empire, 1687–1851.* Cambridge, MA: Harvard University Press.

Jacobi, Tonja, and Barry R. Weingast. 2013. "The Self-Stabilizing Constitution" Working Paper, Hoover Institution, Stanford University.

Jakiela, Pamela. 2011. "Social Preferences and Fairness Norms as Informal Institutions: Experimental Evidence." *American Economic Review Papers and Proceedings,* 101(3): 509–513.

Jakiela, Pamela, Edward Miguel, and Vera te Velde. 2010. "You've Earned It: Combining Field and Lab Experiments to Estimate the Impact of Human Capital on Social Preferences." NBER Working Paper #16449.

Jensen, Merrill. 1940. *The Articles of Confederation; an Interpretation of the Social Constitutional History of the American Revolution.* Madison: University of Wisconsin Press.

Jha, S. 2010. "Financial Innovations and Political Development: Evidence from Revolutionary England." Stanford, CA: Stanford Graduate School of Business.

Jimenez, Emmanuel. 1984. "Tenure Security and Urban Squatting." *Review of Economics and Statistics,* 66(4): 556–567.

Johnson, Dominic D. P. 2009. "The Error of God: Error Management Theory, Religion, and the Evolution of Cooperation." In *Games, Groups, and the Global Good.* Springer Series in Game Theory Part 2, ed. Simon Levin, 169–180. New York and Heidelberg.

Johnson, Dominic D. P., and O. Kruger. 2004. "The Good of Wrath: Supernatural Punishment and the Evolution of Cooperation." *Political Theology,* 5(2): 159–176.

Johnson, Simon, Daniel Kaufmann, and Andrei Shleifer. 1997. "The Unofficial Economy in Transition." *Brookings Papers on Economic Activity,* (2): 159–221.

Johnson, Simon, John McMillan, and Christopher Woodruff. 2002. "Property Rights and Finance." *American Economic Review,* 92(5): 1335–1356.

Jones, Bence. 1871. *The Royal Institution: Its Founder and its First Professors.* London: Longmans Green and Co.

Jones, Eric L. 1981. *The European Miracle.* Cambridge: Cambridge University Press.

Jones, Eric L. 2006. *Cultures Merging: a Historical and Economic Critique of Culture.* Princeton: Princeton University Press.

Jones, J. R. 1992. "The Revolution in Context." In *Liberty Secured? Britain Before and After 1688,* ed. J. R. Jones. Stanford: Stanford University Press.

Jones, Richard Foster. [1936] 1961. *Ancients and Moderns: A Study in the Rise of the Scientific Movement in 17th Century England.* 2nd ed., St. Louis: Washington University Press.

Kamei, Kenju. 2010. "Democracy and Resilient Pro-Social Behavioral Change: An Experimental Study." Mimeo, Brown University.

Kandori, Michihiro. 1992. "Repeated Games Played by Overlapping Generations of Players." *The Review of Economic Studies,* 59(1): 81–92.

Kaplow, Louis. 1992. "Rules Versus Standards: An Economic Analysis." *Duke Law Journal,* 42: 557–623.

Karayalçin, Cem. 2008. "Divided We Stand, United We Fall: the Hume-North-Jones Mechanism for the Rise of Europe." *International Economic Review,* 49(3): 973–999.

Keynes, John Maynard. 1946. "Newton the Man." Available at http://www-groups.dcs. st-and.ac.uk/~history/Extras/Keynes_Newton.html, accessed on September 17, 2010.

Kiernan, Brendan, and Francis X. Bell. 1997. "Legislative Politics and the Political Economy of Property Rights in Post-Communist Russia." In *The Political Economy of Property Rights: Institutional Change and Credibility in the Reform of Centrally Planned Economies,* ed. David L Weimer, 113–138. New York: Cambridge University Press.

Kiser, Larry L., and Elinor Ostrom. 1982. "The Three Worlds of Action: A Metatheoretical Synthesis of Institutional Approaches." In *Strategies of Political Inquiry,* ed. Elinor Ostrom, 179–222. Beverly Hills, CA: Sage.

Kitschelt, Herbert. 2003. "Accounting for Postcommunist Regime Diversity: What Counts as a Good Cause?" In *Capitalism and Democracy in Central and Eastern Europe: Assessing the Legacy of Communist Rule,* ed. Grzegorz Ekiert and Stephen E. Hanson. Cambridge: Cambridge University Press.

Klein, Peter G. 2005. "The Make-or-Buy Decisions: Lessons from Empirical Studies." In *Handbook of New Institutional Economics,* ed. C. Ménard and M. Shirley, 435–464. Berlin: Springer.

Knack, Stephen, and Philip Keefer. 1995. "Institutions and Economic Performance: Cross-Country Tests Using Alternative Institutional Measures." *Economics and Politics,* 7(3): 207–227.

Knack, Stephen, and Philip Keefer. 1997. "Does Social Capital Have an Economic Payoff: A Cross-Country Investigation." *Quarterly Journal of Economics,* 112(4): 1251–1288.

Kopstein, Jeffrey, and David Reilly. 2000. "Geographic Diffusion and the Transformation of the Postcommunist World." *World Politics,* 53(1): 1–37.

Kornai, Janos. 1986. "The Soft Budget Constraint." *Kyklos,* 39(1): 3–30.

Kornai, Janos. 1992. *The Socialist System: The Political Economy of Communism.* Princeton, NJ: Princeton University Press.

Kornai, Janos. 2006. "The Great Transformation of Central Eastern Europe: Success and Disappointment." *Economics of Transition,* 14(2): 207–244.

Kosfeld, Michael, Akira Okada, and Arno Riedl. 2009. "Institution Formation in Public Goods Games." *American Economic Review,* 99(4): 1335–1355.

Kramarz, F. 1996. "Dynamic Focal Points in N-Person Coordination Games." *Theory and Decision,* 40: 277–313.

Krammer, Marius. 2008. "Drivers of National Innovative Systems in Transition: an Eastern European Cross-country Analysis." MPRA Paper 7739, University Library of Munich, Germany.

Kramnick, Isaac. 1992. *Bolingbroke and His Circle.* Ithaca: Cornell University Press.

Krehbiel, Keith. 1991. *Information and Legislative Organization.* Ann Arbor: University of Michigan Press.

Kreps, David. 1990. "Corporate Culture." In *Perspectives on Positive Political Economy,* ed. J. Alt and K. Shepsle. Cambridge: Cambridge University Press.

Kroll, Stephan, Todd L. Cherry, and Jason F. Shogren. 2007. "Voting, Punishment, and Public Goods." *Economic Inquiry,* 45(3): 557–570.

Kuran, Timur. 1987. "Preference Falsification, Policy Discontinuity, and Collective Conservatism." *Economic Journal,* 97(387): 642–665.

Kuran, Timur. 1997. *Private Truths, Public Lies: The Social Consequences of Preference Falsification.* Cambridge, MA: Harvard University Press.

La Porta, Rafael, Florencio Lopez-de-Silanes, and Andrei Shleifer. 1997. "Legal Determinants of External Finance." *Journal of Finance*, 52: 1131–1150.

La Porta, Rafael, Florencio Lopez-de-Silanes, and Andrei Shleifer. 2008. "The Economic Consequences of Legal Origins," *Journal of Economic Literature*, 46: 285–332.

La Porta, Rafael, Florencio Lopez-de-Silanes, Andrei Shleifer, and Robert W. Vishny. 1998. "Law and Finance." *Journal of Political Economy*, 106(6): 1113–1155.

Ladurie, Emmanuel Le Roy. 1976. *The Peasants of Languedoc*. Urbana: University of Illinois Press.

Lamoreaux, Naomi. 2011. "The Mystery of Property Rights." *Journal of Economic History*, 71(2): 275–306.

Landa, Janet Tai. 1981. "A Theory of the Ethically Homogeneous Middleman Group: An Institutional Alternative to Contract Law." *Journal of Legal Studies*, X: 349–376.

Landa, Janet Tai. 1995. *Trust, Ethnicity, and Identity: Beyond the New Institutional Economics of Ethnic Trading Networks, Contract Law, and Gift-Exchange*. Ann Arbor: University of Michigan Press.

Landes, David S. 2000. "Culture Makes Almost All the Difference." In *Culture Matters: How Values Shape Human Progress*, ed. Lawrence E. Harrison and Samuel P. Huntington, 1–13. New York: Basic Books.

Lanjouw, Jean and Philip Levy. 2002. "Untitled: A Study of Formal and Informal Property Rights in Urban Ecuador." *Economic Journal*, 112: 986–1019.

Lazear, Edward P., Ulrike Malmendier, and Roberto A. Weber. 2006. "Sorting in Experiments with Application to Social Preferences." Unpublished.

Lebergott, Stanley. 1985. The Demand for Land: The United States, 1820–1860. *Journal of Economic History*, 45(2): 181–212.

Levine, David I., and Laura D. Tyson. 1990. "Participation, Productivity, and the Firm's Environment." In *Paying for Productivity: A Look at the Evidence*, ed. Alan S. Blinder. Washington: Brookings Institution.

Levine, David K. and Thomas R. Palfrey. 2007. "The Paradox of Voter Participation? A Laboratory Study." *American Political Science Review*, 101(1): 143–158.

Levine, Joseph M. 1981. "Ancients and Moderns Reconsidered." *Eighteenth Century Studies*, 15(1): 72–89.

Levitt, Steven D., and John A. List. 2007. "What Do Laboratory Experiments Measuring Social Preferences Tell Us About the Real World?" *Journal of Economic Perspectives*, 21(2): 153–174.

Levy, Brian, and Pablo Spiller. 1996. *Regulations, Institutions and Commitment. Comparative Studies of Telecommunication*. Cambridge: Cambridge University Press.

Lijphart, Arend. 1984. *Democracies: Patterns of Majoritarian and Consensus Government in Twenty-One Countries*. New Haven, CT: Yale University Press.

Lijphart, Arend, ed. 1992. *Parliamentary Versus Presidential Government*. Oxford: Oxford University Press.

Lijphart, Arend. 1994. *Electoral Systems and Party Systems: A Study of Twenty-Seven Democracies, 1945–1990*. Oxford: Oxford University Press.

Lind, E. Allan, and Tom R. Tyler. 1988. *The Social Psychology of Procedural Justice*. New York: Plenum Press.

Linz, Juan, and Arturo Valenzuela, eds. 1994. *The Failure of Presidential Democracy. Comparative Perspectives*. Baltimore: Johns Hopkins University Press.

Linz, Juan. 1994. "Presidential or Parliamentary Democracy: Does It Make a Difference?" In *The Failure of Presidential Democracy: Comparative Perspectives*, ed. Juan Linz and Arturo Valenzuela. Baltimore: Johns Hopkins University Press.

Locke, John. 1980 [1690]. *Second Treatise of Government*. Indianapolis, IN: Hackett.

Londregan, John. 2000. *Legislative Institutions and Ideology in Chile*. New York: Cambridge University Press.

Lopez, Robert S. 1976. *Commerical Revolution of the Middle Ages, 950–1350*. Cambridge: Cambridge University Press.

Loveman, Brian. 1993. *Constitution of Tyranny: Regimes of Exception in Spanish America*. University of Pittsburgh Press.

Lowengard, Sarah. 2006. *The Creation of Color in Eighteenth-Century Europe*. New York: Gutenberg-ebooks, http://www.gutenberg-e.org/lowengard/index.html, accessed October 4, 2010.

Luban, David. 2007. *Legal Ethics and Human Dignity*. Cambridge: Cambridge University Press.

Lubell, Mark, Mark Schneider, John Scholz, and Mihriye Mete. 2002. "Watershed Partnerships and the Emergence of Collective-Action Institutions." *American Journal of Political Science*, 46(1): 148–163.

Macedo, Stephen. 2010. *Why Public Reason? Citizens' Reasons and the Constitution of the Public Sphere*. Princeton: Princeton University Press.

MacFarlane, Alan. 1991. *The Origins of English Individualism: The Family Property and Social Transition*. London and New York: Wiley.

Mackie, Gerry. 1996. "Ending Footbinding and Infibulation: A Convention Account." *American Sociological Review*, 61(6): 999–1017.

Maclaurin, Colin. 1750. *An Account of Sir Isaac Newton's Philosophical Discoveries*. 2nd ed. London: A. Millar.

Mailath, George. J., Stephen Morris, and Andrew Postlewaite. 2001. "Laws and Authority." Manuscript, University of Pennsylvania.

Mailath, George J., Stephen Morris, and Andrew Postlewaite. 2007. "Maintaining Authority." Manuscript, University of Pennsylvania.

Mandeville, Bernard. [1724] 1755. *The Fable of the Bees*, Part II. Edinburgh: Gray & Peters.

Mantzavanos, C., Douglass C. North, and S. Shariq. 2004. "Learning, Institutions, and Economic Performance." *Perspectives on Politics*, 2: 75–84.

Margreiter, Magdalena, Matthias Sutter, and Dennis Dittrich. 2005. "Individual and Collective Choice and Voting in Common Pool Resource Problem with Heterogeneous Actors," *Environmental & Resource Economics*, 32: 241–271.

Marks, Brian A. 1988. "A Model of Judicial Influence on Congressional Policymaking: Grove City College v. Bell." *Working Papers in Political Science* P-88–7, Hoover Institution.

Marshall, Alfred. 1890. *Principles of Economics*. London: MacMillan and Co.

Marshall, Graham. 2009. "Polycentricity, Reciprocity, and Farmer Adoption of Conservation Practices under Community-Based Governance." *Ecological Economics*, 68(5): 1507–1520.

Martens, Bertin, Uwe Mummert, Peter Murrell, and Paul Seabright. 2002. *The Institutional Economics of Foreign Aid*. Cambridge: Cambridge University Press.

McAdams, Richard H. 2000. A Focal Point Theory of Expressive Law. *Virginia Law Review*, 86: 1649–1729.

McCloskey, Deirdre. 2006. *The Bourgeois Virtues: Ethics for an Age of Commerce. Chicago*: University of Chicago Press.

McCloskey, Deirdre. 2010. *Bourgeois Dignity: Why Economics Can't Explain the Modern World*. Chicago: University of Chicago Press.

McCubbins, M. D. and T. Schwartz. 1987. *A Theory of Congressional Delegation. Congress: Structure and Policy*. New York, Cambridge University Press.

McElreath, Richard, Abigail Barr, Jean Ensminger, Clark Barrett, Alexander Bolyanatz, Juan Camilo Cardenas, Michael Gurven, Edwins Gwako, Natalie Hen-rich, Carolyn Lesorogol, Frank Marlowe, David Tracer, and John Ziker. 2006. "Costly Punishment Across Human Societies." *Science*, 312(5781): 1767–1770.

McInnes, Angus. 1982. "When Was the English Revolution?" *History*. 67(221): 381–383.

McInnes, Angus. 1970. *Robert Harley, Puritan Politician*. London: Littlehampton Book Services Ltd.

McKelvey, Richard D. 1979. "General Conditions for Global Intransitivities in Formal Voting Models." *Econometrica*, 47: 1085–1112.

McKelvey, Richard D., and Norman Schofield. 1986. "Structural Instability of the Core." *Journal of Mathematical Economics*, 15: 179–198.

McKelvey, Richard D., and Norman Schofield. 1987. "Generalized Symmetry Conditions at a Core." *Econometrica*, 55(4): 923–933.

Medina, L. F. 2007. *A Unified Theory of Collective Action and Social Change*. New York, Cambridge University Press.

Megginson, William L., and Jeffrey M. Netter. 2001. "From State to Market: A Survey of Empirical Studies on Privatization." *Journal of Economic Literature*, 39(2): 321–389.

Ménard, Claude. 2004a. "The Economics of Hybrid Organizations." *Journal of Institutional and Theoretical Economics*, 160(3): 345–376.

Ménard, Claude, ed. 2004b. *The International Library of New Institutional Economics*. Cheltenham, UK: Edward Elgar Publisher. 7 vol.

Ménard, Claude. 2006. "Challenges in New Institutional Economics." In *Institutions in Perspective*, ed. U. Bindsell, J. Haucap, and C. Wey, 21–33. Tubingen: Mohr-Siebeck.

Ménard, Claude, and Mary Shirley, eds. 2005/2008. *Handbook of New Institutional Economics*. Dordrecht, the Netherlands: Springer.

Ménard, Claude, and Mary Shirley. 2012a. "From Intuition to Institutionalization: A History of New Institutional Economics." Ronald Coase Institute Working Paper #8. September.

Ménard, Claude, and Mary Shirley. 2012b. "New Institutional Economics: From Early Intuitions to a New Paradigm?" Ronald Coase Institute Working Paper #8. www.Coase.org/research.htm.

Merryman, John, and Regelio Perez-Perdomo. 2007. *The Civil Law Tradition, 3rd Edition: An Introduction to the Legal Systems of Europe and Latin America*. Stanford: Stanford University Press.

Merton, Robert K. [1938] 2001. *Science, Technology, and Society in Seventeenth-Century England*. New York: Howard Fertig Press.

Merton, Robert K. 1973. *The Sociology of Science*. Chicago: University of Chicago Press.

Mesoudi, Alex. 2011. *Cultural Evolution*. Chicago: University of Chicago Press.

Milgrom, Paul R., Douglass C. North, and Barry R. Weingast. 1990. "The Role of Institutions in the Revival of Trade: The Medieval Law Merchant, Private Judges, and the Champagne Fairs." *Economics and Politics*, 2: 1–23.

Minchinton W. E., ed. 1969. *The Growth of Overseas Trade in the Seventeenth and Eighteenth Centuries.* London: Methuen & Co.

Mitchell, William. 1904. *An Essay on the Early History of the Law Merchant.* London: University Press.

Mittal, Sonia, and Barry R. Weingast. 2013. "Self-Enforcing Constitutions: With an Application to Democratic Stability in America's First Century." *Journal of Law, Economics, and Organization* 29(2): 278–302.

Mokyr, Joel. 1990. *The Lever of Riches.* Oxford: Oxford University Press.

Mokyr, Joel. 2002. *The Gifts of Athena.* Princeton: Princeton University Press.

Mokyr, Joel. 2006. "Mobility, Creativity, and Technological Development: David Hume, Immanuel Kant and the Economic Development of Europe." In *Kolloquiumsband of the XX*, ed. G. Abel, 1131–1161. Berlin: Deutschen Kongresses für Philosophie.

Mokyr, Joel. 2007. "The Market for Ideas and the Origins of Economic Growth in Eighteenth Century Europe." [Heineken Lecture]. *Tijdschrift voor Sociale en Economische Geschiedenis*, 4(1): 3–38.

Mokyr, Joel. 2009. *The Enlightened Economy.* New York and London: Yale University Press.

Mokyr, Joel. 2011–2012. "The Commons of Knowledge: A Historical Perspective." In *The Wealth and Well-Being of Nations*, vol. 4, ed. Emily Chamlee-Wright, 29–44.

Mokyr, Joel. 2013. "Cultural Entrepreneurs and the Origins of Modern Economic Growth." [Heckscher Memorial Lecture]. *Scandinavian Economic History Review*, forthcoming.

Montes, Leonidas. 2008. *"Newton's Real Influence on Adam Smith and its Context."* Cambridge Journal of Economics, 32: 555–576.

Moraski, Bryon. 2006. *Elections by Design: Parties and Patronage in Russia's Regions.* DeKalb: Northern Illinois University Press.

Morrill, John. 1991. "The Sensible Revolution," in *The Anglo-Dutch Moment*, ed. Jonathan Israel. New York: Cambridge University Press.

Morris, Ian. 2010. *Why the West Rules for Now.* New York: Farrar, Straus, and Giroux.

Morton, Rebecca B., and Kenneth C. Williams. 1999. "Information Asymmetries and Simultaneous versus Sequential Voting." *American Political Science Review*, 93(1): 51–67.

Munger, Michael, C. 2010. "Endless Forms Most Beautiful and Most Wonderful: Elinor Ostrom and the Diversity of Institutions." *Public Choice*, 143: 263–268.

Murphy, Anne L. 2009. *The Origins of English Financial Markets: Investment and Speculation before the South Sea Bubble.* Cambridge: Cambridge University Press.

Murrell, Peter. 2010. "Design and Evolution in Institutional Development: The Insignificance of the English Bill of Rights." Mimeo.

Mussachio, Aldo. 2008. "Can Civil Law Countries Get Good Institutions? Lessons from the History of Creditor Rights and Bond Markets in Brazil." *Journal of Economic History*, 68(1): 80–108.

Mussachio, Aldo. 2009. *Experiments in Financial Democracy: Corporate Governance and Financial Development in Brazil, 1882–1950.* New York: Cambridge University Press.

Musson, A. E., and Robinson, Eric. 1969. *Science and Technology in the Industrial Revolution.* Manchester: Manchester University Press.

Myerson, Roger. 2004. "Justice, Institutions, and Multiple Equilibria." *Chicago Journal of International Law*, 5: 91–107.

Nenner, Howard. 1997. "Introduction." In *Politics and the Political Imagination in Later Stuart Britain*, ed. Howard Nenner. Rochester, NY: University of Rochester Press.

Nettels, Curtis. 1924. "*The Mississippi Valley and the Constitution, 1815–1829.*" Mississippi Valley Historical Review, 11(3): 332–357.

Newton, Isaac. 1721. *Opticks*. 3rd ed. London: William and John Innys.

North, Douglass C. 1958. "Ocean Freight Rates and Economic Development 1750–1913." *Journal of Economic History*, 18(4): 537–555.

North, Douglass C. 1961. *The Economic Growth of the United States 1790–1860*. Englewood Cliffs, N.J.: Prentice-Hall, Inc.

North, Douglass C. 1966. *Growth and Welfare in the American Past. A New Economic History*. Englewood Cliffs, N.J.: Prentice-Hall, Inc.

North, Douglass C. 1968. "Sources of Productivity Change in Ocean Shipping, 1600–1850." *The Journal of Political Economy*, 76(5): 953–970.

North, Douglass C. 1971. "Institutional Change and Economic Growth." *Journal of Economic History*, 31(1): 118–125.

North, Douglass C. 1974. "Beyond the New Economic History." *Journal of Economic History*, 34(1): 1–7.

North, Douglass C. 1978. "Structure and Performance: The Task of Economic History." *Journal of Economic Literature*, 16: 963–978.

North, Douglass C. 1981. *Structure and Change in Economic History*. Cambridge: Cambridge University Press.

North, Douglass C. 1986. "The New Institutional Economics." *Journal of Institutional and Theoretical Economics*, 142(1): 230–237.

North, Douglass. C. 1990a. *Institutions, Institutional Change, and Economic Performance*. New York: Cambridge University Press.

North, Douglass C. 1990b. "A Transaction Cost Theory of Politics." *Journal of Theoretical Politics*, 2(4): 355–367.

North, Douglass C. 1991. "Institutions." In *The Journal of Economic Perspectives*, 5(1): 97–112.

North, Douglass C. 1993. "Douglass C. North, the Sveriges Riksbank Prize in Economic Sciences in Memory of Alfred Nobel 1993: Autobiography." Vol. 2010. The Nobel Foundation.

North, Douglass C. 1994. "Economic Performance through Time." *American Economic Review*, 84: 359–368.

North, Douglass C. 1995. "The New Institutional Economics and Third World Development," in John Harriss, Janet Hunter, and Colin M. Lewis, eds., *The New Institutional Economics and Third World Development*, New York: Routledge.

North, Douglass C. 2005. *Understanding the Process of Economic Change*. Princeton: Princeton University Press.

North, Douglass C., and Robert Thomas. 1973. *The Rise of the Western World: A New Economic History*. New York: Cambridge University Press.

North, Douglass C., John J. Wallace, and Barry Weingast. 2009. *Violence and Social Orders: A Conceptual Framework for Interpreting Human History*. New York: Cambridge University Press.

North, Douglass C., John J. Wallis, Steven B. Webb, and Barry R. Weingast. 2009. "Limited Access Orders: Rethinking the Problems of Development and Violence." Unpublished working paper, June 8, 2009.

North, Douglass C., and Barry R. Weingast. 1989. "Constitutions and Commitment: The Evolution of Institutions Governing Public Choice in Seventeenth-Century England." *The Journal of Economic History*, 49(4): 803–832.

Noussair, Charles N., and Fangfang Tan. 2011. "Voting on Punishment Systems within a Heterogeneous Group." *Journal of Public Economic Theory*, 13(5): 661–693.

Nunn, Nathan. 2008. "The Long-Term Effects of Africa's Slave Trades," *Quarterly Journal of Economics*, 123: 139–176.

Nunn, Nathan. 2009. "The Importance of History for Economic Development." *Annual Review of Economics*, 1(1): 65–92.

Olken, Benjamin. 2010. "Direct Democracy and Local Public Goods: Evidence from a Field Experiment in Indonesia." *American Political Science Review*, 104(2): 243–267.

Ordeshook, Peter. 1992. "Constitutional Stability." *Constitutional Political Economy*, 3 (Spring/Summer): 137.

Ostrom, Elinor. 1990. *Governing the Commons: The Evolution of Institutions for Collective Action*. New York: Cambridge University Press.

Ostrom, Elinor. 1991. "An Overview of Rule Configurations." Working paper. Bloomington: Indiana University, Workshop in Political Theory and Policy Analysis.

Ostrom, Elinor. 2005. *Understanding Institutional Diversity*. Princeton, NJ: Princeton University Press.

Ostrom, Elinor. 2007. "A Diagnostic Approach for Going beyond Panaceas." *Proceedings of the National Academy of Sciences*, 104(39): 15181–15187.

Ostrom, Elinor. 2009. "A General Framework for Analyzing the Sustainability of Social-Ecological Systems." *Science*, 325(5939): 419–422.

Ostrom, Elinor. 2011. "Background on the Institutional Analysis and Development Framework." *Policy Studies Journal*, 39(1): 7–27.

Ostrom, Vincent. 1980. "Artisanship and Artifact." *Public Administration Review*, 40(4): 309–317.

Ostrom, Vincent. 1991. *The Meaning of American Federalism: Constituting a Self-Governing Society*. San Francisco, CA: ICS Press.

Ostrom, Vincent. 1997. *The Meaning of Democracy and the Vulnerability of Democracies: A Response to Tocqueville's Challenge*. Ann Arbor: University of Michigan Press.

Ostrom, Vincent. 2008. *The Political Theory of a Compound Republic: Designing the American Experiment*. 3rd ed. Lanham, MD: Lexington Books.

Ostrom, Vincent, Charles M. Tiebout, and Robert Warren. 1961. "The Organization of Government in Metropolitan Areas: A Theoretical Inquiry." *American Political Science Review*, 55(4): 831–842.

Paakkonen, Jenni. 2008. "Government and Growth in Transition: The Trajectories of Former Planned Economics since the Collapse of the Iron Wall." Unpublished manuscript.

Pateman, Carole. 1970. *Participation and Democratic Theory*. Cambridge: Cambridge University Press.

Paterson, Timothy H.1987. "On the Role of Christianity in the Political Philosophy of Francis Bacon." *Polity*, 19(3): 419–442.

Persson, Torsten, and Guido Tabellini. 2000. *Political Economics: Explaining Economic Policy*. Cambridge, MA: MIT Press.

Pettigrew, William. 2007. "Free to Enslave: Politics and the Escalation of Britain's Transatlantic Slave Trade, 1688–1714." *William and Mary Quarterly*, 64(1): 3–38.

Pettigrew, William. 2009. "Some Underappreciated Connections Between Constitutional Change and National Economic Growth in England, 1660–1720." Unpublished paper. Canterbury: University of Kent.

Pierson, Arthur. 1994. *Politics in Time: History, Institutions, and Social Analysis*. Princeton, Princeton University Press.

Piketty, Thomas. 1995. "Social Mobility and Redistributive Politics." *Quarterly Journal of Economics*, 110(3): 551–584.

Pincus, Steven. 2009. *1688: The First Modern Revolution*. New Haven: Yale University Press.

Pincus, Steven. n.d. "The Pivot of Empire: the Sir John Neale Lecture." In *Rethinking the British Empire in the Augustan Age*, ed. Jason Peacey, forthcoming.

Pomfret, Richard. 2003. "Lessons from Economies in Transition from Central Planning." *Australian Economic Review*, 36(2): 245–252.

Pop-Eleches, Grigore. 2007. "Historical Legacies and Post-Communist Regime Change." *Journal of Politics*, 69(4): 908–926.

Poteete, Amy R., Marco Janssen, and Elinor Ostrom. 2010. Working Together: Collective Action, the Commons, and Multiple Methods in Practice. Princeton, NJ: Princeton University Press.

Posner, Richard A. 2007. *Economic Analysis of Law*. 7th ed. Austin, TX: Wolters Kluwer.

Potters, Jan, Martin Sefton, and Lise Vesterlund. 2005. "After You – Endogenous Sequencing in Voluntary Contribution Games." *Journal of Public Economics*, 89(8): 1399–1419.

Powell, G. Bingham, and Georg Vanberg. 2000. "Election Laws, Disproportionality and Median Correspondence: Implications for Two Visions of Democracy." *British Journal of Political Science*, 30(3): 383–411.

Przeworski, Adam. 1991. *Democracy and the Market: Political and Economic Reforms in Eastern Europe and Latin America*. New York: Cambridge University Press.

Przeworski, Adam, Michael Alvarez, Jose Antonio Cheibub, and Fernando Limongi. 1996. "What Makes Democracies Endure?" *Journal of Democracy*, 7(1): 39–55.

Putnam, Robert. 1993. *Making Democracy Work: Civil Traditions in Modern Italy*. Princeton, NJ: Princeton University Press.

Putterman, Louis, Jean-Robert Tyran, and Kenju Kamei. 2010. "Public Goods and Voting on Formal Sanction Schemes: An Experiment," mimeo.

Quinn, Stephen. 2001. "The Glorious Revolution's Effect on English Private Finance: A Microhistory, 1680–1705." *Journal of Economic History*, 61(3): 593–615.

Rajan, Raghuram G., and Luigi Zingales. 1998. "Financial Dependence and Growth." *American Economic Review*, 88(3): 559–586.

Rakove, Jack. 1979. *The Beginnings of National Politics: An Interpretive History of the Continental Congress*. Baltimore: Johns Hopkins University Press.

Raz, Joseph. 1977 [1979]. "The Rule of Law and its Virtues." Reprinted in *Authority of Law*, ed. Joseph Raz. Oxford: Clarendon Press.

Reitan, Earl A. 1970. "From Revenue to Civil List, 1689–1702: The Revolutionary Settlement and the 'Mixed and Balanced' Constitution." *The Historical Journal*, 13(4): 569–588.

Richerson, Peter J., and Boyd, Robert. 2005. *Not by Genes Alone: How Culture Transformed Human Evolution*. Chicago: University of Chicago Press.

Riddick, Floyd M. 1981. *Senate Procedure: Precedents and Practices*. Washington, D.C.: U.S. Government Printing Office.

Riker, William H. 1976. "Comments on Vincent Ostrom's Paper." *Public Choice*, 27(1): 13–15.

Riker, William H. 1981. "Implications from the Disequilibrium of Majority Rule for the Study of Institutions." *American Political Science Review*, 74: 432–446.

Riker, William H. 1984. "The Heresthetics of Constitution-Making." *American Political Science Review*, 1978: 1–16.

Riker, William H. 1996. *Campaigning for the American Constitution*. New Haven and London: Yale University Press.

Roberts, Clayton. 1977. "The Constitutional Significance of the Financial Settlement of 1690." *The Historical Journal*, 20(1): 59–76.

Rodrik, Dani. 1999. Where Did All the Growth Go? External Shocks, Social Conflict and Growth Collapses. *Journal of Economic Growth*, 4(4): 385–412.

Rodrik, Dani. 2007. *One Economics, Many Recipes: Globalization, Institutions, and Economic Growth*. Princeton: Princeton University Press.

Rodrik, Dani., A. Subramanian, and F. Trebbi, 2004. "Institutions Rule: The Primacy of Institutions over Geography and Integration in Economic Development" *Journal of Economic Growth*, 9(2): 131–165.

Rodrik, Dani, A. Subramanian, et al. 2002. "Institutions Rule: The Primacy of Institutions Over Integration and Geography in Economic Development." Working paper 9305. Cambridge, MA: National Bureau of Economic Research.

Roland, Gerard. 2000. *Transition and Economics: Politics, Markets, and Firms*. Cambridge, MA: MIT Press.

Rotemberg, Julio. 2002. "Perceptions of Equity and the Distribution of Income." *Journal of Labor Economics*, 20(2): 249–288.

Roth, Alvin E., Vesna Prasnikar, Masahiro Okuno-Fujiwara, and Shmuel Zamir. 1991. "Bar-Gaining and Market Behavior in Jerusalem, Ljubljana, Pittsburgh, and Tokyo: An Experimental Study." *American Economic Review*, 81(5), 1068–1095.

Sala-i-Martin, Xavier. 2002. "15 Years of New Growth Economics: What Have We Learnt?" Unpublished manuscript, Columbia University.

Saviotti, Pier Paolo. 1996. *Technological Evolution, Variety, and the Economy*. Cheltenham: Edward Elgar.

Schelling, Thomas C. 1960/1981. *The Strategy of Conflict*. Cambridge, MA: Harvard University Press.

Schiavo-Campo, Salvatore Giulio de Tommaso, and Amitabha Mukherjee. 1997. "An International Statistical Survey of Government Employment and Wages." Policy research working paper 1806, World Bank.

Schlager, Edella. 1990. "Model Specification and Policy Analysis: The Governance of Coastal Fisheries." PhD diss. Indiana University.

Schlager, Edella. 1994. "Fishers' Institutional Responses to Common-Pool Resource Dilemmas." In *Rules, Games, and Common-Pool Resources*, ed. Elinor Ostrom, Roy Gardner, and James Walker, 247–265. Ann Arbor: University of Michigan Press.

Schlager, Edella, and Elinor Ostrom. 1992. "Property-Rights Regimes and Natural Resources: A Conceptual Analysis." *Land Economics*, 68(3): 249–262.

Schlager, Edella, William Blomquist, and Shui Yan Tang. 1994. "Mobile Flows, Storage, and Self-Organized Institutions for Governing Common-Pool Resources." *Land Economics*, 70(3): 294–317.

Schliesser, Eric. 2007. "Hume's Newtonianism and Anti-Newtonianism." *Stanford Encyclopedia of Philosophy*. http://plato.stanford.edu/entries/hume-newton/, accessed September 2010.

Schmitter, Philippe C., and Terry Lynn Karl. 1994. "The Conceptual Travels of Transitologists and Consolidologists: How Far to the East Should They Attempt to Go?" *Slavic Review*, 53(1):173–185.

Schofield, Norman. 2000. "Core Beliefs and the Founding of the American Republic." *Homo Oeconomicus*, 16(2000): 433–462.

Scholz, John, and Cheng-Lung Wang. 2006. "Cooptation or Transformation? Local Policy Networks and Federal Regulatory Enforcement." *American Journal of Political Science*, 50(1): 81–97.

Schotter, Andrew A. 1981. *The Economic Theory of Social Institutions*. New York: Cambridge University Press.

Schotter, Andrew A. 1998: "Worker Trust, System Vulnerability and the Performance of Work Groups." In *Economics, Values and Organization*, ed. Ben-Ner and Putterman. New York: Cambridge University Press.

Schram, Arthur, and Joep Sonnemans. 1996. "Voter Turnout as a Participation Game: An Experimental Investigation." *International Journal of Game Theory*, 27(3): 385–406.

Schwoerer, Lois G. 1981. *The Declaration of Rights, 1689*. Baltimore: Johns Hopkins University Press.

Scott, Johnathn. 1991. *Algernon Sidney and the Restoration Crisis, 1677–1683*. New York: New York: Cambridge University Press.

Scully, Timothy. 1996. "Chile: The Political Underpinnings of Economic Liberalization." In *Constructing Democratic Governance: South America in the 1990s*, ed. Jorge I. Dominquez and Abraham F. Lowenthal. Baltimore: Johns Hopkins University Press.

Seabright, Paul. 2010. *The Company of Strangers: A Natural History of Economic Life*. Princeton: Princeton University Press.

Seaward, Paul. 2007. "Parliament and the Idea of Accountability in Early Modern Britain." In *Realities of Representation: State-Building in Early Modern Europe and European America*, ed. Maija Jansson. Basingstoke: Palgrave Macmillan: 45–62.

Seki, Motohide, and Ihara, Yasuo. 2012. "The Rate of Cultural Change in One-to-Many Social Transmission when Cultural Variants are not Selectively Neutral." *Letters on Evolutionary Behavioral Science*, 3(2): 12–16.

Sened, Itai. 1997. *The Political Institution of Private Property*. Cambridge: Cambridge University Press.

Shapin, Steven. 1988. "Understanding the Merton Thesis." *Isis*, 79(4): 594–605.

Shariff, Azim F., Ara Norenzayan, and Joseph Henrich. 2009. "The Birth of High Gods: How the Cultural Evolution of Supernatural Policing Agents Influenced the Emergence of Complex, Cooperative Human Societies, Paving the Way for Civilization." In *Evolution, Culture and the Human Mind*, ed. M. Schaller et al. New York: Psychology Press.

Shelanski, Howard, and Peter Klein. 1995. "Empirical Research in Transaction Cost Economics: A Survey and Assessment." *Journal of Law, Economics and Organization*, 11(2): 335–361.

Shepsle, Kenneth A. 1979. "Institutional Arrangements and Equilibrium in Multidimensional Voting Models." *American Journal of Political Science*, 23: 23–57.

Shepsle, Kenneth A. 1986. "Institutional Equilibrium and Equilibrium Institutions." In *The Science of Politics*, ed. Herbert Weisberg. New York: Agathon.

Shepsle, Kenneth A. 2006a. "Old Questions and New Answers about Institutions: The Riker Objection Revisited." In *The Oxford Handbook of Political Economy*, ed. Barry R. Weingast and Donald A. Wittman, 1031–1050. New York: Oxford University Press.

Shepsle, Kenneth A. 2006b. "Rational Choice Institutionalism." In *The Oxford Handbook of Political Institutions*, ed. R. A. W. Rhodes, Sarah A. Binder, and Bert A. Rockman, 23–39. New York: Oxford University Press.

Shepsle, Kenneth. A., and Barry R. Weingast. 1981. "Structure-Induced Equilibrium and Legislative Choice." *Public Choice*, 37: 503–519.

Shepsle, Kenneth A. 1986. "Institutional Equilibrium and Equilibrium Institutions." In Herbert F. Weisberg, ed., *Political Science: The Science of Politics*. New York: Agathon, pp. 51–82.

Shepsle, Kenneth A., and Barry R. Weingast. 1987. "The Institutional Foundations of Committee Power." *American Political Science Review*, 81: 85–104.

Shimanoff, Susan B. 1980. *Communication Rules: Theory and Research*. Beverly Hills: Sage.

Shirley, Mary M., ed. 2002. *Thirsting for Efficiency: The Economics and Politics of Urban Water System Reform*. Oxford: Elsevier Science.

Shirley, Mary M. 2005. "Institutions and Development." In *Handbook of New Institutional Economics*, ed. Claude Ménard and Mary M. Shirley, 611–638. Dordrecht, the Netherlands: Springer.

Shirley, Mary M. 2008. *Institutions and Development*. Cheltenham, UK and Brookfield, VT: Edward Elgar.

Shleifer, Andrei, and Daniel Treisman. 2000. *Without a Map: Political Tactics and Economic Reform in Russia*. Cambridge, MA: MIT Press.

Shleifer, Andrei, and Robert W. Vishny. 1993. "Corruption." *Quarterly Journal of Economics*, 108(3): 599–617.

Shugart, Matthew Soberg, and John Carey. 1992. *Presidents and Assembles. Constitutional Design and Electoral Dynamics*. Cambridge, MA: Cambridge University Press.

Siavelis, Peter. 2008. "Chile: The End of the Unfinished Transition." In *Constructing Democratic Governance in Latin America*, ed. Jorge I. Dominguez and Michael Shifter. Baltimore: Johns Hopkins University Press.

Sills, D. L. 1957. *The Volunteers: Means and Ends in a National Organization*. New York, Free Press.

Simpson, A. W. B. 1986. *A History of the Land Law*, 2nd ed. Oxford: Clarendon Press.

Singleton, Sara. 1998. *Constructing Cooperation: The Evolution of Institutions of Comanagement*. Ann Arbor: University of Michigan Press.

Singleton, Sara, and Michael Taylor. 1992. "Common Property Economics: A General Theory and Land Use Applications." *Journal of Theoretical Politics* 4(3): 309–324.

Smith, A. 1976. *An Inquiry into the Nature and Causes of the Wealth of Nations*. Chicago: University of Chicago Press.

Snobelen, Stephen D. 1999. "Isaac Newton, Heretic: the Strategies of a Nicodemite," *British Journal for the History of Science*, 32, pp. 381–419.

Sonin, Konstantin. 2003. "Why the Rich May Favor Poor Protection of Property Rights." *Journal of Comparative Economics*, 31(4): 715–731.

Soskice, David, Robert. H. Bates, et al. 1992. "Ambition and Constraint: The Stabilizing Role of Institutions." *Journal of Law, Economics, and Organizations*, 8(3): 547–560.

Spadafora, David. 1990. *The Idea of Progress in Eighteenth-Century Britain*. New Haven, CT: Yale University Press.

Spinka, Matthew. 1943. *John Amos Comenius: That Incomparable Moravian*. Chicago: University of Chicago Press.

Sprat, Thomas. 1667. *History of the Royal Society*. London: J. Martyn at the Bell.

Stark, David. 1992. "Path Dependence and Privatization Strategies in East Central Europe." *East European Politics and Societies*, 6(1): 17–53.

Stasavage, David. 2003. *Public Debt and the Birth of the Democratic State*. Cambridge: Cambridge University Press.

Steel, William Anderson. 1894. "The Founders of the Bank of England." *Macmillan's Magazine*, 70(417): 184.

Stepan, Alfred, and Cindy Skach. 1993. "Constitutional Frameworks and Democratic Consolidation: Parliamentarianism Versus Presidentialism." *World Politics*, 46(1): 1–22.

Stinchcombe, A. L. 1968. *Constructing Social Theories*. New York: Harcourt Brace & World.

Strasser, Gerhard F. 1994. "Closed and Open Languages: Samuel Hartlib's Involvement with Cryptology and Universal Languages." In *Samuel Hartlib and Universal Reformation*, ed. Mark Greengrass, Michael Leslie and Timothy Raylor, 151–161. Cambridge: Cambridge University Press.

Sugden, Robert. 1986. *The Economics of Rights, Cooperation and Welfare*. Palgrave, CT: Palgrave-Macmillan.

Sugden, Robert. 2005. *The Economics of Rights, Cooperation and Welfare*. 2nd ed. New York: Palgrave Macmillan.

Sussman, Nathan, and Yishay Yafeh. 2006. "Institutional Reforms, Financial Development and Sovereign Debt: Britain 1690–1790." *Journal of Economic History*, 66(4): 906–935.

Sutter, Matthias, Stefan Haigner, and Martin G. Kocher. 2010. "Choosing the Carrot or the Stick? Endogenous Institutional Choice in Social Dilemma Situations." *Review of Economic Studies*, 77(4): 1540–1566.

Swingen, Abigail. 2007. *The Politics of Labor and the Origins of the British Empire, 1650–1720*. University of Chicago Dissertation.

Szostak, Rick. 1991. *The Role of Transportation in the Industrial Revolution*. Montreal: McGill-Queen's University Press.

Szostak, Rick. 2009. *The Causes of Economic Growth: Interdisciplinary Perspectives*. Berlin: Springer.

Tabellini, Guido. 2008. "Institutions and Culture (Presidential Address)." *Journal of the European Economic Association*, 6(2–3): 255–294.

Taylor, Michael. 1982. *Community, Anarchy, and Liberty*. New York: Cambridge University Press.

Temin, Peter. 1997. "Is it Kosher to Talk about Culture?" *Journal of Economic History*, 57(2): 267–287.

Thibaut, John, and Laurence Walker. 1975. *Procedural Justice: A Psychological Analysis*. New Jersey: Lawrence Erlbaum Associates.

Thomson, Dennis. 1970. *The Democratic Citizen: Social Science and Democratic Theory in the Twentieth Century.* Cambridge: Cambridge University Press.

Tocqueville, Alexis de. 1838. *Democracy in America.* New York: Adlard and Saunders.

Toulmin, Stephen. 1974. "Rules and Their Relevance for Understanding Human Behavior." In *Understanding Other Persons*, ed. Theodore Mischel, 185–215. Oxford: Basil Blackwell.

Traugot, John. 1994. "Review of Joseph Levine, The Battle of the Books: History and Literature in the Augustan Age." *Modern Philology*, 91(4): 501–508.

Treisman, Daniel. 2010. "The Return: Russia's Journey from Gorbachev to Medvedev." Unpublished book manuscript.

Trevor-Roper, Hugh. 1992. *Counter-Reformation to Glorious Revolution.* Chicago: University of Chicago Press.

Tsebelis, George. 2002. *Veto Players: How Political Institutions Work.* Princeton, NJ: Princeton University Press.

Tyran, Jean-Robert, and Lars P. Feld. 2006. "Achieving Compliance When Legal Sanctions are Non-Deterrent." *Scandinavian Journal of Economics*, 108(1): 135–156.

Valenzuela, Arturo. 1994. "Chile: Government and Politics." In *Chile: A Country Study*, ed. Rex A. Hudson. Washington, DC: Federal Research Division, Library of Congress.

Van den Bos, Kees. 1999. "What Are We Talking about When We Talk about No-Voice Procedures? On the Psychology of the Fair Outcome Effect." *Journal of Experimental Social Psychology*, 35(6): 560–577.

Van Huyck, John B., Raymond C. Battalio, and Richard Beil. 1993. "Asset Markets as an Equilibrium Selection Mechanism: Coordination Failure, Game Form Auctions, and Tacit Communication." *Games and Economic Behavior*, 5(3): 485–504.

Voigtländer, Nico, and Voth. Joachim. 2011. "Persecution Perpetuated: the Medieval Origins of Anti-Semitic Violence in Nazi Germany." Unpublished working paper, Barcelona: ICREA/UPF.

Von Hayek, Friedrich A. 1958. "The Creative Powers of a Free Civilization." In *Essays on Individuality*, ed. Felix Morley, 259–290. Philadelphia: University of Pennsylvania Press.

Waldron, J. 2008. "The Concept and the Rule of Law." *Georgia Law Review*, 43(1): 60–71.

Waldron J. 2011. The Rule of Law and the Importance of Procedure. In *Getting to the Rule of Law (NOMOS)* New York: NYU Press

Walker, James M., Roy Gardner, Andrew Herr, and Elinor Ostrom. 2000. "Collective Choices in the Commons: Experimental Results on Proposed Allocation Rules and Votes." *The Economic Journal*, 110(1): 212–234.

Wallis, John Joseph. 2003. "The Property Tax as a Coordinating Device: Financing Indiana's Mammoth System of Internal Improvements, 1835 to 1842." *Explorations in Economic History*, 40:223–250.

Weber, M. 1985. *Basic Concepts in Sociology.* Seacaucus, NJ: Citadel Press.

Weber, Max. [1905] 1958. *The Protestant Ethic and the Spirit of Capitalism.* New York: Charles Scribner's.

Webster, Charles. 1970. *Samuel Hartlib and the Advancement of Learning.* Cambridge: Cambridge University Press.

Webster, Charles. 1975. *The Great Instauration: Science Medicine and Reform, 1626–1660.* London: Duckworth.

Weimer, David L., ed. 1997. *The Political Economy of Property Rights: Institutional Change and Credibility in the Reform of Centrally Planned Economies.* New York: Cambridge University Press.

Weingast, Barry R. 1993. "Constitutions as Governance Structures: The Political Foundations of Secure Markets." *Journal of Institutional and Theoretical Economics,* 149(1): 286–311.

Weingast, Barry R. 1995. "The Economic Role of Political Institutions: Market-Preserving Federalism and Economic Development." *Journal of Law, Economics, and Organization,* 11(1): 1–31.

Weingast, Barry R. 1997. "The Political Foundations of Democracy and the Rule of Law." *American Political Science Review,* 91: 245–263.

Weingast, Barry. 1997. "The Political Commitment to Markets and Marketization." In *The Political Economy of Property Rights: Institutional Change and Credibility in the Reform of Centrally Planned Economies,* ed. David L. Weimer. New York: Cambridge University Press.

Weissing, Franz J., and Elinor Ostrom. 1991a. "Crime and Punishment: Further Reflections on the Counterintuitive Results of Mixed Equilibria Games." *Journal of Theoretical Politics,* 3(3): 343–350.

Weissing, Franz J., and Elinor Ostrom. 1991b. "Irrigation Institutions and the Games Irrigators Play: Rule Enforcement without Guards." In *Game Equilibrium Models II: Methods, Morals, and Markets,* ed. Reinhard Selten, 188–262. Berlin: Springer-Verlag.

Weitzman, Martin. 1980. "The Ratchet Principle and Performance Incentives." *Bell Journal of Economics* 11(1): 302–308.

Wilkins, John. 1648. *Mathematical Magic, or, The Wonders that may be performed by Mechanical Geometry.* London: Printed by M. F. for Gellibrand.

Williamson, Oliver E. 1971. "The Vertical Integration of Production: Market Failure Considerations." *American Economic Review,* 61: 112–123.

Williamson, Oliver E. 1975. *Markets and Hierarchies: Analysis and Antitrust Implications. A Study in the Economics of Internal Organization.* New York: Free Press.

Williamson, Oliver E. 1985. *The Economic Institutions of Capitalism.* New York: The Free Press.

Williamson, Oliver E. 1996. *The Mechanisms of Governance.* Oxford: Oxford University Press.

Wilson, James A. 2002. "Scientific Uncertainty, Complex Systems, and the Design of Common-Pool Institutions." In *The Drama of the Commons, National Research Council, Committee on the Human Dimensions of Global Change,* ed. Elinor Ostrom, Thomas Dietz, Nives Dolšak, Paul C. Stern, Susan Stonich, and Elke Weber, 327–359. Washington, D.C.: National Academies Press.

Wilson, James A., James M. Acheson, Mark Metcalfe, and Peter Kleban. 1994. "Chaos, Complexity, and Community Management of Fisheries." *Marine Policy,* 18: 291–305.

Wilson, Kathleen, 1992. "A Dissident Legacy; Eighteenth Century Popular Politics and the Glorious Revolution." In *Liberty Secured? Britain Before and After 1688,* ed. J. R. Jones. Stanford: Stanford University Press.

Wojcik, Jan. 1997. *Robert Boyle and the Limits of Reason.* Cambridge: Cambridge University Press.

Wolf, Holger C. 1999. *Transition Strategies: Choices and Outcomes.* Princeton, NJ: Princeton Studies in International Finance.

Wolfram, Alice, and Steven Pincus. 2011. "A Proactive State? The Land Bank, Investment and Party Politics in the 1690s." In *Regulating the Augustan Economy*, ed. Perry Gauci. Burlington VT: Ashgate.

Woodruff, Christopher. 2001. "Review of De Soto's The Mystery of Capital." *Journal of Economic Literature*, 39(4): 1215–1223.

Woolf, Virginia. 1928. *Mr Bennett and Mrs Brown*. London: Hogarth Press.

World Bank. 1995. Bureaucrats in Business. Washington, D.C.: Oxford University Press.

World Bank. 2002. World Development Report 2002: Building Institutions for Markets. Washington, D.C.: Oxford University Press.

World Bank. 2006. "Where is the Wealth of Nations? Measuring Capital for the 21st Century." Washington, D.C.: The World Bank.

Wrigley, E. A. 2004. *Poverty, Progress and Population*. Cambridge: Cambridge University Press.

Young, H. Peyton. 1998. "Social Norms and Economic Welfare." *European Economic Review*, 42: 821–828.

Young, H. Peyton. 1990. "Condorcet's Theory of Voting." *Math. Inform. Sci. Humaines*, 111: 45–59.

Zak, Paul J., and Knack, Stephen. 2001. "Trust and Growth." *The Economic Journal*, 111(470): 295–321.

Ziman, John. 2000. "Selectionism and Complexity." In *Technological Innovation as an Evolutionary Process*, ed. John Ziman, 41–51. Cambridge: Cambridge University Press.

Index

action situations, 87–94. *See also* game theory, working rules
Africa, 62–63, 92
  East Africa, 63. *See also* Uganda, Kenya
  economic growth, 62
Alchian, Armen, 15, 16
Argentina, 8, 109, 113, 114, 117
Arrow's impossibility theorem, 4
Articles of Confederation, 45, 72, 73, 82, 143, 144. *See also* United States Constitution

Bacon, Francis, 181, 183–186, 187, 191
Bates, Robert, 5, 7, 14
behavioral social sciences, 2, 14, 17, 224
Black Death, 33, 35, 167. *See also* Western Europe
Buenos Aires, 8, 20, 113, 117, 119. *See also* Argentina

chaos theorems, 4
Charles II of England, 198, 199, 201, 205, 210, 212, 220, 221. *See also* seventeenth century England
Chile, 127, 142, 143, 146
cliometrics, 1, 18, 32
Coase, Ronald, 6, 11, 13, 14–16, 17, 23, 24, 29
  Coase and Williamson, 11, 14, 24, 25
coercion, 6, 52, 53, 136
  environment without coercion, 127
  socially productive coercion, 17, 50, 52, 55, 61
cognition, 43. *See also* cognitive science
  cognition, beliefs and culture, 31, 36, 48
cognitive science, 21, 29, 163
collective choice problem, 3–4, 8, 81, 123

collective punishment, 123, 128–130, 133. *See also* game theory
commitment problem (of self-governing groups), 73, 195
common knowledge of the rules, 123, 126, 128, 135, 149. *See also* constitutions
common logic, 128–131, 135
common pool resources (CPR), 3, 8, 84, 91, 92–99, 102–104, 273. *See also* tragedy of the commons, collective choice problem
  CPR games, 273–277
  large scale CPR, 93, 103
  small scale CPR, 26, 101, 102
constitutional economics, 3. *See also* collective choice problem
constitutional equilibrium, 121, 122, 141
constitutions, 21, 70, 80, 121, 122, 137, 141–150, 227–231, 248
  citizen resistance, 123, 137, 140
  constitutional order, 126, 130, 132, 135, 148, 149
  constitutional rules, 121, 123, 124, 127, 132, 133, 137
  coordination function, 122, 123–127, 128–131, 133, 136, 139, 141–142, 146, 148–150
  emergency powers, 82, 141
  enforcement, 121, 122, 137
  post communist states, 223, 226, 227–236, 246
  public reasoning, 8, 121, 123, 136, 139, 140, 141, 148
  successful constitutions, 121, 122, 136, 142, 149
  unconstitutional behavior, 123, 125, 128, 129, 131–133, 141, 149, 150, 228